T0320747

The Cambridge Handbook of
Artificial Intelligence

Artificial intelligence, or AI, is a cross-disciplinary approach to understanding, modeling, and creating intelligence of various forms. It is a critical branch of cognitive science, and its influence is increasingly being felt in other areas, including the humanities. AI applications are transforming the way we interact with each other and with our environment, and work in artificially modeling intelligence is offering new insights into the human mind and revealing new forms mentality can take. This volume of original essays presents the state of the art in AI, surveying the foundations of the discipline, major theories of mental architecture, the principal areas of research, and extensions of AI such as artificial life. With a focus on theory rather than technical and applied issues, the volume will be valuable not only to people working in AI, but also to those in other disciplines wanting an authoritative and up-to-date introduction to the field.

Keith Frankish is Visiting Senior Research Fellow at The Open University UK and Adjunct Professor with the Brain and Mind Program in Neurosciences at the University of Crete. He is the author of *Mind and Supermind* (Cambridge, 2004) and *Consciousness* (2005). He is co-editor of *In Two Minds: Dual Processes and Beyond* (with Jonathan St B. T. Evans, 2009), *New Waves in Philosophy of Action* (with Jesús H. Aguilar and Andrei A. Buckareff, 2010), and *The Cambridge Handbook of Cognitive Science* (with William M. Ramsey, Cambridge, 2012).

William M. Ramsey is Associate Professor of Philosophy at the University of Nevada, Las Vegas. He is the author of *Representation Reconsidered* (Cambridge, 2007) and co-editor of *Philosophy and Connectionist Theory* (with David Rumelhart and Stephen Stich, 1991), *Rethinking Intuition* (with Michael DePaul, 1998), and *The Cambridge Handbook of Cognitive Science* (with Keith Frankish, Cambridge, 2012).

The Cambridge Handbook of
Artificial Intelligence

EDITED BY

Keith Frankish and William M. Ramsey

CAMBRIDGE
UNIVERSITY PRESS

University Printing House, Cambridge CB2 8BS, United Kingdom

Cambridge University Press is part of the University of Cambridge.

It furthers the University's mission by disseminating knowledge in the pursuit of
education, learning and research at the highest international levels of excellence.

www.cambridge.org
Information on this title: www.cambridge.org/9780521871426

© Cambridge University Press 2014

First published 2014

A catalogue record for this publication is available from the British Library

Library of Congress Cataloguing in Publication data
The Cambridge handbook of artificial intelligence / edited by Keith Frankish and
William M. Ramsey.
    pages   cm
Includes bibliographical references and index.
ISBN 978-0-521-87142-6 (hardback) – ISBN 978-0-521-69191-8 (paperback)
1. Artificial intelligence – Philosophy.   I. Frankish, Keith.
II. Ramsey, William M., 1960– editor of compilation.   III.
Title: Handbook of artificial intelligence.
Q335.C26   2014
006.3 – dc23   2013048906

ISBN 978-0-521-87142-6 Hardback
ISBN 978-0-521-69191-8 Paperback

Contents

Figures

Notes on contributors

Eduardo Alonso is Reader in Computing at the Department of Computer Science, City University London. He has published his research in journals such as *Knowledge Engineering Review* and *Artificial Intelligence Review*, and in various Springer Lecture Notes in Artifical Intelligence (LNAI) and Lecture Notes in Computer Science (LNCS) volumes, and he has edited a special issue of *International Journal of Autonomous Agents and Multi-Agent Systems* on Multi-Agent Learning.

Eyal Amir is Associate Professor of Computer Science at the University of Illinois at Urbana-Champaign (UIUC). His research focuses on AI, specifically reasoning, learning, and decision making with logical and probabilistic knowledge. In 2006 Eyal was chosen by the Institute of Electrical and Electronics Engineers (IEEE) as one of the "10 to watch in AI."

Konstantine Arkoudas is an AI research scientist at Applied Communication Sciences, with a focus on reasoning and knowledge engineering. He has published many articles in AI and computer science, as well as in philosophy, on topics ranging from philosophy of mind and cognitive science to epistemology and philosophy of mathematics.

Mark A. Bedau is Professor of Philosophy and Humanities at Reed College, and Editor-in-Chief of the journal *Artificial Life*. He has co-authored or co-edited *Emergence* (2008), *Protocells: Bridging Non living and Living Matter* (2009), *The Ethics of Protocells: Moral and Social Implications of Creating Life in the Laboratory* (2009), and *The Nature of Life* (Cambridge, 2010).

Randall D. Beer is a Professor of Informatics and Computing in the Cognitive Science program at Indiana University. He is the author of *Intelligence as Adaptive Behavior* (1990) and the editor of *Biological Neural Networks in Invertebrate Neuroethology and Robotics* (1993), as well as numerous articles.

Margaret A. Boden is Research Professor of Cognitive Science at the University of Sussex. She is the author of *The Creative Mind* (2004), *Mind as Machine: A History of Cognitive Science* (2006), *Creativity and Art* (2011), and several other books plus many journal articles.

Nick Bostrom is Professor in the Faculty of Philosophy at Oxford University and Director of the Future of Humanity Institute within the Oxford Martin

School. He is the author of some 200 publications, including *Anthropic Bias* (2002), *Global Catastrophic Risks* (ed., 2008), and *Human Enhancement* (ed., 2009).

Selmer Bringsjord is Professor of Cognitive Science and Professor of Computer Science at Rensselaer Polytechnic Institute. He has written numerous books, including *Superminds: People Harness Hypercomputation and More* (with M. Zenzen, 2003) and over 150 refereed papers.

David Danks is Associate Professor of Philosophy and Psychology at Carnegie Mellon University. He has developed multiple novel machine learning algorithms and has written numerous articles and book chapters on the intersection between machine learning and cognitive science. He is also the author of *Unifying the Mind: Cognitive Representations as Graphical Models* (2014).

Keith Frankish is Visiting Senior Research Fellow at The Open University UK and Adjunct Professor with the Brain and Mind Program in Neurosciences at the University of Crete. He is the author of *Mind and Supermind* (Cambridge, 2004) and *Consciousness* (2005). He is co-editor of *In Two Minds: Dual Processes and Beyond* (with Jonathan St. B. T. Evans, 2009), *New Waves in Philosophy of Action* (with Jesús H. Aguilar and Andrei A. Buckareff, 2010), and *The Cambridge Handbook of Cognitive Science* (with William M. Ramsey, Cambridge, 2012).

Stan Franklin is the W. Harry Feinstone Interdisciplinary Research Professor at the University of Memphis and Co-director of its Institute for Intelligent Systems. He is the author of *Artificial Minds* (1995) as well as numerous articles and book chapters on cognitive modeling, artificial general intelligence, and machine consciousness.

Phil Husbands is Research Professor of Artificial Intelligence and Co-founder of the Centre for Computational Neuroscience and Robotics at the University of Sussex. He has published numerous papers and edited several books on complex adaptive systems, both natural and artificial, bio-inspired approaches to robotics, modeling of neural systems, history of AI and Cybernetics, machine learning and creative systems.

William M. Ramsey is Associate Professor of Philosophy at the University of Nevada at Las Vegas. He is the author of *Representation Reconsidered* (Cambridge, 2007) and co-editor of *Philosophy and Connectionist Theory* (with David Rumelhart and Stephen Stich, 1991), *Rethinking Intuition* (with Michael DePaul, 1998), and *The Cambridge Handbook of Cognitive Science* (with Keith Frankish, Cambridge, 2012).

William S. Robinson is Emeritus Professor of Philosophy at Iowa State University He is the author of *Computers, Minds & Robots* (1992), and two more recent books: *Understanding Phenomenal Consciousness* (Cambridge, 2004) and a work for a general audience, *Your Brain and You: What Neuroscience Means for Us* (2010).

Gerhard Sagerer is Professor of Computer Science at the University of Bielefeld, Germany and head of the research group for Applied Informatics. He is author, co-author, or editor of several books and articles on image and speech understanding and the application of pattern understanding methods to natural science domains as well as social robotics.

Matthias Scheutz is Professor of Computer and Cognitive Science in the Department of Computer Science at Tufts University and Adjunct Professor in the Department of Psychology. He has over 200 peer-reviewed publications in artificial intelligence, artificial life, agent-based computing, natural language processing, cognitive modeling, robotics, human–robot interaction, and foundations of cognitive science.

Ron Sun is Professor of Cognitive Sciences at Rensselaer Polytechnic Institute. He is the author of *Integrating Rules and Connectionism for Robust Commonsense Reasoning* (1994) and *Duality of the Mind* (2001), and the editor of *The Cambridge Handbook of Computational Psychology* (Cambridge, 2008) and many other books, in addition to publishing numerous articles and book chapters.

Markus Vincze leads a group of researchers in the Vision for Robotics laboratory at Technische Universität Wien (TUW). With Gregory Hager he edited a book on Robust Vision for IEEE and is author or co-author of over 250 papers, specializing in particular on computer vision techniques for robotic systems situated in real-world environments.

Sven Wachsmuth is a lecturer at Bielefeld University and is currently heading the Central Lab Facilities of the Center of Excellence Cognitive Interaction Technology (CITEC). He is author or co-author of over 100 papers on human–robot interaction, especially high-level computer vision, as well as system integration and evaluation aspects.

Yorick Wilks is Professor of Artificial Intelligence at the University of Sheffield and Senior Research Scientist at Florida Institute for Human and Machine Cognition (IHMC). He is the co-editor (with Derek Partridge) of *The Foundations of Artificial Intelligence* (Cambridge, 1990), the editor of *Close Engagements with Artificial Companions* (2010), and the author of some 200 papers.

Eliezer Yudkowsky is Research Fellow at the Machine Intelligence Research Institute. His publications include "Timeless decision theory" and "Artificial intelligence as a positive and negative factor in global risk."

Acknowledgments

Many people have contributed to the production of this volume. First, we would like to thank the contributors for their expertise, hard work, patience, and responsiveness to our often exacting requirements. We are also grateful to Hilary Gaskin at Cambridge University Press for inviting us to compile the volume and for her patience when the project took longer than expected; to David Mackenzie for his careful management of the volume's production process; and to Anna Oxbury for her scrupulous and thoughtful copy-editing of the text.

We also wish to thank our home institutions. Keith is grateful to The Open University for support during some difficult personal times; to the Department of Philosophy and Social Studies at the University of Crete for welcoming him as a Visiting Researcher; to Professor Adonis Moschovakis, Professor Helen Savaki, and other members of the Brain and Mind Program at the University of Crete for helping him feel part of the cognitive science community in Crete; and, most importantly, to his partner Maria Kasmirli for her patience, support, and excellent advice on philosophical matters. William is grateful to both the University of Notre Dame and the University of Nevada at Las Vegas, and especially would like to thank Notre Dame for its Associative Professor's Special Leave, which helped support work on this project.

Introduction

Keith Frankish and William M. Ramsey

Overview

Very generally, artificial intelligence (AI) is a cross-disciplinary approach to understanding, modeling, and replicating intelligence and cognitive processes by invoking various computational, mathematical, logical, mechanical, and even biological principles and devices. On the one hand, it is often abstract and theoretical as investigators try to develop theories that will enrich our understanding of natural cognition or help define the limits of computability or proof theory. On the other hand, it is often purely pragmatic as other investigators focus on the engineering of smart machines and applications. Historically, its practitioners have come from such disciplines as logic, mathematics, engineering, philosophy, psychology, linguistics, and, of course, computer science. It forms a critical branch of cognitive science since it is often devoted to developing models that explain various dimensions of human and animal cognition. Indeed, since its inception in the mid twentieth century, AI has been one of the most fruitful new areas of research into the nature of human mentality. Today, it is impossible to be a serious cognitive scientist or philosopher of mind without at least some familiarity with major developments in AI. At the same time, anyone who uses modern technology is probably enjoying features that, in one way or another, had their origin in AI research, and AI technology will undoubtedly play an increasingly large role in our lives in coming decades.

This volume of original essays aims to describe the state of the art in the field of AI and to highlight important theoretical and philosophical applications of current research. The book's focus is on theory rather than technical and applied issues, and the chapters should be useful not only to AI researchers and other cognitive scientists, but also to philosophers and people in the humanities. Each chapter is a specially commissioned survey article from a leading writer in the area – either a philosopher of AI or an AI researcher with strong theoretical interests. There is coverage of the foundations of the discipline, cognitive architectures, the various facets of AI research, and extensions of AI research, such as robotics and artificial life (see the chapter summary below for details about each contribution). The approach is thematic rather than historical, and although the chapters are primarily survey pieces, critical assessment is also included where appropriate. We have worked hard to make the material accessible to non-specialists, and readers are not expected to have any significant background in the subject areas covered.

The volume possesses a number of distinctive features. First, it provides concise and up-to-date coverage of a diverse and rapidly expanding field, written by leading researchers with important perspectives. The contributors include both senior figures who have helped to form the modern discipline and younger researchers doing work that will help shape its future. Second, it presents scientific work in a form that is accessible to a humanities audience and focuses on broad theoretical issues and applications rather than experimental work and technical details. Contributors present logical and mathematical principles in general terms, and the use of symbolic notation has been kept to a minimum. Third, the book includes coverage of important topics that have been relatively neglected by past overviews, including the ethics of artificial intelligence, artificial life, and machine consciousness. Fourth, the discussion is pitched at an intermediate level, suitable for both advanced students and scholars new to the area, and the book includes supporting material, such as a glossary and chapter-specific "Further reading" sections that enhance its value as a teaching text. A companion volume, *The Cambridge Handbook to Cognitive Science* (2012), serves to complement this handbook in both scope and aims.

Artificial intelligence and cross-disciplinarity

As its title indicates, this volume is intended as a guide to AI itself, rather than to the *philosophy* of AI. That is, the primary focus is on first-order research in AI, and on theoretical issues raised directly by that research, rather than on meta-level philosophical questions about the *science* of AI. Yet, as readers will note, several of the chapters are written by people who are usually characterized as philosophers of AI or of cognitive science, and the volume's co-editors both have their homes in philosophy departments and have done no significant first-order research in AI. Why, one might ask, do philosophers have such a large role in a volume about one of the sciences of the mind?

There are a number of reasons why philosophical involvement in a volume on AI is beneficial. First, in truth, the distinction between AI research and philosophical work on mentality is not a sharp one. As a number of the chapters make clear, there are no tidy and well-defined demarcations between, say, programming rationality on the one hand and philosophical work on logic or reasoning on the other. Foundational questions and challenges regarding the development of synthetic minds are unavoidably philosophical in nature, and AI researchers often need to reflect on the broader implications of their findings, speculate about abstract matters such as hidden assumptions and overarching themes, appeal to thought experiments, and invoke traditional philosophical concepts, such as knowledge, representation, and action. In other words, there is a lot of philosophical reasoning involved in being a cutting-edge investigator in AI. At the same time, philosophers of mind need to be well-versed in the theories, models, and major developments in AI, so that their own contributions are informed and useful.

Second, philosophers of mind possess two attributes that provide them with a unique perspective on AI research itself. One is an understanding of the more general metaphysical, epistemological, and even ethical issues that arise in AI. These include questions about the nature of machine intelligence and consciousness, reductionism, levels of explanation, properties of symbols and representations, the moral status of non-humans, and so on. The other attribute is an appreciation of specific foundational issues in various areas of AI research. For centuries, philosophers have been thinking and writing about a wide array of phenomena that AI researchers are now exploring – phenomena such as intelligence, consciousness, rationality, mental representation, perceptual experience, and human action. These are *both* established areas of philosophical analysis *and* the target of increased scientific investigation. The philosophy of mind is itself being transformed by work in AI, and, at the same time, philosophers have a unique vantage from which they can elucidate empirical work, synthesizing ideas, making theoretical connections, and highlighting conceptual and methodological issues.

Despite this overlap, however, there has remained some distance between advanced AI researchers and those working in related disciplines, including philosophy. Consequently, a third and final reason to have input from relative outsiders is to help overcome this. The distance has been especially marked where AI research has been highly technical and focused upon specific applications and tasks. To some degree, AI researchers belong to a tighter, more homogeneous community than researchers in other areas of cognitive science, with a greater emphasis upon investigating precise theoretical problems or producing highly specific applications. This focus has led to considerable progress in many areas, but it has also made much of the work less accessible to those in other disciplines. Thus, one of our aims in compiling the present volume was to help bridge this gap by presenting even technical areas of research in an accessible manner, with a focus on general principles rather than specific details. In our role as editors, we view ourselves as representatives of readers who have a strong interest in AI but who do not currently work in the field and are not familiar with many developments. Consequently, we chose a mix of established figures and up-and-coming researchers, and then pressured them hard to explain the state of the art in a way that others could understand. The end result is a unique volume that allows those without formal training to gain a good overview of even highly complicated areas of AI research. We hope it will help to foster productive communication and collaboration between AI and other disciplines.

Summary of the volume

The volume is composed of fifteen chapters, collected into four sections: *Foundations, Architectures, Dimensions,* and *Extensions.* The focus narrows across the first three sections, which respectively survey foundational issues, general theories of mental architecture, and specific areas of research. The final section then extends the coverage to some related topics and research programs. Each section and each chapter stands alone and can be read individually (and in order to achieve this, we have allowed occasional overlap between chapter contents); but the chapters and sections are designed to complement each other, and the collection as a whole provides a systematic and comprehensive overview of the theoretical landscape of AI. Below we give a brief summary of the contents of each part of the volume.

Part I: Foundations

The essays in this section are devoted to explaining and discussing foundational issues in AI. In the first chapter, Stan Franklin introduces readers to the field, with a concise survey of the discipline's core themes, landmark moments, major accomplishments, main research areas, and recent trends. Chapter 2, by Konstantine Arkoudas and Selmer Bringsjord, looks in detail at the philosophical and conceptual roots of AI. For instance, the functionalist notion that the mind is like a computational program has traditionally served as a metaphysical basis for a great deal of work in AI, but it has also led to various powerful criticisms. Arkoudas and Bringsjord discuss these and other ways in which philosophy and AI intersect. The field of AI has also faced a number of philosophical challenges, both to the general project of creating artificial intelligence and to specific approaches within the field. In Chapter 3, William Robinson discusses the most important of these and the ways in which defenders have responded. For example, Robinson carefully explains Searle's well-known *Chinese Room* argument against the classical symbol-processing approach to AI and the responses that have been offered by proponents of that approach.

Part II: Architectures

This section of the volume looks at the three major architectural views (general theories of the representations and processes involved in intelligent thought and action) that have dominated work in AI. In Chapter 4, Margaret Boden provides an overview of the core features of classic computational architectures, often called GOFAI (for "Good Old-Fashioned AI"). She examines the strengths and weaknesses of the classical approach, and argues that the alleged failure of traditional AI has been grossly overstated, though she grants that it will probably need to be complemented by other approaches. Ron Sun presents a similar review of connectionism and neural networks in Chapter 5. After providing a historical perspective and an analysis of the distinctive features of connectionist models (such as distributed representations), Sun offers his own support for hybrid architectures, which combine both connectionist and traditional symbolic elements. In Chapter 6, Randall Beer gives an in-depth look at the dynamical and embedded approach to AI, or as he puts it, the Situated, Embodied, and Dynamical (SED) framework. As Beer notes, this approach focuses upon the dynamic interaction between intelligent systems and their environment, and leans heavily upon mathematical tools such as dynamical systems theory to capture that interaction through time. Beer provides an analysis of both the unique characteristics of the SED framework and its prospects for providing a radically new way of thinking about intelligent systems.

Part III: Dimensions

In this section, authors provide a glimpse into cutting-edge research in different subfields of AI, corresponding to different dimensions of intelligence: learning, perception, reasoning, language, action, and consciousness.

The section begins with Chapter 7, in which David Danks provides an overview of the different forms of machine learning and the sorts of algorithms and methods that have proven successful. The chapter also provides an interesting analysis of some of the technical and philosophical challenges that confront researchers in this area. In Chapter 8, Markus Vincze, Sven Wachsmuth, and Gerhard Sagerer review work in artificial perception, particularly computer vision. They give a detailed account of recent developments in such critical areas as object recognition and categorization, tracking and visual servoing, and vision-based human–computer interaction, and they offer their assessment of the key challenges that lie ahead. In Chapter 9, Eyal Amir presents a survey of recent work in artificial reasoning and decision making – topics which are central to the AI subfield known as *Knowledge Representation and Reasoning* (KR&R). Amir surveys techniques for representing information and reasoning with it (including ones drawn from propositional logic and probabilistic theory), looks at the various formalisms that have guided work in automated decision making, and highlights some cross-cutting issues such as the emergence of applications combining logic-based and probabilistic methods.

Two other important subfields of AI have been Natural Language Processing and Computational Linguistics, both of which focus on artificial language processing. In Chapter 10, Yorick Wilks provides some of the background to these fields and explains how they relate to core areas of linguistics, including syntactic processing, semantics, and lexical disambiguation. He also explains some of the quantitative and statistical approaches that have recently been employed to develop AI systems with linguistic capacities. In Chapter 11, Eduardo Alonso looks at agency in AI and discusses the strategies used to develop AI systems that function as competent agents in different environments, both as a consequence of stored knowledge and as a result of learning. In particular, Alonso highlights the importance of an emerging agent-centered AI, in which software systems are designed to display behavior that is autonomous, adaptive, and social. The chapter looks at the challenges involved in developing artificial agents that can operate in multi-agent environments by using techniques such as negotiation and argumentation. In the final chapter in this section, Chapter 12, Matthias Scheutz provides an in-depth look at recent work on developing machines that experience emotions and even some form of consciousness. Reviewing the historical and philosophical dimensions of the issue (such as the possible functional role of emotions), Scheutz examines the central challenges to this line of research, noting that we have yet to develop clear criteria for deciding when a system does or does not possess subjective states.

Part IV: Extensions

This final section extends the volume's coverage to topics and research programs that are closely related to AI, including robotics, artificial life, and the ethical dimensions of AI. In Chapter 13, Phil Husbands looks at the recent history of building machines that engage in intelligent behavior, both for industrial applications and for research purposes. He examines efforts to mimic biological systems, especially insects, and surveys evolutionary approaches, which use processes of iterated replication and mutation to generate robotic controllers adapted to specific tasks and environments. Chapter 14, by Mark Bedau, presents a fascinating look at the rapidly growing field of artificial life, which seeks to synthesize life in a variety of different forms, including robotic systems, artificial cells made from biochemical building blocks, and software agents inhabiting virtual eco-systems. After examining the ways in which artificial life is linked to conventional AI, Bedau explores what it has taught us about living systems and highlights some new philosophical issues it raises. In the final chapter of the volume, Chapter 15, Nick Bostrom and Eliezer Yudkowsky explore a wide range of ethical issues associated with the creation of thinking and feeling machines. These include questions about our use of AI algorithms to govern financial or legal transactions, the creation of artificial persons with moral status and rights, and the development of machines that are smarter than humans. As Bostrom and Yudkowsky correctly note, whereas these issues once belonged to the domain of science fiction, they are increasingly becoming real moral dilemmas we must face.

Coverage and scope

We shall add some remarks on the coverage and the scope of the volume. Our first point concerns the relation between the chapters. This handbook can be read straight through by those wanting a broad overview of the field of AI, but we also wanted it to be of use to those seeking to know only about specific topics or particular areas of AI research. Consequently, the chapters are written as stand-alone pieces that can be read individually for a thorough treatment of a given topic. Readers with a particular interest in, say, machine learning can go straight to David Danks' chapter and find an extensive examination of the topic that includes discussion of several closely related issues and does not assume familiarity with the material in earlier chapters. While we regard this as an important virtue of the volume, it also means that there is occasional overlap between different chapters. For example, any chapter on the philosophical foundations of AI, such as Arkoudas and Bringsjord's, would be incomplete without discussion of John Searle's famous Chinese Room argument, since that argument played a significant role in shaping the way some people think about the limits of AI. But, of course, discussion of Searle's argument also belongs in Robinson's chapter on the philosophical challenges to AI and in Boden's chapter on classical ("Good Old-Fashioned") AI as well. The same can be said for a variety of other arguments, ideas, theories, and developments that are critical for understanding the different aspects of AI described in these chapters.

While this overlap is unavoidable, it should be noted that each chapter has a unique focus, emphasizing different aspects of shared topics. Thus, Robinson places Searle's argument in the context of philosophical and conceptual challenges to AI, assessing the scope of the argument (via a useful distinction between flexibility and understanding) and explaining the major replies to the argument and Searle's responses to them. Boden, on the other hand, discusses the argument's impact on classical AI's supposed commitment to Strong AI – the view that running a suitable computer program is sufficient for mentality – and she goes on to discuss the extent to which classical AI is actually committed to that doctrine. Similar points could be made with regard to other topics that surface in different places, such as connectionism, dynamical systems theory, the Turing Test, and the frame problem. Thus, although readers may come across particular themes or topics in more than one chapter, we believe that each encounter will be informative and helpful.

Our second point concerns the scope of the volume. There are some topics relevant to AI research that are not covered in depth here. In particular, there is no systematic coverage of the technical, nuts-and-bolts aspects of AI research, such as programming languages and techniques, information search strategies, different styles of knowledge representation (such as scripts and frames), and so on – though there is some discussion of these matters in the chapters on the subfields of AI research. These "tools" of AI are of course essential topics for those planning to work in the field of AI. However, they are covered in detail in standard textbooks (see the "Further reading" section at the end of this Introduction), and, given space constraints, we decided to focus the volume primarily on what AI researchers are doing and thinking, rather than on how to actually do AI research.

Another area in which the coverage could have been greatly extended is that of applications and implications of AI research. Developments in AI are so far-reaching and have become so interwoven in our lives that our section on the extensions of AI could have been much, much larger. Indeed, whole volumes could be (and have been) devoted to topics such as AI and creativity, AI and the internet, AI on the battlefield, AI in film and literature, and so on. These issues are touched on in many places throughout the volume. However, this is not, strictly speaking, an "AI-And-Something-Else" volume, and we limited the Extensions section to two major research areas that are closely intertwined with AI – robotics and artificial life – and discussion of the major ethical issues arising directly from AI research. These well illustrate the important and fascinating ways in which the field of AI has grown, influenced other areas of inquiry, and generated new topics of enquiry, new problems, and new challenges.

The focus of the volume, then, is on the middle ground – the central conceptual and theoretical issues in AI and the major research programs – excluding technical details of AI system building on the one hand and the wider social, cultural, and economic implications of AI research on the other. We feel this makes for a manageable and accessible volume, which can easily be complemented by other works with a narrower or wider focus. We offer some suggestions for complementary works in the "Further reading" section at the end of this Introduction. Finally, as already mentioned, this volume has a companion, *The Cambridge Handbook of Cognitive Science*, which has a similar structure and scope and was designed to complement this one. That book looks at many of the same topics (the nature of mentality, cognitive architecture, the structure and function of various mental faculties) from the perspective of researchers on human cognition, as well as discussing allied research programs such as evolutionary psychology. AI and cognitive science have influenced each other strongly throughout their history, and the discussions in each volume will give further depth and perspective to those in the other.

General themes

Although the chapters were written individually, the reader will notice a number of common themes appearing throughout the volume. For example, in the past a good deal of AI research involved the promotion of specific architectures or theories, such as classic computationalism or connectionism. Often, simple toy systems were developed, in part to demonstrate how a given type of computational framework could in principle perform a particular task. However, with rapid developments in technology and computing power, it has become possible to build far more sophisticated AI systems that can do real work, and, as a result, pragmatic engineering concerns have become more central. Many researchers today are more concerned with employing whatever works best for the particular job in hand, rather than promoting a particular global architecture. Consequently, an increasing amount of AI work involves hybrid systems, as investigators employ different sorts of architectures for different sub-processes or tasks. This mirrors recent trends in cognitive science, such as "dual-process" theories of cognition, which claim that different types of computational architectures underlie different cognitive capacities. Much of the work discussed in this volume suggests that past theoretical divisions and battles over competing architectures are fading while a growing number of researchers are adopting a more inclusive and ecumenical outlook.

Another trend is a shift in the theoretical, conceptual, and philosophical issues that occupy investigators. Traditional questions about whether a computer could feel pain or about the nature of computational symbols are still important, but we also see new philosophical concerns becoming central. For example, the development of dynamic models in AI has encouraged people to reconsider what counts as a computational or intelligent system, the boundaries of such systems, and how intelligent behavior ought to be explained. At the same time, many investigators are rethinking the need for representations or internal models that in the past were assumed to be essential for guiding the behavior of AI systems. More and more investigators are accepting the importance of situatedness and embodiment and exploring the degree to which a system's interactions with a real-world environment are crucial. Thus, many of the chapters reveal that traditional assumptions are no longer taken for granted, and that radically new ideas and principles are taking center stage.

At the same time, developments in popular culture and technology are having a greater impact on how researchers regard the field, with investigators commonly making reference to the internet, to the explosion of special applications for smart devices, and to the influence of computer gaming. Similarly, many of the chapters reflect a sophisticated awareness of important findings in biology, animal cognition, neuroscience, and the psychology of perception. Thus, one thing that has not changed is the degree to which the field of AI continues to evolve as it assimilates the newest developments in technology and the most recent discoveries in the life sciences.

We have enjoyed putting this volume together and hope it will serve as an entry-point to the fascinating and hugely important work being done in AI. Work in this field already affects our lives in countless ways, and future developments are likely to transform our world radically. On the small scale, AI applications will increasingly pervade our lives, reshaping and enhancing our interactions with our environment and each other, while on a larger scale, theoretical advances in artificially modeling intelligence will not only give us a deeper understanding of our own minds, but may also confront us with new minds with vastly different capacities from ours. We hope this volume will help to make this exciting but often highly technical field more accessible, and that readers will be inspired to learn more about AI, to apply its insights in other fields, and to reflect upon its implications for humanity.

Further reading

As explained earlier, this volume's focus is on the middle ground of AI research – the main conceptual and theoretical issues and the major research programs. As such, the volume is designed to be self-standing. However, some readers may wish to complement it with other reading that has either a narrower focus, on technical matters, or a wider one, on the social and cultural implications of AI research. In this section we offer some brief suggestions for such reading.

Technical matters

One of the most popular undergraduate textbooks of AI concepts and techniques and among the best single-volume introductions to the nuts and bolts of AI is:

Russell, S. and Norvig, P. (2010). *Artificial Intelligence: A Modern Approach* (3rd edn.). Upper Saddle River, NJ: Prentice Hall.

Two other recommended volumes, on more specialized topics, are:

Norvig, P. (1992). *Paradigms of Artificial Intelligence Programming: Case Studies in Common Lisp.* San Francisco, CA: Morgan Kaufmann. A little dated, but still a classic textbook on AI programming, which teaches the reader how to build and debug real AI programs and illustrates important techniques and concepts.
Whitten, I. H., Frank, E., and Hall, M. A. (2011). *Data Mining: Practical Machine Learning Tools and Techniques* (3rd edn.). Burlington, MA: Morgan Kaufmann. A standard textbook on the statistical techniques of machine learning and data mining, which are now central to much AI research. Written at an accessible introductory level.

Wider perspectives

There is a growing literature on the social, economic, and cultural effects of AI research, from which the following is a selection.

Anderson, M. and Anderson, S. L. (eds.) (2011). *Machine Ethics*. Cambridge University Press. A collection of essays on the project of building machines with ethical values, covering the importance of developing machine ethics, the requirements of the task, challenges facing the project, various approaches that have been proposed, and the future of the field.

Boden M. A. (2004). *The Creative Mind: Myths and Mechanisms* (2nd edn.). London: Routledge. Offers a computationalist perspective on human creativity, drawing on work in AI.

Boden M. A (2011) *Creativity and Art: Three Roads to Surprise*. Oxford University Press. A series of essays exploring creativity in art, including discussion of computer art.

Chalmers, D. J. (2010). The singularity: A philosophical analysis, *Journal of Consciousness Studies*, 17(9–10): 7–65. An analysis of the intelligence explosion ("singularity") that some believe will occur when machines surpass humans in intelligence and then proceed to create ever more sophisticated machines themselves. Discusses whether there will be a singularity, how humans should deal with it, and the future for humanity in a post-singularity world.

Lin, P., Abney, K., and Bekey, G. A. (2012). *Robot Ethics: The Ethical and Social Implications of Robotics*. Cambridge, MA: MIT Press. Discusses ethical, social, and legal issues associated with advanced robotics, including ones arising from the use of robots as weapons, sexual partners, and caregivers.

Singer, P. W. (2009). *Wired for War: The Robotics Revolution and Conflict in the 21st Century*. New York: Penguin. A readable account of the emerging military applications of robotics and the effects they may have.

Turkle, S. (2011) *Alone Together: Why We Expect More from Technology and Less from Each Other*. New York: Basic Books. A psychologist's perspective on how robotics and digital technology are affecting human social interaction.

Part I

Foundations

1 History, motivations, and core themes

Stan Franklin

1.1 Introduction

This chapter introduces the field of artificial intelligence (AI) through a review of its core themes, history, major research areas, and current trends. The goal is to provide the reader with sufficient background context for understanding and appreciating the subsequent chapters in the volume.

1.2 Overview of core themes

The history of artificial intelligence may be best understood in the context of its core themes and controversies. Below is a brief listing of such AI distinctions, issues, themes, and controversies. It would be well to keep these in mind during your reading of the rest of this chapter. Each of the themes will be expanded upon and clarified as the chapter progresses. Many of these result from there being, to this day, no agreed upon definition of intelligence within the AI community of researchers.

Smart software vs. cognitive modeling. AI has always been a part of computer science, an engineering discipline aimed at creating smart computer programs – that is, intelligent software products to meet human needs. We shall see a number of examples of such smart software. AI also has its science side, which is aimed at helping us understand human intelligence. This endeavor includes building software systems that "think" in human-like ways, as well as producing computational models of aspects of human cognition. These computational models provide hypotheses for cognitive scientists.

Symbolic AI vs. neural nets. From its very inception AI was divided into two quite distinct research streams: symbolic AI and neural nets. Symbolic AI took the view that intelligence could be achieved by manipulating symbols within the computer according to rules. Neural nets, or connectionism as the cognitive scientists called it, instead attempted to create intelligent systems as networks of nodes each comprising a simplified model of a neuron. Basically, the difference was between a computer analogy and a brain analogy, between implementing AI systems as traditional computer programs and modeling them after nervous systems.

Reasoning vs. perception. Here the distinction is between intelligence as high-level reasoning for decision making, say in machine chess or medical diagnosis, and the lower-level perceptual processing involved in, say, machine vision – the understanding of images by identifying objects and their relationships.

Reasoning vs. knowledge. Early symbolic AI researchers concentrated on understanding the mechanisms (algorithms) used for reasoning in the service of decision making. The assumption was that understanding how such reasoning could be accomplished in a computer would be sufficient to build useful smart software. Later, researchers realized that, in order to scale up for real-world problems, they had to build significant amounts of knowledge into their systems. A medical diagnosis system had to know a great deal about medicine, to be able to draw valuable conclusions.

To represent or not. This knowledge had to be represented somehow within the system; that is, the system had to somehow model its world. Such representation could take various forms, including rules. Later, a controversy arose as to how much of such modeling actually needed to be done. Some claimed that much could be accomplished without extensive internal modeling.

Brain in a vat vs. embodied AI. The early AI systems had humans entering input into the systems and acting on the output of the systems. Like a "brain in a vat" these systems could neither sense the world nor act on it. Later, AI researchers created embodied, or situated, AI systems that directly sensed their worlds and also acted on them directly. Real-world robots are examples of embodied AI systems.

Narrow AI vs. human-level intelligence. In the early days of AI many researchers aimed at creating human-level intelligence in their machines, the so-called "strong AI." Later, as the extraordinary difficulty of such an endeavor became more evident, almost all AI researchers built systems that operated intelligently within some relatively narrow domain such as chess or medicine. Only recently has there been a move back in the direction of systems capable of a more general, human-level intelligence that could be applied broadly across diverse domains.

1.3   Some key moments in AI

1.3.1   McCulloch and Pitts

The neural nets branch of AI began with a very early paper by Warren McCulloch and Walter Pitts (1943). McCulloch, a professor at the University of Chicago, and Pitts, then an undergraduate student, developed a much-simplified model of a functioning neuron, a McCulloch–Pitts unit (Figure 1.1). They showed that networks of such units could perform any Boolean operation (and, or, not) and, thus, any possible computation. Each of these units

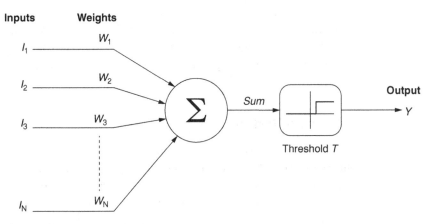

Figure 1.1 A simple artificial neuron.

compared the weighted sum of its inputs to a threshold value to produce a binary output. Neural Nets AI, and also computational neuroscience, thus was born.

1.3.2   Alan Turing

Alan Turing, a Cambridge mathematician of the first half of the twentieth century, can be considered the father of computing (its grandfather was Charles Babbage during the mid nineteenth century) and the grandfather of AI. During World War II in 1939–1944 Turing pitted his wits against the Enigma cipher machine, the key to German communications. He led in developing the British Bombe, an early computing machine that was used over and over to decode messages encoded using the Enigma.

During the early twentieth century Turing and others were interested in questions of computability. They wanted to formalize an answer to the question of which problems can be solved computationally and several people developed distinct formalisms as a result. Turing offered the Turing Machine (1936), Alonzo Church the Lambda Calculus (1936), and Emil Post the Production System (1943). These three apparently quite different formal systems soon proved to be logically equivalent in defining computability, that is, for specifying those problems that can be solved by a program running on a computer. The Turing machine proved to be the most useful formalization and it is the one most often used in theoretical computer science.

In 1950 Turing published the very first paper suggesting the possibility of artificial intelligence (1950). In it he first described what we now call the Turing Test, and offered it as a sufficient condition for the existence of AI. The Turing Test has human testers conversing in natural language without constraints via terminals with either a human or an AI natural language program, both hidden from view. If the testers cannot reliably distinguish between the human and the program, intelligence is ascribed to the program. In 1991 Hugh Loebner established the Loebner Prize, which would award $100,000 to the first AI program to pass the Turing Test. As of this writing, the Loebner Prize has not been awarded.

1.3.3   The Dartmouth Workshop

The Dartmouth Workshop served to bring researchers in this newly emerging field together to interact and to exchange ideas. Held during August of 1956, the workshop marks the birth of artificial intelligence. AI seems alone among disciplines in having a birthday. Its parents included John McCarthy, Marvin Minsky, Herbert Simon, and Allen Newell. Other eventually prominent attendees were Claude Shannon of Information Theory fame, Oliver Selfridge, the developer of Pandemonium Theory, and Nathaniel Rochester, a major designer of the very early IBM 701 computer.

John McCarthy, on the Dartmouth faculty at the time of the Workshop, is credited with having coined the name Artificial Intelligence. He was also the inventor of LISP, the predominant AI programming language for a half century. McCarthy subsequently joined the MIT faculty and later moved to Stanford where he established their AI Lab. He remained an active AI researcher until his death in 2011. Marvin Minsky helped to found the MIT AI Lab where at the time of this writing he remains an active and influential AI researcher. Herbert Simon and Allen Newell brought the only running AI program, the logical theorist, to the Dartmouth Workshop. This operated by means–ends analysis, an AI planning algorithm. At each step it attempted to choose an operation (means) that moved the system closer to its goal (end). Simon and Newell founded the AI research lab at Carnegie Mellon University. Newell passed away in 1992, and Simon in 2001.[1]

1.3.4   Samuel's checker player

Every computer scientist knows that a computer only executes the algorithm it was programmed to run. Hence, it might be thought that it can only do what its programmer told it to do. It cannot know anything its programmer didn't, nor do anything its programmer couldn't. This seemingly logical conclusion is, in fact, simply wrong because it ignores the possibility of a computer being programmed to learn. Such machine learning, later to become a major subfield of AI, began with Arthur Samuel's checker playing program (1959). Though

---

[1] While still a pure mathematician, the present author spent some years on the Carnegie Mellon faculty, where he knew both Simon and Newell. He learned no AI from them, a wasted opportunity.

Samuel was initially able to beat his program, after a few months of learning it is said that he never won another game from it. Machine learning was born.

1.3.5 Minsky's dissertation

In 1951, Marvin Minsky and Dean Edmonds built the SNARC, the first artificial neural network, which simulated a rat running a maze. This work was the foundation of Minsky's Princeton dissertation (1954). Thus one of the founders and major players in symbolic AI was, initially, more interested in neural nets and set the stage for their computational implementation.

1.3.6 Perceptrons and the neural net winter

Frank Rosenblatt's perceptron (1958) was among the earliest artificial neural nets. A two-layer neural net best thought of as a binary classifier system, a perceptron maps its input vector into a weighted sum subject to a threshold, yielding a yes or no answer. The attraction of the perceptron was due to a supervised learning algorithm, by means of which a perceptron could be taught to classify correctly. Thus neural nets contributed to machine learning.

Research on perceptrons came to an inglorious end with the publication of the Minsky and Papert book *Perceptrons* (1969) in which they showed that the perceptron is incapable of learning to classify as true or false the inputs to such simple systems as the exclusive "or" (XOR – either A or B but not both). Minsky and Papert also conjectured that even multi-layered perceptrons would prove to have similar limitations. Though this conjecture proved to be mostly false, the government agencies funding AI research took it seriously. Funding for neural net research dried up, leading to a neural net winter that didn't abate until the publishing of the Parallel Distributing Processing volumes in the mid 1980s (McClelland, Rumelhart, and the PDP Research Group 1986; Rumelhart, McClelland, and the PDP Research Group 1986).

1.3.7 The genesis of major research areas

Early in its history the emphasis of AI research was largely toward producing systems that could reason about high-level, relatively abstract, but artificial problems – problems that would require intelligence if attempted by a human. Among the first of such systems was Simon and Newell's general problem solver (Newell, Shaw, and Simon 1959), which, like its predecessor the logical theorist, used means–ends analysis to solve a variety of puzzles. Yet another early reasoning system was Gelernter's geometry theorem-prover.

Another important subfield of AI is natural language processing, concerned with systems that understand language. Among the first such was SHRDLU (Winograd 1972), named after the order of keys on a linotype machine.

SHRDLU could understand and execute commands in English ordering it to manipulate wooden blocks, cones, spheres, and so on with a robot arm in what came to be known as a "blocks world." SHRDLU was sufficiently sophisticated to be able to use the remembered context of a conversation to disambiguate references.

It was not long, however, before AI researchers realized that reasoning wasn't all there was to intelligence. In attempting to scale their systems up to deal with real-world problems, they ran squarely into the wall of the lack of knowledge. Real-world problems demanded that the solver know something. So, knowledge-based systems (often called expert systems) were born. The name came from the process of knowledge engineering: of having knowledge engineers laboriously extract information from human experts and then encode that knowledge into their expert systems.

Led by chemist Joshua Lederberg and AI researchers Edward Feigenbaum and Bruce Buchanan, the first such expert system, called DENDRAL, was an expert in organic chemistry. DENDRAL helped to identify the molecular structure of organic molecules by analyzing data from a mass spectrometer and employing its knowledge of chemistry (Lindsay, Buchanan, Feigenbaum, and Lederberg 1980). The designers of DENDRAL added knowledge to its underlying reasoning mechanism, an inference engine, to produce an expert system capable of dealing with a complex, real-world problem.

A second such expert system, called Mycin (Davis, Buchanan and Shortliffe 1977), helped physicians diagnose and treat infectious blood diseases and meningitis. Like DENDRAL, Mycin relied on both hand-crafted expert knowledge and a rule-based inference engine. The system was successful in that it could diagnose difficult cases as well as the most expert physicians, but unsuccessful in that it was never fielded. Inputting information into Mycin required about twenty minutes. A physician would spend at most five minutes on such a diagnosis.

1.3.8   Research during the neural net winter

As already noted, Minsky and Papert's *Perceptrons* (1969) mistakenly convinced government funding agencies that the neural net approach was unpromising, leading to a neural net winter that lasted almost twenty years. In spite of this appalling lack of funding, significant research continued to be performed around the world. Intrepid researchers who somehow managed to keep this important research going included Shun-ichi Amari and Satoru Fukushima in Japan, Stephen Grossberg and John Hopfield in the United States, Teuvo Kohonen in Finland, and Christoph von der Malsburg in Germany. Much of this work concerned the self-organization of neural nets, and learning therein. Much was also motivated by the backgrounds of these researchers in neuroscience.

1.3.9   The rise of connectionism

The end of the neural net winter was precipitated by the publication of the two Parallel Distributed Processing volumes (Rumelhart et al. 1986; McClelland et al. 1986). They were two massive edited volumes with chapters authored by members of the PDP research group, then at the University of California, San Diego. These volumes gave rise to the application of artificial neural nets, soon to be called connectionism, in cognitive science. Whether connectionism was up to the job of explaining the mind rapidly became a hot topic of debate among philosophers, psychologists, and AI researchers (Fodor and Pylyshyn 1988; Smolensky 1987; Chalmers 1990). The debate has died down with no declared winner, but with artificial neural nets becoming an established player in the current AI field.

In addition to their success (in the guise of connectionism) for cognitive modeling, artificial neural nets have found a host of practical applications. Most of these involve pattern recognition. They include mutual fund investing, fraud detection, credit scoring, real estate appraisal, and a host of others. This wide applicability has been primarily the result of a widely used training algorithm called backpropagation. Though subsequently traced to much earlier work, backpropagation was rediscovered by the PDP research group and constituted the preeminent tool for the research reported in the two PDP volumes.

1.3.10   The AI winter

Owing to what turned out to be an overstatement of the potential and timing of artificial intelligence, symbolic AI suffered its own winter. As an example, in 1965 Herbert Simon predicted "machines will be capable, within twenty years, of doing any work that a man can do." This and other such predictions did not come to pass. As a result, by the mid 1980s government agency funding for AI began to dry up, and commercial investment became almost non-existent. Artificial intelligence became a taboo word in the computing industry for a decade or more, in spite of the enormous success of expert systems. The AI spring did not arrive until the advent of the next "killer" application, video games (these developments are discussed in Section 1.4).

1.3.11   Soft computing

The term "soft computing" refers to a motley assemblage of computational techniques designed to deal with imprecision, uncertainty, approximation, partial truths, and so on. Its methods tend to be inductive rather than deductive. In addition to neural nets, which we have already discussed, soft computing includes evolutionary computation, fuzzy logic, and Bayesian networks. We shall consider each in turn.

Evolutionary computation began with a computational rendition of natural selection called a genetic algorithm (Holland 1975). A population search algorithm, this process typically begins with a population of artificial genotypes representing possible solutions to the problem at hand. The members of this population are subjected to mutation (random changes) and crossover (the intermixing of two genotypes). The resulting new genotypes are input to a fitness function that measures the quality of the genotype. The most successful of these genotypes constitute the next population, and the process repeats. If well designed, the genotypes in the population tend over time to become much alike, thus converging to a desired solution and completing the genetic algorithm. In addition, evolutionary computation also includes classifier systems, which combine rule-based and reinforcement ideas with genetic algorithms. Evolutionary computation also includes genetic programming, a method of using genetic algorithms to search for computer programs, typically in LISP, that will solve a given problem.

Derived from Zadeh's fuzzy set theory, in which degrees of set membership between 0 and 1 are assigned (1965), *fuzzy logic* has become a mainstay of soft computing. Using if-then rules with fuzzy variables, fuzzy logic has been employed in a host of control applications including home appliances, elevators, automobile windows, cameras, and video games. (References are not given since these commercial applications are almost always proprietary.)

A *Bayesian network*, with nodes representing situations, uses Bayes' theorem on conditional probability to associate a probability with each of its links. Such Bayesian networks have been widely used for cognitive modeling, gene regulation networks, decision support systems, and so on. They are an integral part of soft computing.

1.4 Recent major accomplishments

We shall conclude our brief history of AI with an account of some of its relatively recent major accomplishments. These include expert systems, chess players, theorem provers, natural language processing, and a new killer application. Each will be described in turn.

1.4.1 Knowledge-based expert systems

Though knowledge-based expert systems made their appearance relatively early in AI history, they became a major, economically significant AI application somewhat later. Perhaps the earliest such commercially successful expert system was R1, later renamed XCON (McDermott 1980). XCON saved millions for DEC (Digitial Equipment Corporation) by effectively configuring their VAX computers before delivery, rather than having DEC engineers solve problems after their delivery. Other such applications followed, including diagnostic and maintenance systems for Campbell Soups' cookers and GE locomotives. A Ford Motor Company advertisement for a piece of production machinery stipulated that such a diagnostic and maintenance expert system be a part of every proposal. One book detailed 2,500 fielded expert systems. Expert systems constituted the first AI killer application. It was not to be the last.

1.4.2   Deep Blue beating Kasparov

Early AI researchers tended to work on problems that would require intelligence if attempted by a human. One such problem was playing chess. AI chess players appeared not long after Samuel's checker player. Among the most accomplished of these chess-playing systems was IBM's Deep Blue, which in 1997 succeeded in defeating world champion Gary Kasparov in a six-game match, belatedly fulfilling another of Herbert Simon's early predictions. Though running on a specially built computer and provided with much chess knowledge, Deep Blue depended ultimately upon traditional AI game-playing algorithms. The match with Kasparov constituted an AI triumph.

1.4.3   Solution of the Robbins conjecture

Another, even greater, AI triumph was soon to follow. In a 1933 paper E. V. Huntington gave a new set of three axioms that characterized a Boolean algebra, a formal mathematical system important to theoretical computer science. The third of these axioms was so complex as to be essentially unusable. Thus motivated, Herbert Robbins soon replaced this third axiom with a simpler one, and conjectured that this new three-axiom set also characterized Boolean algebras. This Robbins conjecture remained one of a host of such in the mathematical literature until the prominent logician and mathematician Alfred Tarski called attention to it, turning it into a famous unsolved problem. After resisting the efforts of human mathematicians for over half a century, the Robbins conjecture finally succumbed to a *general-purpose* AI automatic theorem prover called EQP (EQuational Prover). Where humans had failed, EQP succeeded in proving the Robbins conjecture to be true (McCune 1997).

1.4.4   Watson defeats human champions at Jeopardy

Jeopardy is a popular and long-running TV quiz show in which contestants are given clues in the form of answers to wide-ranging trivia questions and must respond with the corresponding questions as quickly as possible. Its twenty-eighth season opened in 2011. In that same year three special episodes of Jeopardy aired in which two of the most successful human champions and record holders were pitted against each other and against an AI system called Watson (in honor of the founder of IBM). Using its AI natural language processing algorithms to query some 200 million pages of content, and replying in conversational English, Watson consistently outperformed its two human opponents.

1.4.5   Games – the killer app

Employing more AI practitioners than any other, the computer and video game industry is enjoying a screaming success. According to one reliable source, the Entertainment Software Association, total US spending on the games industry topped 20 billion dollars in 2012, with 188 million games sold.[2] AI's role in this astounding success is critical; its use is essential to producing the needed intelligent behavior on the part of the virtual characters who populate the games. Wikipedia has an entry entitled "game artificial intelligence" that includes a history of the ever-increasing sophistication of AI techniques used in such games, as well as references to a half-dozen or so books on applying AI to games. At this writing there seems to be an unbounded demand for AI workers in the game industry. This highly successful commercial application is yet another triumph for AI.

1.5   Major AI research areas

There are almost a dozen distinct subfields of AI research, each with its own specialized journals, conferences, workshops, and so on. This section will provide a concise account of the research interests in each of these subfields.

1.5.1   Knowledge representation

Every AI system, be it a classical AI system with humans providing input and using the output, or an autonomous agent (Franklin and Graesser 1997), must somehow translate input (stimuli) into information or knowledge to be used to select output (action). This information or knowledge must somehow be represented within the system so that it can be processed to help determine output or action. The problems raised by such representation constitute the subject matter of research in the AI subfield commonly referred to as knowledge representation.

In AI systems, one encounters knowledge represented using logical formalisms such as propositional logic and first-order predicate calculus. One may also find network representations such as semantic nets whose nodes and links have labels providing semantic content. The underlying idea is that a concept, represented by a node, gains meaning via its relationships (links)

---

[2] www.theesa.com/facts/pdfs/ESA_EF_2013.pdf, pp. 10–11.

to other concepts. More complex data structures such as production rules, frames, and fuzzy sets are also used. Each of these data structures has its own type of reasoning or decision-making apparatus, its inference engine.

The issue of whether to represent or not seems to have been implicitly settled, as the arguments have died down. Rodney Brooks of the MIT AI Lab seems to have made his point that more than was previously thought could be accomplished without representation (1991). His opponents, however, have carried the day, in that representations continue to be widely used. It appears that representations are critical for the process of deciding what action to take, and much less so for the process of executing the action. This seems to be the essence of the issue.

1.5.2   Heuristic search

Search problems have been studied in computer science almost since its inception. For example, in the traveling salesman problem, the task is to find the most efficient route for a salesman to take to visit each of N cities exactly once. All known algorithms for finding optimal solutions to such a problem increase exponentially with N, meaning that for large numbers of cities no optimal solution can be found. However, good enough solutions can be found using heuristic search algorithms from AI. Such algorithms employ knowledge of the particular domain in the form of heuristics, rules of thumb, that are not guaranteed to find the best solution, but that most often find a good enough solution.

Such heuristic search algorithms are widely used for scheduling, for data mining (finding patterns in data), for constraint satisfaction problems, for games, for searching the web, and for many other such applications.

1.5.3   Planning

An AI planner is a system that automatically devises a sequence of actions leading from an initial real-world state to a desired goal state. Planners may be used, for example, to schedule work on a shop floor, to find routes for package delivery, or to assign usage of the Hubble telescope. Research on such planning programs is a major subfield of AI. Fielded applications are involved in space exploration, military logistics, and plant operations and control.

1.5.4   Expert systems

Knowledge-based expert systems were discussed in the previous sections. As a subfield of AI, expert systems researchers are concerned with reasoning (improving inference engines for their systems), knowledge representation (how to represent needed facts to their systems), and knowledge engineering (how to elicit knowledge from experts that is sometimes implicit). As we have seen, their fielded applications are legion.

1.5.5   Machine vision

Machine or computer vision is a subfield of AI devoted to the automated understanding of visual images, typically digital photographs. Among its many applications are product inspection, traffic surveillance, and military intelligence. With images multiplying every few seconds from satellites, high-flying spy planes, and autonomous drones, there are not enough humans to interpret and index the objects in the images so that they can be understood and located. Research toward automating this process is just starting. AI research in machine vision is also beginning to be applied to security video cameras so as to understand scenes and alert humans when necessary.

1.5.6   Machine learning

The AI subfield of machine learning[3] is concerned with algorithms that allow AI systems to learn (see Samuel's checker player above). Though machine learning is as old as AI itself, its importance has increased as more and more AI systems, especially autonomous agents (see below), are operating in progressively more complex and dynamically changing domains. Much of machine learning is supervised learning in which the system is instructed using training data. Unsupervised, or self-organizing systems, as mentioned above, are becoming common. Reinforcement learning, accomplished with artificial rewards, is typical for learning new tasks. There is even a new subfield of machine learning devoted to developmental robotics, robots that go through a rapid early learning phase, as do human children.

1.5.7   Natural language processing

The AI subfield of natural language processing includes both the generation and the understanding of natural language, usually text. Its history dates back to the Turing Test discussed earlier. Today it is a flourishing field of research into machine translation, question answering, automatic summarization, speech recognition, and other areas. Machine translators, though typically only about 90 percent accurate, can increase the productivity of human translators fourfold. Text recognition systems are being developed for the automatic input of medical histories. Voice recognition enables spoken commands to a computer and even dictation.

---

[3] Searching Google with the key words "machine learning" yielded this message: "Google is looking for Engineering experts to join our team. Apply!"

1.5.8   Software agents

An autonomous agent is defined to be a system situated in an environment that senses the environment and acts on it in pursuit of its own agenda, in such a way that its actions can influence what it later senses (Franklin and Graesser 1997). Artificial autonomous agents include software agents and some robots. Autonomous software agents come in several varieties. Some like the author's IDA "live" in an environment including databases and the internet, and autonomously perform a specified task such as assigning new jobs for sailors at the end of a tour of duty. Others, sometimes called avatars, have virtual faces or bodies displaying on monitors that allow them to interact more naturally with humans, often providing information. Still others, called conversational virtual agents, simulate humans, and interact conversationally with them in chat rooms, some so realistically as to be mistaken for human.[4] Finally, there are virtual agents as characters in computer and video games.

1.5.9   Intelligent tutoring systems

Intelligent tutoring systems are AI systems, typically software agents, whose task it is to tutor students interactively one on one, much as a human tutor would. Results from early efforts in this direction were disappointing. Later systems were more successful in domains such as mathematics that lend themselves to short answers from the student. More recently intelligent tutoring systems such as AutoTutor have been developed that can deal appropriately with full paragraphs written by the student. Today the major bottleneck in this research is getting domain knowledge into the tutoring systems. As a result, research in various authoring tools has flourished.

1.5.10   Robotics

In its early days robotics was a subfield of mechanical engineering with most research being devoted to developing robots capable of executing particular actions, such as grasping, walking, and so on. Their control systems were purely algorithmic, with no AI components. As robots became more capable, the need for more intelligent control structures became apparent, and cognitive robotics research involving AI-based control structures was born. Today, robotics and AI research have a significant and important overlap (more below).

---

[4] One such agent, called Julia, interacted so realistically that young men would hit on her.

1.6   Recent trends and directions

As the second decade of the twenty-first century began, artificial intelligence had not only emerged from its AI winter into an AI spring, but that spring had morphed into a full-fledged AI summer with its luxuriant growth of fruit. Flourishing recent trends include soft computing, AI for data mining, agent-based AI, cognitive computing (including developmental robotics and artificial general intelligence), and the application of AI in cognitive science. Let's look at each of these in turn.

1.6.1   Soft computing

In addition to the components described earlier (namely, neural nets, evolutionary computing, and fuzzy logic) soft computing is expanding into hybrid systems merging symbolic and connectionist AI. Prime examples of such hybrid systems are ACT-R, CLARION, and the author's LIDA. Most such hybrid systems, including the three examples, were intended as cognitive models. Some of them underlie the computational architectures of practical AI programs. Soft computing now also includes artificial immune systems with their significant contributions to computer security as well as applications to optimization and to protein structure prediction.

1.6.2   AI for data mining

Along with statistics, AI provides indispensable tools for data mining, the process of searching large databases for useful patterns of data. Many of these tools have been derived from research in machine learning. As databases rapidly increase in content, data mining systems become more and more useful, leading to a trend toward researching AI tools for data mining.

1.6.3   Agent-based AI

The situated, or embodied, cognition movement (Varela, Thompson, and Rosch 1991), in the form of agent-based AI, has clearly carried the day in AI research. Today, most newly fielded AI systems are autonomous agents of some sort. The dominant AI textbook (Russell and Norvig 2010), used in over 1,000 universities in over 100 countries, is the leading text, partially because its first edition was the first agent-based AI textbook. Applications of AI agents abound. Some were mentioned in the section on software agents above.

1.6.4   Cognitive computing

Perhaps the newest, and certainly among the most insistent, current trends in AI research is what has come to be called cognitive computing.[5] Cognitive computing includes cognitive robotics, development robotics, self-aware computing systems, autonomic computing systems and artificial general intelligence. We shall briefly describe each in turn.

As mentioned above, robotics in its early days was primarily concerned with *how* to perform actions, and was mostly a mechanical engineering discipline. More recently this emphasis is shifting to action selection, that is, to deciding *what* action to perform. *Cognitive robotics*, the endowing of robots with more cognitive capabilities, was born, and is becoming an active subfield of AI.

Another closely related new AI research discipline, *developmental robotics*, combines robotics, machine learning, and developmental psychology. The idea is to enable robots to learn continually. as humans do. Such learning should allow cognitive robots to operate in environments too complex and too dynamic for all contingencies to be hand-crafted into the robot. This new discipline is supported by the IEEE Technical Committee on Autonomous Mental Development, as well as its own journal, *Transactions on Autonomous Mental Development*.

Government agencies are investing in cognitive computing in the form of *self-aware computing systems*. DARPA, the Defense Advanced Research Programs Agency, sponsored the Workshop on Self-aware Computer Systems. Ron Brachman, then director of the DARPA IPTO program office, and since the president of AAAI, the Association for the Advancement of Artificial Intelligence, spelled it out thus:

A truly cognitive system would be able to … explain what it was doing and why it was doing it. It would be reflective enough to know when it was heading down a blind alley or when it needed to ask for information that it simply couldn't get to by further reasoning. And using these capabilities, a cognitive system would be robust in the face of surprises. It would be able to cope much more maturely with unanticipated circumstances than any current machine can.[6]

DARPA is currently supporting research on such biologically inspired cognitive systems.

IBM Research is offering commercially oriented support for cognitive computing through what it refers to as *autonomic computing*. The primary interest here is in self-configuring, self-diagnosing, and self-healing systems.

[5] The author heads the Cognitive Computing Research Group at the University of Memphis.
[6] www-formal.stanford.edu/jmc/www.selfawaresystems.org/

A very recent and not yet fully developed trend in AI research is the move toward systems exhibiting a more human-like general intelligence, often now called *artificial general intelligence* (AGI). The development of this AGI trend can be traced through a sequence of special tracks, special sessions, symposia, and workshops:

- AAAI'04 Fall Symposium entitled Achieving Human-Level Intelligence through Integrated Systems and Research
- AAAI'06 Special Track on Integrated Intelligent Capabilities
- WCCI'06 special session entitled A Roadmap to Human-Level Intelligence
- CogSci'06 Symposium on Building and Evaluating Models of Human-Level Intelligence
- AAAI'06 Spring Symposium entitled Between a Rock and a Hard Place: Cognitive Science Principles Meet AI-Hard Problems
- AAAI'09 Fall Symposium entitled Biologically Inspired Cognitive Architectures.
- AAAI'12 Spring Symposium entitled Designing Intelligent Robots: Reintegrating AI
- AGIRI Workshop on Artificial General Intelligence Workshop
- Artificial General Intelligence Conferences – 2008, 2009, 2010, 2011

AGI systems currently being developed include LIDA, Joshua Blue, and Novamente.

1.6.5   AI and cognitive science

The science side of AI is devoted primarily to modeling human cognition. Its application is to provide hopefully testable hypotheses for cognitive scientists and cognitive neuroscientists. In addition to cognitive models with more limited theoretical ambition, integrated models of large portions of cognition have been developed. These include SOAR, ACT-R, CLARION, and LIDA. Some of them have been implemented computationally as software agents, becoming part of embodied cognition. One of them, LIDA, implements several different psychological theories, including global workspace theory, working memory, perception by affordances, and transient episodic memory. The importance of this cognitive modeling subfield of AI has been recognized by a few computer science departments that have begun offering degree programs in cognitive science.

1.7   The core themes – where do they stand now?

Smart software vs. cognitive modeling. As throughout AI history, both pursuits are still active in AI research, the engineering side and the science side. Currently, both are moving toward a more general approach. Smart software is beginning to include AGI. Cognitive modeling is moving toward more integrated hybrid models such as ACT-R, CLARION, and LIDA, in addition to its traditional interest in more specialized models. Another major push on the smart software side is toward more autonomous software agent systems.

Symbolic AI vs. neural nets. Both symbolic AI and neural nets have survived their respective winters and are now flourishing. Neither side of the controversy has won out. Both continue to be quite useful. They are even coming together in such hybrid systems as ACT-R, CLARION, and LIDA. ACT-R melds symbolic and neural net features, CLARION consists of a neural net module interconnected with a symbolic module, and LIDA incorporates passing activation throughout an otherwise symbolic system, making it also quite neural-net-like.

Reasoning vs. perception. Research into AI reasoning continues unabated in such subfields as search, planning, and expert systems. Fielded practical applications are legion. Perception has come into its own in machine vision, agent-based computing, and cognitive robotics. Note that reasoning and perception come together in the last two, as well as in integrated cognitive modeling and AGI.

Reasoning vs. knowledge. In addition to reasoning, knowledge plays a critical role in expert systems, and in agent-based computing, self-aware computing, and autonomic computing also. Again both are alive and flourishing, with the importance of adding knowledge to practical systems ever more apparent. Data mining has become another way of acquiring such knowledge.

To represent or not. Without representation, Brooks' subsumption architecture accords each layer its own senses and ability to choose and perform its single act. A higher level can, when appropriate, subsume the action of the next lower level. With this subsumption architecture controlling robots, Brooks successfully made his point that much could and should be done with little or no representation. Still, representation is almost ubiquitous in AI systems as they become able to deal more intelligently with ever more complex, dynamic environments. It would seem that representation is critical to the process of action selection in AI systems, but much less so to the execution of these actions. The argument over whether to represent seems to have simply died away.

Brain in a vat vs. embodied AI. For once we seem to have a winner. Embodied, or situated, AI has simply taken over, as most of the new research into AI systems is agent based. Perusal of the titles of talks at any of the general AI conferences such as AAAI or IJCAI (International Joint Conference on Artificial Intelligence) makes this abundantly clear.

Narrow AI vs. human-level intelligence. Narrow AI continues to flourish unabated, while the pursuit of human-level intelligence in machines is gaining momentum via AGI.

Except for the strong move of AI research toward embodiment, each side of every issue continues to be strongly represented in today's AI research. Research into artificial intelligence is thriving as never before, and promises continuing contributions, both practical to engineering and theoretical to science.

Further reading

Franklin, S. (1995). *Artificial Minds*. Cambridge MA: MIT Press. In this book for the intelligent layperson, the reader will find expanded discussions of most of the major themes and ideas of this chapter.

Russell, S. and Norvig, P. (2010). *Artificial Intelligence: A Modern Approach* (3rd edn.). Upper Saddle River, NJ: Prentice Hall. This best-selling text offers the most comprehensive, state-of-the-art introduction to the theory and practice of artificial intelligence. It is both readable and monumentally complete, perfect for a general reference to the various topics in this chapter.

Timeline: A Brief History of Artificial Intelligence. An online chronology of significant events in the History of AI prepared by the Association for the Advancement of Artificial Intelligence. www.aaai.org/AITopics/pmwiki/pmwiki.php/AITopics/BriefHistory

References

Brooks, R. A. (1991). Intelligence without representation, *Artificial Intelligence* 47: 139–59.

Chalmers, D. (1990). Why Fodor and Pylyshyn were wrong: The simplest refutation, in *Proceedings of the 12th Annual Conference of the Cognitive Science Society* (pp. 340–7). Hillsdale, NJ: Lawrence Erlbaum.

Church, A. (1936). An unsolvable problem of elementary number theory, *American Journal of Mathematics* 58: 345–63.

Davis, R., Buchanan, B., and Shortliffe, E. (1977). Production rules as a representation for a knowledge-based consultation program, *Artificial Intelligence* 8: 15–45.

Fodor, J. A. and Pylyshyn, Z. W. (1988). Connectionism and cognitive architecture, *Cognition* 28: 3–71.

Franklin, S. and Graesser, A. (1997). Is it an agent, or just a program?: A taxonomy for autonomous agents, in J. Müller, M. J. Wooldridge, and N. R. Jennings (eds.), *Intelligent Agents III: Agent Theories, Architectures, and Languages* (pp. 21–35). Berlin: Springer Verlag.

Holland, J. H. (1975). *Adaptation in Natural and Artificial Systems*. Ann Arbor: University of Michigan Press.

Lindsay, R. K., Buchanan, B. G., Feigenbaum, E. A., and Lederberg. J. (1980). *Applications of Artificial Intelligence for Organic Chemistry: The Dendral Project*. Columbus, OH: McGraw-Hill.

McClelland, J. L., Rumelhart, D. E., and the PDP Research Group. (1986). *Parallel Distributed Processing: Explorations in the Microstructure of Cognition*, vol. 2: *Psychological and Biological Models*. Cambridge, MA: MIT Press.

McCulloch, W. S. and Pitts, W. H. (1943). A logical calculus of the ideas immanent in nervous activity, *Bulletin of Mathematical Biophysics* 5: 115–33.

McCune, W. (1997). Solution of the Robbins problem, *Journal of Automated Reasoning* 19: 263–76.

McDermott, J. P. (1980). R1: The formative years, *AI Magazine* 2: 21–9.

Minsky, M. (1954). *Neural Nets and the Brain Model Problem*. PhD. Dissertation, Princeton University.

Minsky, M. and Papert, S. (1969). *Perceptrons*. Cambridge, MA: MIT Press.

Newell, A., Shaw, J. C., and Simon, H. A. (1959). Report on a general problem-solving program, *Proceedings of the International Conference on Information Processing, Paris* (pp. 256–64). Paris: UNESCO.

Post, E. L. (1943). Formal reductions of the general combinatorial decision problem, *American Journal of Mathematics* 65: 197–215.

Rosenblatt, F. (1958). The perceptron: A probabilistic model for information storage and organization in the brain, *Psychological Review* 65: 386–408.

Rumelhart, D. E., McClelland, J. L., and the PDP Research Group (1986). *Parallel Distributed Processing: Explorations in the Microstructure of Cognition*, vol. 1: *Foundations*. Cambridge, MA: MIT Press.

Russell, S. and Norvig, P. (2010). *Artificial Intelligence: A Modern Approach* (3rd edn.). Upper Saddle River, NJ: Prentice Hall.

Samuel, A. L. (1959). Some studies in machine learning using the game of checkers, *IBM Journal of Research and Development* 3: 211–29.

Smolensky, P. (1987). The constituent structure of connectionist mental states: A reply to Fodor and Pylyshyn, *Southern Journal of Philosophy*, 26 (Supplement): 137–63. Reprinted in T. Horgan and J. Tienson (eds.), (1991), *Connectionism and the Philosophy of Mind* (pp. 281–308). Dordrecht: Kluwer Academic.

Turing, A. M. (1936). On computable numbers, with an application to the Entscheidungsproblem, *Proceedings of the London Mathematical Society* 42: 230–65.

(1950). Computing machinery and intelligence, *Mind* 59: 433–60. Reprinted in E. A. Feigenbaum and J. Feldman (eds.) (1963), *Computers and Thought* (pp. 11–35). New York: McGraw-Hill.

Varela, F. J., Thompson, E., and Rosch, E. (1991). *The Embodied Mind*. Cambridge, MA: MIT Press.

Winograd, T. (1972). *Understanding Natural Language*. San Diego: Academic Press.

Zadeh, L. A., (1965). Fuzzy sets, *Information and Control* 8: 338–53.

2 Philosophical foundations

Konstantine Arkoudas and Selmer Bringsjord

2.1 Introduction

Much work in artificial intelligence has built on concepts and theories developed by philosophers and logicians. This chapter introduces this foundational work, surveying different conceptions of AI, the philosophical dream of mechanizing human reasoning, the conceptual roots of AI, and the major theories of mind that have underpinned different strands of AI research.

2.2 What is AI?

That is itself a deep philosophical question, and attempts to systematically answer it fall within the foundations of AI as a rich topic for analysis and debate. Nonetheless, a provisional answer can be given: AI is the field devoted to building artifacts capable of displaying, in controlled, well-understood environments, and over sustained periods of time, behaviors that we consider to be intelligent, or more generally, behaviors that we take to be at the heart of what it is to have a mind. Of course this answer gives rise to further questions, most notably, what exactly constitutes intelligent behavior, what it is to have a mind, and *how* humans actually manage to behave intelligently. The last question is empirical; it is for psychology and cognitive science to answer. It is particularly pertinent, however, because any insight into human thought might help us to build machines that work similarly. Indeed, as will emerge in this article, AI and cognitive science have developed along parallel and tightly interwoven paths; their stories cannot be told separately. The second question, the one that asks what is the mark of the mental, is philosophical. AI has lent significant urgency to it, and conversely, we will see that careful philosophical contemplation of this question has influenced the course of AI itself. Finally, the first challenge, that of specifying precisely what is to count as intelligent behavior, has traditionally been met by proposing particular behavioral tests whose successful passing would signify the presence of intelligence.

The most famous of these is what has come to be known as the *Turing Test* (TT), introduced by Turing (1950). In TT, a woman and a computer are sequestered in sealed rooms, and a human judge, ignorant as to which of the two rooms contains which contestant, asks them both questions by email (actually, by *teletype*, to use the original term). If, on the strength of the returned answers, the judge can do no better than 50/50 when delivering a verdict as to which room houses which player, we say that the computer in question has *passed* TT. According to Turing, a computer able to pass TT should be declared a *thinking* machine.

His claim has been controversial, although it seems undeniable that linguistic behavior of the sort required by TT *is* routinely taken to be at the heart of human cognition. Part of the controversy stems from the unabashedly behaviorist presuppositions of the test. Block's "Aunt Bertha" thought experiment (1981) was intended to challenge these presuppositions, arguing that it is not only the behavior of an organism that determines whether it is intelligent. We must also consider *how* the organism achieves intelligence. That is, the internal functional organization of the system must be taken into account. This was a key point of *functionalism*, another major philosophical undercurrent of AI, to which we will return later. (For more discussion of Block's thought experiment, under its other name, "the Blockhead argument," see Chapter 3.)

Another criticism of TT is that it is unrealistic and may even have obstructed AI progress insofar as it is concerned with *disembodied* intelligence. As we will see, many thinkers have concluded that disembodied artifacts with human-level intelligence are a pipe dream, practically impossible to build, if not downright conceptually absurd. Accordingly, Harnad (1991) insists that sensorimotor capability is required of artifacts that would spell success for AI, and he proposes the *Total* TT (TTT) as an improvement over TT. Whereas in TT a bodiless computer program could, at least in principle, pass, TTT-passers must be robots able to operate in the physical environment in a way that is indistinguishable from the behaviors manifested by embodied human persons navigating the physical world.

When AI is defined as the field devoted to engineering artifacts able to pass TT, TTT, and various other tests,[1] it can be safely said that we are dealing with *weak* AI. Put differently, weak AI aims at building machines that *act* intelligently, without taking a position on whether or not the machines actually *are* intelligent.

There is another answer to the "What is AI?" question: AI is the field devoted to building persons, period. This brand of AI is so-called *strong* AI,[2] an ambitious form of the field aptly summed up by Haugeland:

The fundamental goal [of AI research] is not merely to mimic intelligence or produce some clever fake. Not at all. AI wants only the genuine article: *machines with minds*, in the full and literal sense. This is not science fiction, but real

---

[1] More stringent tests than TT and TTT are discussed by Bringsjord (1995).

[2] To the best of our knowledge, the distinction between strong and weak AI was first made (in those terms) by Searle (1980).

science, based on a theoretical conception as deep as it is daring: namely, we are, at root, *computers ourselves*. (Haugeland 1985, p. 2)

This "theoretical conception" of the human mind as a computer has served as the bedrock of most strong-AI research to date. It has come to be known as the computational theory of the mind; we will discuss it in detail shortly. On the other hand, AI engineering that is itself informed by philosophy, as in the case of the sustained attempt to mechanize reasoning, discussed in the next section, can be pursued in the service of both weak and strong AI.

2.3 Philosophical AI: The example of mechanizing reasoning

It would not be unreasonable to describe Classical Cognitive Science as an extended attempt to apply the methods of proof theory to the modelling of thought. (Fodor and Pylyshyn 1988, pp. 29–30)

This section is devoted to a discussion of an area that serves as an exemplar of AI that is bound up with philosophy (as opposed to philosophy *of* AI). This is the area that any student of both philosophy and AI ought to be familiar with, first and foremost. Part of the reason for this is that other problems in AI of at least a partially philosophical nature are intimately connected with the attempt to mechanize human-level reasoning.[3]

Aristotle considered rationality to be an essential characteristic of the human mind. Deductive thought, expressed in terms of syllogisms, was the hallmark of such rationality, as well as the fundamental intellectual instrument (*organon*) of all science. Perhaps the deepest contribution of Aristotle to artificial intelligence was the idea of *formalism*. The notion that certain patterns of thought are valid by virtue of their syntactic *form*, independently of content, was an exceedingly powerful innovation, and it is that notion that remains at the heart of the contemporary computational theory of the mind (Pylyshyn 1989) and what we have called *strong* AI above.

In view of the significance that was historically attached to deduction in philosophy (starting with Aristotle and continuing with Euclid, and later Bacon, Hobbes, Leibniz, and others), the very idea of an intelligent machine was often tantamount to a machine that can perform logical inference: one that can validly extract conclusions from premises. *Automated theorem proving* (ATP), as the field is known today, has thus been an integral part of AI from the very beginning, although, as we will see, its relevance has been hotly debated, especially in recent decades. Broadly speaking, the problem of

---

[3] Many examples can be given. One is the *frame problem*, which we discuss in Section 2.6. Another is *defeasible reasoning*, which is the problem of how to formalize inference given that much everyday reasoning only temporarily commits us to conclusions, in light of the fact that newly arrived information often defeats prior arguments.

mechanizing deduction has at least three different layers. Listed in order of increasing difficulty, we have:

- *Proof checking*: Given a deduction D that purports to derive a conclusion P from a number of premises $P_1, \ldots, P_n$, decide whether or not D is correct.
- *Proof discovery*: Given a number of premises $P_1, \ldots, P_n$ and a putative conclusion P, decide whether P follows logically from the premises, and if it does, produce a formal derivation of it.
- *Conjecture generation*: Given a number of premises $P_1, \ldots, P_n$, generate an "interesting" conclusion P that is likely to follow logically from the premises.

Technically speaking, the first problem is the easiest. In the case of predicate logic with equality, the problem of checking the correctness of a given deduction is not only algorithmically solvable, but efficiently so. Nevertheless, the problem is pregnant with interesting philosophical and technical issues, and its relevance to AI was realized early on by McCarthy (1962), who wrote that "checking mathematical proofs is potentially one of the most interesting and useful applications of automatic computers."

The second problem is considerably harder. Early results in recursive function theory (Church 1936; Turing 1936) established that there is no Turing machine which can decide whether an arbitrary formula of first-order logic is valid (that was Hilbert's *Entscheidungsproblem*). Therefore, by Church's thesis, it follows that the problem is algorithmically unsolvable – there is no general mechanical method that will always make the right decision in a finite amount of time. However, humans have no guarantee of always solving the problem either (and indeed often fail to do so). Accordingly, AI can look for conservative approximations that perform well in practice: programs that give the right answer as often as possible, and otherwise do not give an answer at all (either failing explicitly, or else going on indefinitely until we stop them). The problem was tackled early on for weaker formalisms with seemingly promising results: The Logic Theorist (LT) of Newell, Simon, and Shaw, presented at the inaugural 1956 AI conference at Dartmouth, managed to prove thirty-eight out of the fifty-two propositional-logic theorems of *Principia Mathematica*. Other notable early efforts included an implementation of Presburger arithmetic by Martin Davis in 1954 at Princeton's Institute for Advanced Studies (Davis 2001), the Davis-Putnam procedure (Davis and Putnam 1960), variations of which are used today in many satisfiability-based provers, and an impressive system for first-order logic built by Wang (1960). It should be noted that whereas LT was intentionally designed to simulate human reasoning and problem-solving processes, the authors of these other systems believed that mimicking human processes was unnecessarily constraining, and that better results could be achieved by doing away with cognitive plausibility. This was an early manifestation of a tension that is still felt in the field and which parallels the distinction between strong and weak forms of AI: AI as science, particularly as the study of human thought, vs. AI as engineering – the construction of intelligent systems whose operation need not resemble the internal workings of human cognition.

Robinson's discovery of unification and the resolution method (Robinson 1965) provided a major boost to the field. Most automated theorem provers today are based on resolution. Other prominent formalisms include semantic tableaux and equational logic (Robinson and Voronkov 2001). While there has been impressive progress over the last ten years, the most sophisticated ATPs today continue to be brittle, and occasionally fail on problems that would be trivial for college students.

The third problem, that of conjecture generation, is the most difficult, but it is also the most interesting. Conjectures do not fall from the sky, after all. Presented with a body of information, humans – particularly mathematicians – regularly come up with interesting conjectures and then set out to prove those conjectures, often with success. This discovery process (along with new concept formation) is one of the most *creative* activities of the human intellect. The sheer difficulty of simulating this creativity computationally is surely a chief reason why AI has made little progress here. But another reason is that throughout most of the previous century (and really beginning with Frege in the nineteenth century), logicians and philosophers were concerned almost exclusively with *justification* rather than with *discovery*. This applied not only to deductive reasoning but to inductive reasoning as well, and indeed to scientific theorizing in general (Reichenbach 1938). It was widely felt that the discovery process should be studied by psychologists, not by philosophers and logicians. Interestingly, this was not the case prior to Frege. Philosophers such as Descartes (1988), Bacon (2002), Mill (1874), and Peirce (1960) had all attempted to study the discovery process rationally and to formulate rules for guiding it. Beginning with Hanson (1958) in science and with Lakatos (1976) in mathematics (the latter having been heavily influenced by Pólya (1945)), philosophers started re-emphasizing discovery. AI researchers also attempted to model discovery computationally, both in science (Langley et al. 1987) and in mathematics (Lenat 1976, 1983), and this line of work has led to machine-learning innovations in AI such as genetic programming (Koza 1992) and inductive logic programming (Muggleton 1992). However, the successes have been limited, and fundamental philosophical objections to algorithmic treatments of discovery and creativity in general – for example, such as put forth by Hempel (1985) – remain trenchant. A major issue is the apparently holistic character of higher cognitive processes such as creative reasoning, and the difficulty of formulating a rigorous characterization of relevance. Without a precise notion of relevance, one that is amenable to computational implementation, there seems to be little hope for progress on the conclusion-generation problem, or on any of the other similar problems, including concept generation and abductive hypothesis formation.

Faced with relatively meager progress on the hard reasoning problems, and influenced by various critiques of symbolic AI (see Section 2.6), some AI researchers (such as Minsky 1986, p. 167) launched serious attacks on formal logic, criticizing it as an overly rigid system that does not provide a good model of the eminently flexible mechanisms of human reasoning. They have accordingly tried to shift the field's attention and efforts away from rigorous deductive and inductive reasoning, turning them toward "commonsense reasoning" instead. A good deal of work has been aimed at developing *formal* systems for modeling commonsense reasoning (Davis and Morgenstern 2004). However, critics charge that such efforts miss the greater point. For instance, Winograd writes that

Minsky places the blame for lack of success in explaining ordinary reasoning on the rigidity of logic, and does not raise the more fundamental questions about the nature of all symbolic representations and of formal (though possibly non-logical) systems of rules for manipulating them. There are basic limits to what can be done with symbol manipulation, regardless of how many "different, useful ways to chain things together" one invents. The reduction of mind to decontextualized fragments is ultimately impossible and misleading. (Winograd 1990, p. 172)

As we will see in the sequel, similar criticisms have been made by Dreyfus (1992) and others, who have argued that symbol manipulation cannot account for such essential human traits as intuition, judgment, and imagination, all of which can play a key role in inference and problem solving in general; and that human reasoning will never be matched by any decontextualized and unembodied (or "unsituated") system that works by formally representing and manipulating symbolic information.

2.4   Historical and conceptual roots of AI

AI officially started in 1956, launched by a small but now-famous summer conference at Dartmouth College, in Hanover, New Hampshire. (The fifty-year celebration of this conference, AI@50, was held in July 2006 at Dartmouth, with five of the original participants making it back. Some of what happened at this historic conference figures in the final section of this chapter.) Ten thinkers attended, including John McCarthy (who was working at Dartmouth in 1956), Claude Shannon, Marvin Minsky, Arthur Samuel, Trenchard Moore (apparently the youngest attendee, and the lone note-taker at the original conference), Ray Solomonoff, Oliver Selfridge, Allen Newell, and Herbert Simon. From where we stand now, some years into the new millennium, the Dartmouth conference is memorable for many reasons, including this pair: (1) the term "artificial intelligence" was coined there (and has long been firmly entrenched, despite being disliked to this day by some of the attendees, e.g., Moore); (2) Newell and Simon revealed a program – Logic Theorist (LT) – agreed by those at the conference (and, indeed, by nearly all those who learned about it soon after the Dartmouth event) to be a remarkable achievement. LT, as we have mentioned, was capable of proving elementary theorems in the propositional calculus, and was regarded as a remarkable step toward the rendering of human-level reasoning in concrete computation.

From the standpoint of philosophy, however, neither the 1956 conference nor the aforementioned Turing *Mind* paper of 1950 come close to marking the start of AI. Hobbes had already anticipated strong AI back in the seventeenth century, when he famously proclaimed that "ratiocination is computation." Roughly in that same era, Leibniz dreamed of a "universal calculus" in which all disputes could be settled by rote calculation. And Descartes had already considered something like the Turing Test long before Turing, albeit adopting a rather pessimistic view of the matter in perhaps a somewhat glib fashion:

[I]f there were machines which bore a resemblance to our body and imitated our actions as far as it was morally possible to do so, we should always have two very certain tests by which to recognise that, for all that, they were not real men. The first is, that they could never use speech or other signs as we do when placing our thoughts on record for the benefit of others. For we can easily understand a machine's being constituted so that it can utter words, and even emit some responses to action on it of a corporeal kind...But it never happens that it arranges its speech in various ways, in order to reply appropriately to everything that may be said in its presence, as even the lowest type of man can do. And the second difference is, that although machines can perform certain things as well as or perhaps better than any of us can do, they infallibly fall short in others, by the which means we may discover that they did not act from knowledge, but only from the disposition of their organs. (Descartes 1911, p. 116)

But while the ceremonial inauguration of AI was the 1956 Dartmouth conference, and while philosophers have ruminated on machines and intelligence for centuries, the key conceptual origins of AI can be found at the intersection of two of the most important intellectual developments of the twentieth century:

- the "cognitive revolution"[4] that started in the mid 1950s and which overthrew behaviorism and rehabilitated mentalistic psychology;

---

[4] Speaking of the cognitive revolution has become somewhat of a banality, particularly after the 1980s saw the publication of two books on the subject (Baars 1986; Gardner 1985).

- the theory of computability that had been developed over the preceding couple of decades by pioneers such as Turing, Church, Kleene, and Gödel.

The significance of each for AI will be briefly discussed below.

The cognitive revolution is typically associated with the work of George Miller and Noam Chomsky in the 1950s, particularly with the latter's notorious review of Skinner's theory of language (Chomsky 1996). It had been anticipated in the 1940s by McCulloch and Pitts (1943) and other cybernetics pioneers, who had already been pointing out the similarities between human thought and information processing, as well as by experimental results obtained by psychologists such as Tolman (1948), who, studying maze navigation by rats, presented evidence for the existence of "cognitive maps." Particularly influential was Chomsky's famous "poverty of stimulus" argument to the effect that the efficiency and rapidity of language acquisition during childhood cannot be explained solely by appeal to the meager data to which children are exposed in their early years; rather, they compel the postulation of innate mental rules and representations that encode linguistic competence. Strong cases for the existence of mental representations were also made by experimental findings pertaining to memory, such as the results of Sperling (1960), which indicated that humans typically *store* more information than they can report. Memory, after all, provides perhaps the clearest case of mental representation; it seems absurd to deny that people store information, that is, that we have some sort of internal representation of information such as the year we were born or the names of our parents. That much is commonsensical to the point of triviality, as is the claim that people routinely talk as if they really have beliefs, hopes, desires, and so on; and indeed most behaviorists would not have denied these claims. What they denied was the *theoretical legitimacy* of explaining human behavior by positing unobservable mental entities (such as memories), or that intentional terminology had any place in a *science* of the mind. Essentially a positivist doctrine, behaviorism had a distrust of anything that could not be directly observed and a general aversion to theory. It had been the dominant paradigm in psychology for most of the twentieth century, up until the mid 1950s, until it was finally dethroned by the new "cognitive" approach.

2.5 Computational theories of mind and the problem of mental content

Once the first steps were taken and mental representations were openly allowed in scientific theorizing about the mind, the "computer metaphor" – with which researchers such as Newell and Simon had already been flirting – became ripe for explosion. After all, computers were known to store structured data in their memories and to solve problems by manipulating that data in systematic ways, by executing appropriate instructions. Perhaps a similar model could explain – and eventually help to duplicate – human thought. Indeed, the postulation of mental representations would not by itself go far if their causal efficacy could not be explained in a mechanistic and systematic manner. Granted that structured mental representations are necessary for higher-order cognition; but *how* do such representations actually *cause* rational thought and action? The theory of computation was enlisted precisely in order to meet this important theoretical need. The result became known as the *computational theory of mind* (CTM for short), a doctrine that has been inextricably linked with strong AI. In the next paragraph we briefly discuss the main tenets of CTM.

The first core idea of CTM is to explain intentional mental states by giving a computational spin to Russell's analysis (1940) of intentional sentences such as "Tom believes that 7 is a prime number" as *propositional attitudes* that involve a psychological attitude A (in this case believing) toward a proposition P (in this case, that 7 is prime). More precisely, to be in a mental state involving an attitude A and proposition P is to be in a certain relationship R_A with a mental representation M_P whose meaning is P. To put it simplistically, to have a belief that 7 is a prime number is to have a mental representation in your "belief box" which means that 7 is prime. The representation itself is symbolic. That is, your "belief box" contains a *token of a symbolic structure* whose meaning (or "content") is that 7 is prime. Thus, mental representations have both syntax and semantics, much like the sentences of natural languages. They constitute a "language of thought," so to speak, or *mentalese*. But it is only their syntax – syntax ultimately being reducible to physical shape – that makes them causally efficacious. This is a plausible story because, as work in logic and computability has shown, there exist purely syntactic transformations of symbolic structures that are nevertheless sensitive to semantics. Deductive proofs provide perhaps the best example: By manipulating formulas exclusively on the basis of their syntactic properties, it is possible to extract from them other formulas which *follow logically* from them. Syntax can thus mirror semantics, or, as Haugeland (1985, p. 106) put it, "if you take care of the syntax, the semantics will take care of itself." On this model, a mental process is a sequence of tokenings of mental representations which express the propositional content of the corresponding thoughts. The causes and effects of each mental representation, what it can actually *do*, are determined by its syntax "in much the way that the geometry of a key determines which locks it will open" (Fodor 1987, p. 19). And the entire process is orchestrated by an algorithm, a set of instructions that determines how the representations succeed one another in the overall train of thought. That is the second core idea of CTM. The mind is thus viewed as a "syntactic engine" driving a semantic engine, and, at least in principle, its operation could be duplicated on a computer.

A natural extension of CTM is Turing-machine functionalism, which was first adumbrated by Putnam (1960) in an influential paper that helped to drive the cognitive revolution forward (at least in philosophical circles), to undermine behaviorism, and to shape the outlook of strong AI. Functionalism in general is, roughly, the idea that the essence of a mental state is not to be found in the biology of the brain (or in the physics that underwrites the hardware of its central processing unit, in the case of a machine) but rather in the *role* that the state plays in one's mental life (or computations), and particularly in the causal relations that it bears to stimuli (inputs), behavior (outputs), and other mental (computational) states. Turing-machine functionalism, in particular, is the idea that the mind is essentially a giant Turing machine whose operation is specified by a set of instructions dictating that if the mind is in a certain state s and receives a certain input x, a transition is made to a state s' and an output y is emitted. The most popular – and least implausible – versions of Turing-machine functionalism allow for probabilistic transitions.

Also closely related to CTM (in fact stronger than it) is the *physical symbol system hypothesis* (PSSH) put forth by Newell and Simon (1976). According to it, a physical symbol system "has the necessary and sufficient means for general intelligent action" (1976, p. 116), where a physical symbol system is "a machine that produces through time an evolving collection of symbol structures" – a symbol structure being a collection of symbol tokens "related in some physical way (such as one token being next to another)" and subject to a variety of syntactic operations, most notably "creation, modification, reproduction, and destruction." Newell and Simon regarded machines executing list-processing programs of the LISP variety as the prototypical examples of physical symbol systems. While there have been various internal disagreements (e.g., pertaining to questions of innateness), in some form or other CTM, PSSH, and Turing-machine functionalism together loosely characterize "classical" or "symbolic" AI, or what Haugeland (1985, p. 112) has dubbed GOFAI ("good old-fashioned AI"). All three were posited as substantive empirical theses, CTM and Turing-machine functionalism about the human mind and PSSH about intelligence in general (GOFAI too, was explicitly characterized by Haugeland as an empirical doctrine of cognitive science). They set the parameters and goals for most AI research for at least the first three decades of the field, and they continue to be a dominant influence, although, as we will see, they are no longer the only game in town, having suffered considerable setbacks as a result of forceful attacks that have elaborated serious conceptual and empirical problems with the GOFAI approach.

According to CTM, complex thoughts are represented by complex symbolic structures in much the same way that, in natural languages and formal logics alike, complex sentences are recursively built up from simpler components. Thus the mental representation of a complex thought such as "All men are mortal" contains component mental representations for concepts such as "mortal" and "men," as well as "all" and "are." These components are somehow assembled together (and eventually science should be able to spell out the details of how such symbolic operations are carried out in the brain) to form the complex thought whose content is that all men are mortal. That is how complex thoughts attain their meaning, by combining the meanings of their components. Now, a compositional story of this sort – akin to the compositional semantics championed by Frege and Tarski – is only viable if there is an inventory of primitives that can be used as the ultimate building blocks of more complex representations. The central question for CTM, which has a direct analogue in AI, is how these primitives acquire meaning. More precisely, the question is how mentalese primitives *inside* our brains (or inside a robot's central processing unit) manage to be about objects and states of affairs *outside* our brains – objects that may not even exist and states of affairs that may not even obtain. This is also referred to as the *symbol grounding* problem (Harnad 1990). It is not merely a philosophical puzzle about the human mind, or even a protoscientific question of psychology. It has direct engineering implications for AI, since a plausible answer to it might translate into a methodology for building a robot that potentially averts some of the most devastating objections to CTM (these will be discussed in the next section). Such a robot would "think" by performing computations over formal symbolic structures (as we presumably do, according to CTM), but nevertheless be sufficiently grounded in the real world that it could be said to attain extra-symbolic understanding (as we do). Clearly it is not tenable to suggest that evolution has endowed us with all the right primitive symbols having all the right meanings built in, since evolution could not have foreseen such things as thermostats or satellites.

A number of theories have been expounded in response, all falling under the banner of "naturalizing content," "naturalizing semantics," or "naturalizing intentionality." The objective is to provide a physicalistic account of how mentalese symbol tokens in our heads manage to be about things that are external to us (or, framing the issue independently of CTM, how mental states can achieve meaning). The type of account that is sought, in other words, is reductive and materialistic; it should be expressed in the non-intentional vocabulary of pure physical science. In what follows we will briefly review three of the most prominent attempts to provide naturalized accounts of meaning: informational theories, evolutionary theories, and conceptual-role semantics.

The gist of informational theories is the notion of covariance. The idea is that if a quantity x covaries systematically with a quantity y, then x carries information about y. A car's speedometer covaries systematically with the car's speed and thus carries information about it. Accordingly, we can view the speedometer as an intentional system, in that its readings are *about* the velocity of the car. Likewise, we say that smoke "means" fire in that smoke carries information about fire. This is a sense of the word "means" that Grice called *natural meaning*, a notion that presaged theories of informational semantics. Again, because smoke and fire are nomologically covariant, we can say that one is about the other. Here, then, we have the beginnings of a naturalized treatment of meaning that regards intentionality as a common natural phenomenon rather than a peculiarly mental one. Concerning mentalese semantics, the core insight of such theories – put somewhat simplistically – is that the meaning of a symbol is determined by whatever the tokenings of that symbol systematically (nomologically) covary with. If a token of a certain mentalese symbol H pops up in our brains whenever a horse appears in front of us, then H carries information about horses and thus means *horse.*

Evolutionary theories maintain, roughly, that intentional states are adaptations, in the same way that livers and thumbs are adaptations, and that the content (meaning) of an intentional state is the function for which it was selected, that is, the purpose that it serves. Like all adaptationist theories, this too is susceptible to charges of Panglossianism (Gould and Lewontin 1979). Nevertheless, the basic story is not implausible for, say, beliefs to the effect that there is a predator nearby or for desires to get and eat some bananas that appear in one's visual field. The content of such a belief would be something like "there is a tiger under that tree over there," which would presumably be the function for which such beliefs were selected (to correlate with tigers under trees), and the content of such a desire would be "I want to eat those bananas over there," which would again coincide with the purpose served by such desires (obtaining food and surviving).

Conceptual-role semantics (CRS) takes its cue from Wittgenstein's famous "use" theory of meaning, according to which the meaning of a linguistic item (expression, sentence, etc.) is the way in which that item is used by speakers of the language. The main thesis of CRS is that the meaning of a mentalese symbol S is fixed by the role that S plays in one's cognitive life, and particularly by the relations that it bears to other symbols, to perception, and to action. It is thus very similar to functionalism about mental states. Logical connectives such as *and* provide the standard illustrations for the use theory of linguistic meaning, and, likewise, the meaning of a mentalese symbol equivalent to *and* would be the role it plays in our heads, for example, the set of mentalese inferences in which it participates. The theory has notable similarities to the *operational semantics* of programming languages in theoretical computer science. In cognitive science, CRS has been known as *procedural semantics*. It was primarily advocated by Johnson-Laird (1977), and roundly criticized by Fodor.

Related to this is the whole issue of externalism. CRS makes the meaning of a symbol a thoroughly internal matter, contingent only on the relations it bears to other symbols and states (including perceptual and behavioral states). But clearly there is more to meaning than that. At least on the face of it, meaning seems to hook symbols to the world, not just to other symbols. The meaning of the term *dog* must have something to do with its *reference*, that is, with actual dogs, and the meaning of *Aristotle* must have something to do with the actual Aristotle. More sophisticated externalist challenges were presented by Putnam and Burge, arguing respectively that meaning is a function of the overall physical and social environment in which one is embedded. So-called *two-factor* CRS were developed in response, in an attempt to distinguish between *narrow* and *wide* mental content. Narrow meaning is "in the head" and does not depend on the surrounding circumstances, while wide meaning hinges on reference and has truth conditions. An entire industry has grown around this distinction, and we do not have the space to delve into it here.

Incidentally, it was precisely the lack of a connection between mentalese and the world (or between a computer's symbols and the world) that was the chief objection of Fodor (1978) when he argued against the AI-style "procedural semantics" advocated by Johnson-Laird. The latter had written that the "artificial languages, which are used to communicate programs of instructions to computers, have both a syntax and semantics. Their syntax consists of rules for writing well-formed programs that a computer can interpret and execute. *Their semantics consists of the procedures that the computer is instructed to execute*" (Johnson-Laird 1977, p. 189, our italics).

In an important critique of Johnson-Laird's article that in some ways presaged Searle's Chinese Room argument, Fodor protested that:

> The computer models provide no semantic theory *at all*, if what you mean by semantic theory is an account of the relation between language and the world. In particular, procedural semantics doesn't supplant classical semantics, it merely begs the questions that classical semanticists set out to answer.
>
> . . .
>
> a machine can compile 'Did Lucy bring dessert?' and have not the foggiest idea that the sentence asks about whether Lucy brought dessert. (Fodor 1978, p. 229, p. 235, his italics)

2.6 Philosophical issues

The three principal philosophical criticisms of strong AI that helped to change the tide in the AI community and point to new research directions are the following:

1 The critique of Hubert Dreyfus;
2 Block's critique of machine functionalism via the *China brain* thought experiments; and
3 Searle's *Chinese Room* thought experiment.

All three surfaced within ten years of one another. There had been several other philosophical criticisms of strong AI before these (e.g., the ones by Lucas and Penrose; see Chapter 3 of the present volume[5]), and there have been others since.[6] But these three generated the most debate and have had the greatest impact.

Dreyfus' critique was the first (Dreyfus 1972). It was a mixture of empirical and philosophical arguments. Empirically, his main charge was that AI researchers had simply failed to deliver the goods. Despite exceedingly optimistic – and often grandiose – early forecasts, they had not managed to build general-purpose intelligent systems. This line of criticism was generally dismissed as invalid and unfair: invalid because at best it showed that AI had not succeeded *yet*, not that it could not *ever* succeed; and unfair because AI was a very young field, and revolutionary technological breakthroughs could not be expected from a field in its infancy, despite the overly enthusiastic proclamations of some of its pioneers. Philosophically, Dreyfus argued that our ability to understand the world and other people is a non-declarative type of *know-how skill* that is not amenable to GOFAI-style propositional codification. It is inarticulate, preconceptual, and has an indispensable phenomenological dimension that cannot be captured by any rule-based system. Dreyfus also stressed the importance of capacities such as imagination, ambiguity tolerance, and the use of metaphor, as well as phenomena such as fringe consciousness and gestalt perception, all of which were – and continue to be – resistant to computational treatment. Most importantly, in our view, Dreyfus stressed the importance of *relevance*, emphasizing the ability of humans to distinguish the essential from the inessential, and to effortlessly draw on relevant aspects of their experience and knowledge in accordance with the demands of their current situation, as required by their ongoing involvement with the world.[7] He correctly felt that imparting the same ability to a digital computer would be a major stumbling block for AI – what he called the "holistic context" problem. The problem of relevance remains, in our view, the key technical challenge to AI, both strong and weak, and to computational cognitive science as well.

The claim that people do not go about their daily activities by following rules points to a concern that has been a recurrent issue for strong AI and CTM, and even for general mentalistic theories such as Chomsky's generative linguistics, and merits a brief discussion here before we move on to Block's

---

[5] See also Bringsjord 1992 for a sustained, detailed updating of all these criticisms.

[6] For instance, see Bringsjord and Zenzen 1997.

[7] It may be of historical interest to note that much of what Dreyfus had to say was couched in the language of continental phenomenology and existentialism, heavily influenced by thinkers such as Heidegger and Merleau-Ponty. That, unfortunately, was not conducive to facilitating communication with AI researchers, or with analytic philosophers for that matter.

thought experiment. The objection has been made under somewhat different guises by many philosophers, from Wittgenstein and Quine to Dreyfus, Searle, and others. It has to do with the so-called *psychological reality* of rule-based explanations of cognition, and particularly with computerized simulations of mental processes. The issue hinges on the distinction between description and causation, and also between prediction and explanation. A set of rules (or a fortiori a computer program) might adequately *describe* a cognitive phenomenon, in that the rules might constitute a veridical model of the gross observational regularities associated with that phenomenon. They might fit all available experimental data and make all the right predictions. But this does not mean that there is actually an encoded representation of the rules (or the program) inside our heads that is causally implicated in the production of the phenomenon. A set of grammatic rules R might correctly describe certain constraints on English syntax, for instance, but that does not mean that English speakers have an encoding of R inside their brains which causes them to produce speech in accordance with R. So even though R might correctly predict behavior,[8] it does not necessarily explain it.

The distinction is also known in the terminology of Pylyshyn (1991, p. 233) as the difference between *explicit* and *implicit* rules. Implicit rules merely describe behavioral regularities, whereas explicit rules have encoded representations, presumably in our brains, which play a causal role in the production of the regularities. The issue of psychological reality gives rise to serious epistemological problems. What evidence would count as substantiating the claim that certain rules are explicitly encoded in our brains? How do we distinguish between different sets of rules or different computer programs that are nevertheless descriptively equivalent? What parts of a computerized model should be ascribed psychological significance and what parts should be ignored? Those who are sympathetic to Quine's arguments about the radical indeterminacy afflicting the study of language are likely to entertain similar misgivings about computational approaches to cognitive science and to conclude that the above difficulties are insurmountable. (Although it is not necessary to accept Quine's indeterminacy arguments or his behaviorism in order to reach such conclusions.) Chomsky views such fears as manifestations of empirical prejudices about the human mind and of a deep-seated but unwarranted methodological dualism which presupposes a sharp distinction between the physical and mental realms. To him, the foregoing epistemological problems amount to nothing more than the usual inductive underdetermination issue that regularly confronts all sciences. Computational cognitive scientists such as Newell, Pylyshyn, and others have responded more concretely by developing the notion of different levels of system description. Nevertheless,

---

[8] In fact rules do not even do that, at least in Chomskyan linguistics, as they are supposed to model idealized human competence rather than actual performance.

serious issues with computational cognitive modeling remain, and many continue to feel that the epistemological difficulties facing such modeling do not stem from the usual underdetermination problem found in the physical sciences, but from a fundamentally different sort of problem that is much more challenging.

A second influential criticism was directed specifically against machine functionalism. It was delivered by Block (1978) in the form of a thought experiment which asks us to imagine the entire population of China simulating a human mind for one hour. The citizens of China are all supplied with two-way radios that connect them to one another in the right way. We can think of the individual Chinese citizens as neurons, or whatever brain elements we care to regard as atomic. The people are also connected, via radio, to an artificial body, from which they can receive sensory stimuli and to which they can deliver output signals for generating physical behavior such as raising an arm. According to machine functionalism, one would have to conclude that if the Chinese simulated the right transition table faithfully, then by virtue of being properly related to one another and to inputs and outputs, they would in fact amount to a conscious mind. But this strikes us as counterintuitive, if not patently absurd. The resulting system might well be isomorphic to the brain, at some level of description, but it would not seem to harbor any sensations, pains, itches, or beliefs and desires for that matter. For similar reasons it would follow that no purely computational AI system could ever be said to have a genuine mind. Some functionalists have chosen to bite the bullet and concede that the "China brain" (or a properly programmed robot) would in fact possess genuine mental contents, chalking up our contrary intuitions to brain chauvinism, our propensity to regard only neurological wetware as capable of sustaining a mental life. But this is hard to swallow, and the thought experiment convinced many that unabashed functionalism is too liberal and must be either abandoned or significantly circumscribed.

The third seminal philosophical attack on strong AI was launched by Searle (1980) with his now-famous Chinese Room argument (CRA). CRA has generated a tremendous amount of discussion and controversy, and we will only provide a very cursory review of it here; for a detailed discussion the reader is referred to Cole (2009; see also Chapter 3). CRA is based on a thought experiment in which Searle himself stars. He is inside a room; outside the room are native Chinese speakers who don't know that Searle is inside it. Searle-in-the-room, like Searle-in-real-life, doesn't know any Chinese but is fluent in English. The Chinese speakers send cards into the room through a slot; on these cards are written questions in Chinese. The room, courtesy of Searle's secret work therein, returns cards to the native Chinese speakers as output. Searle's output is produced by consulting a rulebook: this book is a lookup table that tells him what Chinese to produce based on what is sent in. To Searle, the Chinese is all just a bunch of – to use Searle's language – squiggle-squoggles. The gist of the argument is rather simple: Searle-in-the-room is supposed to be everything a computer can be, and because he doesn't understand Chinese, no computer could have such understanding. Searle is mindlessly moving squiggle-squoggles around, and, according to the argument, that's all computers do, fundamentally. Searle has given various more general forms of the argument. For example, he summarizes the argument as one in which from the premises

1. Syntax is not sufficient for semantics.
2. Computer programs are entirely defined by their formal, or syntactical, structure.
3. Minds have mental contents; specifically, they have semantic contents.

it is supposed to follow that

No computer program by itself is sufficient to give a system a mind. Programs, in short, are not minds, and they are not by themselves sufficient for having minds. (Adapted from Searle 1984, p. 39)

Many replies have been given to CRA, both in its original incarnation and in the general form expressed above; perhaps the two most popular ones are the *systems reply* and the *robot reply*. The former is based on the claim that though Searle-in-the-room doesn't understand Chinese, the overall system that includes him as a proper part does. This means that the premise to the effect that Searle-in-the-room is everything a computer can be is called into question. The latter objection is based on the claim that though, again, Searle-in-the-room doesn't understand Chinese, this deficiency stems from the fact that Searle is not causally connected to the outside environment in the right manner. The claim is that in a real robot, meaning would be built up on the basis of the robot's causal transactions with the real world. So, though Searle may in some sense be functioning in the room as a computer, he is not functioning as a full-fledged robot, and strong AI is in the business of aiming at building persons as full-fledged robots. Searle has put forth replies to the replies, and the controversy continues. Regardless of one's opinions on CRA, the argument has undeniably had a tremendous impact on the field.

At the same time that philosophical criticisms like the above were being made, serious technical problems with classical AI began to emerge. One of them was the *frame problem*. By now the term has become quite vague. Sometimes it is understood as the relevance problem that was mentioned earlier (how to tell whether a piece of information might be relevant in a given situation); sometimes it is understood to signify the apparent computational intractability of holistic thought processes; and occasionally it is even misunderstood as a generic label for the infeasibility of symbolic AI. Perhaps the widest and least inaccurate reading of it is this: it is the problem of spelling out the conditions under which a belief should be updated after an action has been undertaken. In its original incarnation the problem was more technical and narrow, and arose in the context of a specific task in a specific framework: reasoning about action in the *situation calculus*. The latter is a formal system, based on first-order logic, for representing and reasoning about action, time, and change. Its basic notion is that of a *fluent*, which is a property whose value can change over time, such as the temperature of a room or the position of a moving object. Fluents are reified, and can thus be quantified over. Importantly, Boolean properties of the world are themselves treated as fluents. Such a *propositional fluent* might represent whether or not an object is to the left of another object, or whether the light in a room is on. The world at any given point in time can be exhaustively described by a set of formulas stating the values of all fluents at that point; such a description is said to represent the *state* of the world at that point in time. Actions are also reified. Each action has a set of preconditions and effects, both of which are described in terms of fluents. If the preconditions of an action are satisfied in a given state, then the action can be carried out and will result in a new state satisfying the effects of the action. Starting from an initial state, which presumably represents the world when a robot first enters it, many different sequences of states are possible depending on the different courses of action that may be undertaken.

To rule out outlandish models in which, for example, an action has effects that are unrelated to it, we need to explicitly specify the non-effects of each action via so-called "frame axioms." While succinct ways of stating frame axioms have been devised, the computational complexity of reasoning with them remains a challenge. Several other proposed solutions have been put forth, ranging from circumscription to altogether different formalisms for representing and reasoning about action and change. It is noteworthy that none of the proposed solutions so far comes anywhere near approaching the efficiency with which young children reason about action. It has been suggested that humans do not run into the problem of reasoning about the non-effects of actions because they take it for granted that an action does not affect anything unless they have evidence to the contrary. However, the real problem, onto which philosophers such as Fodor have latched, is this: How can we tell whether or not a piece of information constitutes "evidence to the contrary"? There are at least two separate issues here. First we need to be able to determine whether or not a piece of information is potentially relevant to some of our beliefs. That is again the relevance problem. And second, we need to be able to determine whether or not the information falsifies the belief. These are both engineering problems for GOFAI and general philosophical problems. On the engineering front, it is not too difficult to build a symbolic system that reaches a reasonable verdict *once the right background beliefs have been identified*. The major practical difficulty is quickly zeroing in on relevant information. Many have come to believe it highly unlikely that any symbol-manipulating system can overcome this difficulty.

2.7 Connectionism and dynamical systems

Conceptual and engineering problems such as the above, combined with the disillusionment that followed a brief period of excitement over expert systems and the grand "fifth-generation" project launched in Japan during the 1980s, helped to pave the way for a backlash against GOFAI approaches, both in AI and in cognitive science. To a large extent that backlash was manifested in the very rapid ascension of *connectionism* during the 1980s. Connectionism had been around at least since the 1940s (the foundations had been laid by McCulloch and Pitts (1943)), but only in the 1980s did it begin to emerge as a serious alternative to GOFAI, largely due to the efforts of Rumelhart, McClelland, and the PDP Research Group (1986).

The basic conceptual and engineering tool of connectionists is the neural network. A neural network consists of a number of nodes (or "units") that resemble brain neurons. Each node receives a number of input signals and delivers an output signal. The nodes are connected to one another so that the output of one node becomes an input to another node. Input and output values are typically represented by real numbers. The connections have weights attached to them, which are also represented by real numbers. Intuitively, the weight of a connection represents the influence that one node has on the output of another. The output of each node is a simple linear function of the inputs; typically, the weighted sum of the input values is calculated, and an output of 1 or 0 produced depending on whether or not the sum exceeds a certain threshold. If the output is 1, the node is said to be activated, or to fire; otherwise it is inhibited. Certain units are designated as the input and output nodes of the entire network; typically there is only one output node. Neural networks are capable of a certain type of learning; they can be trained to compute – or approximate – a target function. General-purpose learning algorithms exist, such as backpropagation, which, starting with random weights, repeatedly expose the network to different inputs in a training set and adjust the weights so as to bring the output closer to the correct value. Neural networks have been constructed that perform well on various nontrivial cognitive tasks, such as learning the past tense of English verbs or synthesizing speech from written text.

Neural networks have a number of remarkable features that set them apart from GOFAI systems. One of them is the absence of a central processing unit, or of any explicitly coded instructions that determine the behavior of the system. There are only individual nodes, and an individual node has only a small amount of entirely local information: the input values it receives from its neighbors. Owing to this massive locality and interconnectedness, neural networks are capable of graceful degradation, meaning that if some parts of the network are damaged, the network as a whole continues to function, with a performance drop that is more or less proportional to the amount of damage. In contrast, symbol-manipulating systems are usually brittle; a small deviation from the programmed course of events can lead to catastrophic failure. Such brittleness is atypical of human intelligence. Like the performance of neural networks, human cognition will suffer a continuous and graceful degradation under adverse conditions, instead of an abrupt general failure. Second, representation is distributed, in that pieces of information are not encoded by concrete symbolic structures; rather, a piece of information is essentially represented as a pattern of activity over the entire network: the firings of the various nodes. And the overall "knowledge" encoded by a neural network essentially resides in the weights of the various connections; it is sub-symbolic and highly distributed. An important corollary of distributed representation is that neural networks end up sidestepping the vexing question of content that arises for classical CTM. The question of how atomic symbols manage to acquire their meaning does not arise – because there are no atomic symbols.

These interesting features of neural networks, in combination with the fact that they appear to be more biologically plausible than digital computers, continue to appeal to many cognitive scientists and AI engineers, and intensive research in the field is continuing unabated, although so far there have been relatively few outstanding achievements. The problem of common sense, however, resurfaces in the setting of neural networks in a different guise. The intelligence exhibited by a (supervised) neural network is pre-built into the system by the human modeler who trains the network. But this is not enough to sufficiently circumscribe the space of possible hypotheses so as to rule out generalizations which are legitimate from the perspective of the training data but inept and inappropriate from the human perspective. There are legions of stories about neural networks which, after intensive training, came up with generalizations which had learned to distinguish features that were entirely irrelevant to the human modeler (indeed, features which had not even been noticed by the modeler). Moreover, in terms of computational power, anything that can be done by neural networks can be done by Turing machines, and therefore, by Church's thesis, there is nothing that neural networks can do which cannot also be done, say, by LISP programs. This entails that even if brains turned out to be giant neural networks of sorts, it would be possible in principle to simulate them with perfect precision using classical GOFAI techniques. It would follow, for instance, that there do exist rule-based systems capable of passing the Turing Test, even if those systems are so incredibly vast and unwieldy that it is practically impossible to build them. (Although, should brains turn out to be nothing but neural networks, that would certainly prove that it is not *necessary* for a system to deploy a symbolically encoded rule-based theory of a domain in order to achieve competence in that domain.) There are other issues related to the question of whether neural networks could ever manage to achieve general intelligence, including the famous *systematicity debate*, which was started by Fodor and Pylyshyn (1988) and is still ongoing, but we will not take these up here (see Chapter 3).

Closely related to connectionism is the *dynamical-systems* approach to intelligence (Port and van Gelder 1995). This approach draws on the general theory of nonlinear dynamical systems, conceiving of the mind as a continuous dynamical system – essentially a set of variables whose values evolve concurrently over time. The evolution of the system is typically described by a set of laws, usually expressed by differential or difference equations. The state of the system at a given moment in time is described by the values of the variables at that moment. The values of the variables at subsequent times (i.e., the dynamic trajectory of the system through the space of all possible states) is determined by the present state and the dynamical laws. Dynamical systems theory, however, is used to do pure cognitive science, not AI. That is, it provides a set of conceptual resources for understanding cognition and for modeling aspects of it as dynamical systems, but not for *building* intelligent systems. Accordingly, we will not have much to say on it here (though see Chapter 6). Nevertheless, the advocates of the dynamical-systems approach to cognition typically emphasize the importance of time, context, interaction, embodiment, and the environment, and have thus been natural allies of situated and embedded AI, to which we turn next.

2.8   AI from below: Situated intelligence

As disillusionment with GOFAI began to take hold in the 1980s, AI researchers such as Rod Brooks of MIT were coming to the conclusion that systems which relied on detailed symbolic representations of the world, baked in ahead of time by the engineers, and on action generation via detailed logical planning, were infeasible, brittle, and cognitively implausible. They encouraged a shift of focus from higher-order symbolic tasks such as deductive reasoning to lower-level, ostensibly "simple" perceptual and motor tasks, such as sensing, moving, turning, grasping, avoiding obstacles, and so on. They maintained that only fully embodied agents capable of carrying out these tasks adeptly can be truly validated as artificial agents, and that only full embodiment has any hopes of properly "grounding" an artificial agent in the real world. GOFAI had either completely ignored or minimized the importance of such activities. Perceptual and motor faculties were seen as mere "transducers," peripherally useful and relevant only inasmuch as they delivered symbolic representations of the world to the central thought processes or deployed effectors to translate the outcomes of such processes into bodily movements.

Surely what differentiates humans from insects, GOFAI advocates thought, is our capacity for rational thought.

Brooks and his co-workers argued that bodily capacities were far from trivial – indeed, GOFAI had proved inept at building systems that had them. Moreover, they held that the study of such capacities could lend us valuable insights on how higher-order cognition could emerge from them. Language and the capacity for symbolic thought have emerged very recently in human history, a consideration which suggests that evolution has put most of its effort into building up our sensory and motor systems. Once we understand the seemingly simple and mundane workings of such systems, the puzzle of intelligence might begin to dissolve. Language and reasoning will become simple once we know how to build a robot that can successfully navigate the physical world, for, according to Brooks, the "prime component of a robot's intellect" is not to be found in reasoning but rather in "the dynamics of the interaction of the robot and its environment." Essentially, the AI research program pursued by Brooks and his followers, which became known as *situated* AI,[9] amounted to "looking at simpler animals as a bottom-up model for building intelligence" (Brooks 1991, p. 16). To borrow a phrase from historians, this was, in a sense, AI "from below."

A key point made by Brooks and his team was that intricate symbolic representations of the world are unnecessary for solving a wide variety of problems. Many problems can be more efficiently tackled by doing away with representations and exploiting the *structure of the surrounding environment,* an idea captured in the slogan "the world is its own best representation." Continuously sensing and interacting with the world in a closed feedback loop was thought to be a much more promising approach than building a static symbolic "model" of it (described, say, as a state in the situation calculus) and reasoning over that. Brooks and his team demonstrated their approach by building a robot named Herbert, whose task was to roam the halls of the MIT AI Lab with the goal of identifying and disposing of empty soda cans. Herbert was built on a so-called subsumption architecture, consisting of a number of independent modules, each of them specialized for performing a specific task, such as moving forward. At any given time, a module might become activated or suppressed depending on the stimuli dynamically received by Herbert. The overall system relied on little or no internal representations and symbolic manipulation, but managed to exhibit surprisingly robust behavior (see also Chapter 13).

By turning the spotlight away from internal representations and processes toward external behavior and continuous interaction with the environment,

---

[9] Also known as *embedded* or *embodied* AI.

Table 2.1 **The main differences between GOFAI and situated/embodied AI**

Classical	Embodied
representational	non-representational
individualistic	social
abstract	concrete
context-independent	context-dependent
static	dynamic
atomistic	holistic
computer-inspired	biology-inspired
thought-oriented	action-oriented

the work of Brooks and other situated-AI researchers marked a reverse shift away from the cognitive revolution and back towards behaviorism. Indeed, some have spoken about a "counter-revolution" in AI and cognitive science. We believe that such claims are exaggerated; the majority of researchers in these fields are not willing to renounce the scientific legitimacy of representations in explaining the mind or their usefulness as engineering tools. Nor should they, in our view. The points made by the situation theorists have been well taken, and AI as a whole now pays considerably more attention to environmental context and embodiment. That is a positive development, and the trend is likely to persist. But the existence of mental representations seems as undeniable now as ever. People can simply close their eyes, shut their ears, and do some very nontrivial thinking about the possible effects of their actions, the tenth prime number, logical consequences of their beliefs, the structure of our solar system or water molecules, unicorns, and so on. The premise that such "classical" thinking will become straightforward once we understand how we tie shoelaces is dubious, and has been called into question (Kirsh 1991). In summary, Table 2.1 provides a rough graphical depiction of the main differences between GOFAI and situated/embodied AI.

It is noteworthy that the advent of situational theories in AI and cognitive science had already been mirrored – or has since been mirrored – by similar movements in several areas of philosophy. In philosophy of language, for instance, the ordinary-language turn that started to occur in Oxford in the 1950s, primarily as a reaction against logical positivism, can be seen as a precursor to the behavioral backlash against cognitivism. Speech-act theory, in particular, initiated by Austin and then taken up by Strawson, Searle, and others, was the first to emphasize that the key unit of linguistic meaning was not an abstract sentence but rather an utterance, thereby shifting attention from an isolated theoretical entity (the sentence) to a concrete *act* carried out by real people in real time. The trend has continued and strengthened, particularly as seen in the subsequent development of pragmatics and the growing recognition of the extensive and very intricate dependence of meaning on deictic and other contextual factors.

Roughly similar developments took place in the philosophy of science and mathematics, again to a large extent as a reaction against positivism. In science, philosophers such as Thomas Kuhn and Joseph Agassi emphasized that abstract systems of justification (essentially inductive and deductive logics) are poor models of scientific practice, which is, above all, a human *activity* that is highly contingent on social interaction and cultural and political factors. In mathematics, philosophers such as Lakatos (1976) and social constructivists such as Barnes and Bloor (1982) launched vigorous attacks against "Euclideanism," the formal style of doing mathematics whereby a seemingly indubitable set of axioms is laid down as the foundation and deductive consequences are then derived cumulatively and monotonically. That style, it was claimed, is too neat to reflect "real" mathematics. In fact it completely disregarded the process of *doing* mathematics (actually coming up with results), the dynamic and live aspects of the field.

We do not claim that all these threads necessarily influenced one another, or that there was anything inexorable about any of them. Nevertheless, the existence of certain salient common points of reference and underlying similarities is undeniable. There has been an overall trend away from statics and toward dynamics, from the abstract and decontextualized to the concrete and context-bound, from justification to discovery, from isolated contemplation to social interaction, and from thinking to doing. A dominant and recurrent theme has been the conviction that genuine understanding will never be attained by taking something that is dynamic and evolving, reactive, plastic, flexible, informal, highly nuanced, textured, colorful, and open-ended; and modeling it by something static, rigorous, unbending, and inflexible – that is, essentially by replacing something alive by something that is dead. The trends in question are not unrelated to the increasing prominence of social sciences, cultural anthropology, feminist studies, and so on, and to a large extent the conflict between GOFAI and situated AI can be seen as a reflection of the infamous science wars, the clash between traditional "objectivist" metaphysics and social constructivism, and more recently, in the case of cognitive science, the rationality wars, where situational theorists have been questioning the "ecological validity" of classical cognitive science and psychology laboratory experiments, and calling for a greater focus on ethology, ecological validity, and "real" behavior exhibited in the "real" world (as opposed to the supposedly artificial and highly constrained conditions of the laboratory). Our remarks here are not intended as a commentary on the science wars, but merely as an effort to provide a greater context for understanding the back-lash against GOFAI and the emergence of situational approaches to AI and the study of the mind.

2.9 The future of AI

If past predictions are any indication, the only thing we know today about tomorrow's science and technology is that it will be radically different from whatever we predict. Arguably, in the case of AI, we may also know today that progress will be much slower than what most expect. After all, at the 1956 kickoff conference at Dartmouth College, Herb Simon predicted that thinking machines able to match the human mind were "just around the corner" (for relevant quotes and informative discussion, see the first chapter of Russell and Norvig 2003). As it turned out, the new century would arrive without a single machine able to converse at even the toddler level. When it comes to building machines capable of displaying human-level intelligence, Descartes, not Turing, seems today to be the better prophet. That has not stopped people from continuing to issue exceedingly optimistic predictions. For example, Moravec (1999) declared that because the speed of computer hardware was doubling every eighteen months (in accordance with Moore's Law, which has apparently held in the past), "fourth-generation" robots would soon enough exceed humans in all respects, from running companies to writing novels. These robots, so the story goes, will evolve to such lofty cognitive heights that we will stand to them as single-cell organisms stand to us today.

Moravec is by no means singularly Pollyannaish. Many others in AI predict the same sensational future unfolding just as rapidly. In fact, at the fiftieth anniversary celebration at Dartmouth of the 1956 AI conference at the university, host and philosopher Jim Moor posed the question "Will human-level AI be achieved within the next 50 years?" to five thinkers who attended the original conference: John McCarthy, Marvin Minsky, Oliver Selfridge, Ray Solomonoff, and Trenchard Moore. McCarthy and Minsky gave firm, unhesitating affirmatives, and Solomonoff seemed to suggest that AI provided the one ray of hope in the face of the fact that our species seems bent on destroying itself. (Selfridge's reply was a bit cryptic. Moore returned a firm, unambiguous negative, and declared that once his computer is smart enough to interact with him conversationally about mathematical problems, he might take this whole enterprise more seriously.)

Moor's question is not just for scientists and engineers; it is also a question for philosophers. This is so for two reasons: (1) research and development designed to validate an affirmative answer must include philosophy, for reasons expressed above; (2) philosophers might be able to provide arguments that answer Moor's question now, definitively. If any of the strong critiques of AI that we have discussed is fundamentally correct, then of course AI will not manage to produce machines having the mental powers of persons. At any rate, time marches on, and will tell.

Further reading

Introductions

Braddon-Mitchell, D. and Jackson, F. (2006). *Philosophy of Mind and Cognition: An Introduction* (2nd edn.). Malden, MA: Wiley-Blackwell. An introductory philosophy-of-mind text which also contains excellent discussions of various philosophical issues in AI.

Carter, M. (2007). *Minds and Computers: An Introduction to the Philosophy of Artificial Intelligence.* Edinburgh University Press. An accessible general introduction to philosophical issues in artificial intelligence (sympathetic to computationalism).

Haugeland, J. (1985) *Artificial Intelligence: The Very Idea.* Cambridge, MA: MIT Press. Another lucid exposition of the big AI questions at a generally introductory level.

Stich, S. P. and Warfield, T. A. (eds.) (2003). *The Blackwell Guide to Philosophy of Mind.* Malden, MA: Blackwell. A collection of survey articles on the central themes of philosophy of mind, written by leading scholars.

Anthologies

Boden, M. (ed.) (1990). *The Philosophy of Artificial Intelligence.* Oxford University Press. A general collection that also includes various replies to Searle's Chinese Room argument.

Chalmers, D. J. (ed.) (2002) *Philosophy of Mind: Classical and Contemporary Readings.* New York: Oxford University Press.

Haugeland, J. (ed.) (1981). *Mind Design: Philosophy, Psychology, Artificial Intelligence.* Cambridge, MA: MIT Press.

(ed.) (1997). *Mind Design II: Philosophy, Psychology, Artificial Intelligence.* Cambridge, MA: MIT Press.

Specific topics

Bringsjord, S. (1992) *What Robots Can and Can't Be.* Dordrecht: Kluwer. Contains further discussion of Searle's Chinese Room argument, among other topics.

Clark, A. (1998) *Being There: Putting Brain, Body, and World Together Again.* Cambridge, MA: MIT Press. Argues for a situated/embodied approach to cognition.

Cole, D. (2004, revised 2009). The Chinese Room argument, in E. N. Zalta (ed.), *The Stanford Encyclopedia of Philosophy*, http://plato.stanford.edu/entries/chinese-room. A scholarly overview of work on the CRA.

Horgan, T. and Tienson, J. (1996). *Connectionism and the Philosophy of Psychology.* Cambridge, MA: MIT Press. Argues that the mind is best understood as a dynamical system realized in a neural network.

Horst, S. W. (1996). *Symbols, Computation, and Intentionality: A Critique of the Computational Theory of Mind.* Berkeley, CA: University of California Press. An in-depth discussion of computational theories of mind.

Johnson, M. (1987). *The Body in the Mind: The Bodily Basis of Meaning, Imagination, and Reason.* University of Chicago Press. Further arguments for the importance of physical embodiment in cognition.

Ramsey, W., Rumelhart, D. E., and Stich, S. P. (eds.) (1991). *Philosophy and Connectionist Theory.* Hillsdale, NJ: Lawrence Erlbaum. A collection of essays on philosophical issues related to connectionism.

Roitblat, H. L. and Meyer, J.-A. (eds.) (1995). *Comparative Approaches to Cognitive Science.* Cambridge, MA: MIT Press. A collection of essays on cognitive-science work from a situated/embodied angle.

References

Baars, B. J. (1986). *The Cognitive Revolution in Psychology.* New York: Guilford Press.

Bacon, F. (2002). *The New Organon.* Cambridge University Press.

Barnes, B. and Bloor, D. (1982). Relativism, rationalism, and the sociology of science, in M. Hollis and S. Lukes (eds.), *Rationality and Relativism* (pp. 21–47). Oxford: Blackwell.

Block, N. (1978). Troubles with functionalism, in C. W. Savage (ed.), *Perception and Cognition: Issues in the Foundations of Psychology* (pp. 261–325). Minneapolis, MN: University of Minnesota Press.

(1981). Psychologism and behaviorism, *Philosophical Review* 90: 5–43.

Bringsjord, S. (1992). *What Robots Can and Can't Be.* Dordrecht: Kluwer.

(1995), Could, how could we tell if, and why should–androids have inner lives? in K. Ford, C. Glymour, and P. Hayes (eds.), *Android Epistemology* (pp. 93–122). Cambridge, MA: MIT Press.

Bringsjord, S. and Zenzen, M. (1997). Cognition is not computation: The argument from irreversibility, *Synthese* 113: 285–320.

Brooks, R. A. (1991). Intelligence without reason, Technical report 1293, MIT Artificial Intelligence Laboratory.

Chomsky, N. (1996). A review of B. F. Skinner's "Verbal Behavior," in H. Geirsson and M. Losonsky (eds.), *Readings in Language and Mind* (pp. 413–41). Oxford: Blackwell.

Church, A. (1936). An unsolvable problem of elementary number theory, *American Journal of Mathematics* 58: 345–63.

Cole, D. (2009). The Chinese Room argument, in E. N. Zalta (ed.), *The Stanford Encyclopedia of Philosophy (Winter 2009 Edition)*, http://plato.stanford.edu/archives/win2009/entries/chinese-room.

Davis, E. and Morgenstern, L. (2004). Progress in formal commonsense reasoning, Introduction to the special issue on formalization of common sense, *Artificial Intelligence Journal* 153: 1–12.

Davis, M. (2001). The early history of automated deduction, in A. Robinson and A. Voronkov (eds.), *Handbook of Automated Reasoning*, vol. I (pp. 3–15). Amsterdam: Elsevier.

Davis, M. and Putnam, H. (1960). A computing procedure for quantification theory, *Journal of the Association for Computing Machinery* 7: 201–15.

Descartes, R. (1911). *The Philosophical Works of Descartes*, vol. I (trans. E. S. Haldane and G. R. T. Ross). Cambridge University Press.

(1988). *Descartes: Selected Philosophical Writings*, Cambridge University Press.

Dreyfus, H. L. (1972). *What Computers Can't Do: A Critique of Artificial Reason.* New York: Harper & Row.

(1992). *What Computers Still Can't Do: A Critique of Artificial Reason.* Cambridge, MA: MIT Press.

Fodor, J. A. (1978). Tom Swift and his procedural grandmother, *Cognition* 6: 229–47.

(1987). *Psychosemantics: The Problem of Meaning in the Philosophy of Mind.* Cambridge, MA: MIT Press.

Fodor, J. A. and Pylyshyn, Z. W. (1988). Connectionism and cognitive architecture: A critical analysis, *Cognition* 28: 139–96.

Gardner, H. (1985). *The Mind's New Science: A History of the Cognitive Revolution.* New York: Basic Books.

Gould, S. J. and Lewontin, R. (1979). The spandrels of San Marco and the Panglossian paradigm: A critique of the adaptationist paradigm, *Proceedings of the Royal Society of London B* 205: 581–98.

Hanson, N. R. (1958). *Patterns of Discovery.* Cambridge University Press.

Harnad, S. (1990). The symbol grounding problem, *Physica D* 42: 335–46.

(1991). Other bodies, other minds: A machine incarnation of an old philosophical problem, *Minds and Machines* 1: 43–54.

Haugeland, J. (1985). *Artificial Intelligence: The Very Idea.* Cambridge, MA: MIT Press.

Hempel, C. G. (1985). Thoughts on the limitations of discovery by computer, in K. Schaffner (ed.), *Logic of Discovery and Diagnosis in Medicine* (pp. 115–22). Berkeley, CA: University of California Press.

Johnson-Laird, P. N. (1977). Procedural semantics, *Cognition* 5: 189–214.

Kirsh, D. (1991). Today the earwig, tomorrow man?, *Artificial Intelligence* 47: 161–84.

Koza, J. R. (1992). *Genetic Programming: On the Programming of Computers by Means of Natural Selection.* Cambridge, MA: MIT Press.

Lakatos, I. (1976). *Proofs and Refutations: The Logic of Mathematical Discovery.* Cambridge University Press.

Langley, P. W., Simon, H. A., Bradshaw, G. L., and Zytkow, J. M. (1987). *Scientific Discovery: Computational Explorations of the Creative Process.* Cambridge, MA: MIT Press.

Lenat, D. B. (1976). *AM: An Artificial Intelligence Approach to Discovery in Mathematics as Heuristic Search*. Ph.D. thesis, Stanford University.

(1983). EURISKO: A Program that learns new heuristics and domain concepts: The nature of Heuristics III: Program design and results, *Artificial Intelligence* 21: 61–98.

McCarthy, J. (1962). Computer programs for checking mathematical proofs, in *Proceedings of the Symposium in Pure Math, Recursive Function Theory* (pp. 219–28). Providence, RI: American Mathematical Society.

McCulloch, W. S. and Pitts, W. A. (1943). A logical calculus of the ideas immanent in nervous activity, *Bulletin of Mathematical Biophysics* 5: 115–33.

Mill, J. S. (1874). *System of Logic*. New York: Harper and Brothers.

Minsky, M. (1986). *The Society of Mind*. New York: Simon and Schuster.

Moravec, H. (1999). *Robot: Mere Machine to Transcendent Mind*. Oxford University Press.

Muggleton, S. (1992). Inductive logic programming, in S. Muggleton (ed.), *Inductive Logic Programming* (pp. 3–27), London: Academic Press.

Newell, A. and Simon, H. A. (1976). Computer science as empirical inquiry: Symbols and search, *Communications of the Association for Computing Machinery* 19: 113–26.

Peirce, C. S. (1960). *Collected Papers of C. S. Peirce*. Cambridge, MA: Harvard University Press.

Pólya, G. (1945). *How to Solve It: A New Aspect of Mathematical Method*. Princeton University Press.

Port, R. F. and van Gelder, T. (1995). *Mind as Motion: Explorations in the Dynamics of Cognition*. Cambridge, MA: MIT Press.

Putnam, H. (1960). Minds and machines, in S. Hook (ed.), *Dimensions of Mind* (pp. 138–64). New York University Press.

Pylyshyn, Z. (1989). Computing in cognitive science, in M. I. Posner (ed.), *Foundations of Cognitive Science* (pp. 49–92). Cambridge, MA: MIT Press.

(1991). Rules and Representations: Chomsky and representational realism, in A. Kasher (ed.), *The Chomskyan Turn* (pp. 231–51). Oxford: Blackwell.

Reichenbach, H. (1938). *Experience and Prediction*. University of Chicago Press.

Robinson, J. A. (1965). A machine-oriented logic based on the resolution principle, *Journal of the Association for Computing Machinery* 12: 23–41.

Robinson, J. A. and Voronkov, A. (eds.) (2001). *Handbook of Automated Reasoning*, vol. 1. Amsterdam: Elsevier.

Rumelhart, D. E., McClelland, J. L., and the PDP Research Group. (1986). *Parallel Distributed Processing: Explorations in the Microstructure of Cognition*, vol. I: *Foundations*. Cambridge, MA: MIT Press.

Russell, B. (1940). *An Inquiry into Meaning and Truth*. London: George Allen and Unwin.

Russell, S. and Norvig, P. (2003). *Artificial Intelligence: A Modern Approach* (2nd edn.). Upper Saddle River, NJ: Prentice Hall.

Searle, J. (1980). Minds, brains and programs, *Behavioral and Brain Sciences* 3: 417–24.

(1984). *Minds, Brains, and Science.* Cambridge, MA: Harvard University Press.

Sperling, G. (1960). The information available in brief visual presentations, *Psychological Monographs: General and Applied* 74: 1–29.

Tolman, E. C. (1948). Cognitive maps in rats and men, *Psychological Review* 55, 189–208.

Turing, A. M. (1936). On computable numbers with applications to the Entscheidungsproblem, *Proceedings of the London Mathematical Society* 42, 230–65.

(1950). Computing machinery and intelligence, *Mind* 59: 433–60.

Wang, H. (1960). Toward mechanical mathematics, *IBM Journal of Research and Development* 4: 2–22.

Winograd, T. (1990). Thinking machines: Can there be? Are we?, in D. Partridge and Y. Wilks (eds.), *The Foundations of Artificial Intelligence* (pp. 167–89). Cambridge University Press.

3 Philosophical challenges

William S. Robinson

Descartes (1637/1931, p. 116) held that our reason was a "universal instrument." Since he believed that any mechanism has to have some special purpose, and that no collection of special purpose mechanisms could be large enough to encompass all that reason can do, he concluded that no mechanism could instantiate human reason. Aquinas (1265–72, I, Q.75, a. 2) also argued that intellect was not provided by a material organ. He believed that a disease-induced bitter humor could interfere with our tasting sweetness, or any taste different from bitter. Analogously, he thought that if our intellects were material, they would be prevented from knowing material things of different natures.

Most contemporary philosophers would accept that our intelligence is provided by our material brains, and thus would be disinclined to challenge the possibility of artificially intelligent devices on the ground of their materiality. The questions and problems about artificial intelligence that remain can be divided into those that are largely independent of particular approaches to AI, and those that are prompted by more specific ideas about artificially realizable cognitive architectures. We shall begin with the more general issues.

3.1 General questions

3.1.1 Terminological preliminaries

Some tasks would be generally agreed to require intelligence for their execution – for example, finding the quotient of 231 divided by 42. One may say that a device has artificial intelligence just in case it can be used by us to carry out a task that would be agreed to require intelligence for execution by a human being. I shall call possession of intelligence in this sense "task intelligence." Calculators can be used to find the quotient of 231 divided by 42, so, evidently, even calculators have task intelligence. Artificial task intelligence is not controversial; not even Aquinas or Descartes would have reason to object to task intelligence. We must note, however, that calculators do not know what the answers to arithmetic problems are, nor do they know they are doing arithmetic. It is thus clear that we are not entitled to move from possession of task intelligence to grander claims about the intelligence of the *thing* that we can use to carry out a task.

The intended contrast to task intelligence is "thing intelligence." If a device has artificial thing intelligence, then it – the device – is intelligent. Controversial contemporary questions concern the possibility of artificial thing intelligence, and various approaches to its design.

We may distinguish between two species of thing intelligence by borrowing some terminology from the gas station. Let us say that a device has *premium*, artificial, thing intelligence (or "premium AI") if it has its intelligence in a way that is enlightening about how humans have their thing intelligence. If a device has its intelligence in a way that is not enlightening about how humans have their intelligence, let us say that it has *regular*, artificial, thing intelligence (or "regular AI"). It is to be noted that regular gasoline is real gasoline; likewise, regular AI is real intelligence.

Compatibly with these definitions, it could turn out that there is no real difference between regular and premium AI; that is, it could turn out that the only way to provide thing intelligence in a device is to provide it in a way that would be enlightening about how we have intelligence. But it is not an a priori truth that this is so, and so we need both terms.

Searle (1980) introduced a distinction between strong AI and weak AI. Strong AI is the thesis that "the appropriately programmed computer really *is* a mind, in the sense that computers given the right programs can be literally said to *understand* and have other cognitive states" (p. 417; emphases in original). Weak AI claims only that computers provide a useful tool for rigorous formulation and testing of hypotheses about the mind.

Searle's distinction enabled him to readily focus his argument which, as we shall see later, was directed only against the strong AI thesis. But for more general purposes, we need the further distinctions just introduced. The regular/premium distinction enables us to recognize two possibilities within strong AI. And the task/thing distinction permits us to agree with most writers in what counts as work in AI research while recognizing that philosophical challenges are generally directed at claims that a device could itself be genuinely intelligent, or have cognitive states of its own.

Since there is no real issue about the possibility of task intelligence, unqualified occurrences of "intelligence" in what follows will always mean "thing intelligence."

3.1.2   The Turing Test

If we suppose that an artificially intelligent device is possible, the question arises as to how we might know when we had succeeded in producing one. Although Alan Turing (1950) suggested that we *replace* such questions with questions about the performance in his "imitation game," his proposal has often been treated as a test, the "passing" of which would show that a device possessed intelligence.

In its standard interpretation, the Turing Test (as it has come to be known) consists of a series of trials in which an interrogator interacts with both a machine and a human, and, after some specified finite time, renders a judgment, either "X is human, Y is a machine" or "Y is human, X is a machine." Turing's examples (ranging from analysis of poetry to arithmetic problems) show that interrogators are presumed to understand their task to be correct identification and that they are to have the widest latitude in what they might ask. The only limitation he put on required performance was that it be exhibited via teletype. A 50 percent success rate for interrogators' declarations would mean that they were learning nothing from comparing human and machine responses to their probes, and rates close to that would plausibly count as "passing" the Turing Test. Provided it is agreed that engaging in conversation requires extensive use of our intelligence, the argument can be advanced that successful devices (devices that "pass") are exercising intelligence. Such an ability would resist being classified as mere task intelligence, because the range of allowable probes is so wide.

Interestingly, it was conversational ability that Descartes predicted artifacts would never be able to achieve. In contrast, Turing (1950) made a famous prediction that by 2000, devices would exist for which interrogators would not do better than 70 percent correct after five minutes of questioning. This failed prediction is, of course, to be distinguished from the view that doing well on the Turing Test would show that a device possessed intelligence, if such an achievement were actually attained. Since 1990, an annual competition for the Loebner Prize has sought to stimulate work toward this goal.

Alternative interpretations of Turing's description of his procedure have been advanced, and several suggestions have been made for improving it. The journal *Minds and Machines* published fiftieth anniversary issues in 2000 that contain discussions of several of these interpretations and suggestions.

Ned Block (1981) described a machine that appears to undercut the acceptability of the Turing Test. Workers begin by listing all gambits with which an interrogator might begin. These openers are alphabetized, and for each one a response is composed for the machine such that the combination of interrogator's opener and machine response is plausible as a human conversation. The workers then list and alphabetize all possible next probes by interrogators. (Since interrogators may change the subject whenever they please, later probes will include almost all earlier ones.) Again, responses are composed such that each combined series of opener + response + further probe + response is plausible as a human conversation. The workers continue in this fashion until conversations of the predetermined finite length are reached. During a Turing Test trial, the machine simply finds the interrogator's probes in the alphabetized list and returns the stored responses.

The argument that proceeds from this description is that Block's machine would pass the Turing Test, but is evidently not intelligent. (It is just canning plus a mere look-up device and has no more intelligence than a grocery store bar code reader system.) Therefore, the Turing Test is not a good test for intelligence.

Dissenters from this argument can concede that the logical possibility of Block's machine (aka, the Blockhead) prevents the Turing Test from being used as a *definition* of intelligence. But they may still claim that the vastness of the space of possible probes makes the probability of the actual existence of Block's machine vanishingly small and that, consequently, Turing's procedure can still be a highly effective *test* of intelligence.

3.1.3   Purpose, consciousness, and intentionality

Intelligent behavior is purposive; it implies some sort of goal, even if only that of giving a correct answer to a question. It is difficult to imagine an action's having a point unless, sooner or later, someone's pleasant or unpleasant bodily sensation, emotion, religious transport, elation or depression is contingent upon that action. Arguably, none of the terms for such states can be fully understood by beings that cannot be in any of them. These states are, however, conscious states. Thus, it may be held that artificial intelligence would require artificial consciousness. Since most approaches to AI are not aimed at producing consciousness, it may be doubted that typical approaches to AI can really succeed.

Most AI researchers, however, would be satisfied if they could provide appropriate responses to purposes*, where purposes* are just like purposes except that they do not involve consciousness. That is, purposes* function as goal states by reference to which activities may be organized. The purpose* of a chess-playing machine is to win, and success by this standard will likely be counted as a success for task AI even if no one supposes that the machine feels elation upon winning, or is desolated by losing. If the range of tasks for which similar remarks would apply were sufficiently wide and varied, thing intelligence would plausibly be achieved. For example, a robot that could do one's grocery shopping, including separating ripe from unripe fruit, adjusting to changes in bus schedules, weather-related delays, and so on, would plausibly be counted as artificially (thing) intelligent, without there being any supposition that it has conscious tastes or feelings of satisfaction for a job well done.

A deeper line of argument holds that thoughts can be about things only if they are products of an evolutionary history in which survival functions as a naturally provided goal (Dretske 1995). Since robots lack the required kind of evolutionary history, it might be concluded that their "thoughts" cannot really be about anything. It is, however, controversial whether such a history is required for genuine intentionality (aboutness). And even if it were agreed that it is required, many thinkers would be quite happy to settle for intentionality*, that is, to claim success in providing artificial intelligence for any robot that could not only talk well but also suit its actions to its words while engaging with real-world objects and processes in real time.

Possession of intentionality (or even intentionality*) suggests possession of internal states or events that *represent* worldly objects and their properties. We shall see that questions about representations and their use play an important role in many challenges to AI.

A further doubt about machine intentionality and robotic thing intelligence has been raised by Searle (1992). His view is that computation is not intrinsic to any physical system; instead, it is "observer relative," that is, assigned by possessors of genuine intentionality such as ourselves. We can, for example, view a light switch as a computer by assigning 0 to "Off", 1 to "On" and regarding each movement of the switch as taking 0 or 1 as input and giving 1 or 0, respectively, as output. By suitable choice of assignments, we could regard any sufficiently complex system as computing anything we like. Since, as Searle puts it, syntax is not intrinsic to physics, no physical account of a robot's states could determine that any of them are about anything, even if *we* could choose an assignment that would make the robot useful to us.

Dissenters from Searle's view argue, in brief, that we can achieve a non-arbitrary assignment of meanings to a robot's linguistic and non-linguistic behaviors, provided that the robot is sufficiently complex and competent; that we include causal relations between its states and its external environment; and that we further include what its behavior would have been under counterfactual conditions. Success in this line would support attribution of thing intelligence to such a device. Useful further discussions of this somewhat technical issue can be found in Chalmers (1996) and Piccinini (2010).

3.1.4   Mechanism vs. rationality

Intelligence worthy of the name ought to approximate rationality. Rationality has sometimes been held to be in conflict with mechanism. If there really is such a conflict, then artificial intelligence will not be possible.

The putative conflict is that rationality is normative and causation of the kind found in devices such as computers and robots is not. To explain: Being rational requires proceeding according to norms of correct inference, including deductive cases (e.g., accepting *modus ponens* and rejecting affirming the consequent) and inductive cases (e.g., inferring high probability from high frequency in observed samples, or applying the principle of total evidence). But mechanical causation as such is no respecter of logical norms; it is as easy to cause a device to print out $2 + 2 = 5$ as it is to cause it to produce a correct statement.

An alternative formulation of the same point goes this way. A rational being may be characterized as one that adjusts its beliefs in light of evidence *because* that evidence is understood to be relevant to the belief. But computers and robots change their internal states only because of their inputs and their wiring. Therefore, none of their changes of state can be regarded as exhibiting rationality.

In response to this challenge, proponents of AI can concede that the class of artificial devices contains many examples that do not respect rationality. Other members of the class, however, may be designed in such a way that their mechanistic operations parallel correct principles of inference. (*Mechanistic* operations are changes or series of changes in physical systems that proceed in accordance with natural laws. *Mechanical* systems – e.g., pendulum clockworks – are paradigmatically mechanistic, but electrical systems, neural systems, etc. are mechanistic without being mechanical. See Dennett 1973.) Proponents of AI may hold that evolution has designed our brains in just this way – that is, that our brains are neural mechanisms that are ordered so as to constrain our beliefs by logical principles. That such a design is possible is illustrated by devices as simple as calculators, which clearly work mechanistically and also clearly respect the principles of arithmetic. From this point of view, the problem of AI is the problem of finding designs whose mechanistic operations parallel application of logical principles over a wide range of cases. (Perfect rationality is not required for AI because it is generally conceded that human beings are intelligent, but not perfectly rational.)

Devices of the kind just indicated may not have their state changes caused by logical or evidential relations; but it will be held that it is just as good if a design makes an addition to its set of beliefs only in cases where the proper logical or evidential relation holds. In support of this conception, it may be argued that this must be how it is with human beings. Logical and evidential relations are abstract entities and thus cannot be causes of particular events. It is only devices whose designs constrain events within themselves to conform to logical and evidential principles that can have causes of changes that respect those principles.

Free will has often been associated with rationality (Aquinas 1265–72/1945, I, Q83, a. 1; Hasker 1999), and this association can generate a challenge to AI. Robots, no matter how sophisticated, would be governed by deterministic laws and thus some would say they lack rationality because, according to one tradition, deterministic systems lack free will. Of course, such a stance would be incompatible with regarding human intelligence as completely explainable by reference to the activity of our material brains. There is, however, a long standing "compatibilist" tradition according to which free will is not in conflict with deterministic mechanism. (Hume 1748, viii; Ayer 1954; Dennett 1973.) Broadly speaking, this tradition holds free will to be present when reasoning processes have their normal effects on behavior. Deprivations of free will occur only when reasoning processes (such as deriving consequences of actions) are interfered with by being damaged, bypassed, or overruled by brute force. This distinction between reasoning processes that are operating normally, and reasoning processes that are interfered with in sundry ways, would seem to be applicable to the operations of robots. Thus, if the compatibilist tradition can be sustained on independent grounds, the suspicion of conflict between robotic intelligence and free will may be able to be allayed.

3.1.5   Gödelian arguments

Gödel (1931) proved a mathematical result that has sometimes been held to imply a limitation on machine intelligence. To understand the plausibility of this view, we may begin by imagining a treatment for arithmetic modeled on Euclid's treatment of geometry. That is, we may imagine a system that begins with some axioms that (given a standard scheme of interpretation of the signs in the system) are about addition and multiplication. For example, one of the axioms might be a formula whose standard interpretation is "There is a number n such that, for any number m, n times m equals m." The further development of the system would then consist of formulas derived from the axioms, whose standard interpretations would be statements of arithmetic.

Gödel was concerned with *formal* systems, that is, systems in which *proof* can be defined in terms of explicit rules for adding formulas to the system. An example of such a rule is that if statements p and $p \rightarrow q$ are already theorems of the system, then q may be added to the list of theorems.

Intuitively, two properties would seem to be desirable in a formal system for arithmetic. One, it should be consistent; that is, our system should not contain proofs for two formulas whose standard interpretations are contradictions of each other. Two, we would like our system to be complete; that is, we would like to have a system such that for each and every true arithmetical statement, there is a formula, derivable in the system, whose standard interpretation is that statement.

Gödel's amazing result was that no formal system for arithmetic can be both consistent and complete. To condense a long and difficult story, Gödel showed how each formula of a proposed formal system for arithmetic could be assigned a unique number (its "Gödel number"). He further showed that any system that provided for a certain portion of arithmetic could be used to construct formulas whose standard interpretation would say that the formula with Gödel number N is not a theorem of that system. Finally, he was able to show that any system, s, that provided for that portion of arithmetic would contain some formula (let us call it G(s), the Gödel sentence for system s) whose interpretation was "The formula with Gödel number N is not provable in s" *and* whose Gödel number was N. If this formula were provable in s, then formulas standardly interpretable as "G(s) is provable" and "G(s) is not provable" would both be derivable, and the system would be inconsistent. If, however, G(s) is not provable in the system, then what it says is a true arithmetical statement that is not derivable in the system, and thus the system is incomplete.

The argument that has been based on this result begins with the observation that any mechanism can be represented as a formal system in which the outputs of the mechanism correspond to theorems of that formal system. So, since all formal systems must be either inconsistent or incomplete for arithmetic, any mechanism must either produce inconsistent outputs or be unable to produce all the truths of arithmetic. In particular, a mechanism would be unable to produce G(s), where "s" is the formal system that represents that mechanism.

However, some thinkers (e.g., Lucas 1961; Penrose 1989, 1994) have argued that by using ideas contained in Gödel's method of proving his theorem, human mathematicians could come to understand the truth of any arithmetical proposition, including the Gödel sentence of whatever formal system one might propose as representing their cognitive abilities. And they could do this without thereby contradicting themselves. If this is right, then human cognitive ability outstrips the capabilities of any possible mechanism.

Many philosophers (e.g., Putnam 1960; Robinson 1992, 1996) have criticized various aspects of this attempt to apply Gödel's work. A key point of dissent begins with the observation that the supposed limitation on abilities of mechanisms requires the demonstration that there is something that we can do, but machines cannot. However, both a mechanism that is represented by system s, and we (if we study Gödel's work) can prove that

1 If s is consistent, then s cannot prove G(s).

But neither we nor the mechanism represented by s can prove that

2 s cannot prove G(s).

Of course, if human mathematicians could prove that they were consistent, they could argue that substituting themselves for 's' would enable them to derive (2). That would lead to a contradiction (since G(s) says that s cannot prove G(s)), and so they would be in a position to reject the supposition that they are substitutable for 's'. Since, in this argument, s can be any mechanism, the result would be that human mathematicians could always legitimately reject the supposition that they are equivalent to a mechanism.

However, this line of defense rests on the premise that human mathematicians can prove themselves to be consistent. It is far from evident that this can be done. Further, another of Gödel's results is that if a formal system is consistent, it cannot contain a proof that it is. If we cannot prove we are consistent, then it remains open that (1) is provable by both machines and us, and (2) is provable by neither; and a difference in what is possible for us and what is possible for machines will not have been shown.

3.2   The classical approach to AI

If doubts about the possibility of machine intelligence are thought to be answerable, the question arises as to how machine intelligence might be produced. In this and the next two sections, we will consider the three leading approaches to this question.

The classical approach to AI (aka GOFAI, or Good Old-Fashioned Artificial Intelligence, after Haugeland 1981) developed from factors discussed in the preceding sections. Logical principles (or, rules) apply to propositions and, in general, depend on the terms and internal structure of those propositions. (For example, accepting "All bats are mammals, all mammals are warm-blooded, therefore, all bats are warm-blooded" depends on appreciating the force of "all" and the identity and order of the subject and predicate terms that occur in these statements.) It seems natural, therefore, to conceive intelligence (whether natural or artificial) as involving states that correspond to terms and structures of terms, and rules for operations on these terms and structures. And rules seem very naturally embodied in programs – indeed, the form "If condition X is satisfied, do Y, otherwise do Z" can be described as a rule to do Y if X, and Z if not X. Continuing this conception, one can regard data entries as (structured) representations of facts, and programs as ways of embodying rules for manipulation of such representations.

The classical approach to AI has received a number of well-known challenges, which we will now consider.

3.2.1   Searle's Chinese Room

Schank and Abelson (1977) related understanding to scripts, which consist of stored knowledge about the structure of specific situations – for example, eating in a restaurant, or going to a theatrical performance. A brief remark or story can invoke a script, and the knowledge in the script can then be used to guide expectations and responses. Schank and Abelson held that we acquire many scripts, and that "most of understanding is script-based" (p. 67).

Schank and Abelson's work provided some of the background for a famous article by John Searle (1980). Searle envisaged himself in a room containing scripts in Chinese, stories in Chinese, and a program (in English) that permitted operations on Chinese characters solely in virtue of their shapes (i.e., neither translations nor the means of making translations were provided). Searle imagined receiving questions written in Chinese and executing the program. Sometimes the program would command the copying of a shape onto a piece of paper, and a series of these would eventually be passed to native Chinese speakers outside the room. Searle allowed that these answers could be as good (from the point of view of the questioners) as one pleases, so that people on the outside would have every reason to think that something in the room had understood the questions. But in fact Searle knew no Chinese and understood nothing; from his point of view, there was nothing more than the identifying of squiggles and squoggles in various positions and sequences, and the occasional copying of shapes onto the output paper. If a paper is passed in that says, in Chinese, "Yell if you want a hamburger," Searle might pass out a paper with the Chinese for "Yes, I'd like a hamburger" but he would have no reason to yell, even if he were ravenously hungry.

Searle's argument concedes the possibility of a certain kind of achievement, and it will be convenient to have a term for this achievement. For this purpose, I introduce the term "flexibility", as follows.

"X has flexibility" $=$ $_{df}$ X can respond appropriately to a wide range of novel circumstances.

"Appropriate," "wide range," and "novel" are not precise terms, but they are not obviously less precise than "intelligence" and it appears that flexibility as just defined captures at least part of what would be expected from anything that is said to have intelligence.

What Searle characteristically denies to programs is not flexibility, but *understanding*, and one way of expressing his conclusion is that flexibility can be achieved without understanding. Another is that formal symbol manipulation (i.e., manipulation of symbols in virtue of their shapes alone) is inadequate to the task of providing understanding. Mere syntactical proficiency, however appropriate and wide ranging, cannot provide semantic content (meaning; understanding). Demonstration of flexibility is thus not demonstration of intelligence, if "intelligence" is taken to require understanding. Formal symbol manipulation is exactly what computers do, so what computers do is inadequate to providing understanding. They may provide words that *we*, who have understanding, can take to be about things in the world; but for them, there is no intentionality – that is, for them their symbols are just shapes and are not *about* anything at all.

Searle considered a number of objections to his argument. A prominent one is the *Systems Reply*. We can think of the Systems Reply as a claim about where to draw the proper shortest boundary of an understander; namely, it is to be drawn around the whole system, where the whole system includes not only the man inside, but also the program and the scripts. It is whole persons who understand stories and questions, not their language centers or their frontal lobes. Similarly, says the Systems Reply, it is irrelevant that a certain part of the system (i.e., the man inside the Chinese Room) is not an understander; it is the whole Chinese Room to which understanding is to be attributed.

Searle's response to the Systems Reply was to imagine himself memorizing the program and the scripts, and executing the program by consulting his memory. The effect of internalizing the program and scripts in memory is that the boundary of the system is now the same as the boundary of Searle's body. But, Searle argued, he would still not understand a word of Chinese, even though the results of his prodigious mental program execution would be written products that native Chinese speakers regarded as impeccably correct. The Chinese instruction "Yell if you want a hamburger" would still give Searle no reason to yell, even as he wrote, in Chinese, "Yes, I'd like a hamburger."

Another prominent reply that Searle considered is the *Robot Reply.* This reply makes an important concession to Searle's argument, namely, that a mere computer has no understanding, no matter how good its verbal responses. But, it says, if the computer's outputs were used to drive a robot, in such a way that actions fit the words, the whole robot would understand. For in that case, there would be analogues of perception and action that would connect the words to objects and situations in the world. For example, a computer that answered "What should you do if you smell smoke?" with "Leave the room" might not understand at all. But suppose a robot has a smoke detector, and suppose its ability to generate its good answer is connected to transducing mechanisms that also drive it to leave the room when its smoke detector is stimulated. Such a robot might then be said not only to talk a good game, but to understand what it says. The plausibility of this suggestion becomes stronger, the wider the range of novel responses accompanied by appropriate actions that we imagine.

Searle's response to the Robot Reply was to imagine a scenario in which he is inside a Chinese Room that is inside a robot. He proceeds just as before; but now, unbeknownst to him, the messages he passes out of the Chinese Room drive not only the robot's speech, but also its appropriate actions. Searle noted that in this scenario, he would still not understand any of the words that he processes, and concludes that the robot he is (unknowingly) controlling has no intentionality.

Unfortunately, despite devoting a section to what he calls the "Combination Reply," Searle does not really address the result of putting together the Systems Reply and the Robot Reply. This combination permits the objection that the relevant boundary for an understander in the robot case is not the man inside, but the whole robot. Moreover, Searle's internalizing move in response to the Systems Reply will not work here; the robotic analogue of internalizing the scripts and program would require internalizing the mechanisms that drive appropriate actions. For example, the robot that is being run by Searle's program executions might not only give verbal output "When batteries are low, it's best to go to the nearest recharger," but also proceed to the nearest recharger when its batteries are low. Searle's lack of explicit consideration of this possibility leaves his argument open to the objection that, while he was right that *computers* do not understand, he has not shown that properly organized *robots* could not understand what they say.

The question of what it would take to give artificially produced words genuine semantic content has been discussed by others, notably by Harnad (1990) under the phrase "the symbol grounding problem."

3.2.2   Dreyfus' work

Hubert Dreyfus (1972/1979) raised an influential series of related challenges for the classical approach to AI. We may begin to understand them by returning to our example of calculators. It is true that such devices embody arithmetical principles; however, they are arguably not (thing) intelligent. What took intelligence was the discovery of arithmetical principles, and calculators make no start on that project at all. They can be plausibly regarded as mere tools in which we have stored a certain product of our intelligence and, as such, they throw no light on what it takes to actually be intelligent. More complex devices may store more impressive products of our intelligence, but the conclusion to be drawn is essentially the same. Intelligence requires the ability to figure out what rules to apply – and when they can be applied – and machines that merely store rules do not begin to do this, no matter how useful they may be as tools.

This challenge can be deepened by noting that intelligence is exhibited in the ability to recognize what is relevant to whatever task is at hand. But, in general, relevance depends on all features present (or absent!) in a situation. Thus, achieving recognition of relevance by applying rules to representations of features would seem to require exhaustive rule sets that apply to every contingency. On the one hand, this project does not seem remotely feasible. On the other hand, if it could be carried out, it would be plausible to object that *intelligence* had not been embodied in the resulting device, which, at best, would be a repository of the results of our intelligence.

The problem of bringing to bear what is relevant to current tasks is sometimes called the "frame problem." This problem is sometimes regarded as merely empirical, that is, a problem to be solved by finding a suitable compromise between restrictions on the range of cases to which a program may be applied (which can reduce the size of spaces that have to be searched for relevant data or operations), and the complexity of the program needed to deal adequately with the intended problem space. The philosophical challenge is an addition to the empirical difficulties (which are considerable); it suggests that the whole idea of approaching intelligence through representations and rules can never provide a device that exhibits true intelligence. And it offers an explanation of the difficulties repeatedly encountered in attempts to "scale up" elegant solutions to relatively simple problems so they can be applied to complex, real-world problems (Dreyfus 1972/1979; McDermott 1976). The explanation is that efficiency implies restriction on the size of search spaces, but success in providing flexibility requires allowing potential access to any piece of data. It is not evident how the tension between these two demands can be resolved in the case of real-world problems in which many features may become relevant to successful coping.

For some practical purposes, these problems can be handled by hardware advances in memory size and processing speed. However, the more solutions rely on these means, the more plausible it becomes that there must be an alternative approach to intelligence; for, although our brains' storage capacity is large, its processing speed, at the level of individual elements, is slow (roughly 100 processing steps per second [Feldman 1985] vs. millions for computers). In the terminology introduced above, the more classical approaches to AI base their improvements in performance on hardware advances, the more it looks as if they will at most yield regular AI. This reflection suggests that aiming at premium AI might be useful, even for practical applications, and has led many in the AI community to explore more biologically inspired approaches.

3.3   Connectionism

Connectionist devices (parallel distributed processors, artificial neural networks) typically consist of *units* whose output to other units is a function of the sum of weighted inputs that they receive from other units. A weighted input to a unit *B* is the output of the projecting unit *A* times the weight of the connection (positive or negative) between unit *A* and unit *B*. Networks of units are characterized, in part, by their patterns of connectivity. Many such patterns have been investigated, including strictly "feedforward" networks and networks with lateral ("feedsideways") and recurrent (feedback) connections.

Connectionist devices are further characterized by their rule for finding a set of connection weights that will yield patterns on their output units that are appropriate to each pattern on their input units. In many cases, differences between actual outputs and correct outputs for patterns in a training set are used to generate an error signal that, in turn, is used to incrementally adjust weights. After many such cycles of adjustment, correct input–output pattern pairings are achieved.

Connectionist devices have several properties that have stimulated interest. For example, they generalize, in the sense that, once trained, a novel input pattern that is similar to a training pattern, P1, will generate an output that is similar to the output for P1. Their "memories" are "content addressable" – that is, the input pattern together with the existing set of weights directly produces the output, and there is no process of "searching" for information that is relevant to the input–output relation. They degrade gracefully – that is, damage to some of a network's units does not immediately destroy the input-output relation. Instead, there is a range in which damage makes the generalization gradually worse but not completely useless. (For further details on connectionist devices and their properties, see Chapter 5.)

3.3.1   Rule-like results without rules?

The properties just listed have generated interest in part because they resemble our own psychological properties, and thus suggest that connectionist studies can provide some insight into premium AI. This suggestion is present in the case of a further and somewhat controversial property of some connectionist devices; namely, they appear to be able to provide rule-like relations between input and output patterns without having corresponding internal representations of rules.

For example, it appears that when children learn how to form the past tense in English, they learn a rule that applies to the majority of verbs: "add '-ed'." In a much-discussed experiment, however, Rumelhart and McClelland (1986) trained a connectionist device to associate phonetic representations of verbs with phonetic representations of their past-tense forms. Both regular and irregular verbs were included, and the results of the training generalized fairly well for both. There was even a reproduction of an interference effect on past tenses for irregular verbs that is observed in children and that is usually attributed to their over-applying the rule for past tenses of regular verbs. But the training was simply association of present- and past-tense phonetic representations. One could describe the results in terms of rules, but there was no representation of rules within the system that generated the results.

However, this experiment has been criticized on several grounds (Pinker and Prince 1988; for continuing discussion see Clark 1993; McClelland and Patterson 2002a, 2002b; Pinker and Ullman 2002a, 2002b.) The most generalizable of these criticisms concerns the extent to which apparent success in providing rule-like results without explicit rules depends on particular features of the course of training. If the rule-like results turn out to depend on features of the training set that are not common in human experience, then their relevance to the possibility of premium AI would be significantly weakened.

3.3.2   Systematicity

Fodor and Pylyshyn (1988; see also Fodor 2000) have advanced a line of criticism of connectionism based on their concept of *systematicity*. Natural languages are learned in systems of sentences. For example, if one can understand and apply "John loves Mary," one can also understand and apply "Mary loves John," "Tom loves Jane," and so on. Systematicity is easily accounted for in terms of rules that apply to structured representations – for example, the meaning of "X loves Y" is that the first item mentioned loves the second item mentioned. But if sentences and meanings are merely associated in a trained network, there is no reason to expect to find systematicity.

Connectionists (e.g., Smolensky 1995) may reply that there are some kinds of networks that will yield systematicity. This kind of response, however, raises the question whether the attractive properties of connectionist networks really contribute to our understanding of how intelligence is produced or whether, as Fodor suggests, connectionist networks are merely capable of implementing a classical architecture – in which case it is really the latter that explains how we manage to be intelligent. If that is right, premium intelligence could, in principle, be implemented in a non-connectionist device after all.

3.3.3   Psychological realism

One can, of course, distinguish between the questions "Are connectionist devices steps on a road leading to premium AI?" and "Can connectionist devices be used to provide regular artificial intelligence?" A negative answer to the first would be compatible with the possibility of a robot that is driven by a connectionist-style brain and that responds flexibly to obstacles and exhibits a constant tendency toward achieving its goal states. However, some of the inspiration for connectionism comes from the idea that since our brains presumably make us intelligent, a brain-inspired device should also be able to provide premium artificial intelligence. To the extent that there are doubts that connectionist devices succeed in capturing the way we work, this inspiration is weakened, and alternative support for the probability of their providing even regular artificial intelligence is fairly demanded.

One doubt of this kind concerns the use of error signals (differences between correct output and actual output of a unit or set of units) to find a set of weights that will be useful for a given purpose. There is an algorithm (commonly known as backpropagation) that can be shown to be effective, and that is frequently used in connectionist research. Unfortunately, it is not clear how a brain could apply this algorithm to the adjustment of synaptic connections among neurons.

An alternative approach to weight adjustment is *reinforcement learning.* The core idea in reinforcement learning is that no one needs to know correct solutions to the problem of what actions to take; action choices can be shaped by the (positive or negative) value of consequences upon an agent of actions recently taken (e.g., Kaebling, Littman, and Moore 1996; Sutton and Barto 1998; Porta and Celaya 2005). It seems evident that we can learn in this way, and a very promising suggestion is to design devices that can also learn through reinforcement.

Those who have taken Dreyfus' critique of GOFAI to heart, however, may have some analogous doubts concerning reinforcement learning. Work in this area at present focuses on small problems and it is not clear whether results can be scaled up to handle real-world complexity. Behaviors can be well defined, and easily distinguished. Intelligence, however, (whether regular or premium) will likely have to deal with actions whose proper classification depends on circumstances – for example, the same running behavior might be fleeing or chasing, depending on whether a predator is behind the runner, or prey is in front of it. It may be that working on problems that permit easy classification of actions bypasses an essential element of intelligence; namely, learning how circumstances affect the significance of a behavior.

A further problem in assessing current work on reinforcement learning is that many schemes require updating the value, not only of actions, but of states that are parts of sequences of states leading up to actions. There are algorithms for doing this, but they require significant calculation and it is not evident how they, or equivalents, could be executed in the brain. This is not a problem for regular AI. However, to the extent that research on reinforcement learning forgoes plausible connection with premium AI, it loses the support of the argument that since we humans exhibit reinforcement learning, (regular) AI will be achievable by (current) approaches to reinforcement learning.

3.3.4   Representation

The attractive properties of connectionism depend on the use of distributed representations; that is, representations that depend on the pattern of activation across more than one unit. The "knowledge" of a connectionist device is also distributed across the weights of its connections. Outputs are dependent on combined effects of many weights, and each weight contributes to many outputs. The distributed character of the representations and "knowledge" in connectionist devices leads to two kinds of questions.

Ramsey, Stich, and Garon (1990) have noted that the distributed character of a network's "knowledge" makes it difficult to see how a connectionist network could ever model the seemingly obvious truth that people can act for one reason rather than another, even when they have beliefs and desires corresponding to two or more reasons for that action. For if the relevant beliefs are stored in a single network, the connections grounding both would make a contribution to any outcome. One could, of course, hold that different beliefs are stored in different networks; but to apply this strategy generally would be to give up the putative advantages of connectionist networks.

Connectionists may, however, respond that a distinction among reasons for an output can be adequately made by attending to whatever differences give us grounds for believing that an action was done for one, rather than the other, of two good reasons (Robinson 1995). For example, it might be that only one of two possible inputs was present (or salient) on a given occasion. If it is I1 that causes O, the reason that goes with I1 might be the reason for the output, even if the network would have yielded O if input I2 had been present (or more salient). It is, however, controversial whether analogues of this strategy can be provided for all relevant cases.

A second, widely discussed issue concerns the processing of representations in connectionist systems. There are several ingenious schemes for creating and storing information in connectionist devices. (See, e.g., Pollack 1988, 1990; Smolensky and Legendre 2006.) But if stored representations have to be decoded, (i.e., retrieved and represented separately) in order to be used in cognitively useful processing, then the idea that connectionism makes a *distinctive* contribution to our understanding of cognition is put in some doubt.

In an ingenious experiment, Chalmers (1993) showed that connectionist representations could be processed without decoding. This experiment involved two networks. The first network was trained to form a compressed representation of active-voice sentences and passive-voice sentences, and to decode those representations into their original full sentences. A second network was trained to convert the compressed representations of active-voice sentences into compressed representations of their passive-voice equivalents. When these latter compressed representations were decoded by the first network, the result was a correct passive-voice equivalent of the corresponding active-voice sentence. Most interestingly, the same result was obtained for compressed representations that had never been presented to the second network during its training phase. In effect, the second network was able to apply what it had "learned" about the active-/passive-voice relation to new (i.e., unseen) cases; and it was able to do this without first decoding the compressed active-voice representations.

However, as Chalmers explicitly noted, this result was not psychologically realistic. The training set was more than half of the total set of cases, and the sentences were all of the same simple form (subject, verb, object). Thus, while Chalmers' experiment provides an existence proof for the possibility of useful processing without decoding, it remains an open question whether psychologically realistic examples can be found.

From a broad perspective, GOFAI and connectionism agree that intelligence involves the processing of representations. Their disagreement concerns the nature of that processing, and, in light of the difficulties in both approaches, it is perhaps not surprising that suspicion has fallen on the idea of representation itself.

3.4 Dynamical systems theory

Dynamical systems theory (DST) views cognition as depending on a continuous interaction of a cognitive agent with its surroundings. Intelligent action does not arise in virtue of first representing the environment and then executing processes upon that representation. Instead, environmental inputs directly drive activities that react back upon the environment, resulting in new inputs and new reactions. Intelligence arises from a design that can exploit the information present in an environment without first converting that information into an internal representation.

A key feature of dynamical systems is their relation to time. If a device works by operating on representations, its operations can vary in their time course, subject only to the constraint that a representation of an action must be delivered in time for the action to be useful. If a device's processing is tightly coupled to external inputs, rather than representations of them, then the timing of the process is dependent on the timing of the arrival of those inputs, and there is no arbitrariness in the time course of the processing.

These ideas have been illustrated by considering the Watt governor (see van Gelder 1997). This device links a spindle to the drive shaft of a steam engine. The spindle supports a pair of weights that rotate with the spindle, and that are mounted so that they change their height as fluctuations in engine speed vary their distance from the spindle's axis. The arms supporting the weights are mechanically linked to a valve that varies steam pressure inversely to the height of the weights. The result of this arrangement is to keep the engine speed within a narrow range, even when load on the drive shaft varies.

Van Gelder suggested that if we are trying to understand cognition, the Watt governor is a better inspiration than computers. The key point of contrast is that the governor's system of linkages performs its useful function without having any part that applies rules to representations. The speed of the drive shaft is mechanically coupled to the governor, which in turn is mechanically coupled to the valve. The result is a dynamical system that involves no calculation of appropriate valve state from a record of drive shaft speed.

Brooks' (1991) robotic examples are more complex than the Watt governor, but the inspiration – visible from his title, "Intelligence without Representation" – is the same. Brooks regards navigation as a significant problem, which has been solved in evolutionary time prior to development of the ability to do explicit calculations. His work suggests that we will understand intelligence best by constructing devices that dynamically connect inputs to actions, that is, devices that are always under constraints similar to those that have been present throughout the course of evolution. Brooks decisively rejects any conception in which there is a division of labor between devices that embody intelligence and devices that turn the resulting output into actions. The problems of transducing sensory inputs to computer representations, and computer representations to motor outputs, are formidable at best (and intractable at worst). Such an approach is therefore to be abandoned in favor of devices in which the sensory input to motor output connection is built in at every stage. (For further details of DST and related approaches, see Chapter 6.)

3.4.1   Questions for DST

Downplaying representations naturally focuses attention on what is to count as a "representation." The weakest interpretation of this term would equate it to "tracking" – that is, high correlation between occurrences of states of a system that are regarded as representations, and the presence of objects or properties that are held to be represented. A much richer conception of "representation" (Grush 1997) requires an internal model that can be used to predict future states from present inputs. It seems clear that dynamical systems can work without representations in this stronger sense. It is not so clear, however, that devices of the kind featured in dynamical systems theory dispense with "representations" in the sense of mere tracking. For example, the height of the weights in the Watt governor could be regarded as representing the speed of the drive shaft (see Bechtel 1998).

A further question (also raised by Bechtel 1998) concerns the extent to which dynamical systems theory offers a distinctive explanation of cognition, as opposed to a distinctive type of description of what cognitive systems do. To illustrate: The relation between the height of the weights in the Watt governor and the speed of the engine can be given an elegant description by using differential equations. We can, however, still ask how the device works, and can give an answer by pointing to the spindle, valve, drive shaft, and the mechanical linkages between them. If this distinction between description and explanatory mechanism can be applied to cognitive systems, then the contribution of dynamical systems theory, while valuable at the descriptive level, may not offer a radical departure at the level of explaining cognition.

Finally, a problem for dynamical systems theory arises from the observation that many instances of intelligent performance rely heavily on memory. Use of memory would seem to require representations, and these representations must have their effects on behavior independently of the time at which the memory representation was created. Research on robot controllers that work without memory (e.g., Nolfi and Floreano 2000) has shown some surprising abilities to solve problems; nonetheless, it is not plausible that there will be devices that will be widely accepted as exhibiting (thing) intelligence but do not rely on memory. To be sure, it may be that memory representations can be incorporated into DST (as van Gelder 1997, suggests). It is, however, not clear how this can be done without returning us to the previously discussed questions about how representations can be processed to yield intelligent outcomes.

Further reading

Carter, M. (2007). *Minds and Computers: An Introduction to the Philosophy of Artificial Intelligence*. Edinburgh University Press. Introduces basic concepts in philosophy of mind and the computational theory of mind, which is defended.

Chalmers, D. and Bourget, D. (Repeatedly updated.) "Philosophy of Artificial Intelligence," http://consc.net/mindpapers/6/all. A comprehensive bibliography of papers, organized by many sections and subsections covering all aspects under its title.

Cole, D. (2004, rev. 2009). The Chinese Room argument, in E. N. Zalta (ed.), *The Stanford Encyclopedia of Philosophy*, http://plato.stanford.edu/entries/ chinese-room. Explains the argument and the replies to it, and makes connections to larger philosophical issues.

Garson, J. (1997, rev. 2010). Connectionism, in E. N. Zalta (ed.), *The Stanford Encyclopedia of Philosophy*, http://plato.stanford.edu/entries/connectionism. Explanation of connectionist devices, strengths and weaknesses, and issues between connectionism and classical approaches to AI.

Horst, S. (2003, rev. 2009). The computational theory of mind, in E. N. Zalta (ed.), *The Stanford Encyclopedia of Philosophy*, http://plato.stanford.edu/entries/ computational-mind. Explains why the mind has been regarded as a computer, and reviews criticisms of that view.

References

Aquinas, T. (1265–72/1945). *Summa Theologica*, in A. C. Pegis (tr.), *Basic Writings of St. Thomas Aquinas*. New York: Random House.

Ayer, A. J. (1954). Freedom and necessity, in A. J. Ayer, *Philosophical Essays* (pp. 271–84). London and Basingstoke: Macmillan.

Bechtel, W. (1998). Representation and cognitive explanations: Assessing the dynamicist's challenge in cognitive science, *Cognitive Science* 22: 295–318.

Block, N. (1981). Psychologism and behaviorism, *The Philosophical Review* 90: 5–43.

Brooks, R. (1991). Intelligence without representation, *Artificial Intelligence* 47: 139–59.

Chalmers, D. J. (1993). Connectionism and compositionality: Why Fodor and Pylyshyn were wrong, *Philosophical Psychology* 6: 305–19.

(1996). Does a rock implement every finite-state automaton?, *Synthese* 108: 309–33.

Clark, A. (1993). *Associative Engines: Connectionism, Concepts, and Representational Change*. Cambridge, MA: MIT Press.

Dennett, D. C. (1973). Mechanism and responsibility, in T. Honderich (ed.), *Essays on Freedom of Action* (pp. 157–84). London: Routledge and Kegan Paul. Reprinted in Dennett, D. C. (1978) *Brainstorms* (pp. 233–55). Cambridge, MA: Bradford Books.

Descartes, R. (1637/1931). *Discourse on the Method of Rightly Conducting the Reason and Seeking for Truth in the Sciences*, in E. Haldane and G. R. T. Ross (trs.), *The Philosophical Works of Descartes*, vol 1. Cambridge University Press.

Dretske, F. (1995). *Naturalizing the Mind.* Cambridge, MA: MIT Press.

Dreyfus, H. L. (1972; rev. edn. 1979). *What Computers Can't Do.* New York: Harper & Row.

Feldman, J. A. (1985). Connectionist models and their applications: Introduction, *Cognitive Science* 9: 1–2.

Fodor, J. A. (2000). *The Mind Doesn't Work That Way.* Cambridge, MA: MIT Press.

Fodor, J. A. and Pylyshyn, Z. (1988). Connectionism and cognitive architecture: A critical analysis, in S. Pinker and J. Mehler (eds.), *Connections and Symbols* (pp. 3–71). Cambridge, MA: MIT Press.

Gödel, K. (1931). Über formal unentscheidbare Sätze der Principia Mathematica und verwandter Systeme I, *Monatshefte für Mathematik und Physik* 38: 173–98.

Grush, R. (1997). The architecture of representation, *Philosophical Psychology* 10: 5–23.

Harnad, S. (1990). The symbol grounding problem, *Physica D* 42: 335–46.

Hasker, W. (1999). *The Emergent Self.* Ithaca and London: Cornell University Press.

Haugeland, J. (ed.) (1981). *Mind Design.* Montgomery, VT: Bradford Books.

Hume, D. (1748). *An Enquiry Concerning Human Understanding.* Full text available online at http://eserver.org/18th/hume-enquiry.html.

Kaebling, L. P., Littman, M. L., and Moore, A. W. (1996). Reinforcement learning: A survey, *Journal of Artificial Intelligence Research* 4: 237–85.

Lucas, J. R. (1961). Minds, machines and Gödel, *Philosophy* 36: 120–34.

McClelland, J. L. and Patterson, K. (2002a). 'Words or Rules' cannot exploit the regularity in exceptions: A reply to Pinker and Ullman, *Trends in Cognitive Science* 6: 464–65.

(2002b). Rules or connections in past-tense inflections: What does the evidence rule out?, *Trends in Cognitive Science* 6: 465–72.

McDermott, D. (1976). Artificial intelligence meets natural stupidity, *SIGART Newsletter*, no. 57: 4–9.

Nolfi, S. and Floreano, D. (2000). *Evolutionary Robotics: The Biology, Intelligence and Technology of Self-Organizing Machines.* Cambridge, MA: MIT Press.

Penrose, R. (1989). *The Emperor's New Mind.* Oxford University Press.

(1994). *Shadows of the Mind.* Oxford University Press.

Piccinini, G. (2010). Computation in physical systems, in E. N. Zalta (ed.), *The Stanford Encyclopedia of Philosophy* (Fall 2010 edn.), http://plato.stanford.edu/archives/fall2010/entries/computation-physicalsystems/.

Pinker, S. and Prince, A. (1988). On language and connectionism: Analysis of a parallel distributed model of language acquisition, in S. Pinker and J. Mehler (eds.), *Connections and Symbols* (pp. 73–193). Cambridge, MA: MIT Press.

Pinker, S. and Ullman, M. T. (2002a). The past and future of the past tense, *Trends in Cognitive Science* 6: 456–63.

(2002b). Combination and structure, not gradedness, is the issue: Reply to McClelland and Patterson, *Trends in Cognitive Science* 6: 472–4.

Pollack, J. (1988). Recursive auto-associative memory: Devising compositional distributed representations, *Proceedings of the 10th Annual Conference of the Cognitive Science Society*. Mahwah, NJ: L. Erlbaum.

(1990). Recursive distributed representations, *Artificial Intelligence* 46: 77–105.

Porta, J. M. and Celaya, E. (2005). Reinforcement learning for agents with many sensors and actuators acting in categorizable environments, *Journal of Artificial Intelligence Research* 23: 79–122.

Putnam, H. (1960). Review of Nagel and Newman, Gödel's Proof, *Philosophy of Science* 27: 205–7.

Ramsey, W., Stich, S., and Garon, J. (1990). Connectionism, eliminativism and the future of folk psychology, in J. E. Tomberlin (ed.), *Philosophical Perspectives* 4: 499–533.

Robinson, W. S. (1992). *Computers, Minds and Robots*. Philadelphia: Temple University Press.

(1995). Mild realism, causation, and folk psychology, *Philosophical Psychology* 8: 167–87.

(1996). Review of Roger Penrose, Shadows of the Mind, *Philosophical Psychology* 9: 119–22.

Rumelhart, D. E. and McClelland, J. L. (1986). On learning the past tenses of English verbs, in D. E. Rumelhart, J. L. McClelland, and the PDP Research Group, *Parallel Distributed Processing: Explorations in the Microstructure of Cognition*, vol. 2 (pp. 216–71). Cambridge, MA: MIT Press.

Schank, R. C. and Abelson, R. P. (1977). *Scripts, Plans, Goals, and Understanding*. Hillsdale, NJ: L. Erlbaum.

Searle, J. (1980). Minds, brains, and programs, *The Behavioral and Brain Sciences* 3: 417–24.

(1992). *The Rediscovery of the Mind*. Cambridge, MA: MIT Press.

Smolensky, P. (1995). Constituent structure and explanation in an integrated connectionist/symbolic cognitive architecture, in C. MacDonald and G. MacDonald (eds.), *Connectionism: Debates on Psychological Explanation* (pp. 223–90). Oxford: Blackwell.

Smolensky, P. and Legendre, G. (2006). *The Harmonic Mind*. Cambridge, MA: MIT Press.

Sutton, R. S. and Barto, A. G. (1998). *Reinforcement Learning: An Introduction*. Cambridge, MA: MIT Press.

Turing, A. (1950). Computing machinery and intelligence, *Mind* 59: 433–60.

van Gelder, T. (1997). Dynamics and cognition, in J. Haugeland (ed.), *Mind Design II* (pp. 421–50). Cambridge, MA: MIT Press.

Part II

Architectures

4 GOFAI

Margaret A. Boden

4.1 Introduction

Good Old-Fashioned AI – GOFAI, for short – is a label used to denote classical, symbolic, AI. The term "AI" is sometimes used to mean only GOFAI, but that is a mistake. AI also includes other approaches, such as connectionism (of which there are several varieties: see Chapter 5), evolutionary programming, and situated and evolutionary robotics. Indeed, most work in artificial life (A-Life) falls within AI broadly defined, despite A-Lifers' tendency to distance themselves from it (see Chapter 14). Here, however, we are concerned with symbolic AI alone.

Both technological and psychological AI employ the full range of AI methodologies, GOFAI included. But they are driven by different motivations. The goal of the former is to build useful computer systems, doing, or assisting with, tasks that humans want done. The goal of the latter – which can also be called computational psychology – is to develop explanatory theories of mind. Sometimes (according to "strong" AI: see Section 4.4), it also aims to build computer systems that are genuinely intelligent in themselves. Accordingly, psychological AI is the more likely to raise questions of interest for the philosophy of mind.

4.2 GOFAI outlined

The GOFAI methodology employs programmed instructions operating on formal symbolic representations. It is well suited to the binary, serial nature of the von Neumann digital computer. From the mid 1950s to the mid 1980s, it was the dominant (though not the only) approach in AI. Functionalism in the philosophy of mind was developed with these programs, and/or abstract Turing machines, in mind (Putnam 1960; Newell and Simon 1963; Fodor 1968; see Chapter 3).

A GOFAI symbol is an item in a formal language (a programming language). Like the symbols of mathematics or logic, GOFAI symbols – and programs composed of them – can be regarded as purely formal (meaningless) structures. In practice, however, they are normally interpreted by the user in terms of some particular semantic content: verbal, numerical, visual, auditory, and so on. Atomic symbols can be combined to form complex symbols, according to specific formal rules of symbol manipulation. What happens when a GOFAI program is run is that symbols of various kinds, structured in various ways, are built, stored, retrieved, compared, and transformed. In short, GOFAI computation involves the construction and transformation of symbolic data structures.

The key concepts that structure GOFAI programs are heuristic search and planning. These closely connected ideas were pioneered in the 1950s (Newell, Shaw, and Simon 1958a; Newell, Shaw, and Simon 1958b, 1959; Samuel 1959; Boden 1977/87, ch. 12). They are still crucial to GOFAI work today (see Russell and Norvig 2003, especially ch. 4). A GOFAI problem, or task, is represented as a search space: a set of possibilities (defined by a finite set of generative rules), within which the solution lies – and within which it must be found. Examples include the set of legal moves in chess, or of permissible word strings given some particular grammar and vocabulary. The specific locations in the search space do not have to be detailed beforehand, but can be generated by the program.

In many cases, a systematic "brute force" search through the space is impractical, because there are too many possibilities to be individually considered. Moreover, there is often no utterly reliable rule for picking out all (and only) the "promising" candidates. If so, the search must be guided by heuristics: rules of thumb that are usually helpful in guiding the program toward the solution and away from dead ends but which are not guaranteed to solve the problem. (Compare "Protect your queen" in chess: This is a very useful heuristic, but it is occasionally advisable to sacrifice your queen.) Planning is a GOFAI technique wherein the problem is analyzed by the program as a hierarchical structure of goals, subgoals, and sub-subgoals ... In the paradigm case, the final goal is specified at the beginning, and the program's task is to reduce the differences between the current state and the goal state until no such differences remain. (The general idea that purposive behavior is rooted in the reduction of differences was inherited from cybernetics, the mid-century study of feedback systems, such as biological homeostasis and guided missiles; but cybernetics did not specify structured representations of goal states; Rosenblueth, Wiener, and Bigelow 1943.) The program is provided before it starts with a number of possible differences, a list of actions (operators) that can eliminate the various differences, lists of prerequisites that must hold if a certain operator is to be used, and heuristics for ordering the actions when more than one action is possible in the current circumstances. Indeed, most of the "intelligence" involved lies in the choices of actions, operators, and heuristics specified by the programmer. If the program, when it is run, decides that a particular operator is needed to achieve the current goal, it may have to set up a new subgoal to satisfy the relevant prerequisites. This process can be repeated on indefinitely many hierarchical levels. In many cases, finely detailed planning can be left until the point of execution, so that – up to a point – unanticipated factors can be dealt with.

In the earliest GOFAI research, the goal hierarchy was clearly explicit and "up-front." In other words, the program would be focused on one goal at a certain moment, and would switch to another only if (1) a new subgoal had to be set up in order to achieve it, or (2) the original goal was attained – in which case the program would "pop" up to the next goal level, or exit if the top level had been reached.

A later AI methodology made the goal hierarchy implicit within a large set of logically independent Condition-Action rules (Newell and Simon 1972). (The individual rules were called "productions," so programs built out of them were called production systems.) The Condition and the Action within a rule could each be a single item, or a conjunction (or disjunction) of several – even of many – different items. For instance, one of the rules in a program for solving alphabetically coded addition problems, such as "DONALD + GERALD = ROBERT," read as follows: "IF the current goal is to evaluate a set of letters, THEN find one of the letters (by means of the production rule called FIND-LETTER) AND set up the (new) goal of evaluating it." What had earlier been represented as separate lists of heuristics, actions, and prerequisites were now tacitly included within the productions. So the Condition might include the specification that such-and-such a goal has already been set up. Similarly, the Action could include an item setting up a new goal or subgoal. Conflict resolution techniques were provided to deal with cases where more than one Condition was satisfied at the same time. For instance, a Condition specifying a longer, more inclusive, conjunction would take priority over one which specified only a single conjunct.

One advantage of this general approach was that a new rule could be added at any time (provided that it was consistent with the existing rule set), without having to rewrite a complex hierarchical procedure. In addition, this methodology enabled interrupts: instant changes of goal, promoted by sudden changes in the environment or elsewhere in the running of the program. GOFAI search was thereby rendered less inflexible and "single-minded" than in the early days.

The development of expert systems – for medical diagnosis, for example, or advice on geological prospecting (Michie 1979; Feigenbaum and McCorduck 1983) – depended heavily on production systems. In general, an expert system is a program that represents the knowledge of the human expert as a set of IF-THEN rules, and which can be used to offer advice to non-experts in the domain concerned. For instance, a rule for medical diagnosis might be: "IF *these* symptoms are observed in the patient, AND the patient is an adult male, THEN infer that *this* bacterium is responsible, AND recommend *this* drug, given in *that* dosage for *that* length of time, as the treatment." The expert-systems researchers introduced inferential techniques for "forward chaining" and "backward chaining" within production systems. The former is used bottom-up, to generate conclusions from data. The latter is used top-down, to find evidence for a supposition, and/or to explain an item of advice already given by the program to the human user by recapitulating the previously fired rules. In general, "bottom-up" processing starts from a collection of disparate data items and tries to make overall sense of them in some way – perhaps by GOFAI techniques (such as production systems), or perhaps by PDP (parallel distributed processing) connectionism or other forms of self-organization (see Chapter 5). "Top-down" processing, by contrast, starts with some high-level goal or structure, and uses this to interpret – and sometimes to alter – input at lower levels. For example, a GOFAI visual program searching for cubes may decide to "hallucinate" the missing corner of input showing an incomplete drawing of a cube.

As the notions of *search, planning,* and *heuristic* may suggest, GOFAI programs often simulate the conscious deliberations of high-level human thought. That is partly because they can represent propositions with specific semantic content, and partly because they can include top-down executive control and self-monitoring processes. Even when they model unconscious processes, they typically represent these as being similar in kind to conscious deliberations. Visual recognition in GOFAI, for example, is often taken to be analogous to problem solving in logic. And logical problem solving, a fortiori, is seen as logic all the way down. However, the type of logic used varies. It may be the propositional calculus, expressed by simple logic gates implementing the basic logical operations (McCulloch and Pitts 1943) or by hierarchical planners like those sketched above (Newell et al. 1958a, 1958b, 1959). More often, it is predicate logic (McCarthy and Hayes 1969). In that case, it may be supplemented by various modal logics (McCarthy and Hayes 1969; Hayes 1979, 1985), or by special methods designed to combat the combinatorial explosion – such as resolution theorem proving (Robinson 1968). Or it may be a production system, whose Condition-Action pairs are based on a logic of IF-THEN rules (Post 1943). GOFAI's roots in logic provide it with both strengths and weaknesses, as we shall see in Section 4.3.

A further subvariety of GOFAI is evolutionary programming (Holland 1975; Ray 1992). More accurately, evolutionary programming was initially developed within GOFAI, and is often used in a GOFAI context – although it can also be used for evolving connectionist networks. Here, so-called "genetic algorithms" make random changes in the program's own rules, inspired by the processes of point mutation and crossover in biology. (In point mutation, a single element within the symbol-string that codes the rule is altered, so that ABCDE may give ABFDE; in crossover, a set of adjacent units on one rule string – comparable to adjacent genes on a chromosome – is swapped for a set of adjacent units on another string, so that ABCDEFGH and PQRSTUVW give ABCSTUFGH and PQRDEFUVW.) At each "generation," one or two of the more successful newly hatched programs are selected as (asexual or sexual) parents for the next generation. Usually, the selection is done automatically by a pre-defined fitness function; but it can be done interactively, by a human being. Where the problem is sufficiently well understood for slight improvements in performance to be recognized automatically, this methodology enables optimization of the task concerned. For example, if one wants a program that will sort a list of numbers into ascending order, or put names into alphabetical order, then an evolutionary approach will be able to find the most efficient algorithm whereas a human programmer may not.

4.3   Strengths and weaknesses of GOFAI

The major strengths of GOFAI are its abilities to model hierarchy and sequential order, to allow for precision in problem solving, and to represent specific propositional contents. Each of these features was illustrated in the pioneering SHRDLU program (Winograd 1972), which captured the attention of many psychologists and philosophers previously unfamiliar with AI. Unlike the simple keyword matchers that preceded it, SHRDLU could parse sentences of some significant complexity, such as "How many eggs would you have been going to use in the cake if you hadn't learned your mother's recipe was wrong?" In engaging in "conversation," SHRDLU's parser was closely integrated with semantic analysis, problem solving, and world knowledge. To decide the reference of the human speaker's phrase "the pyramid," for instance, it would ask itself whether there was more than one pyramid in the scene, and if so whether any specific pyramid had already been mentioned in the conversation. In general, SHRDLU – like GOFAI programs today – could alternate between different tasks and/or knowledge bases in order to solve what seems superficially like "one" problem.

The "How many eggs . . . ?" example illustrates the importance of hierarchy and sequential order: The parsing simply could not be accomplished without getting these right. And precision, too, is crucial – for a single letter can sometimes make a huge difference. (Compare a telegram saying "Our son is dead" with one saying "Your son is dead.") However, precision can be overdone. The early GOFAI programs were notoriously brittle, in the sense that missing and/or contradictory data would result in a nonsensical response from the computer – if it did not halt altogether. (Even SHRDLU was less powerful than it appeared, for its "conversation" was not a continuous exchange but was cobbled together from a number of separate occasions.)

A special case of brittleness is the *frame problem* (McCarthy and Hayes 1969; Dennett 1984; Boden 2006, ch. 10.iii). This term is widely used to mark two difficulties: first, knowing which aspects of a situation would be changed by a particular action, and which would not; second, reasoning with incomplete knowledge, due to our inevitable ignorance about the facts of the real world and to the vagueness of ordinary-language concepts. For instance, the puzzle of how stranded explorers can cross a river in a jungle might be solved not (as one might predict) by their laboriously building a raft, but by their being unexpectedly rescued by the helicopter of a film crew working nearby. GOFAI roboticists tried to distinguish between changeable and unchangeable states of affairs, with respect to planned actions, but often some relevant instances were overlooked. And the logic of resolution theorem proving – which proved theorems in predicate logic by showing that their negations were inconsistent, on the assumption that not-not-X implies X – was so unforgiving that it threatened to undermine any real-world plan or "commonsense" problem solver. Various types of "nonmonotonic" logic were developed, in which a statement could be taken as true *until it was shown to be false* (Boden 2006, ch. 13.i.a). Even so, these "default assumptions" had to be specified beforehand.

(The exigencies of the frame problem later encouraged the development of situated robotics [Brooks 1991]. GOFAI robots had planned their performance beforehand, guided top-down by a complex model of the world, which needed to be laboriously updated if the world suddenly changed, and by assumptions about what would happen if this or that action was taken. By contrast, situated robots did not rely on internal world models. Instead, they worked bottom-up by responding directly in simple "reflex" ways to specific environmental cues whenever they happened to encounter them; if the world suddenly changed, the newly relevant responses would be elicited as a matter of course.)

Some critics of GOFAI seem to believe that unrelieved brittleness is essential to it, but that is not so. There are several ways in which a GOFAI program can be prevented, up to a point, from making irreversible inferences that may turn out to be false. Special anticipatory measures, of which the default assumptions mentioned above are a special case, and a variety of interacting *temporary* (i.e., provisional) representations (e.g., Sloman 1978, ch. 9), have been developed to reduce the brittleness of GOFAI systems. And, as we have seen, techniques for conflict resolution have been identified which enable a program to choose between two (or more) individually allowable actions. It is true, however, that symbolic AI programs do tend to be brittle. They do not "naturally" show what is called graceful degradation – in which imperfections in the data lead to proportionally imperfect *but often acceptable* performance. A main strength of PDP connectionist systems is that they have this property simply because of the way they work: It does not have to be specifically built in (see Chapter 5).

Explicitness has its drawbacks, too. If one wants a GOFAI program to learn something, one has to provide the defining features of that "something" (Boden 2006, ch. 13.iii.f). Often, this is not possible. For example, you may want to teach a program to recognize cats. But can you define "cat"? Can you even identify and list the relevant features seen in photographs of a dozen cats? GOFAI programs can sometimes learn new concepts, to be sure: for instance, a more efficient method for diagnosing a certain disease (Michalski and Chilausky 1980). But the defining features of those concepts have to be explicitly specified beforehand, even if they are merely included within a longer list of features.

It is not the case (although it is often believed) that GOFAI programs always work top-down, rather than bottom-up. However, they often do involve some central executive, or high-level control. This is less obvious in production systems, where the control hierarchy is not made explicit and where interrupts can switch the system's attention to a different area. But the ability, in principle, to model hierarchies does often lead, in practice, to the modeling of hierarchical phenomena – such as complex planning, or natural language. And it has become increasingly clear, over the years, that some forms of intelligence (within both individuals and groups) do not involve any central executive. Rather, the intelligence, and the control, is distributed over the whole system. In such cases, the traditional GOFAI approach must be modified, or even wholly abandoned. Modification occurs, for instance, when a number of largely autonomous systems ("agents") are programmed, whose collective behavior emerges from their many interactions rather than from some high-level executive. The agents may be virtual "softbots" or physical robots, and their interactions may include communication, negotiation, cooperation, bidding, and even bargaining (Boden 2006, ch. 13.iii.d–e; see also Chapter 11 of the present volume).

Abandonment occurs, for example, when PDP connectionism is used instead of GOFAI. PDP systems are described in the following chapter. Here, what is relevant is that – besides avoiding the imposition of a top-down central controller – the PDP methodology avoids some other weaknesses of GOFAI. Above all, PDP avoids the brittleness that threatens the symbolic approach. Instead of deducing a clear conclusion by logical means, a PDP program settles into an equilibrium state in which a majority of (potentially contradictory) constraints are simultaneously satisfied. Contaminated and/or partly missing data can therefore be allowed, up to a point. In other words, noise tolerance and pattern completion, both of which are problematic for GOFAI, result "naturally" from the design of PDP networks. For example, a "messy" or incomplete drawing/photograph of a cube will be recognized by a PDP system as representing a cube even if the messiness and/or incompleteness had not been expected, still less deliberately anticipated, by the programmer. Similarly, patterns (concepts), which are not accessible to GOFAI learners and which were not suspected by the humans who built the system, can be learnt by example. (This is why PDP is used for expert systems that identify subtle patterns in financial information, such as stockmarket movements.)

However, PDP is no panacea. It lacks GOFAI's key strengths in modeling multi-level hierarchy, sequential order, and inferential relations between specific propositional contents. Moreover, it is not well suited to tasks where absolute precision, as opposed to graceful degradation, is required. Indeed, much of the connectionist research of the last twenty years has sought to acquire those very strengths – so far, with only limited success (Boden 2006, ch. 12.viii–ix).

Some researchers therefore employ "hybrid" systems, in which GOFAI is combined with PDP connectionism (see Chapter 5). One example of this approach is the model of action, and action errors, developed by Donald Norman and Timothy Shallice, respectively a cognitive psychologist and a clinical neurologist, and by AI researchers working with them (Norman and Shallice 1986; Cooper et al. 1996). Briefly, this "Supervisory Attentional System" uses connectionism to model perceptual recognition and associative memory/reminding, and GOFAI to model deliberate choice and planning. Both of these aspects are crucial to (much) human action, and – according to some leading AI experts – to successful robotics too (Sahota and Mackworth 1994). Since both aspects are crucial, it follows that situated robotics (see above, and Chapters 6 and 13) cannot always be substituted for GOFAI either. The hope expressed by Rodney Brooks (1991), that AI can be fully situated and GOFAI abandoned, is illusory. It is true that "direct" responsiveness to the environment can provide a surprising degree of order in behavior. This point was made in the 1960s by one of GOFAI's high priests, with respect to the path of an ant walking over cluttered ground (Simon 1969, ch. 3). Insect locomotion may be amenable to purely situationist modeling, relying only on inbuilt reflex responses to environmental cues (Beer 1990). But where human-level behavior is concerned, planning, and internal representation, is sometimes essential (Kirsh 1991; Vera and Simon 1993).

It is also true that the "embodiment" of a physical robot negotiating the material world (see Chapter 6) offers problems and solutions over and above those typical of "disembodied" GOFAI. For a robot is a material thing moving in the real world, as opposed to a program merely representing that world, so it encounters physical obstacles – and also opportunities – that do not arise in the case of a programmed simulation. That is why it has been suggested that GOFAI be superseded by GOFAIR: GOFAI and Robotics (Sahota and Mackworth 1994). GOFAIR is doubly hybrid. On the one hand, much of the robot's response is situated; on the other hand, connectionist methods are combined with GOFAI. The point of importance here, however, is that GOFAI – though supplemented – is maintained. That is not surprising, since the strengths and weaknesses of GOFAI and PDP, and of classical GOFAI and situated robotics, are largely complementary.

The motto of both psychological and technological AI today might be "Let a hundred flowers blossom – or anyway, four." Those four are the approaches of GOFAI, connectionism, situated AI, and dynamical systems (all of which sometimes employ evolutionary computation).

4.4 GOFAI as philosophy

When the GOFAI label was coined by the philosopher John Haugeland (1985, p. 112), his word "old-fashioned" implied that this type of AI had been superseded. And in a sense, it had: For PDP connectionism was on the rise, and would soon enthuse the philosophers (Clark 1989) – and the journalists too. However, Haugeland apparently knew nothing of that, for connectionism was not even mentioned in his book. His critique of GOFAI as *passé* was based rather in the philosophy of phenomenology, as Hubert Dreyfus' (1965) had been twenty years earlier. Haugeland argued that twenty years of philosophical critique had shown GOFAI to be false. "False," not just impractical, or limited. For his definition of the term did not merely pick out an AI methodology (symbolic computation). It also specified a commitment to what John Searle (1980) had called strong AI: the view that a suitably programmed computer would be really intelligent – and by implication, really emotional and really conscious too. Haugeland believed strong AI to have been refuted, in different ways, by both Searle and Dreyfus (and by his own arguments as well). Anyone who still accepted it was not only mistaken but behind the times (i.e., old-fashioned).

It is not clear that all GOFAI researchers are committed to strong AI. (By Haugeland's definition, then, not all GOFAI researchers are GOFAI researchers.) But some certainly are. For instance, Allen Newell and Herbert Simon explicitly stated a form of strong AI in their theory of Physical Symbol Systems, or PSSs (Newell and Simon 1963; Newell 1980). They claimed that intentionality (i.e., meaning, or "aboutness") is achieved, in both minds and computers, by implementing certain types of formal computation in PSSs. These were seen as "the necessary and sufficient means for general intelligent action." In other words, the mind (or mind/brain) *is* a PSS. Their commitment to strong AI was crystal clear.

Newell and Simon's AI programs specified formal computational systems of the type defined by Alan Turing in 1936. As psychologists, however, they were interested in computations that are responsive to the world and capable of directing behavior in it. Unlike Turing himself, then, they defined computation in causal terms. A *symbol*, they said, is a physical pattern with causal effects. The meaning of a symbol is the set of changes it enables the information processing system to effect, either *to* or *in response to* some object or process (outside or inside the system itself). Analogously, concepts such as *representation, interpretation, designation, reference, naming, standing for,* and *aboutness* were causally defined. In short, their semantic theory presented meaning as computational – and computation as intentional.

It was their statement of strong AI which Searle was attacking in his famous paper on the Chinese Room (1980; see also Chapter 3). Just in case there are any readers who have not already come across this example, it can be stated very briefly here. Searle imagines himself sitting in a windowless room, with a slot through which paper slips with "squiggles" and "squoggles" on them are occasionally passed in. On the table is a box of slips carrying similar doodles, of various shapes; and there is a rulebook, saying that if a squiggle is passed in then Searle should find a blingle-blungle and pass it out, or perhaps go through a long sequence of doodle pairings before passing some shape out. Unknown to Searle-in-the-room, the doodles are Chinese writing, the rulebook is an AI program for answering questions in Chinese, and the Chinese people outside the room are happily using Searle to answer their questions about some topic or other. The key point, says Searle, is that he entered the room unable to understand Chinese and, no matter how long he stays there, he still will not understand a word of it when he comes out. And his anti-GOFAI conclusion is that formal computation alone (which is what Searle-in-the-room is doing) cannot generate meaning, or intentionality. As he put it, programs are "all syntax and no semantics." So strong AI is impossible.

Searle's key premise was that GOFAI systems are defined in terms of abstract (uninterpreted) Turing computation. It follows, he said, that such programs are mere shufflers of meaningless shapes (i.e., formal symbols). Those shapes could in principle be interpreted as (mapped onto) many different activities: maths, music, mousetrap design, and so on. As regards the program itself, however, the choice between "meanings" is arbitrary. Any meaning it appears to have is derived entirely from us. So although we cannot help speaking of computers in intentional terms, they do not "intrinsically" merit such ascriptions. Strong AI is an illusion.

As for "weak" AI (that is, AI used in formulating, developing, and testing psychological theories), Searle doubted that brains generally implement formal computations. If they do not, then GOFAI-based computational psychology cannot even begin to explain our mental life – although psychological theories based on connectionist AI might do so. (When Searle defined weak AI he used "AI" to mean only GOFAI; the connectionist renaissance hadn't yet happened.) But even if our brains do implement formal computations, he said, the Chinese Room argument shows that something more was needed for intentionality. And that "something" was the causal powers of neuroprotein. This was a very poor argument, which most commentators politely ignored; for how neuroprotein, considered as a biochemical substance, can possibly ground intentionality is a philosophical mystery (Boden 2006, ch. 16.v.d).

The Chinese Room spawned a thriving philosophical industry whose mills are still spinning merrily. Many readers agreed that Searle's empty-symbolism argument proved just what he said it proved, while just as many saw it as fundamentally wrong-headed. Moreover, those who saw it as wrong-headed gave different accounts of just what was wrong with it. This is not the place to summarize the ever-lengthening debate. But two points must be mentioned.

First, it is arguable that Searle was attacking a straw man. Newell and Simon, and their GOFAI co-pioneers Marvin Minsky and John McCarthy too, undoubtedly believed that AI systems of a certain complexity would be really intelligent. But, contrary to what Searle assumed, they did not have abstract, uninterpreted, Turing computation solely in mind. Most philosophers take it for granted that all computation is Turing computation, and as such semantically empty. If that is so, then PSS theory holds that causation grounds the interpretation of computations once implemented, not that it is involved in defining computation as such. However, Newell and Simon's semantic theory sketched above suggests that they were not primarily concerned with computation as uninterpreted Turing computation. (In effect, their causal approach was tacitly offering what Searle termed "the Robot reply.") What is more, other AI scientists have also offered causal/intentional accounts of computation, sometimes explicitly denying that AI is primarily concerned with Turing computation (Sloman 2002). Their definitions are admittedly much less clear than Turing's, and in one case (Smith 1996) metaphysically maverick too. Without going into detail here (but see Boden 2006, ch. 16.ix), the point is that practising AI scientists do not think of computation only in the way that Turing did in his 1936 paper. It follows that the familiar "all syntax and no semantics" attack on GOFAI is not so obviously well-aimed as is usually assumed.

Second, some philosophers have argued that intentionality is grounded in our evolutionary history (Millikan 1984). If that is so, then only evolved AI systems/robots (including GOFAI-based examples) could even be candidates for the possession of intentionality. Some of the meanings attributed to evolved robots are not "arbitrary," as Searle would have it, but are grounded in their particular evolutionary history. For instance, a mini-network in a robot's "brain" may plausibly be seen as an orientation detector evolved for navigating the task environment (Harvey, Husbands, and Cliff 1994; Husbands, Harvey, and Cliff 1995). It is true, however, that whether these meanings – albeit not arbitrary – are real meanings remains controversial.

As remarked above, the empty-program argument was not the only reason why Haugeland rejected GOFAI. Even more important in his eyes (and Dreyfus') was the lack of embodiment of GOFAI programs. This feature was grounded in the Cartesian separation of mind, body, and world – with its picture of mental life as a sort of relay race, where the baton is passed along by a series of analytically distinct stages of perception, thinking, and motor action. That picture had imbued (most) experimental psychology and neurophysiology long before GOFAI came on the scene. But GOFAI made it even more evident, for instance in the 1960s/1970s programs of scene analysis that studied "vision" as a disembodied, and quasi-intellectualist, matter (Boden 1977/87, chs. 8–9). Haugeland prefers the phenomenological approach, wherein bodily presence and action in a material (and social) world are the source of all meaning and consciousness. This approach, with an accompanying emphasis on dynamical systems, was brought into cognitive science by Francisco Varela (Varela, Thompson, and Rosch 1991). Today, the phenomenological critique is hugely more influential within the field. Martin Heidegger is now more of a name to conjure with than is Bertrand Russell, whose works on logic (and logicist philosophy of language) were so important in the foundation of symbolic AI. But these two philosophers could hardly be more different.

As a result of this sea change, GOFAI is even more out of fashion now than it was in the heyday of PDP. In terms of philosophical interest, only GOFAI work on robotics and distributed cognition is still considered important. Whether any robot, GOFAI or not, can properly be said to be "embodied" is a highly germane question that we cannot go into here (see Chapter 6). But we have already seen (in Section 4.3) that a robot may be situated in, and challenged by, the physical world in a way in which typical (cerebral/intellectualist) GOFAI programs are not.

Some readers may feel that to say that GOFAI is "out of fashion" does not go nearly far enough. After all, fashions can be revived – and admired anew. But many people believe that GOFAI is out of favor forever, not to say dead. Why do they think this? And are they right?

4.5   The myth of GOFAI failure

We saw in Section 4.3 that the strengths and weaknesses of GOFAI and connectionism, and of GOFAI and situated robotics, are complementary. In the minds of the general public (and some AI researchers), however, GOFAI's weaknesses are more often noted than its strengths. Indeed, many commentators take it for granted that GOFAI has failed, and should be written off accordingly.

For example, Dreyfus, who predicted the failure of GOFAI some forty years ago (1965), now regards himself as vindicated. His Houston University lecture in 1998 was called "Why Symbolic AI Failed," and he had already expressed this unequivocal judgment in print: "The rationalist tradition had finally been put to an empirical test, and it had failed" (Dreyfus and Dreyfus 1988, p. 34). This view has percolated so widely that many people now regard it as a cliché.

To be sure, GOFAI has not lived up to its early hype. Simon's 1950s prediction that it would provide the world chess champion by 1967, for instance, was not borne out. (Deep Blue's trouncing of Gary Kasparov happened thirty years later, thanks to special-purpose chips enabling an eight-move lookahead.) And many other early predictions, such as near-faultless machine translation, have not been borne out either. The more recent examples of GOFAI hype include confident predictions of a robotic world soccer champion by 2050. My own view is that such promises will not be fulfilled for hundreds of years, if ever. But that doesn't spell "failure." For the success of the field should not be assessed by focusing on its most extravagant promises – especially since many AI researchers, past and present, have not shared those hype-ridden hopes. Nor should it be assessed in terms of passing the Turing Test. This has never been an appropriate criterion of success in AI – nor was it intended as such by Turing himself (Boden 2006, ch. 16.ii.c). So the fact that it has not been passed is neither here nor there. Nevertheless, many people still assume that it is highly relevant. Dreyfus' "Failure" lecture, for example, opened with a reference to Turing's prediction of close human–computer similarity by 2000. Rather, our assessment should be based on whether GOFAI has made significant progress toward the goals expressed in less careless moments. And here, we must recall the distinction between technological and psychological AI.

As regards technological GOFAI, the charge of failure is absurd. The frame problem itself, though admittedly not solved (and probably insoluble) for the general case, has been solved for practical purposes in many different contexts. Expert systems have been developed in a wide range of domains. They are used, for instance, for commercial, administrative, educational, medical, and military purposes. Some of them are capable of highly complex planning, occasionally scaling up to tens of thousands of steps (Russell and Norvig 2003, p. viii). GOFAI planning is even important in video games and Hollywood animation, for example, to prevent the virtual reality characters from bumping into one another. Moreover, the longed-for Semantic Web – typically regarded as a futuristic project *for computer science* rather than AI (see below) – will require advances in computerized ontologies, a topic pioneered by GOFAI (McCarthy and Hayes 1969).

Expert systems, VR games, and internet search engines such as Google all illustrate the fact that, in industrial societies, there are a host of invisible AI applications of which the general public are not even aware. Avid video-gamers do not know that there is a GOFAI planner in their favorite system. Workers in call centers often offer advice taken from a GOFAI expert system that is unseen by the customer at the other end of the telephone line. And many domestic machines, from cars to cookers, rely on inbuilt GOFAI (and connectionist) technology.

Invisibility is only one reason why GOFAI's successes go largely unsung. Another is unidentifiability. Many aspects of AI have been so successful that people (including other computer scientists) think of them merely as part of mainstream computer science. These include computing techniques that are now taken for granted, such as time sharing, personal computers with windows and mice, and object-oriented programming. Their roots in AI are forgotten. In this, AI is comparable to philosophy. It bravely asks the unanswered, almost unaskable, questions – but when it finds a reliable way of answering them, they are relabeled as questions for "respectable" science. In short, the charge that GOFAI has failed as a technology cannot be sustained. But what of GOFAI as a psychological enterprise?

As regards weak AI, there is no question but that this has led to many psychological discoveries. Some GOFAI-based work, to be sure, has led to what the philosopher Karl Popper called "refutations" of apparently promising "conjectures." For instance, GOFAI turned out to be inappropriate for modeling low-level vision, and for dealing with multiple partially conflicting constraints. But that is par for the course: The conjecture/refutation dialectic is what drives science forward.

What is more, GOFAI-based computational psychology has not met only with refutations. It has led to new psychological data and/or a deeper theoretical understanding regarding many topics (Boden 2006, ch. 7). These include emotions, hypnosis, and psychopathology, as well as cognitive phenomena such as reasoning, problem solving, action errors, and language. Even more important than specific data and theories, AI in general – GOFAI included – has led psychologists to appreciate the previously unsuspected subtlety and computational power of the human mind. Poets and novelists (and Sigmund Freud, too) had long had an intuitive sense of this richness. But pre-computational *theorists* had no notion of the extent to which they were failing to capture it.

Strong AI is another matter. As remarked in the previous section, the original definition of GOFAI included a commitment to strong AI. Here, there are two broad reasons why one cannot claim that GOFAI has succeeded – although whether it has "failed" is a more delicate judgment.

On the one hand, the notion (put forward by Newell and Simon, for instance) that symbolic computation can explain/implement all aspects of intelligence is mistaken. Connectionist computation is crucial too. However, we saw in Section 4.3 that GOFAI has strengths which other AI methodologies cannot yet rival, and which are highly relevant to certain aspects of human minds. So if strong AI (interpreted broadly, as the claim that *some computational system or other* could be genuinely intelligent) is correct, then GOFAI can form part of a truly intelligent system.

On the other hand, it is not clear that strong AI is correct. Indeed, it is as controversial as ever – not least because it would involve a naturalistic (scientific) explanation of intentionality, or meaning. Those philosophers who are committed to finding such an explanation disagree over how this is to be done. The most promising attempt, in my view, is an evolutionary one; but even its proponents admit that their position is counterintuitive in various ways (Millikan 1984, pp. 93, 337–8). Furthermore, many philosophers – including most of those who favor phenomenology – argue that a naturalistic account of intentionality is impossible in principle (Boden 2006, ch. 16.vi–viii). Even Hilary Putnam, whose philosophy of functionalism (1960) fuelled the rise of GOFAI-grounded strong AI, now accepts a version of this view – and accordingly refers to cognitive science as "science fiction" (Putnam 1997, 1999).

The core anti-naturalist claim is that human language, meaning, and consciousness are the fount of all our concepts and all our knowledge (science included), so that these phenomena themselves could never be explained by science. Strong AI, on that view, is philosophically topsy-turvy.

The naturalist/anti-naturalist schism is the deepest divide in philosophy (Boden 2006, chs. 1.iii.b, 16.vi.b). It has led to the vituperative "science wars," in which science in general has been scathingly attacked and hotly defended. Given its claim to explain mental phenomena, psychological AI – whether GOFAI or not – is the first in the firing line. Most scientists are realists: They believe that a real world exists independently of human beings, with its own properties that much of human thought, and especially science, attempts to describe. Realists typically accuse the anti-naturalists of being irrational and self-defeating, and incapable of accounting for the many successes of science. My own view is that the realists are right. However, there is no knock-down argument on either side. For sure, this philosophical battle will not be decided soon.

In sum: Considered as technology, GOFAI is a hugely impressive, though largely invisible (and therefore unrecognized), success. From expert systems to the internet, daily life in industrial societies would be very different without it. Considered as psychology, it is partially successful but needs to be complemented by other AI methodologies. It has thrown light on a very wide range of psychological phenomena, from everyday cognition (including language use) to action errors, hypnosis, and hallucinations (Boden 2006, chs. 7, 12, and 14). Considered as philosophy, it is partly mistaken (see Chapter 3), and some (i.e., the anti-naturalists) would say that it is fundamentally on the wrong track. If that last charge is correct, however, all other forms of AI/A-Life – and even neuroscientific explanations of mind, too – fall with it (Boden 2006, chs. 1.iii.b, 16.vi–viii). In other words, people who oppose GOFAI on philosophical grounds often use arguments which – although they do not always realize this – cast doubt also on the legitimacy of neuroscience, and even of physics. In short, GOFAI is in good company.

Further reading

Boden, M. A. (ed.) (1990). *The Philosophy of Artificial Intelligence*. Oxford University Press. This collection contains some of the classical and some more recent papers on AI, focusing on theoretical/philosophical issues rather than practical methodologies. (A companion volume in the same series focuses on A-Life.)

Boden, M. A. (2006). *Mind as Machine: A History of Cognitive Science*, 2 vols. Oxford University Press. This book describes the past history and some current state-of-the-art work in all the disciplines of cognitive science. The parts especially relevant to GOFAI are chapters 10, 11, and 13 – plus sections 4.i–iv, 6.iii, 7.i.e–g, 7.iv–v, and 9.x–xi. (Cybernetics, connectionism, and artificial life are discussed in Chapters 12, 14, and 15, and in Sections 4.v–ix and 5.iv.)

Dreyfus, H. L. (1992). *What Computers Still Can't Do: A Critique of Artificial Reason.* Cambridge, MA: MIT Press. An updated version of Dreyfus' classic (1972) attack on GOFAI. Its statements about the achievements and limitations of AI in practice are not always reliable (see Boden 2006, ch. 11.ii). However, it offers a well-written account of a common set of philosophical objections to AI in general, and GOFAI in particular.

Graubard, S. (ed.) (1988). *The Artificial Intelligence Debate: False Starts, Real Foundations.* Cambridge, MA: MIT Press. This collection of papers (including one by the Dreyfus brothers) is an attack on GOFAI, in favor of connectionism. It underestimates the former while overestimating the latter, but is a good example of a common view outside the field.

Russell, S. and Norvig, P. (2010). *Artificial Intelligence: A Modern Approach* (3rd edn.). Upper Saddle River, NJ: Prentice Hall. An up-to-date and comprehensive textbook of technical work in AI. The book includes both connectionism and GOFAI, but is weighted more heavily towards GOFAI.

Simon, H. A. (1969). *The Sciences of the Artificial.* Cambridge, MA: MIT Press. A classic account of the fundamental assumptions and methodology of GOFAI, which also includes the core idea of situated robotics (in the now-famous example of Simon's ant).

Sloman, A. (1978). *The Computer Revolution in Philosophy: Philosophy, Science, and Models of Mind.* Brighton: Harvester Press. Out of print, but available – and continually updated – online at www.cs.bham.ac.uk/research/cogaff/crp/. This text, and the papers accompanying it on Sloman's CogAff website, is a rich and insightful account of how GOFAI and other types of AI relate to the mind, whether animal or human. Sloman is an accomplished philosopher, as well as an AI leader. Among other things, he offers a stimulating view (and mini-programs for simulation) of the role of emotions in mental architecture.

References

Beer, R. D. (1990). *Intelligence as Adaptive Behavior: An Experiment in Computational Neuroethology.* Boston: Academic Press.

Boden, M. A. (1977/87). *Artificial Intelligence and Natural Man.* New York: Basic Books. (2nd edn. 1987, London: MIT Press.)

(2006). *Mind as Machine: A History of Cognitive Science,* 2 vols. Oxford University Press.

Brooks, R. A. (1991). Intelligence without representation, *Artificial Intelligence* 47: 139–59.

Clark, A. J. (1989). *Microcognition: Philosophy, Cognitive Science, and Parallel Distributed Processing.* Cambridge, MA: MIT Press.

Cooper, R., Fox, J., Farringdon, J., and Shallice, T. (1996). Towards a systematic methodology for cognitive modelling, *Artificial Intelligence* 85: 3–44.

Dennett, D. C. (1984). Cognitive wheels: The frame problem of AI, in C. Hookway (ed.), *Minds, Machines and Evolution: Philosophical Studies* (pp. 129–52). Cambridge University Press.

Dreyfus, H. L. (1965). *Alchemy and Artificial Intelligence*. Santa Monica, CA: Rand Corporation, Research Report P-3244, December.

Dreyfus, H. L. and Dreyfus, S. E. (1988). Making a mind versus modelling the brain: Artificial Intelligence back at a branch point, in S. Graubard (ed.), *The Artificial Intelligence Debate: False Starts, Real Foundations* (pp. 15–43). Cambridge, MA: MIT Press.

Feigenbaum, E. A. and McCorduck, P. (1983). *The Fifth Generation: Artificial Intelligence and Japan's Computer Challenge to the World*. London: Addison-Wesley.

Fodor, J. A. (1968). *Psychological Explanation: An Introduction to the Philosophy of Psychology*. New York: Random House.

Harvey, I., Husbands, P., and Cliff, D. (1994). Seeing the light: Artificial evolution, real vision, in D. Cliff, P. Husbands, J.-A. Meyer, and S. W. Wilson (eds.), *From Animals to Animats 3: Proceedings of the 3rd International Conference on Simulation of Adaptive Behavior* (pp. 392–401). Cambridge, MA: MIT Press.

Haugeland, J. (1985). *Artificial Intelligence: The Very Idea*. Cambridge, MA: MIT Press.

Hayes, P. J. (1979). The naive physics manifesto, in D. M. Michie (ed.), *Expert Systems in the Micro-Electronic Age* (pp. 242–70). Edinburgh University Press.

(1985). The second naive physics manifesto, in J. R. Hobbs and R. C. Moore (eds.), *Formal Theories of the Commonsense World* (pp. 1–36). Norwood, NJ: Ablex.

Holland, J. H. (1975). *Adaptation in Natural and Artificial Systems*. Ann Arbor: University of Michigan Press.

Husbands, P., Harvey, I., and Cliff, D. (1995). Circle in the round: State space attractors for evolved sighted robots, *Journal of Robotics and Autonomous Systems* 15: 83–106.

Kirsh, D. (1991). Today the earwig, tomorrow man?, *Artificial Intelligence* 47: 161–84.

McCarthy, J. and Hayes, P. J. (1969). Some philosophical problems from the standpoint of Artificial Intelligence, in B. Meltzer and D. M. Michie (eds.), *Machine Intelligence 4* (pp. 463–502). Edinburgh University Press.

McCulloch, W. S. and Pitts, W. H. (1943). A logical calculus of the ideas immanent in nervous activity, *Bulletin of Mathematical Biology* 5 (4): 115–33. Reprinted in W. S. McCulloch (ed.) (1965), *Embodiments of Mind* (pp. 19–39). Cambridge, MA: MIT Press.

Michalski, R. S. and Chilausky, R. L. (1980). Learning by being told and learning from examples: An experimental comparison of the two methods of knowledge acquisition in the context of developing an expert system for soybean disease diagnosis, *International Journal of Policy Analysis and Information Systems* 4: 125–61.

Michie, D. M. (ed.) (1979). *Expert Systems in the Micro-Electronic Age*. Edinburgh University Press.

Millikan, R. G. (1984). *Language, Thought, and Other Biological Categories: New Foundations for Realism*. Cambridge, MA: MIT Press.

Newell, A. (1980). Physical symbol systems, *Cognitive Science* 4: 135–83.

Newell, A., Shaw, J. C., and Simon, H. A. (1958a). Chess-playing programs and the problem of complexity, *IBM Journal of Research and Development*, 2: 320–35. Reprinted (1963) in E. A. Feigenbaum and J. A. Feldman (eds.), *Computers and Thought* (pp. 39–70). New York: McGraw-Hill.

(1958b). Elements of a theory of human problem-solving, *Psychological Review* 65: 151–66.

(1959). Report on a general problem-solving program, *Proceedings of the International Conference on Information Processing, Paris* (pp. 256–64. Paris: UNESCO.

Newell, A., and Simon, H. A. (1963). GPS, a program that simulates human thought, in E. A. Feigenbaum and J. A. Feldman (eds.), *Computers and Thought* (pp. 279–293). New York: McGraw-Hill.

(1972). *Human Problem Solving*. Englewood Cliffs, NJ: Prentice Hall.

Norman, D. A. and Shallice, T. (1986). Attention to action: Willed and automatic control of behavior, in R. Davidson, G. E. Schwartz, and D. Shapiro (eds.), *Consciousness and Self Regulation: Advances in Research and Theory*, vol. 4 (pp. 1–18). New York: Plenum.

Post, E. L. (1943). Formal reductions of the general combinatorial decision problem, *American Journal of Mathematics* 65: 197–215.

Putnam, H. (1960). Minds and machines, in S. Hook (ed.), *Dimensions of Mind: A Symposium* (pp. 148–179). New York University Press.

(1997). Functionalism: Cognitive science or science fiction?, in D. M. Johnson and C. E. Erneling (eds.), *The Future of the Cognitive Revolution* (pp. 32–44). New York: Oxford University Press.

(1999). *The Threefold Cord: Mind, Body, and World*. New York: Columbia University Press.

Ray, T. S. (1992). An approach to the synthesis of life, in C. G. Langton, C. Taylor, J. D. Farmer, and S. Rasmussen (eds.), *Artificial Life II* (pp. 371–408). Redwood City, CA: Addison-Wesley.

Robinson, J. A. (1968). The generalized resolution principle, in D. M. Michie (ed.), *Machine Intelligence 3* (pp. 77–93). Edinburgh University Press.

Rosenblueth, A., Wiener, N., and Bigelow, J. (1943). Behavior, purpose, and teleology, *Philosophy of Science* 10: 18–24.

Russell, S. and Norvig, P. (2003). *Artificial Intelligence: A Modern Approach* (2nd edn.). Upper Saddle River, NJ: Prentice Hall.

Sahota, M. and Mackworth, A. K. (1994). Can situated robots play soccer?, *Proceedings of the Canadian Conference on Artificial Intelligence* (pp. 249–54). Banff, AB: Morgan Kaufmann.

Samuel, A. L. (1959). Some studies in machine learning using the game of checkers, *IBM Journal of Research and Development* 3: 210–29. Reprinted in

Feigenbaum E. A. and Feldman J. A. (eds.) (1963), *Computers and Thought* (pp. 71–108). New York: McGraw-Hill.

Searle, J. R. (1980). Minds, brains, and programs, *Behavioral and Brain Sciences* 3: 417–24.

Simon, H. A. (1969). *The Sciences of the Artificial*. Cambridge, MA: MIT Press.

Sloman, A. (1978). *The Computer Revolution in Philosophy: Philosophy, Science, and Models of Mind*. Brighton: Harvester Press. Out of print, but available – and continually updated – online at www.cs.bham.ac.uk/research/cogaff/crp/.

(2002). The irrelevance of Turing Machines to artificial intelligence, in M. Scheutz (ed.), *Computationalism: New Directions* (pp. 87–127). Cambridge, MA: MIT Press.

Smith, B. C. (1996). *On the Origin of Objects*. Cambridge, MA: MIT Press.

Varela, F. J., Thompson, E., and Rosch, E. (1991). *The Embodied Mind: Cognitive Science and Human Experience*. Cambridge, MA: MIT Press.

Vera, A. H. and Simon, H. A. (1993). Situated action: A symbolic interpretation, *Cognitive Science* 17: 7–48.

Winograd, T. (1972). *Understanding Natural Language*. Edinburgh University Press.

5 Connectionism and neural networks

Ron Sun

Connectionism and neural networks have become a mainstay of artificial intelligence and cognitive science. Nowadays, conferences on neural networks from the perspective of artificial intelligence (or computational intelligence, as some would put it) are held regularly and are usually fairly well attended (such as International Joint Conferences on Neural Networks). At major cognitive science conferences, work based on connectionist models usually occupies a major place. In many engineering conferences and journals, work utilizing neural network models is commonplace. Their popularity and appeal have reached a stable state in a sense. In other words, they have become an integral part of the study and the exploration of intelligence and cognition.

In this chapter, I will first review briefly the history of connectionist models, identifying major ideas and major areas of applications, and then move on to address the issue of symbolic processing in connectionist models; finally, I will expand the discussion to hybrid connectionist models, which incorporate both connectionist and symbolic processing methods.

5.1 The connectionist revolution of the 1980s

Connectionist models – that is, models that consist of networks of simple processing units interconnected through connectivity patterns of various kinds – re-emerged in the 1980s as a major paradigm for cognitive science and AI after a period of dormancy in the late 60s and the 70s. This connectionist revolution in the 1980s brought with it new paradigms, new approaches, new ideas, and new techniques, as well as new excitement and new controversies (Rumelhart, McClelland, and the PDP Research Group 1986). The excitement and controversies have largely died down by now, but many ideas and techniques of connectionism are staying and they have become an integral part of the AI and cognitive science toolkit.

5.1.1 Overview of connectionism

Generally speaking, connectionism is a way of capturing and understanding the mechanisms and processes of cognition through building models using networks of simple, neuron-like processing elements (units), each of which performs simple numerical computations. Connectionist models have been applied to many different tasks: for example, perceiving objects and events (e.g., Carpenter and Grossberg 1992); pronouncing English texts (e.g., Sejnowski and Rosenberg 1987); storing and retrieving (contextually appropriate) information from memory (e.g., Rumelhart et al. 1986; McClelland, McNaughton, and O'Reilly 1995); producing and understanding language (e.g., Rumelhart et al. 1986; St. John and McClelland 1990); skill learning (Sun, Slusarz, and Terry 2005); reasoning (e.g., Sun 1994; Sun and Zhang 2006), and so on.

Connectionist models (neural networks) are based on the assumption that cognition emerges through the interactions of a large number of simple processing elements or units (i.e., "neurons"). The basic idea is that the brain consists of a vast number of such units, and that together they are capable of extremely complex cognitive processing (such as perception, language, motor control, and so on). Although connectionists often claim to capture principles of biological neural processes in their models, the units (nodes) in connectionist models nevertheless rarely correspond to individual biological neurons. Often this was necessitated by practical computational considerations or was due to our lack of complete knowledge of the biology of neural processes.

In a connectionist model, a "representation" is often a pattern of activation over the set of processing units in the model (although there are many variations as well as alternatives to this; more later). Processing is accomplished through the propagation of activations among the processing units (nodes), via the interconnections among them. What mediates the propagation of activations is the numerical connection "weights" between pairs of processing units. Learning takes place through the (usually gradual) change of the connection "weights," as a function of the activity in the network. Learning happens sometimes with "error" signals provided from external sources, in the form of either a success/failure signal (Sun et al. 2005; Sutton and Barto 1998) or a signal indicating the degree of mismatch between the actual result from the network and the desired outcome, or target (Rumelhart et al. 1986).

Here are a few particularly interesting (and potentially useful) properties of connectionist models, as enumerated in Rumelhart et al.'s 1986 book, as well as in other relevant literatures:

- Parallelism (that is, the fact that nodes may perform computation simultaneously and links may propagate information simultaneously in most of these models).
- Adaptivity (that is, the built-in learning ability in most of these models, e.g., through modification of weights on the links connecting nodes).
- Graceful degradation (that is, being able to avoid catastrophic breakdowns in the face of errors in processing or in input).

- Automatic completion of (novel or familiar) patterns (as an inherent property of many of these models).
- Spontaneous generalization (that is, the ability to spontaneously apply existing knowledge to different situations).
- Robustness (that is, inherent fault tolerance due to the preceding five properties, as a result of the structuring of such models).
- Content addressability (that is, the ability to retrieve information based on partial knowledge of its content).
- Optimization and constraint satisfaction (that is, the ability to find optimal or near-optimal solutions that satisfy multiple "soft" constraints, as an inherent property of some of these models).

See the connectionist literature for more detailed discussions of these properties of neural networks (e.g., Rumelhart et al. 1986; Waltz and Feldman 1986; Bechtel and Abrahamsen 1990; Ramsey, Stich, and Rumelhart 1991; Sun 1994).

Historically, connectionism rose from several disparate strands of research. Some of the early research involved networks of binary units. Other early research focused on adaptive systems. Work on dynamic programming and reinforcement learning also contributed to neural networks. In particular, McCulloch and Pitts in the 1940s explored simple networks of binary threshold "neurons" in terms of logical operations. Donald Hebb developed a cell assembly theory of cognition, and proposed in particular the idea that specific synaptic changes might underlie psychological principles of learning. Frank Rosenblatt in the 1950s formulated learning rules for neural networks to associate arbitrary patterns through adjusting weights (i.e., the idea of the perceptron). Bernard Widrow proposed models for adaptive linear systems. (See Rumelhart et al. 1986 for further details of the history.)

Neural networks were revived in the 1980s as the result of the negative reaction against the then prevailing symbolic approach in artificial intelligence and cognitive science and its perceived failure. This movement of the 1980s was known as the "connectionist revolution." Espousing models that do away with centralized sequential symbol manipulation, and often involving distributed processing (in massively parallel architectures), connectionism was frequently referred to in those days as "parallel distributed processing." On this view, cognition should be approached more in terms of mechanisms of constraint satisfaction, pattern recognition, and weight adaptation, rather than explicit symbol manipulation (see Chapters 2 and 4).

5.1.2   Connectionist learning

A brief review of major paradigms of learning in neural networks is in order here. We shall look in particular at the following types of learning: supervised learning, unsupervised learning, and reinforcement learning. Although these types of learning can also be carried out in other types of models, they are particularly prominent in neural networks.

Supervised learning algorithms (Rumelhart et al. 1986) require a feedback signal (from external sources) for each of the output nodes of a network in order to get learning going. A typical example of such learning occurs within a three-layered feedforward neural network (where a feedforward network means a network with no feedback connections between layers and no lateral connections within a layer). In such a network, input patterns are presented at the first layer (the input layer), and each subsequent layer (the hidden layer and the output layer) is updated in turn (through activation propagation), resulting in an output pattern at the final (output) layer. This output pattern is compared to a desired output pattern, and thus an error signal is computed. The error signal is propagated backward through the network to compute updates to the weights between layers in order to reduce the error. The famed *backpropagation* learning algorithm is one class of such learning algorithms, which has been widely applied in all areas of cognitive science and AI (Rumelhart et al. 1986).

In this regard, interesting theoretical results have been obtained concerning neural network computation. Layered feedforward neural networks have been shown to be universal approximators, that is, able to represent essentially any function. Recurrent neural networks (i.e., networks with feedback connections) have been shown to be Turing-equivalent (i.e., equivalent to the Turing machine – a general model of computation) and able to represent a large class of nonlinear dynamic systems. A variety of results have been obtained for supervised learning in neural networks. For example, for classification, neural network learning algorithms have been shown to converge to the posterior probabilities of the classes. These algorithms have been utilized in both cognitive modeling and practical applications. Bayesian statistical methods have been utilized in analyzing supervised learning and in designing new learning algorithms.

On the other hand, unsupervised learning (Rumelhart et al. 1986) does not require error signals or the distinction among input, hidden (internal), and output nodes. It is thus applicable to many settings where supervised learning is not. For instance, self-organizing networks, a form of unsupervised learning, have been widely explored and utilized in cognitive modeling as well as in industrial applications. They are based on self-organization of nodes and links in response to data from the environment. Another approach to unsupervised learning is through specifying a model of the way in which the environment generates data. Unsupervised learning thus becomes the statistical problem of finding the best model to fit the data.

Reinforcement learning is somewhere between supervised and unsupervised learning: It does not require an exact error signal, but only an indication of whether the current output is good or bad (or how good or bad it is), usually in the form of a number. Thus, it is more widely applicable than supervised learning, and often more useful than unsupervised learning (due to the availability of feedback). Reinforcement learning has been used in modeling animal learning and human skill learning (Sun et al. 2005), as well as in control engineering and other industrial applications. Many theoretical results have been produced concerning various reinforcement learning algorithms (see Sutton and Barto 1998).

Neural network models based on probability theory have also been explored. Many neural network learning models have been shown mathematically to be related to probabilistic computation (i.e., corresponding to probability theory). This provides, in a way, a mathematically rigorous basis for neural network learning. In particular, it is worth noting that some of the unsupervised learning algorithms studied in the neural network literature can be derived from Bayesian networks (for Bayesian statistical methods, see Chapters 7 and 9).

5.1.3   Connectionist representations

There are, in general, two rough categories of connectionist representations: (1) localist representation, in which each node represents an individual concept; and (2) distributed representation, in which each concept is represented by an activation pattern over a set of nodes, each of which may not be interpretable (cognitively penetrable).[1] However, beyond these two rough categories, there is an entire spectrum of different representational techniques available:

- Fully localist representation. As mentioned earlier, this is characterized by representing each concept with an individual, dedicated node in a network. In other words, it is one node for one concept (i.e., there is a one-to-one mapping between nodes and concepts).
- Distributed localist representation. Instead of one node for one concept, it is possible to use a set of nodes for one concept, each of which does the same processing, so that knocking out one node will not drastically affect the performance of a system. This set of nodes is dedicated to represent this particular concept only, and none of these nodes participate in the representation of any other concepts. This representation may be considered as a variation of localist representation. It is a set of nodes for one concept (i.e., there is a one-to-one mapping between sets of nodes and concepts).
- Locally distributed representation. This form of representation is characterized by dividing the representational space (the set of all the available

[1] It is also called coarse coding, although later on the term came to mean a particular type of distributed representation.

nodes) into several subspaces (i.e., subsets of nodes), and a distributed representation is used for each of these subspaces. That is, a set of concepts is represented in a distributed manner within a representational subspace. But outside that particular representational subspace, whether a node is active or not is irrelevant to the representation of the concepts within that set. The representation is localized with respect to a set of concepts, but is distributed within the set.[2] It can be termed a set of nodes for a set of concepts (i.e., there is a one-to-one mapping between sets of nodes and sets of concepts).

- Fully distributed representation. Each node participates in the representation of all the concepts involved, and each concept is represented by all the nodes used in a network.[3] It can be termed all the nodes for all the concepts.
- Other types of distributed representation. In addition, there are other types of distributed representation that do not fit into any of the foregoing descriptions (see, e.g., Sun 1994).

Each of these representational techniques has its own characteristics and its advantages and disadvantages, and therefore each is suitable for some specific situations (Sun 1994).

5.1.4   Connectionism and cognition

Next, a brief survey is in order of different areas of connectionist modeling in relation to understanding cognition, in correspondence with the useful properties of connectionist models mentioned earlier.

While neuroscience addresses phenomena at levels often no higher than cellular and local networks, cognitive models have to address human behavior of higher levels (e.g., as studied in psychology). Some simplification is therefore warranted. In this way, although biological plausibility is compromised to some extent, we may nevertheless posit that simplified models may share the same general approach toward computation as biological neural systems.

Because of their distinctive characteristics, connectionist models have offered new cognitive theories and generated explanations that are often radically different from those of previous theories. I shall briefly review some examples.

---

[2] In this way, one may avoid some unnecessary interference (crosstalk), because, by dividing up a representational space into subspaces and by correspondingly dividing up concepts to be represented into sets, there are fewer concepts represented in each subspace, and thus the chance for interference (crosstalk) is reduced.

[3] Removing a small number of nodes will not affect the system performance drastically and the performance will degrade gradually in proportion to the number of nodes removed (i.e., the property of fault tolerance and graceful degradation mentioned before). Such representation is also capable of generalization (another property mentioned before).

Memory. In connectionist models, memory is often a constructive process involving the interactions of simple processing units (nodes). For example, recall may be a process of constructing a pattern of activation over a set of units that is similar to some pattern previously experienced. It is often subject to the influences resulting from the interactions of the units, which may fill in missing details or correct inaccuracies. One useful property of connectionist models trained with, for example, backpropagation is that they can learn what basis within a distributed representation to use for representing concepts internally, so that similarity-based processes (e.g., generalization) can be based on relevant features. Thus far, connectionist models have been applied to issues of semantic memory (Rogers 2008), episodic memory (Norman, Detre, and Polyn 2008), concept learning (Gluck and Bower 1988), categorization (Kruschke, 2008), and so on.

Implicit and explicit learning. Connectionist models have been shown to be suitable for addressing the psychological distinction between explicit and implicit learning, as developed from empirical psychological research. As demonstrated by Sun et al. (2005), the distinction may be captured by the use of localist versus distributed representation in connectionist networks. In localist (or symbolic) representations, each unit is easily interpretable and has a clear conceptual meaning. This characteristic captures the property of explicit knowledge being more accessible and more manipulable (Sun 1994). In contrast, representational units in a distributed representation are together capable of accomplishing tasks but are generally not individually meaningful (Rumelhart et al. 1986; Sun 1994, 2002). Sun et al. (2005) carefully demonstrated how effects of the interaction of implicit and explicit learning might be captured in models based on this distinction. Relatedly, Cleeremans and McClelland (1991), as well as others, addressed modeling of psychological data of purely implicit learning.

Implicit and explicit memory. Connectionist models have also addressed the distinction between explicit and implicit memory. (Implicit memory refers to the effect of an experience without explicit reference to that prior experience – sometimes even without any conscious recollection of that experience.) Explicit memory for recent experiences may be impaired in some brain-damaged patients who nevertheless show good implicit memory, suggesting a special brain system may be required for the formation of new explicit memories. Connectionist models generally account for implicit memory based on connections among a large pool of units in a network with distributed representations (e.g., McClelland, McNaughton, and O'Reilly 1995).

Language. Connectionist models have suggested viable alternatives to the idea that cognitive processes for language must be represented as a system of rules. Connectionists have produced models of morphological inflection, spelling–sound conversion, sentence processing and comprehension, and a variety of other aspects, which account for many important psycholinguistic phenomena often neglected by rule-based theories. One issue is the sensitivity of language patterns to frequency and consistency. Rule-based approaches failed to account for the fact that the exceptions are not arbitrary. For example, exceptions to the regular past tense of English verbs come in clusters that share phonological characteristics. A connectionist model (see Rumelhart et al. 1986) showed that such a model, which learned connection weights to generate the past tense of a word from the present tense, could capture a number of psychological aspects of the acquisition of the past tense. In connectionist models, language processing is often a constraint-satisfaction process subject to semantic, contextual, syntactic, and other constraints. In addition, connectionist work on learning grammatical structures of sentences has been carried out in recurrent neural networks (e.g., Elman 1990; see Section 5.2.3 below).

Reasoning. For addressing higher-level cognition, such as reasoning and problem solving, connectionist models (of pure forms) fall short in many ways. However, there has been some relevant work in this area. For example, work has been done in the area of analogical reasoning (Holyoak and Thagard 1989). Some other work has also been done in the areas of rule-based reasoning and even logical reasoning (e.g., Shastri and Ajjanagadde 1993; Sun 1992, 1994). In this regard, researchers often opt for "hybrid" models. Hybrid models (which will be discussed later) often involve, in one way or another, traditional symbolic methods. For example, they may assign units and connections using symbolic algorithms and then carry out constraint-satisfaction processes or backpropagation learning in a connectionist fashion. Or, they may implement symbolic reasoning using connection weights directly (Sun 1992).

Binding. Researchers often view the so-called "binding problem" as a fundamental problem in connectionist models of reasoning, as well as in other areas of cognitive science. "Binding" refers to the combination of multiple arbitrary items in processing or representation, including, for example, the assignment of an arbitrary item to a slot in a structured description (e.g., assigning "CPU-213" to the "CPU" slot in a structured description of "computer" that includes slots for CPU, memory, disk, and so on). To address this problem, several (partial) solutions have been proposed (e.g., Shastri and Ajjanagadde 1993; Sun 1992, 1994). However, devising neural networks that learn to form their own bindings, in either familiar or unfamiliar domains, remains a difficult issue.

5.2   The issue of symbolic processing

5.2.1   The importance of symbolic processing

The connectionist revolution has spurred vigorous theoretical debates about the nature of cognition and the various approaches toward understanding it. Among them, the debate between classical connectionism and symbolism has been one of the most fundamental underlying philosophical currents, which has spurred the development of connectionist models within cognitive science, and also to some extent within the AI communities (see Fodor and Pylyshyn 1988; Pinker and Prince 1988; Smolensky 1988, Sun 1994).

The perceived importance of symbol processing lies, at least in part, in a fundamental tenet of symbolic AI and symbolic cognitive science. The physical symbol system hypothesis introduced by Newell and Simon (1976) clearly articulated this tenet. They defined a physical symbol system as follows:

A physical symbol system consists of a set of entities, called symbols, which are physical patterns that can occur as components of another type of entity called an expression (or symbol structure). Thus, a symbol structure is composed of a number of instances (or tokens) of symbols related in some physical way (such as one token being next to another). (Newell and Simon 1976, p. 116)

They further claimed that symbols can designate arbitrarily: "A symbol may be used to designate any expression whatsoever... it is not prescribed a priori what expressions it can designate... There exist processes for creating any expression and for modifying any expression in arbitrary ways" (1976, p. 116). Based on this, they concluded: "A physical symbol system has the necessary and sufficient means for general intelligent action" (1976, p. 116), which is the well-known physical symbol system hypothesis.

The physical symbol system hypothesis has spawned enormous research efforts in traditional AI and also in cognitive science. This approach (classical symbolicism) typically uses discrete symbols as primitives, and performs symbol manipulation in a sequential and deliberative manner.

Major ideas in the symbolicist AI tradition include "search" and "knowledge representation" (Newell and Simon 1976). Search refers to a systematic exploration of a space of problem states, as a means of conceptualizing or conducting problem solving. Among different types of symbolic knowledge representations, the most prominent ones are logic-based representations, structured representations (such as scripts, frames, and semantic networks), and production rules (see Chapters 2, 3, and 4).

5.2.2   Examples of connectionist symbolic processing

Given the significance of symbols in cognitive processes, connectionist models need to be able to capture symbols and symbolic processing, especially search and knowledge representation. There have been many attempts at enabling connectionist models to perform symbolic processing. Various schemes have been proposed, which collectively may be labeled connectionist implementationism. They range from models of variable binding, to implementations of production systems and of first-order logic, and further on to the incorporation of modal logic and fuzzy logic, all based on typical connectionist

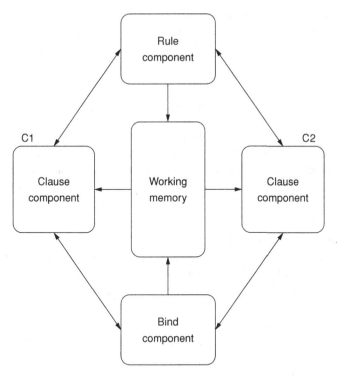

Figure 5.1 The overall structure of a connectionist production system.

network models, such as multi-layered feedforward networks with backpropagation learning. Techniques used for implementing symbolic processing in such networks vary a great deal from model to model.

An early example of connectionist implementationism is Touretzky and Hinton's (1988) distributed connectionist production system (DCPS), which implemented a production system using connectionist models. In DCPS, there was a working memory, which stored facts; there were two clause components, each of which was used to match one of the two conditions of a rule (where each rule was restricted to have two conditions); there was also a rule component, which was used to execute the action of a matching rule that changed the working memory; in addition, a bind component was used to enforce constraints regarding variables that might exist in a rule. Each of these components was implemented as a connectionist network. See Figure 5.1. Overall, it was a complex modular connectionist system designed specifically for implementing a limited production system, as a demonstration of possibilities of implementing complex symbolic systems in classical connectionist models with distributed representation.

In addition to this approach, there are many other methods and techniques that have been proposed and explored for implementing rule-based reasoning and symbolic processing in neural networks, including, for example, recurrent auto-associative memory (RAAM), holographic representation, and tensor product representation (see Wermter and Sun 2000 for surveys as well as details).

5.2.3   Emergent symbolic processing in connectionist models

From both the connectionist and the symbolicist side, some researchers believe that high-level cognition, especially that which is temporally extended or involves explicit verbal reasoning, can often be better captured through the use of a more symbolic framework (more on this in the next section). However, many connectionists believe, rightly or wrongly, that connectionist processes underlie all aspects of human cognition. They believe that human reasoning and problem solving often arise from insight or intuition, or directly from perception, and thus a connectionist, rather than a symbolic, approach may be needed to capture all their subtleties.

For example, Elman (1990) showed how regularities of language could arise without explicit representation of linguistic rules, and how learning could lead to the discovery of internal representations that could capture linguistic structures on the basis of the co-occurrences of words. In Elman's simple recurrent networks (SRNs), on time step t, an input was presented to the network and caused a pattern of activation on hidden and output layers. On time step $t + 1$, the next input in a sequence was presented to the network, and a copy of the activation of the hidden units on time step t is also fed back to the hidden units. Each input to the SRN was therefore processed in the context of what came before. In his experiments, Elman trained an SRN to predict the next word in a sentence. During training, the network's output came to approximate the transition probabilities between words in sentences. For example, following the first noun, the verb units would be more active as the possible next word, and verbs that tended to be associated with this particular noun would be more active than those that did not. Elman examined the structure of the internal representations of the SRN, and found that the internal representations were sensitive to syntactic differences, as well as to a range of semantic distinctions. An SRN was thus able to develop representations of entities that varied according to their context of use, in contrast to traditional symbolic representations, which maintained their identity irrespective of the combinations into which they were put. In sum, Elman's work demonstrated how simple networks can learn statistical regularities over temporal sequences, and how they may be sufficient to produce many of the behaviors that linguists have ascribed to grammatical rules.

For another example, Miikkulainen (1993) showed what a set of interconnected multi-layered feedforward networks with the backpropagation learning algorithm can accomplish in terms of natural language understanding. Instead of just implementing scripts and frames, his models showed how these symbolic representations (scripts and frames) might emerge through backpropagation learning from training data. Because these representations emerged from neural networks through learning, they were able to generalize to novel situations (at least to some extent). This work thus expanded the scope of symbolic representation within connectionist models.

5.3   Hybrid connectionist models

5.3.1   The idea of a hybrid model

In contrast to connectionist implementationism, hybrid connectionist models may be considered a synthesis of connectionist models and traditional symbolic models. Such models thus aim to move us away from the old debate of connectionism versus symbolicism towards a new and productive synthesis. As a result of combining a variety of representations and processes, symbolic or connectionist, they tend to be more expressive, more powerful, often more efficient, and thus more useful, in both cognitive modeling and practical (industrial) applications (Sun 1994, 2002; Sun and Bookman 1995; Wermter and Sun 2000).

The basic rationale for hybrid models can be succinctly summarized as "using the right tool for the right job." More specifically, it should be apparent that cognitive processes are not homogeneous; a wide variety of representations and processes are likely employed, playing different roles and serving different purposes. Some cognitive processes and representations are best captured by symbolic models, others by connectionist models (Dreyfus and Dreyfus 1986; Sun 1994, 2002). There is thus a need for pluralism in the modeling of human cognition, which leads naturally to the development of hybrid connectionist models, to provide necessary computational tools and conceptual frameworks. For instance, to capture a full range of human skill-learning capabilities, a cognitive architecture needs to incorporate both implicit and explicit knowledge (Sun et al. 2005). An architecture incorporating both processes can be implemented computationally by a combination of symbolic models (which capture explicit knowledge) and connectionist models (which capture implicit knowledge). The development of intelligent systems for various practical applications can also benefit from a proper combination of different techniques, as no one single technique can currently do everything efficiently and successfully.

The relative advantages of connectionist versus symbolic models have been amply argued for (see, for example, Dreyfus and Dreyfus 1986; Smolensky 1988; Sun 1994, and Sun 2002, for various views). The advantages of connectionist models include massive parallelism, learning capabilities, and fault tolerance, as enumerated earlier. The advantages of symbolic models include crisp representation and processing, ease of specifying symbolic processing steps, and the resulting precision in processing. With these relative advantages in mind, the combination of connectionist and symbolic models can be justified relatively easily.

Some existing cognitive dichotomies are very relevant in this regard. Psychologists have proposed a host of dichotomies on the basis of empirical data. These dichotomies include implicit vs. explicit learning, implicit vs. explicit memory, automatic vs. controlled processing, incidental vs. intentional learning, and so on. There is also the well-known distinction of procedural vs. declarative knowledge. The evidence for these dichotomies lies in experimental data that elucidate various dissociations and differences in performance under different conditions. Although there is no consensus regarding the details of the dichotomies, there is a consensus on the qualitative difference between different types of cognition. Moreover, most researchers believe in the necessity of incorporating both sides of the dichotomies, since each serves a unique function and is thus indispensable. Cognitive architectures incorporating both connectionist and symbolic techniques have been structured around some of these dichotomies (e.g., Anderson and Lebiere 1998; Sun et al. 2005).

Related to the above dichotomies, Smolensky (1988) proposed a more abstract distinction of conceptual vs. subconceptual processing, and linked the distinction to that between connectionist and symbolic models. Conceptual processing involves knowledge that possesses the following characteristics: (1) public access, (2) reliability, and (3) formality. They are what symbolic models capture in his view. On the other hand, there are other kinds of cognitive capacities, such as skill and intuition, that are not expressible in linguistic forms and do not conform to the above criteria. According to Smolensky and many other researchers, it has been futile to try to model such capacities in symbolic terms, and they should be viewed as being at a different level in cognition – the subconceptual level. This level is better dealt with by connectionist models, which overcome some serious problems that symbolic models encounter in modeling subconceptual processing. Thus, the combination of the two types of models can lead to significant advantages in capturing a full range of cognitive capacities. These ideas provide a foundation for building hybrid connectionist-symbolic models.

5.3.2   Examples of hybrid models

An example of hybrid connectionist-symbolic models is CLARION (e.g., Sun 2002; Sun et al. 2005), which consists of two levels: a symbolic level and a connectionist level. The two levels work rather independently, but their outcomes are combined. The connectionist level consists of neural networks, which work through spreading activation and learn based on reinforcement

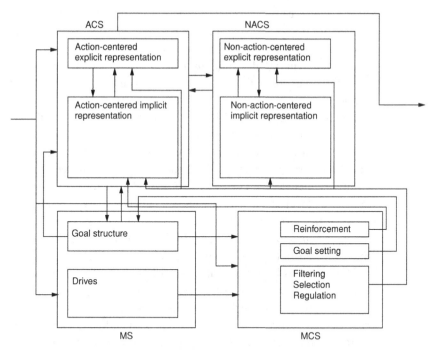

Figure 5.2 The CLARION architecture.

learning methods. The symbolic level works according to symbolic rules. Through integrating the outcomes of the two types of processes, the model was able to capture a variety of human skill learning, reasoning, and other data.

Specifically, CLARION is an integrative architecture composed of a number of distinct subsystems, with a dual representational structure in each subsystem. Its subsystems include the action-centered subsystem (ACS), the non-action-centered subsystem (NACS), the motivational subsystem (MS), and the metacognitive subsystem (MCS). The role of the action-centered subsystem is to control actions, regardless of whether the actions are for external physical movements or for internal mental operations. The role of the non-action-centered subsystem is to maintain general knowledge. The role of the motivational subsystem is to provide underlying motivations for perception, action, and cognition, in terms of providing impetus and feedback. The role of the metacognitive subsystem is to monitor and modify the operations of the other subsystems.

Each of these interacting subsystems consists of two levels of representation. In each subsystem, the top (symbolic) level encodes explicit knowledge and the bottom (connectionist) level encodes implicit knowledge. The distinction of implicit and explicit knowledge was based on psychological data (as discussed earlier; see also, e.g., Sun 2002). See Figure 5.2.

The action-centered subsystem is the central part of CLARION. In it, the process for action decision making is essentially the following: Observing the current state of the world, the two levels of processes (implicit and explicit) make their separate decisions in accordance with their own knowledge, and their outcomes are "integrated." Thus, a final selection of an action is made and the action is then performed. The action changes the world in some way. Comparing the changed state of the world with the previous state, the system learns (e.g., in accordance with reinforcement learning). The cycle then repeats itself.

At the bottom (connectionist) level, implicit knowledge (reactive routines) develops. Reactive routines developed through reinforcement learning can exhibit sequential behaviors without explicit (symbolic) planning. In the top (symbolic) level of the action-centered subsystem, explicit knowledge is captured in the form of symbolic rules. There are many ways in which explicit knowledge may be learned, including independent hypothesis testing learning and "bottom-up learning" (see Sun 2002 for details).

CLARION has been used for a variety of purposes, including, for example, understanding human skill learning. A number of well-known skill-learning tasks have been simulated and explained using CLARION, ranging from simple reactive skills to complex cognitive skills. In addition, many reasoning tasks, metacognitive tasks, motivational tasks, and social interaction tasks have been modeled and explained within CLARION (Sun 2002).

While accounting for various psychological data, CLARION provides detailed explanations of the human data that shed new light on cognitive phenomena. For example, in accounting for skill-learning tasks, CLARION attributed certain performance variations to the differing ways of interaction between implicit and explicit processes (at the two levels respectively). With this simple notion, CLARION explained a large variety of human skill-learning data that had not been explained before in a unified way (see Sun et al. 2005 for details).

In addition to the work above, there are several other approaches that combine connectionist and symbolic methods in a variety of different ways (for detailed accounts, see Sun 1994; Sun and Bookman 1995; Anderson and Lebiere 1998; and Wermter and Sun 2000, among others).

5.3.3   Issues concerning hybrid models

In adopting and developing hybrid connectionist-symbolic models, many questions need to be addressed in order to forge principled approaches. Chief among them are:

- What are the relative advantages and disadvantages of each approach to developing hybrid models?
- How cognitively plausible is each of these approaches?

More specifically, a range of questions arise concerning architectures of hybrid models, as well as learning in these models. First of all, hybrid models usually involve a variety of different types of processes and representations, and, therefore, multiple heterogeneous mechanisms interacting in complex ways. It is necessary to consider ways of structuring these different components, or, in other words, to consider architectures. Some architecture-related issues include:

- How does one decide whether the representation of a particular part of an architecture should be symbolic, localist, or distributed?
- What are the appropriate and principled ways to bridge the likely heterogeneity in hybrid models?
- How do representation and learning interact in hybrid models (because in such models both aspects are likely to be more complex)?
- How does one structure different parts of a hybrid model to achieve optimal results (in whatever sense is appropriate to the task at hand)?

Second, although purely connectionist models, which constitute a part of any hybrid model, are known to excel in their learning abilities, hybridization makes learning more difficult. In a way, hybrid models inherit the difficulty with learning from the symbolic side and forgo to some extent the advantage that purely connectionist models have in this respect. Some of the learning-related issues include:

- What kind of learning can be carried out in each type of hybrid architecture?
- How can complex symbolic structures, such as rules, frames, and semantic networks, be learned in hybrid models? (This is particularly a problem for highly structured hybrid models, in which learning is especially difficult.)
- In developing hybrid models, what should the relationship be among symbolic learning methods, knowledge elicitation/acquisition methods, and neural network learning algorithms?
- How can each type of architecture be formed with various combinations of the above-mentioned methods?

Despite the diversity that exists in the research on hybrid connectionist-symbolic models, there is a clear unifying theme: the search for computational models that bring together symbolic and connectionist techniques to achieve synthesis and synergy of the two seemingly different paradigms. The various methods, models, and architectures proposed manifest the common belief that connectionist and symbolic methods can be usefully integrated, and that such integration may lead to advances in the understanding of cognition and intelligence.

5.3.4   Hybrid models in cognitive modeling

Hybrid models, such as CLARION, have been used to address a wide variety of issues in cognitive science and artificial intelligence, including human learning, reasoning, problem solving, creativity, motivational dynamics, metacognitive processes, and above all, human consciousness (see, e.g., Sun 1999). The modeling and explanation of human learning have already been touched upon. In relation to understanding human reasoning, CLARION has been shown to be able to capture both implicit and explicit reasoning and their interaction (Sun 1994; Sun and Zhang 2006). Through detailed modeling of human reasoning data, CLARION provided interpretations of human reasoning data on the basis of the interaction of implicit and explicit processes, which led to new insights about human reasoning, beyond those to be gained from implementing a limited form of production system, as in the connectionist implementationist work discussed earlier. In relation to understanding human consciousness, CLARION has been useful in generating explanatory hypotheses. In particular, the representational difference between the two levels of representations in CLARION has been hypothesized to capture the fundamental difference between the conscious and the unconscious (Sun 1999), which could not have been conceived without the availability of the technical tools of both symbolic and connectionist approaches. Similarly, John Anderson's ACT-R architecture has been used to understand and model the interaction of perception and cognition in a variety of ways (see Anderson and Lebiere 1998).

5.4   Concluding remarks

In this chapter, three types of connectionist models have been discussed: classical connectionist, connectionist symbolic processing (implementationist), and hybrid connectionist. While classical connectionism brought forth interesting and novel ideas, it is limited by its simplicity and uniformity. Symbolic processing within such connectionist models has been extensively explored, but has yielded limited results thus far. Therefore, it appears necessary, at least for the short run, to develop hybrid connectionist models incorporating symbolic methods (and possibly other methods, such as Bayesian or fuzzy logic ones).

Looking into the future of this field, some trends are discernible. For instance, while there are domain-specific applications to modeling various cognitive processes, such as natural language processing, reasoning and decision making, memory and learning, vision, and so on, there may also be more integrative connectionist models that cross boundaries of narrow domains and functionalities. Another likely trend is that connectionist models may be increasingly linked to statistical (Bayesian) approaches to learning and reasoning, which may provide principled strategies (but are also likely to incur higher computational costs). Another, related, trend is the increasing hybridization of connectionist models; more connectionist models may incorporate symbolic components, fuzzy logic components, and other components that are outside the realm of classical connectionist models. In the reverse direction, symbolic models may also increasingly incorporate connectionist techniques and approaches. Finally, connectionist models may be increasingly linked to work on biological neural systems, including accounting for brain imaging data. In particular, in the future more models may be inspired by biological neural networks, which are not only computationally feasible but also biologically realistic, and may thus help to move the field forward.

Further reading

Carpenter, G. A. and Grossberg, S. (eds.) (1992). *Neural Networks for Vision and Image Processing*. Cambridge, MA: MIT Press. An early collection of work on neural networks for vision and image processing.

Rumelhart, D. E., McClelland, J. L., and the PDP Research Group (1986). *Parallel Distributed Processing: Explorations in the Microstructure of Cognition*, vol. 1: *Foundations*. Cambridge, MA: MIT Press. Provides an introduction to early classic work in connectionism.

Sun, R. and Bookman, L. A. (eds.) (1995). *Computational Architectures Integrating Neural and Symbolic Processes: A Perspective on the State of the Art*. Norwell, MA: Kluwer Academic Publishers. An anthology of work on connectionist and hybrid connectionist models.

Wermter, S. and Sun, R. (eds.) (2000). *Hybrid Neural Systems*. Berlin: Springer. A more recent collection of major work in connectionist and hybrid connectionist models.

References

Anderson, J. and Lebiere, C. (1998). *The Atomic Components of Thought*. Mahwah, NJ: Lawrence Erlbaum Associates.

Bechtel, W. and Abrahamsen, A. (1990). *Connectionism and the Mind: An Introduction to Parallel Processing in Networks*. Cambridge, MA: Blackwell.

Carpenter, G. A. and Grossberg, S. (eds.) (1992). *Neural Networks for Vision and Image Processing*. Cambridge, MA: MIT Press.

Cleeremans, A. and McClelland, J. L. (1991). Learning the structure of event sequences, *Journal of Experimental Psychology: General* 120: 235–53.

Dreyfus, H. L. and Dreyfus, S. E. (1986). *Mind Over Machine: The Power of Human Intuition and Expertise in the Era of the Computer*. New York: The Free Press.

Elman, J. L. (1990). Finding structure in time, *Cognitive Science* 14: 179–211.

Fodor, J. A. and Pylyshyn, Z. W. (1988). Connectionism and cognitive architecture: A critical analysis, *Cognition* 28: 3–71.

Gluck, M. A. and Bower, G. H. (1988). Evaluating an adaptive network model of human learning, *Journal of Memory and Language* 27: 166–95.

Holyoak, K. J. and Thagard, P. (1989). Analogical mapping by constraint satisfaction, *Cognitive Science* 13: 295–355.

Kruschke, J. K. (2008). Models of categorization, in R. Sun (ed.), *The Cambridge Handbook of Computational Psychology* (pp. 267–301). New York: Cambridge University Press.

McClelland, J. L., McNaughton, B. L., and O'Reilly, R. C. (1995). Why there are complementary learning systems in the hippocampus and neocortex: Insights from the successes and failures of connectionist models of learning and memory, *Psychological Review* 102: 419–57.

Miikkulainen, R. (1993). *Subsymbolic Natural Language Processing: An Integrated Model of Scripts, Lexicon, and Memory*. Cambridge, MA: MIT Press.

Newell, A. and Simon, H. A. (1976). Computer science as empirical inquiry: Symbols and search, *Communications of the ACM* 19: 113–26.

Norman, K. A., Detre, G., and Polyn, S. M. (2008). Computational models of episodic memory, in R. Sun (ed.), *The Cambridge Handbook of Computational Psychology* (pp. 189–225). New York: Cambridge University Press.

Pinker, S. and Prince, A. (1988). On language and connectionism: Analysis of a parallel distributed processing model of language acquisition, *Cognition* 23: 73–193.

Ramsey, W., Stich, S. P., and Rumelhart, D. E. (1991). *Philosophy and Connectionist Theory*. Hillsdale, NJ: Lawrence Erlbaum Associates.

Rogers, T. T. (2008). Computational models of semantic memory, in R. Sun (ed.), *The Cambridge Handbook of Computational Psychology* (pp. 226–266). New York: Cambridge University Press.

Rumelhart, D. E., McClelland, J. L., and the PDP Research Group (1986). *Parallel Distributed Processing: Explorations in the Microstructure of Cognition*, vol. 1: *Foundations*. Cambridge, MA: MIT Press.

St. John, M. F. and McClelland, J. L. (1990). Learning and applying contextual constraints in sentence comprehension, *Artificial Intelligence* 46: 217–57.

Sejnowski, T. J. and Rosenberg, C. S. (1987). Parallel networks that learn to pronounce English text, *Complex Systems* 1: 145–68.

Shastri, L. and Ajjanagadde, V. (1993). From simple associations to systematic reasoning: A connectionist representation of rules, variables, and dynamic bindings using temporal synchrony, *Behavioral and Brain Sciences* 16: 417–94.

Smolensky, P. (1988). On the proper treatment of connectionism, *Behavioral and Brain Sciences* 11: 1–74.

Sun, R. (1992). On variable binding in connectionist networks. *Connection Science* 4: 93–124.

(1994). *Integrating Rules and Connectionism for Robust Reasoning.* New York: John Wiley and Sons.

(1999). Accounting for the computational basis of consciousness: A connectionist approach, *Consciousness and Cognition* 8: 529–65.

(2002). *Duality of the Mind: A Bottom-Up Approach Toward Cognition.* Mahwah, NJ: Lawrence Erlbaum Associates.

Sun, R. and Bookman, L. A. (eds.) (1995). *Computational Architectures Integrating Neural and Symbolic Processes: A Perspective on the State of the Art.* Norwell, MA: Kluwer Academic Publishers.

Sun, R., Slusarz, P., and Terry, C. (2005). The interaction of the explicit and the implicit in skill learning: A dual-process approach, *Psychological Review* 112: 159–92.

Sun, R. and Zhang, X. (2006). Accounting for a variety of reasoning data within a cognitive architecture, *Journal of Experimental and Theoretical Artificial Intelligence* 18: 169–91.

Sutton, R. S. and Barto, A. G. (1998). *Reinforcement Learning: An Introduction.* Cambridge, MA: MIT Press.

Touretzky, D. S. and Hinton, G. E. (1988). A distributed connectionist production system, *Cognitive Science* 12: 423–66.

Waltz, D. and Feldman, J. (eds.) (1986). *Connectionist Models and Their Implications: Readings from Cognitive Science.* Norwood, NJ: Ablex.

Wermter, S. and R. Sun (eds.) (2000). *Hybrid Neural Systems.* Berlin: Springer.

6 Dynamical systems and embedded cognition

Randall D. Beer

6.1 Introduction

The conceptual frameworks that we bring to our study of cognition can have a tremendous impact on the nature of that study. They provide a set of filters through which we view the world, influencing our choice of phenomena to study, the language in which we describe these phenomena, the questions we ask about them, and our interpretations of the answers we receive. For much of the last fifty years, thinking about thinking has been dominated by the computational framework, the idea that systems are intelligent to the extent that they can encode knowledge in symbolic representations which are then algorithmically manipulated so as to produce solutions to the problems that these systems encounter (see Chapter 4 of this volume). More recently, the connectionist framework forced an important refinement of the computational framework, in which representation and computation could be distributed across a large number of loosely neuron-like units (see Chapter 5).

Beginning around the mid 1980s, just as the popularity of connectionism was rising, another conceptual framework appeared (or, as in the case of connectionism, reappeared) on the scene. This framework, which, for want of a catchier label, I will call the situated, embodied, dynamical (SED) framework, focuses on concrete action and emphasizes the way in which an agent's behavior arises from the dynamical interaction between its brain, its body, and its environment. In this chapter, I will attempt to trace some of the history of the individual intellectual threads of situated activity, embodiment, and dynamics that underlie the SED approach. I will particularly focus on the years 1985–1995. Although there were important precursors to the SED approach (some of which I will briefly mention), and work in this area has grown rapidly in recent years, many of the pivotal ideas were first given their modern form during this ten-year period.

6.2 Situated activity

The first intellectual thread making up the SED approach is *situated activity*. Roughly speaking, situated activity stresses three ideas that have been traditionally neglected in AI and cognitive science.

S1 *Concrete action*. Actually taking action in the world is more fundamental than the abstract descriptions that we sometimes make of it. While conscious deliberation clearly has its role, the ultimate job of an intelligent agent is to *do* something, to take some concrete action with consequences beyond its own skull.

S2 *Situatedness*. An agent's immediate environment plays a central role in its behavior. This environment is not only a rich source of constraints and opportunities for the agent, but also a context that gives meaning to the agent's actions.

S3 *Interactionism*. An agent's relationship with its environment is one of ongoing interaction. The environment does not serve merely as a source of isolated problems for the agent to solve, but rather a partner with which the agent is fully engaged in moment-to-moment improvisation.

The philosophical roots of situated activity can be traced to phenomenology, especially the work of Martin Heidegger (1927/1962), which was brought into AI and cognitive science primarily through the criticisms of Hubert Dreyfus (1972/1992). One of Heidegger's key insights was the distinction he drew between objects being *zuhanden* ("ready-to-hand") and *vorhanden* ("present-at-hand"). In our normal daily experience, we usually encounter things as resources for immediate action in the service of achieving our goals. For example, to someone in the act of hammering a nail, the hammer in some sense ceases to exist. Rather, like any tool, it becomes merely an extension of the arm (i.e., it is ready-to-hand). It is only when we explicitly adopt an intellectual attitude toward the hammer (e.g., because the handle has broken and the hammer is suddenly unable to perform its normal function), that the hammer emerges from the unarticulated background of things as a distinct object characterized by its own set of properties (i.e., it becomes present-at-hand). A number of authors have carefully articulated the challenges that phenomenological ideas pose to the cognitivist worldview that has dominated thinking in AI and cognitive science, which not only conceives of cognition as the rule-governed manipulation of symbolic representations, but also makes fundamental distinctions between the physical and the mental, between the body and the mind and between the environment and the agent (Dreyfus 1972/1992; Winograd and Flores 1986; Varela, Thompson, and Rosch 1991; Clark 1997; Wheeler 2005).

Another important precursor to situated activity was James Gibson's Ecological Psychology (Gibson 1979). Based on his studies of vision in World War II pilots, Gibson emphasized the structure inherent in an organism's environment and the importance of the organism/environment relation to a theory of perception. For example, the way in which an animal's visual field changes as it moves through its environment carries a great deal of information about the direction and speed of motion, distances to objects, orientations of surfaces, and so on. Gibson's views eventually encompassed a wide-ranging rejection of cognitivism. However, for our purposes here, Gibson's most important contribution is his notion of *affordances* – the possibilities for action that an environment presents to an agent. For example, Heidegger's hammer affords pounding nails due to the graspability of its handle and the shape and hardness of its head. Furthermore, Gibson argued that, although affordances are perceivable facts about the world, they are ecological in the sense that their significance is relative to the capabilities of a particular organism. For example, an opening that affords passability to a mouse does not necessarily afford passability to a human being.

A third important influence on situated activity came from work in the social sciences. For example, Lucy Suchman, an anthropologist studying man-machine interaction, traced breakdowns in communication between a person and a help system for a photocopy machine to mistaken assumptions made by the designers of the system about the nature of action (Suchman 1987). She rejected the traditional view in AI and cognitive science that action results from the execution of a plan, and argued instead that action must be understood as situated, in the sense that it is contingent upon the actual circumstances as they unfold. On this view, explicit plans are best interpreted as resources for communicating about action rather than as mechanisms for action. Based on his studies of the navigation team of a large naval vessel, another anthropologist, Edwin Hutchins, similarly concluded that cognition "in the wild" must often be understood as a culturally constituted activity among a group of individuals depending heavily on the unfolding situation in which it occurs (Hutchins 1995).

Within AI, situated ideas came to the fore in the mid 1980s. Earlier demonstrations of how rich behavior could arise from simple mechanisms interacting with complex environments include W. Grey Walter's robotic "tortoises" (Walter 1953) and Valentino Braitenburg's simple "vehicles" (Braitenburg 1984). However, situated activity research within AI arose mainly as a reaction against the traditional planning view of action, in which agents represent the current situation and available actions, formulate a symbolic plan of action, and then execute this plan. Philip Agre and David Chapman stressed the inability of classical planning techniques to scale to complex, uncertain, real-time environments and proposed instead that routine activity arises from the interaction of simple internal machinery with the immediate situation (Agre and Chapman 1987). Agre and Chapman demonstrated the utility of this idea in a series of programs, the best-known of which was Pengi, an agent that played the video arcade game Pengo in real time despite having to deal with hundreds of often unpredictable objects. Stanley Rosenschein and Leslie Kaelbling showed how a specification of an agent's goals could be "compiled away" into simple machinery such that, although it still made sense for an external observer to talk about the agent's knowledge and beliefs, these states no longer played any direct role in the agent's actions (Rosenschein and Kaelbling 1986). Rodney Brooks' influential work on autonomous robots rejected the traditional sense-model-plan-act cycle, emphasizing that often "the world is its own best model" (Brooks 1986, 1991a; see also Chapter 13 of this volume). He developed a layered control system known as the subsumption architecture, in which networks of simple machines interact with one another and the immediate circumstances to produce behavior, and deployed it on a variety of different robots. David Cliff (Cliff 1991) and I (Beer 1990) demonstrated the significant potential for interaction between work on the neural basis of animal behavior and situated agents, developing models of a hoverfly and a cockroach, respectively.

Presumably, no one would deny that the environmental situation has an important role to play in an agent's behavior, but just how fundamental this observation is remains controversial (Kirsch 1991; Vera and Simon 1993; Hayes, Ford, and Agnew 1994; Clancey 1997; Anderson 2003). To some, situated activity smacks of behaviorism, but this charge depends a great deal on what exactly one means by "behaviorism." It is certainly true that work in situated activity exhibits a renewed emphasis on concrete behavior over abstract reasoning. However, abstract reasoning is not rejected by situated approaches, but rather relegated to a supporting role as an evolutionarily recent elaboration of a more basic capacity for getting around in the world. It is also true that much work in situated activity has tended to emphasize reactive architectures, in which an agent's actions are completely determined by its sensations, and to either reject or at least significantly reconstrue the idea of internal representations. Reactive architectures are strongly reminiscent of the stimulus–response paradigm embraced by behaviorism, and have well-known limitations when it comes to, for example, anticipatory behavior. However, as we shall see later in this chapter, a commitment to purely reactive architectures is unnecessary, and it is possible to articulate a role for internal state that is both essential and interestingly different from the representational role that such state plays in traditional AI and cognitive science.

Perhaps the most controversial idea that has emerged from research on situated cognition in recent years is the notion of the extended mind (Clark 1997; Clark and Chalmers 1998). This idea is grounded in the observation that not only does an agent's environment play an essential role in its behavior, but the agent itself can manipulate that role by actively organizing its environment so as to increase its problem-solving ability. For example, we lay out the ingredients for a recipe in the order in which they will be needed, and we use maps to find our way through sprawling cities. Such scaffolding allows us to offload significant parts of our cognitive processing into the environment. Furthermore, through language, we can coordinate the activities of many people so that they can collectively accomplish things that no individual person may be able to, such as navigating a large naval vessel (Hutchins

1995). Extended mind advocates argue that if memory, problem solving, and so on can be spread across many agents and artifacts, then cognition itself must be understood as a distributed phenomenon that transcends the skull of an individual agent, and properly belongs only to the larger system of agents and artifacts of which that individual is a part. Indeed, even social insects are known to collectively accomplish complex construction tasks such as nest-building by modifying their environment in such a way as to appropriately organize the flow of workers and material, a process referred to as *stigmergy* (Turner 2000).

6.3   Embodiment

A second intellectual thread in the SED approach is *embodiment*. There are at least three somewhat distinct ideas that have been advanced by advocates of embodied cognitive science.

E1   *Physical embodiment.* The uniquely physical aspects of an agent's body are crucial to its behavior, including its material properties, the capabilities for action provided by the layout and characteristics of its degrees of freedom and effectors, the unique perspective provided by the particular layout and characteristics of its sensors, and the modes of sensorimotor interaction that the sensors and effectors collectively support. In some ways, this aspect of embodiment is a special case of situatedness. Whereas situatedness includes any kind of interaction with the environment, embodiment emphasizes those specifically physical interactions mediated by the body.

E2   *Biological embodiment.* Not only are the physical characteristics of bodies important, but the specifically biological facts of an organism's existence must also be taken into account, including the relevant neuroscience, physiology, development, and evolution.

E3   *Conceptual embodiment.* Even when engaged in pure ratiocination, our most abstract concepts are still ultimately grounded in our bodily experiences and body-oriented metaphors.

The philosophical roots of embodiment can also be traced to phenomenology, especially the work of Maurice Merleau-Ponty (1962), who made bodily involvement in the world central to his phenomenology of lived experience. To take but one example, Merleau-Ponty's argument that how we perceive an object is shaped by the kinds of interactions with it that our body allows can be seen as an early precursor to Gibson's (1979) notion of affordances. Merleau-Ponty's thought also played a major role in Dreyfus' critique of computational theories of mind (Dreyfus 1972/1992).

Within AI and cognitive science, the importance of physical embodiment was first emphasized by Brooks (1991b). Brooks argued that AI needed to move beyond the abstract microworlds that had been its primary concern and begin to address the sorts of problems encountered by real robots moving around in real environments. In this way, Brooks suggested, the extent to which most classical AI techniques are simply untenable in realistic situations would become clear. In its milder form, the argument of physical embodiment is simply that the material properties of the body and environment play a key role in its behavior and, by building robots, we get this physics "for free" rather than having to painstakingly model it. In its most radical form, the claim is that only physically instantiated AI systems will exhibit truly intelligent behavior. Coupled with the contemporaneous trends in situated cognition reviewed in the previous section, Brooks' arguments unleashed an explosion of work in behavior-based robotics (Arkin 1998), active perception (Ballard 1991; Churchland, Ramachandran, and Sejnowski 1994; Noë 2004), embodied cognitive science (Pfeifer and Scheier 1999), autonomous agents (Maes 1990), some aspects of artificial life (Langton 1989), and the philosophy of mind (Clark 1997).

Biological embodiment takes the arguments of physical embodiment one step further. Not only are the physical characteristics of bodies important, but so are the biological facts of an organism's existence. The conditions necessary to maintain our living state fundamentally constrain our behavioral and cognitive capacities. In addition, the specific properties of bone, muscle, and skin, the specific characteristics of biological sensors, and the ways these sensory and motor capabilities are knitted together in human bodies fundamentally define our own particular mode of embodiment. Furthermore, the fact that we have gone through the particular evolutionary and developmental history that we have may also have important consequences for our behavioral and cognitive architecture. For example, Esther Thelen and Linda Smith have argued for the importance of understanding the sensorimotor origins of cognition in development, both in studies of the development of walking in infants (Thelen and Smith 1994) and, more recently, in studies of Jean Piaget's classic A-not-B error, in which an infant repeatedly shown an object being hidden under box A will still reach for A even after being shown the object being hidden under a second box B (Thelen et al. 2001). A similar argument can be made for the emergence in evolution of uniquely human cognitive capacities from simpler precursors. Finally, there has been a very strong push toward incorporating more neurobiological realism into embodied agents (Arbib 1987; Beer 1990; Edelman et al. 1992). Conversely, neuroscience has begun to take seriously the role of the body and of neuromechanical interactions in the production of behavior (Chiel and Beer 1997).

Thus, the conventional claim of biological embodiment is that the biological features of organisms matter to their behavior and cognition. A more radical claim that is sometimes associated with biological embodiment is that the living state itself is fundamental to cognition (Maturana and Varela 1980; Varela et al. 1991; Di Paolo 2005). The idea here is generally not that the material or biochemistry of life is essential, but rather that the organization of living systems is indispensable to their cognitive capabilities. The relevant notion of living organization is generally derived from Humberto Maturana and Francisco Varela's concept of *autopoiesis* (roughly, a self-producing network of components and processes, i.e., a kind of organizational homeostasis) (Maturana and Varela 1980).

Finally, conceptual embodiment concerns the way in which even abstract concepts are often grounded in bodily experience and metaphor. For example, Stevan Harnad defined the *symbol grounding problem* as the problem of how words, and ultimately mental states, get their meaning (Harnad 1990), and he proposed that a way to address this problem is to ground them in sensorimotor signals. Furthermore, George Lakoff and Mark Johnson have argued that the structure of our reason is grounded in the details of our embodiment, and that many abstract concepts are metaphors derived from sensorimotor domains (Lakoff and Johnson 1999). For example, we speak of understanding something as "grasping" it and we speak of failing to understand something as a failure to "grasp" it or it "going over our heads." Likewise, bad things "stink" and the "pieces" of a theory "fit" together.

6.4   Dynamics

The final intellectual thread constituting the SED approach is *dynamics*, within which we must distinguish at least three ideas.

D1 *Dynamical systems theory* (DST). A mathematical theory that can be applied to any system characterized by a state that changes over time in some systematic way.

D2 *The dynamical framework.* A collection of concepts, intuitions, and metaphors involved in taking a dynamical perspective on some system of interest.

D3 *The dynamical hypothesis.* A specific hypothesis, put forward by Timothy van Gelder (1998), for how DST and the dynamical framework could be combined into a rigorous counterproposal to the traditional computational hypothesis in AI and cognitive science.

A dynamical system is a mathematical abstraction that unambiguously describes how the state of some system evolves over time (Abraham and Shaw 1992; Strogatz 1994). It consists of a state space S, an ordered time set T, and an evolution operator ϕ that transforms a state at one time to another state at some other time. A dynamical system whose evolution depends on its internal state only is called autonomous, while one whose evolution also depends on external inputs is called nonautonomous. S can be numerical or symbolic, continuous or discrete (or a hybrid of the two), and of any topology and dimension (including infinite dimensional). T is typically either the set of integers or the set of real numbers. The evolution operator may be given explicitly or defined implicitly, and it may be deterministic or stochastic.

The most common examples of dynamical systems are sets of ordinary differential equations and iterated maps, but many other kinds of mathematical systems can also be fruitfully described and analyzed in dynamical terms. For any mathematical system that can be put into this form, DST offers a wide variety of tools for analyzing its temporal behavior, many of which were first developed by the French mathematician Henri Poincaré in support of his work in celestial mechanics. These tools include the identification of invariant sets (sets of points in the state space that the evolution operator does not change, i.e., fixed points and limit cycles), the characterization of their local behavior (how they respond to perturbations, i.e., their stability) and their global behavior (how they are interconnected, i.e., their saddle manifolds), and their dependence on parameters (how they change as parameters are changed, i.e., their bifurcations). It is important to reiterate that, just like the formal theory of computation, DST is a body of mathematics, and not itself a scientific theory of the natural world.

Despite the fact that DST is not itself a scientific theory, taking a dynamical perspective on some natural phenomenon brings with it a set of concepts, intuitions, and metaphors – a certain worldview – that influences the questions we ask, the analyses we perform, and how we interpret the results (van Gelder 1995). When one approaches some system from a computational perspective, one is concerned with what function the system is trying to compute, in what format the problem input is specified, in what output format the answer is required, how the relevant features of the problem are to be represented, by what algorithms these representations are to be transformed, and how the performance of these algorithms scales with problem size. In contrast, when one approaches some system from a dynamical perspective, one seeks to identify a minimal set of state variables whose evolution can account for the observed behavior, the dynamical laws by which the values of these variables evolve in time, the overall spatiotemporal structure of their possible evolution, and the sensitivity of this structure to variations in inputs, states, and parameters.

The dynamical perspective has been found to be a fruitful one in many areas of cognitive science (Port and van Gelder 1995; Beer 2000). A dynamical perspective on brain and behavior was first explicitly articulated by W. Ross Ashby (Ashby 1960). Within neural networks, Stephen Grossberg has long emphasized the importance of dynamical ideas (Grossberg 1969). Indeed, DST is now an essential tool in computational neuroscience (Izhikevich 2007) for analyzing, not just individual nerve cells or small circuits, but also entire brain systems (Skarda and Freeman 1987). Dynamical ideas were first brought into ecological psychology by Peter Kugler (Kugler, Kelso, and Turvey 1980; for reviews see Turvey 1990 and Warren 2006). Scott Kelso and colleagues have pursued a dynamical perspective on brain and behavior for many years, especially emphasizing the role of self-organization in the creation of behavioral patterns and the transitions between them (Kelso 1995). Thelen and Smith have argued for a dynamical approach to cognitive development, in which processes and change are studied using the same tools across a range of timescales (Thelen and Smith 1994). Jeffrey Elman emphasized the fundamentally temporal character of language understanding, with preceding words strongly influencing the interpretation of subsequent ones, and has developed a dynamical approach to language (Elman 1995). Finally, I argued that dynamical systems theory provides the appropriate theoretical language and tools for analyzing the kinds of autonomous agents that were being developed in AI and robotics (Beer 1995a), and Timothy Smithers (1995) and Gregor Schöner (Schöner, Dose, and Engels 1995) advocated a dynamical approach to the design of autonomous robots.

A specific formulation that has received a great deal of attention is the dynamical hypothesis put forward by van Gelder (van Gelder 1995; 1998). Van Gelder defines a dynamical system as a quantitative system, that is, a system whose state space, time set, and evolution law involve numerical quantities. As we saw above, this is a significant restriction of the mathematical definition of a dynamical system. His dynamical hypothesis then has two components: (1) the nature hypothesis and (2) the knowledge hypothesis. The claim of the nature hypothesis is ontological: Cognitive systems are dynamical systems. In contrast, the knowledge hypothesis claims only that cognitive systems are best understood using the tools of dynamical systems theory. Given that even many advocates of the dynamical approach do not fully support van Gelder's dynamical hypothesis, it is unfortunate that most critical discussion of the dynamical approach to cognition has focused on van Gelder's specific formulation (Eliasmith 1997; Grush 1997; Bechtel 1998; Van Leeuwen 2005). Nevertheless, it is an historically important attempt to formulate a dynamical alternative to the computational hypothesis.

6.5   Toward an integrated perspective

To this point, I have treated situatedness, embodiment, and dynamics as relatively separate intellectual threads. I did this both because the historical development of these ideas occurred somewhat independently and because they are logically independent – that is, people can and do hold each of them individually without necessarily also subscribing to the others. However, it will not have escaped the careful reader's attention that there is a great deal of potential overlap and synergism between them. The goal of this section is to articulate an integrated theoretical framework that combines the insights from situatedness, embodiment, and dynamics. In contrast to previous sections, I will also adopt a more personal viewpoint in this section, describing my own

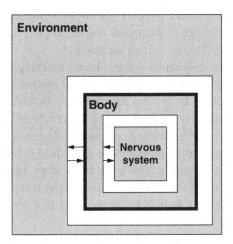

Figure 6.1 An agent and its environment are coupled dynamical systems. The agent in turn is composed of coupled nervous system and body dynamical systems.

particular integrative view (Beer 1995a; 1995b; 2003) rather than attempting a general survey of all such views.

The basic situated, embodied, dynamical (SED) framework is quite simple and is illustrated in Figure 6.1. It consists of the following three postulates:

SED1 *Brains, bodies, and environments are dynamical systems* (cf. S2, E1, E2, D1, D2). Nervous systems, bodies, and environments are all conceptualized as dynamical systems, by which I mean only that we assume that each can be characterized by a set of states whose temporal evolution is governed by dynamical laws.

SED2 *Brain, body, and environment dynamics are coupled* (cf. S1, S3, D1, D2). Nervous systems are embodied in bodies, which are in turn situated within environments, leading to dense interaction between these three component systems. The coupled brain–body subsystem will be termed the "agent." Coupling that flows from the environment to the agent will be termed "sensory," and coupling that flows in the opposite direction will be termed "motor." The "behavior" of an agent will be defined as its trajectory of motor actions.

SED3 *The agent is subject to viability constraints* (cf. E2). There are conditions on the dynamics of the agent that determine its viability. If these viability constraints are violated, then the agent ceases to exist as an independent entity and can no longer engage in behavioral interactions with its environment. (We will not consider this postulate further here; for discussion of its role in the SED framework, see Beer 2004.)

The a priori theoretical commitments of this framework are quite minimal. Indeed, it is hard to imagine a theoretical framework that makes fewer commitments than this. What could possibly follow from such a small set of claims? In fact, quite a number of nontrivial consequences follow almost immediately if we take these three postulates seriously.

Perhaps the most important conclusion is this: Strictly speaking, *behavior is a property of the entire coupled brain–body–environment system*, and cannot in general be properly attributed to any one subsystem in isolation from the others. We have defined behavior to be only the trajectory of an agent's motor actions. However, because the brain, body, and environment dynamics are coupled, they form a single larger autonomous dynamical system with its own trajectories of temporal evolution. The trajectories of an agent's motor actions are merely projections of the full trajectories of the complete brain–body–environment system, and it is these full trajectories that are the proper objects of study within the SED framework.

Even though behavior is a property of the entire coupled system, it is still meaningful to ask about the relative contributions of brain, body, and environment to some particular feature of a behavioral trajectory. In order to do so, we must open the coupled brain–body–environment system by cutting one or more of the coupling pathways in order to isolate the component we wish to study. This component then becomes a nonautonomous dynamical system, and our analysis involves examining how its own intrinsic dynamics interacts with the inputs it receives from the other components of the coupled system in the production of the behavioral feature of interest. This has many interesting consequences for the way we conceive of traditional behavioral and cognitive phenomena.

For example, perception is generally viewed as a means by which an agent extracts information about its surroundings from the raw sensory signals it receives and internally represents the structure of its environment. But a dynamical system follows a trajectory specified by its own internal state and dynamical laws. Sensory inputs cannot in general place a nonautonomous dynamical system into some state uniquely characteristic of a given external object. Rather, the most that they can do is bias the intrinsic tendencies of the agent dynamics by selecting some particular trajectory from the set of possible trajectories that the agent's dynamical laws allow from its current state. This suggests a more behavior-oriented view of perception that is reminiscent of Gibson (1979). On this view, perception is a process whereby agent dynamics that are appropriately sensitive to environmental influences become perturbed by the trajectory of sensory inputs that the system receives and transforms into behavior appropriate to the circumstances. Furthermore, because the coupling between an agent and its environment is two-way, an agent's action can shape its own perception. Agents not only perceive in order to act, but they also act in order to perceive.

Because agents in the SED framework are dynamical, they are not vulnerable to the criticisms that have been leveled against reactive agents. A reactive agent is one whose motor outputs depend only on its sensory inputs; it is merely a function from sensation to action. Although such an agent can participate in complex interactions when coupled to a dynamic environment, its behavior is always subordinated to that environment since it possesses no dynamics of its own. In contrast, the response of a dynamical agent is determined at least in part by its own internal dynamics. Because it possesses an internal state, a dynamical agent can respond differently to the same sensory stimulus at different times, it can initiate behavior independently of its immediate environment, it can modify its behavior based on its history of interactions, and it can exploit long-term correlations in its environment to organize its behavior in anticipation of future events.

One significant advantage of the SED framework is that it offers the possibility of a uniform treatment of disparate behavioral and cognitive phenomena that have often been seen as irreconcilable. At one extreme, some basic sensorimotor behavior may be mostly reactive in character, with internal state playing only a small role in "coloring" the agent's responses to its environment. At the other extreme, some of our most cognitive behavior can be conceived as being nearly decoupled from the immediate environmental circumstances, driven primarily by the temporal evolution of internal state. Of course, most behavior is usually a mixture of external and internal influences, with the relative importance of the two varying, sometimes substantially, from moment to moment. Indeed, the interesting questions of how higher cognitive processes arose from more basic sensorimotor competence during the course of evolution and development seems much more approachable within a theoretical framework that places them both on a common footing. On this view, higher cognition does not necessarily alter our fundamentally situated, embodied, and dynamic character, but instead augments it with a vastly increased reservoir of internal dynamics.

How are we to understand the nature and role of this internal state within a dynamical agent? The traditional computational interpretation of such states would be as internal representations. But possessing an internal state is a property of physical systems in general, and these states can covary with states outside the system in quite complicated ways. Unless we wish to grant representational status to all physical states (does a thunderstorm represent the topography of the terrain over which it passes?), there must be additional conditions that license the modifier "representational." Unfortunately, despite the fundamental role that the notion of representation plays in computational approaches, there is very little agreement about what those additional conditions might be. These considerations have led me to adopt a position of representational skepticism (not, as some have suggested, anti-representationalism) (Beer 2003). I view the representational status of an internal state as an empirical question, to be settled according to the precise definition of the particular representational notion on offer. Thus, by not taking representation for granted, a dynamical perspective offers a broader theoretical playing field. On the one hand, it offers the possibility of understanding what representations are and when and how they arise. On the other hand, we may find that, at least in some cases, the roles played by the internal states of a dynamical agent simply cannot be usefully interpreted as representational.

What is the relationship between a SED approach to cognition and the more familiar computational and connectionist approaches? Such a comparison is fraught with difficulties. For example, we must distinguish between the bodies of mathematics that underlie each of these approaches and the theoretical claims that these approaches make. As mathematical formalisms, computational, connectionist, and dynamical systems are all of roughly equivalent power in the sense that they can each be used to construct models of the same class of phenomena. Thus, there is no useful *mathematical* distinction to be drawn between these different approaches. This, I think, is one of the ways in which van Gelder's dynamical hypothesis goes wrong (Beer 1998).

In addition, we must recognize that computationalism, connectionism, and dynamicism are not really scientific theories at all, because they themselves do not make sharply falsifiable predictions. Rather, they are what I have called theoretical frameworks (Beer 1995b). They provide a set of pretheoretical intuitions, a theoretical vocabulary, a style of explanation, a worldview within which particular falsifiable theories of specific cognitive phenomena are formulated and analyzed. The computationalist framework, for example, emphasizes the structure and content of the internal representations used by an agent and the algorithms by which those representations are manipulated. In contrast, the connectionist framework emphasizes the network architecture, the learning algorithm, the training protocol, and the intermediate distributed representations that are developed. In this sense, many connectionist models are still disembodied, unsituated, and computational (albeit distributed) in nature (Harvey 1992/1996). Finally, the SED framework emphasizes the structure of the space of all possible trajectories of the brain–body–environment system and the various forces, both internal and external to the agent, that shape those trajectories so as to stabilize some particular pattern of behavior. It is likely that all three perspectives will be important in any future theory of behavior and cognition. For example, since the neural components of a SED model are often recurrent connectionist networks, and since deliberative reasoning is one of the cognitive phenomena that must eventually be addressed, ideas and mathematical tools from both connectionism and computationalism are likely to play an essential role even in a SED-centered theory. The exact mix of insights from these three theoretical frameworks (or other frameworks yet unimagined!) that will ultimately prove to be the most fruitful remains an open question that only ongoing empirical investigation can resolve.

6.6   Methodological issues

Taking the SED framework seriously raises many difficult methodological issues. Studying just one component of a brain–body-environment system is difficult enough, but studying the interactions of all three simultaneously is a daunting task. Experimentally, we currently lack the instruments to monitor and manipulate the activity of all the relevant neurons within the nervous systems of intact, behaving animals, let alone the relevant properties of the animal's body and environment. Theoretically, we currently lack the mathematical tools necessary to understand large networks of densely interconnected, heterogeneous, nonlinear dynamical elements, particularly in systems that were evolved for their behavioral efficacy and not for their intelligibility in terms of traditional engineering design principles of modularity and hierarchical decomposition.

For these reasons, a number of researchers have turned to the study of model agents using dynamical neural networks and evolutionary algorithms (Beer and Gallagher 1992; Cliff, Husbands, and Harvey 1993; Nolfi and Floreano 2000). In this approach, a model "nervous system" is embodied in a model body, which is in turn situated in a model environment. The entire system is evolved to perform some behavior of interest. A common choice of nervous system model is continuous-time recurrent neural networks, which are known to be universal approximators of smooth dynamics. Typically, only the neural parameters are evolved, but in some work, network architecture and body properties are also evolved. One significant advantage of an evolutionary approach is that it minimizes a priori theoretical assumptions and thus allows the space of possible brain–body-environment systems capable of generating a particular behavior to be explored.

This evolutionary methodology has already been applied successfully to a wide range of interesting behavior (Nolfi and Floreano 2000). A great deal of work has focused on sensorimotor behavior, such as orientation, legged locomotion, object avoidance, and navigation (Beer and Gallagher 1992; Kodjabachian and Meyer 1998; Vickerstaff and Di Paolo 2005). Another line of work has focused on the evolution of learning behavior (Yamauchi and Beer 1994; Floreano and Mondada 1996; Tuci, Quinn, and Harvey 2002; Izquierdo-Torres and Harvey 2006). In addition, there has been considerable work on visually guided behavior (Cliff et al. 1993) and its application to categorical perception, selective attention, and other cognitively interesting tasks (Beer 2003; Di Paolo and Harvey 2003; Ward and Ward 2006). Finally, the evolution of communication has also been an active area of research (Di Paolo 2000; Marocco, Cangelosi, and Nolfi 2003; Steels 2003; Nolfi 2005). Thus, although there are difficult open issues in scaling evolutionary approaches to increasingly complicated behavior, one could argue that the agents that have already been evolved are interesting enough that their careful analysis could teach us many things about the dynamics of brain–body–environment systems.

Indeed, for me, the main interest is not in evolving such model agents per se, but rather in analyzing the resulting brain–body–environment systems using the tools of dynamical systems theory (Beer 1995a, 1995b, 2003; Husbands, Harvey, and Cliff 1995). The primary purpose of such an analysis is to build the intuitions, theoretical concepts, and mathematical and computational tools necessary for understanding the dynamics of brain–body–environment systems. While DST provides a solid foundation for such investigations, many additional issues must be addressed. For example, there are different levels at which the dynamics of a brain–body–environment system can be analyzed, including the autonomous dynamics of the entire coupled system, how the coupled behavior arises from the interaction between the nonautonomous environment and agent dynamics, how the nonautonomous agent dynamics arises from the interaction between the nonautonomous body and neural dynamics, and how the nonautonomous neural dynamics arises from the architecture, intrinsic and synaptic parameters of the neural elements.

A final issue that must be addressed is understanding nonautonomous dynamics. The mathematical tools of DST are most highly developed in the case of autonomous dynamical systems, when the analysis can focus on attractors and their bifurcations. However, as mentioned above, when we wish to understand the contribution of a particular component of a brain–body-environment system, we must decompose the coupled system into interacting nonautonomous subsystems, and study their transient responses to time-varying inputs received from the other components. Unfortunately, the mathematical tools for analyzing transient dynamics require significant further development.

6.7   Prospects

Like both computationalism and connectionism, the situated, embodied, and dynamical framework described in this chapter has its roots in ideas first articulated in the 1940s and 1950s. However, because the modern form of the SED framework only emerged in the years 1985–1995, it has had far less time for development than have the computational and connectionist frameworks. The number of people working within the SED framework is also considerably smaller at present. Despite these disadvantages, situated, embodied, and dynamical ideas are having a major impact on thinking in cognitive science, AI and robotics, neuroscience, developmental psychology, and philosophy of mind.

In order to further explore the scope and limits of the SED framework, and to clarify the best mix of computational, connectionist, and SED ideas necessary for understanding the mechanisms of behavior and cognition, considerable further development is necessary. First and foremost, this will require the construction and analysis of many more concrete model agents, especially those of a more cognitively interesting nature. This in turn will require the continued development of techniques for scaling evolutionary techniques and dynamical analysis to larger systems and the further development of techniques for analyzing the transient dynamics of nonautonomous dynamical systems. Finally, there is a need for improved education in dynamical systems concepts within the cognitive science community, and for software to support the dynamical analysis of brain–body–environment systems.

Further reading

Clark, A. (1997). *Being There: Putting Brain, Body and World Together Again.* Cambridge, MA: MIT Press. An early philosophical treatment of situated, embodied and dynamical approaches to cognition.

Nolfi, S. and Floreano, D. (2000). *Evolutionary Robotics: The Biology, Intelligence, and Technology of Self-Organizing Machines.* Cambridge, MA: MIT Press. A comprehensive overview of the use of evolutionary algorithms to produce control systems for model agents and robots.

Pfeifer, R. and Bongard, J. (2006). *How the Body Shapes the Way We Think: A New View of Intelligence.* Cambridge, MA: MIT Press. This book provides a gentle introduction to the crucial role that embodiment plays in cognition.

Port, R. F. and van Gelder, T. (eds.) (1995). *Mind as Motion: Explorations in the Dynamics of Cognition.* Cambridge, MA: MIT Press. An early collection of papers on the dynamical approach to cognition, with contributions from most of the major players.

Spivey, M. (2007). *The Continuity of Mind.* New York: Oxford University Press. This book assembles an impressive array of behavioral and neurophysiological evidence that demonstrates the many ways in which continuous processes play an essential role in cognition.

References

Abraham, R. H. and Shaw, C. D. (1992). *Dynamics: The Geometry of Behavior* (2nd edn.). Reading, MA: Addison-Wesley.

Agre, P. E. and Chapman, D. (1987). Pengi: An implementation of a theory of activity, in *Proceedings of the 6th National Conference on AI (AAAI'87)* (pp. 268–72). Seattle, WA : Morgan Kaufmann.

Anderson, M. L. (2003). Embodied cognition: A field guide, *Artificial Intelligence* 149: 91–130.

Arbib, M. A. (1987). Levels of modeling of mechanisms of visually guided behavior. *Behavioral and Brain Sciences* 10: 407–65.

Arkin, R. C. (1998). *Behavior-Based Robotics.* Cambridge, MA: MIT Press.

Ashby, W. R. (1960). *Design for a Brain: The Origin of Adaptive Behaviour* (2nd edn.). New York: John Wiley and Sons.

Ballard, D. H. (1991). Animate vision, *Artificial Intelligence* 48: 57–86.

Bechtel, W. (1998). Representations and cognitive explanations: Assessing the dynamicist's challenge in cognitive science, *Cognitive Science* 22: 295–318.

Beer, R. D. (1990). *Intelligence as Adaptive Behavior: An Experiment in Computational Neuroethology.* San Diego, CA: Academic Press.

(1995a). A dynamical systems perspective on agent-environment interaction, *Artificial Intelligence* 72: 173–215.

(1995b). Computational and dynamical languages for autonomous agents. In R. F. Port and T. van Gelder (eds.), *Mind as Motion: Explorations in the Dynamics of Cognition* (pp. 121–47). Cambridge, MA: MIT Press.

(1998). Framing the debate between computational and dynamical approaches to cognitive science, *Behavioral and Brain Sciences* 21: 630.

(2000). Dynamical approaches to cognitive science, *Trends in Cognitive Sciences* 4: 91–9.

(2003). The dynamics of active categorical perception in an evolved model agent (with commentary and response), *Adaptive Behavior* 11: 209–43.

(2004). Autopoiesis and cognition in the game of life, *Artificial Life* 10: 309–26.

Beer, R. D. and Gallagher, J. C. (1992). Evolving dynamical neural networks for adaptive behavior, *Adaptive Behavior* 1: 91–122.

Braitenburg, V. (1984). *Vehicles: Experiments in Synthetic Psychology.* Cambridge, MA: MIT Press.

Brooks, R. A. (1986). A robust layered control system for a mobile robot, *IEEE Journal of Robotics and Automation* 2: 14–23.

(1991a). Intelligence without representation, *Artificial Intelligence* 47: 139–59.

(1991b). New approaches to robotics, *Science* 253: 1227–32.

Chiel, H. J. and Beer, R. D. (1997). The brain has a body: Adaptive behavior emerges from interactions of nervous system, body and environment, *Trends in Neurosciences* 20: 553–7.

Churchland, P. S., Ramachandran, V. S., and Sejnowski, T. J. (1994). A critique of pure vision, in C. Koch and J. L. Davis (eds.), *Large-Scale Neuronal Theories of the Brain* (pp. 23–60). Cambridge, MA: MIT Press.

Clancey, W. J. (1997). *Situated Cognition: On Human Knowledge and Computer Representations.* Cambridge University Press.

Clark, A. (1997). *Being There: Putting Brain, Body and World Together Again.* Cambridge, MA: MIT Press.

Clark, A. and Chalmers, D. J. (1998). The extended mind, *Analysis* 58: 7–19.

Cliff, D. (1991). Computational neuroethology: A provisional manifesto, in J. A. Meyer and S. W. Wilson (eds.), *From Animals to Animats: Proceedings of the First International Conference on Simulation of Adaptive Behavior* (pp. 29–39). Cambridge, MA: MIT Press.

Cliff, D., Husbands, P., and Harvey, I. (1993). Explorations in evolutionary robotics, *Adaptive Behavior* 2: 73–110.

Di Paolo, E. A. (2000). Behavioral coordination, structural congruence and entrainment in a simulation of acoustically coupled agents, *Adaptive Behavior* 8: 27–48.

    (2005). Autopoiesis, adaptivity, teleology, agency, *Phenomenology and the Cognitive Sciences* 4: 429–52.

Di Paolo, E. A. and Harvey, I. (2003). Decisions and noise: The scope of evolutionary synthesis and dynamical analysis, *Adaptive Behavior* 11: 284–8.

Dreyfus, H. L. (1972/1992). *What Computers Still Can't Do: A Critique of Artificial Reason.* Cambridge, MA: MIT Press. (Revised edition of *What Computers Can't Do*, 1972.)

Edelman, G. M., Reeke, G. N., Gall, W. E., Tononi, G., Williams, D., and Sporns, O. (1992). Synthetic neural modeling applied to a real-world artifact, *Proceedings of the National Academy of Sciences of the United States of America* 89: 7267–71.

Eliasmith, C. (1997). Computation and dynamical models of mind, *Minds and Machines* 7: 531–41.

Elman, J. L. (1995). Language as a dynamical system, in R. Port and T. van Gelder (eds.), *Mind as Motion: Explorations in the Dynamics of Cognition* (pp. 195–225). Cambridge, MA: MIT Press.

Floreano, D. and Mondada, F. (1996). Evolution of plastic neurocontrollers for situated agents, in P. Maes, M. J. Mataric, J.-A. Meyer, J. Pollack, and S. W. Wilson (eds.), *From Animals to Animats 4: Proceedings of the 4th International Conference on Simulation of Adaptive Behavior* (pp. 402–10). Cambridge, MA: MIT Press.

Gibson, J. J. (1979). *The Ecological Approach to Visual Perception.* Boston, MA: Houghton Mifflin.

Grossberg, S. (1969). Embedding fields: A theory of learning with physiological implications, *Journal of Mathematical Psychology* 6: 209–39.

Grush, R. (1997). Review of Port and van Gelder's Mind as Motion, *Philosophical Psychology* 10: 233–42.

Harnad, S. (1990). The symbol grounding problem, *Physica D: Nonlinear Phenomena* 42: 335–46.

Harvey, I. (1992/1996). Untimed and misrepresented: Connectionism and the computer metaphor, *AISB Quarterly* 96: 20–7. Originally published 1992 as University of Sussex Cognitive Science Research Paper 245.

Hayes, P. J., Ford, K. M., and Agnew, N. (1994). On babies and bathwater: A cautionary tale. *AI Magazine* 15(4): 15–26.

Heidegger, M. (1927/1962). *Being and Time.* New York: Harper and Row. Originally published in 1927.

Husbands, P., Harvey, I., and Cliff, D. (1995). Circle in the round: State space attractors for evolved sighted robots, *Robotics and Autonomous Systems* 15: 83–106.

Hutchins, E. (1995). *Cognition in the Wild.* Cambridge, MA: MIT Press.

Izhikevich, E. M. (2007). *Dynamical Systems in Neuroscience: The Geometry of Excitability and Bursting.* Cambridge, MA: MIT Press.

Izquierdo-Torres, E. and Harvey, I. (2006). Learning on a continuum in evolved dynamical node networks. In L. M. Rocha, L. S. Yaeger, M. A. Bedau, et al. (eds.), *Artificial Life X: Proceedings of the 10th International Conference on the Simulation and Synthesis of Living Systems* (pp. 507–12). Cambridge, MA: MIT Press.

Kelso, J. A. S. (1995). *Dynamic Patterns: The Self-Organization of Brain and Behavior.* Cambridge, MA: MIT Press.

Kirsch, D. (1991). Today the earwig, tomorrow man? *Artificial Intelligence* 47: 161–84.

Kodjabachian, J. and Meyer, J.-A. (1998). Evolution and development of neural controllers for locomotion, gradient-following, and obstacle avoidance in artificial insects, *IEEE Transactions on Neural Networks* 9: 796–812.

Kugler, P. N, Kelso, J. A. S., and Turvey, M. T. (1980). On the concept of coordinative structures as dissipative structures, in G. E. Stelmach and J. Requin (eds.), *Tutorials in Motor Behavior* (pp. 3–47). Amsterdam: North Holland.

Lakoff, G. and Johnson, M. (1999). *Philosophy in the Flesh.* New York: Basic Books.

Langton, C. G. (ed.) (1989). *Artificial Life.* Reading MA: Addison-Wesley.

Maes, P., (ed.) (1990). *Designing Autonomous Agents: Theory and Practice from Biology to Engineering and Back.* Cambridge, MA: MIT Press.

Marocco, D., Cangelosi, A., and Nolfi, S. (2003). The emergence of communication in evolutionary robots, *Philosophical Transactions of the Royal Society London A* 361: 2397–421.

Maturana, H. R. and Varela, F. J. (1980). *Autopoiesis and Cognition: The Realization of the Living.* Dordrecht: D. Reidel Publishing.

Merleau-Ponty, M. (1962). *Phenomenology of Perception.* New York: Humanities Press.

Noë, A. (2004). *Action in Perception.* Cambridge, MA: MIT Press.

Nolfi, S. (2005). Emergence of communication in embodied agents: Co-adapting communicative and non-communicative behaviors, *Connection Science* 17: 231–48.

Nolfi, S. and Floreano, D. (2000). *Evolutionary Robotics: The Biology, Intelligence, and Technology of Self-Organizing Machines.* Cambridge, MA: MIT Press.

Pfeifer, R. and Scheier, C. (1999). *Understanding Intelligence.* Cambridge, MA: MIT Press.

Port, R. F. and van Gelder, T. (eds.) (1995). *Mind as Motion: Explorations in the Dynamics of Cognition.* Cambridge, MA: MIT Press.

Rosenschein, S. J. and Kaelbling, L. P. (1986). The synthesis of digital machines with provable epistemic properties, in J. Y. Halpern (ed.), *Proceedings of the Conference on Theoretical Aspects of Reasoning about Knowledge* (pp. 83–98). Los Altos, CA: Morgan Kaufmann.

Schöner, G., Dose, M., and Engels, C. (1995). Dynamics of behavior: Theory and applications for autonomous robot architectures. *Robotics and Autonomous Systems* 16: 213–45.

Skarda, C. A. and Freeman, W. J. (1987). How brains make chaos in order to make sense of the world, *Behavioral and Brain Sciences* 10: 161–95.

Smithers, T. (1995). Are autonomous agents information processing systems?, in L. Steels and R. Brooks (eds.), *The Artificial Life Route to Artificial Intelligence* (pp. 123–62). Hillsdale, NJ: Lawrence Erlbaum.

Steels, L. (2003) Evolving grounded communication for robots, *Trends in Cognitive Sciences* 7: 308–12.

Strogatz, S. H. (1994). *Nonlinear Dynamics and Chaos.* Reading, MA: Addison-Wesley.

Suchman, L. A. (1987). *Plans and Situated Actions: The Problem of Human-Machine Communication.* Cambridge University Press.

Thelen, E., Schöner, G., Scheier, C., and Smith, L. B. (2001). The dynamics of embodiment: A field theory of infant preservative reaching. *Behavioral and Brain Sciences* 24: 1–86.

Thelen, E. and Smith, L. B. (1994). *A Dynamic Systems Approach to the Development of Cognition and Action.* Cambridge, MA: MIT Press.

Tuci, E., Quinn, M., and Harvey, I. (2002). An evolutionary ecological approach to the study of learning behavior using a robot-based model, *Adaptive Behavior* 10: 201–21.

Turner, J. S. (2000). *The Extended Organism: The Physiology of Animal-Built Structures.* Cambridge, MA: Harvard University Press.

Turvey, M. T. (1990). Coordination, *American Psychologist* 45: 938–53.

Van Gelder, T. (1995). What might cognition be, if not computation?, *Journal of Philosophy* 91: 345–81.

(1998). The dynamical hypothesis in cognitive science, *Behavioral and Brain Sciences* 21: 615–65.

Van Leeuwen, M. (2005). Questions for the dynamicist: The use of dynamical systems theory in the philosophy of cognition, *Minds and Machines* 15: 271–333.

Varela, F. J., Thompson, E., and Rosch, E. (1991). *The Embodied Mind: Cognitive Science and Human Experience.* Cambridge, MA: MIT Press.

Vera, A. H. and Simon, H. A. (1993). Situated action: A symbolic interpretation, *Cognitive Science* 17: 7–48 (with commentary and responses).

Vickerstaff, R. J. and Di Paolo, E. A. (2005). Evolving neural models of path integration, *Journal of Experimental Biology* 208: 3349–66.

Walter, W. G. (1953). *The Living Brain.* New York: W. W. Norton.

Ward, R. and Ward, R. (2006). Cognitive conflict without explicit conflict monitoring in a dynamical agent, *Neural Networks* 19: 1430–6.

Warren, W. H. (2006). The dynamics of perception and action, *Psychological Review* 113: 358–89.

Wheeler, M. (2005). *Reconstructing the Cognitive World: The Next Step.* Cambridge, MA: MIT Press.

Winograd, T. and Flores, F. (1986). *Understanding Computers and Cognition: A New Foundation for Design.* Norwood, NJ: Ablex Publishing.

Yamauchi, B. and Beer, R. D. (1994). Sequential behavior and learning in evolved dynamical neural networks. *Adaptive Behavior* 2: 219–46.

Part III

Dimensions

7 Learning

David Danks

7.1 Introduction

Learning by artificial intelligence systems – what I will typically call machine learning – has a distinguished history, and the field has experienced something of a renaissance in the past twenty years. Machine learning consists principally of a diverse set of algorithms and techniques that have been applied to problems in a wide range of domains. Any overview of the methods and applications will inevitably be incomplete, at least at the level of specific algorithms and techniques. There are many excellent introductions to the formal and statistical details of machine learning algorithms and techniques available elsewhere (e.g., Bishop 1995; Mitchell 1997; Duda, Hart, and Stork 2000; Hastie, Tibshirani, and Friedman 2001; Koller and Friedman 2009). The present chapter focuses on machine learning as a general way of "thinking about the world," and provides a high-level characterization of the major goals of machine learning. There are a number of philosophical concerns that have been raised about machine learning, but upon closer examination, it is not always clear whether the objections really speak against machine learning specifically. Many seem rather to be directed towards machine learning as a particular instantiation of some more general phenomenon or process. One of the general morals of this chapter is that machine learning is, in many ways, less unusual or peculiar than is sometimes thought.

7.2 Three broad classes of inference

At a very high level, one can distinguish between three different, not necessarily exhaustive, inferential strategies: analogical, domain-specific, and structural. As an example of the generality of this taxonomy, both deductive and inductive logics are types of structural inference. Analogical inference aims to map some situation or problem onto salient historical examples, whether well known or personal; inferences are then made by using the analogical mapping to translate the historical outcomes onto the present problem. The problems and outcomes need not be large or significant: If one has previous experiences with light switches and light bulbs, then one can use analogical inference to make a decision about how to turn on the lights when entering a new room.

If the analogies are suitable, then analogical inference can support inferences for very rare situations or phenomena, or inferences from very limited data. The reliability of analogical inference is, however, highly dependent on the analogical cases and mappings, and there is little known about search for such cases, or development of suitable mappings. With regards to the focus of this chapter, analogical inference is rarely done by machine; usually, we do analogical inference in our minds.

Domain-specific inference uses techniques that are specifically tailored to knowledge about the particular problems, environments, and responses that occur in a domain. By using specialized algorithms and constraints, one can often make quite powerful inferences, even given only limited amounts of data. Domain-specific methods, however, can only be developed and used with substantial prior domain knowledge, which may preclude the widespread use of such methods. Domain-specific machine learning and inference can often be understood as part of the particular domain, rather than as a distinctive and novel inference strategy. Also, since any technique must use some domain-specific information (e.g., the possible values of a variable), it is unclear whether any sharp line can be drawn to delimit exactly the "domain-specific" methods, though there are clearly many inference algorithms that are applicable only for highly specific situations.

Structural inference uses (relatively) domain-general algorithms whose success depends on the internal structure of the data, rather than features of the semantic content of the data. That is, structural inference focuses on the relationships among the variables, objects, or predicates, rather than on any intrinsic properties of them. This type of inference is necessarily domain-general, as such methods are explicitly designed not to use any domain information except "structural" information about the objects of inference (e.g., number of variable values, whether spatial location of objects is relevant, and so on). The advantage of structural inference is obvious: The methods are applicable for any domain in which the appropriate structural features hold and can be discovered from data. These methods are thus not restricted to domains in which we happen to have substantial prior knowledge, nor do we need to have any significant experience with situations of this type. The disadvantages of such inferences are equally obvious: One cannot infer domain-specific mechanisms (since domain-specific information is excluded), and inference from small datasets can be quite difficult.

Structural inference is the basis of many, and arguably most, machine learning frameworks and methods, including many well-known ones such as various forms of regression, neural-network learning algorithms such as back-propagation, and causal learning algorithms using Bayesian networks. In all of these methods, the algorithm works by extracting – and exploiting – structural relationships among the variables without regard to the meaning or domain of the variables. For example, if doing classification using an artificial neural network, one might be provided with a dataset containing measurements of various features of widgets, as well as some target category. The neural-net learning algorithm (e.g., standard backpropagation) then uses only the statistical regularities in the dataset to learn the relevant inter-variable structure, which can then be used to predict the target category (e.g., "functional" vs. "defective") for future widgets. The precise "meaning" of the variables is irrelevant to the learning algorithm. For all of these methods, one need not know much about the underlying domain in order to apply the methods, though domain-specific information (e.g., variable X takes on a value before variable Y) can typically be incorporated in various ways. The domain-generality of machine learning methods partly explains their popularity in relatively novel scientific domains, such as bioinformatics, in which there is substantial uncertainty about what models or methods are appropriate.

There is a natural division among structural inference methods between logical and statistical methods. Logical methods typically aim to model the structure in terms of deductive relationships, perhaps supplemented with various representations of one's lack of precise knowledge about a situation. The methods often use various types of modal logic to help represent and infer uncertain possibilities. The most common use of logical machine learning methods is for inference from prior knowledge, where that prior knowledge encodes structural information about the particular domain. This chapter will focus more closely on statistical methods, which use larger amounts of data to infer structural relationships. Most of these methods use data to determine which variables are informationally relevant for which other ones, and then use the absence of such informational connections to develop simple but accurate models with significant predictive power.

There is an obvious difference between the learning algorithms and the learned model. For example, some particular neural network (with connection weights, etc.) is a learned model; backpropagation is the algorithm by which the model is learned. Machine learning algorithms are a type of structural inference because the *learning* makes no intrinsic reference to the domain under study; in particular, the learning algorithm does not use (significant) semantic information about the variables. This observation leaves open the question of whether the learned *model* does have interesting semantic content. We will return to that question later in this chapter. In the meantime, however, it is important to bear the "learning algorithm vs. learned model" distinction in mind when thinking about these processes.

7.3 A rough taxonomy of machine learning

Suppose one has a dataset D: a collection of datapoints, each of which has measurements of the values of variables V for a particular individual or unit. There might be many complications with the dataset: The variable values might be imputed or inferred; it might not be obvious how to specify the variables or individuals; the datapoints might not be independent (e.g., if one has time series data); there might be unmeasured factors that influence variables in the dataset; and so on. In terms of developing a rough taxonomy of machine learning methods, these subtleties are largely irrelevant. That being said, essentially all machine learning methods assume that the situation is "well posed" in various ways, such as using well-defined variables.

At the coarsest level, machine learning algorithms can be divided into two classes (with a small middle ground) based on whether the algorithm requires the specification of a target variable in the dataset. *Supervised learning* algorithms assume that some variable X is designated as the target for prediction, explanation, or inference, and that the values of X in the dataset constitute the "ground truth" values for learning. That is, supervised learning algorithms use the known values of X to determine what should be learned. The most common type of supervised learning algorithm aims to develop a classification or categorization model: Given information about various individuals and the categories to which they belong, the algorithm produces a learned model that can be used to predict the category membership of new individuals. For example, one might want to predict which widgets being produced in a factory are most likely to fail. If one has data on the performance of many different widgets as well as measurements of other relevant features, then one can use a machine learning algorithm to learn a model that will predict the performance of future widgets. Under the right conditions, classification algorithms can yield models that can make novel, warranted generalizations about the groups based on the inter-feature relationships. Classification algorithms can also be used for recognition or identification by classifying into a "category" with exactly one member. Examples of supervised learning algorithms include learning algorithms for artificial neural networks, decision trees, and support vector machines; the many forms of regression; and most reinforcement learning methods.

Unsupervised learning algorithms do not single out any particular variables as a target or focus, and so aim to provide a general characterization of the full dataset. Probably the most common use of unsupervised learning is in clustering algorithms: separating the various individuals into "natural" groups according to one or another metric. These algorithms will sometimes draw relatively arbitrary lines between individuals, but they can be quite effective at discovering groups when they actually exist. For example, one might measure people's attitudes about various political issues, and then want to determine whether there are natural groups that can be defined by those beliefs. The output of a clustering algorithm can, in certain conditions, subsequently serve as the target variable for a supervised learning algorithm. It is typically quite difficult to validate the output or model from an unsupervised learning algorithm, precisely because one usually has no "ground truth" against which to compare the performance of the model. There is rarely a single correct, true way to cluster various individuals, only better and worse ways. Various methods for probability distribution or density estimation also fall under the heading of unsupervised learning.

The standard view of learned models is that their semantic content is entirely statistical: Connections between variables provide information that can be used for prediction, but no further semantic content – for example, causal structure – is thought to be attributable to these models. In recent years, however, there has been a significant surge of interest in machine learning algorithms that avoid the use of domain-specific assumptions, but produce learned models with rich semantic content. In particular, the learned models can be used to predict the future behavior or features given interventions or manipulations from outside of the system. These machine learning algorithms are typically unsupervised learning methods, although one often wants to learn the causal structure in order to affect or bring about a change in some particular variable. One might wonder how such causal inference is possible, given the completely standard maxim in the sciences and philosophy that "correlation is not causation." Machine learning methods for causal discovery must make assumptions with some causal content, but they typically use only domain-general assumptions about the ways in which causation and correlation are connected. For example, the widely discussed causal Markov assumption (e.g., Hausman and Woodward 1999, 2004; Cartwright 2002) asserts that a variable provides no information about its non-effects, if one already knows the values of the variable's direct causes. This assumption has causal content, but at a very high level of generality.

This type of causal learning is more difficult than purely statistical learning (e.g., clustering, classification, density estimation, function approximation) in which one is simply trying to find informational connections between the variables. Except in highly unusual circumstances, the set of causal relationships among some features will be a strict subset of the set of informational relationships. That is, (almost all) causal relationships are informational relationships, but not all informational relationships are causal. Given this asymmetry in learnability for the different types of models, one might hope that statistical models could suffice for all interesting applications. Purely statistical information, though, is insufficient for prediction when the system changes, whether because of one's actions or policies, or perhaps because the causal structure breaks in various ways. One needs causal information to predict the likely effects of most interventions, policy decisions, or other exogenous changes in the system. We must sometimes tackle the harder learning problem.

Machine learning algorithms must balance three factors: (1) complexity of the learned model, which provides increased accuracy in representing the input dataset; (2) generalizability of the learned model to new data, which enables the use of the model in novel contexts; and (3) computational tractability of learning and using the model, which is a necessary precondition for the algorithms to have practical value. The complexity of the world will sometimes be greater than the complexity of the models that are practical for a particular situation, which suggests that no single model will be sufficient. One might hope that there are "sub-problems" that are not more complex than the available models. If that is the case, then one could plausibly learn more about the world by (1) determining the scope of the sub-problems; (2) learning an appropriate model (or models) for each sub-problem; and then (3) integrating the model outputs in a principled manner. Various "meta-learning" techniques implement this three-step proposal. As an illustration, consider the case of boosting (Schapire 1990; Freund 1995; and subsequent work) for simple binary classification: for example, whether or not a widget is defective. Rather than trying to learn a complete model in one step, a boosting algorithm first learns a simple classification model that works reasonably well, though typically not as well as the user wants or requires. The system then extracts all of the cases for which this simple model makes an *incorrect* prediction, and learns a second classification model just for those cases. The outputs of those two models can be integrated in various ways to get a classifier for all of the cases. That unified classifier will make incorrect predictions for other cases, and so one can learn a third classifier for those misclassified cases, integrate the new classifier into the unified one, and iterate.[1] In this way, boosting builds a unified classifier consisting of a number of "weak" classifiers, each of which focuses on accurate classification of a reduced subset of the data. Hierarchical models such as mixtures of experts (e.g., Jordan and Jacobs 1994) function similarly.

No overview of machine learning would be complete without a discussion of Bayesian learning. A Bayesian learning algorithm requires specification of a (possibly infinite) set of possible hypotheses or models, as well as a probability distribution – the "prior probability distribution" – over those hypotheses. When provided with data, the learning algorithm then uses Bayes' Rule to determine the correct (by the probability calculus) probability distribution over the hypotheses given that data. Bayesian reasoning captures the intuition that beliefs after observing some data should be given by the probability of each possible explanation given that data. Expressed in ordinary language, Bayes' Rule states: The probability of a hypothesis after observing some data $[P(H \mid D)]$ is equal to (1) the prior probability of the hypothesis $[P(H)]$, multiplied by (2) the likelihood of seeing data like that if the hypothesis actually were true $[P(D \mid H)]$, divided by (3) the probability of seeing that data in the first place $[P(D)]$. The idea that Bayesian learning is rational has a long

---

[1] For technically minded readers, boosting techniques rarely focus on *only* the misclassified datapoints at each stage. Rather, the currently misclassified datapoints are simply weighted more heavily for training of the next classifier.

philosophical history. Bayesianism had relatively little practical impact for many years, however, because of a simple fact: Except in toy examples, the computations required for Bayesian learning quickly become too difficult to do analytically or by hand. The development of modern digital computers has made it possible to carry out or approximate Bayesian learning for more realistic situations, and so Bayesianism has re-emerged as a dominant theme in learning. Many machine learning algorithms can be viewed as implementing or approximating Bayesian learning under various assumptions or constraints on the hypothesis space, prior probability distribution, likelihood functions, and so on.

7.4 Scope and limits of machine learning

As with human learning, the value of machine learning is less in the output, and more in the way that the output can be used for future tasks: prediction, planning, classification, recognition, and so on. As a community, we know how to do quite a lot with machine learning. Machine learning is a large part of present-day computer science, and there are many different algorithms and techniques that are suitable for a wide range of conditions. For clustering, classification, and causal learning, there are of course algorithms for the simple situations: datasets containing all relevant variables, clean measurements, simple relationships (e.g., linear), and no missing datapoints. But there are also algorithms that are robust to variations along all of these dimensions: noisy data, unmeasured variables, complex relationships, missing data, sample selection bias, and so on. There are numerous success stories for each of these algorithms in terms of real-world applications. There are also algorithms for handling time series data, and in particular, for conducting systems monitoring and fault detection. There are quite powerful text and image classification algorithms that are highly specialized for these purposes (though they typically still fall short of human performance in accuracy). Information fusion – the integration of information from multiple distinct sources – has emerged more recently as a central component of real-world machine learning.

At the same time, there are known theoretical limits to machine learning, many of which mirror the limits on human learning. For example, if the data are too noisy – if they are essentially random – then learning will be nearly impossible. Machine learning algorithms employ structural inference, and so if there are no patterns in the data, then there is nothing that can be inferred. Learning also requires some variation in the world, either between individuals, or between times, or between places. Machine learning algorithms cannot learn anything about a constant-valued feature, since there is nothing to learn: The constant feature is always the same. And although some situations are clearly easier for learning than others, learning is almost always difficult in the worst case. More precisely, essentially all interesting machine learning problems are sufficiently hard that they require (we think) an algorithm with exponentially many computational steps in the worst case.

A more interesting constraint on machine learning is the inability, even under seemingly easy conditions, to infer features of the causal or informational structure of an individual from group-level measurements. Suppose that we want to learn something about the individual (e.g., how does education influence subsequent income?), but we only measure features at the group level (e.g., the averages in various groups of education, income, and other relevant variables). Further suppose that every individual has exactly the same type of underlying relationships (though not necessarily the same values), and the group-level features are simple, deterministic functions of the individual-level features (e.g., average or total value). Even under these strong simplifying assumptions, there are many interesting cases for which the informational relationships between the group-level features are *not* the same as the relationships among the corresponding individual-level features (Chu et al. 2003). That is, the learned model for the group-level features is not necessarily the same as the model for the individual, even when every individual has the same model. This possibility raises a serious methodological challenge to the use of machine learning for domains in which individuals are the primary focus, but data collection principally occurs for groups (e.g., parts of economics, other social sciences, and bioinformatics).

7.5   Philosophical challenges to machine learning

Machine learning is a major area of research in computer science and statistics, and so many, and perhaps almost all, of the most prominent problems in machine learning are computational and algorithmic (e.g., "what can one learn under certain conditions?" or "can this algorithm run faster?"), rather than necessarily philosophical. Even notions from machine learning that might appear philosophical often turn out to be less philosophical than one might have thought. As just one example, consider the so-called "no-free-lunch" theorems (e.g., Wolpert 1996; Wolpert and Macready 1997), which are sometimes colloquially stated as: "Algorithms are successful only when they are 'tuned' to their domain; there are no universal learning algorithms." This phrasing suggests various philosophical arguments, but all trade on a misunderstanding of the actual theorems. For example, one might be tempted to argue that machine learning is pointless, since one might think that the no-free-lunch theorems imply that proper algorithm choice requires that one already know the underlying truth, which would obviate the need for any learning. This suggested argument fails to understand the sense in which no algorithm has an advantage over others. The no-free-lunch theorems are, in many ways, just a precise statement of the ancient skeptical observation that any future is consistent with the past. If any future is possible given the past observations, then no learning algorithm has any advantage over others. But one can now straightforwardly see that almost any restriction on the possibility space suffices to defeat the no-free-lunch theorems; for example, a single weak regularity assumption can suffice to define a "domain," and so pick out a privileged class of superior algorithms. One certainly need not a priori know the actual, underlying truth.

Of course, as with many bad arguments, there is a kernel of truth inside this suggested objection. Any interesting machine learning method makes assumptions about the nature of the world, and algorithms can readily fail if those assumptions turn out to be false. An important part of machine learning is to investigate whether the assumptions of one's algorithm actually hold, at least approximately (e.g., by checking to see whether the data distribution is approximately Gaussian). Such tests are often missing from both the practice and rhetoric of machine learning. If the relevant assumptions are false, then one should turn to other methods that do not make those assumptions, even though those other methods will typically be correspondingly weaker. It is incorrect to think about machine learning as a "black box" that simply takes data as input and returns the truth. The practice of machine learning is instead much closer to the use of statistics in science – as a tool to investigate more precisely the structure of one's data. The appropriate tool (i.e., machine learning algorithm) should be chosen for a particular task, and tools can be used with varying degrees of skill (e.g., by interpreting the output of the algorithm in various ways). One might hope for a sophisticated system that could take the input, determine the best algorithm for that type of data, and then apply the algorithm, but such a meta-learner currently remains largely a hope.

One of the least-discussed "assumptions" of machine learning algorithms is that they all require one to provide well-specified variables with precise, possibly infinite, sets of values. The variables need not be numeric – they can range over various categories, such as "large" and "small" – but they must be clearly stated: In some sense, there must be some, possibly unknown, fact about the "true" value of each variable for each datapoint. Machine learning relies on structural inference, and so it must be possible to find patterns and structure within the data. It is not clear what it even means to talk about "structure" among variables that are not well defined. This concern is not a serious challenge in practice, as one is essentially always concerned with datasets that result from measurement processes that specify the variables; metaphysical realists of various types will also typically be untroubled by this concern. If, however, one questions whether there is any stable underlying structure to be measured, then machine learning will seem to be a futile enterprise.

All of the observations in this section raise a natural question: If machine learning is roughly analogous to statistics, then in what sense is it "learning"? A more contentious framing would be: Is the machine doing any learning, or is it really the human who uses the algorithm who learns? There are two different aspects to the "is it learning?" question: The first is a general philosophical concern, and the second points toward gaps in our understanding of cognition. The first concern was most famously presented by Searle (1980) using his Chinese Room, but has arisen in many different forms (e.g., Harnad 1994). The argument starts with the general claim that computation involves only symbol manipulation while cognition involves something more. The "something more" of cognition differs between authors, but is often some semantic notion, such as a particular property of our concepts or a "grounding" for them. Symbol manipulation is then characterized as a purely syntactic notion: According to this argument, one can manipulate symbols correctly solely by examining features of the physical representation and without any understanding of the semantics or meaning of the symbol. The argument then concludes that computation cannot be cognition, as the former lacks any semantic content or grounding in the world while the latter necessarily has it.

This argument is offered as a general one against the idea of "cognition as computation," and machine learning is clearly a relevant type of computation. The successes of machine learning result from structural inference; these methods use patterns or statistical regularities in the data, and are (relatively speaking) indifferent to the semantics of the input variables. A more specific version of the previous argument would conclude that machine "learning" might be useful, but it cannot be *true* learning, at least in so far as true learning requires cognition. In other words, there might be some actual learning, but the human being who processes the machine "learning" output is the one who does it. The machine simply makes certain patterns in the data salient, though that might be a computationally nontrivial task. This is a serious objection to at least the title "machine learning" for these algorithms, since this argument calls into question the use of all cognitive terms to refer to machine operations. However, this argument does not seem to provide any specific objection to machine learning itself, but rather it applies to machine learning *qua* machine operation. That is, one's particular response to (or acceptance of) this argument – for example, appeal to some symbol-grounding process, special causal powers of the brain, or rejection of some premise – will arise from more general philosophical grounds, and not from some deeper reflection on the nature of machine learning in isolation. The overall objection is clearly relevant to machine learning, but it seems just as clear that any solution to it must take into consideration many issues that lie outside of the scope of machine learning.

There is a more specific form of the "is this learning?" objection that does speak directly to machine learning. Insight and creativity are often held up as a central feature of human learning, if not *the* central feature. Our learning seems to depend at times on crucial intuitive leaps that we do not seem to be able to explain or predict. Introspectively, there seems to be something "non-algorithmic" about creative insight. Machine learning algorithms seem to offer no such capacity for insight, as they are "just" complex sequences of simple operations. The practice of machine learning inevitably involves some human element to specify and control the algorithm, test various assumptions, and interpret the algorithm output. These observations suggest the conclusion that machine learning is (again) not true learning at all, but rather fast, useful detection of various patterns in data. On this account, the human who controls and validates the algorithms does the "real" learning. This objection is notably different from the previous one: No claims are made here about the impossibility of machine cognition, but only about the failure of *current* machine learning algorithms to rise to the level of true learning. This objection is entirely consistent with the possibility that more sophisticated and reflective algorithms, supplemented with appropriate background knowledge, could perform real learning. The argument depends instead on the claim that none of the currently available algorithms meet that standard for true learning.

The previous paragraph used the phrases "human learning" and "true learning" without exposition; the reader was simply assumed to understand what was intended by them. One might wonder, however, if our understanding of the nature of human learning is sufficiently clear to provide a standard of "true learning" that machine learning fails to satisfy. There is no well-established model for how people actually do learn, and so it is not clear what criteria would need to be met for a machine algorithm to be considered "learning." There is no question that – for certain situations – human learning is far superior to machine learning. Our ability to assemble disparate pieces of background knowledge and information, whether by analogy, accident, or some other process, is unmatched in machine learning (despite many attempts to build systems for commonsense reasoning). That observation, however, is not sufficient to conclude that we use some wholly different process in our learning; one can only conclude that there is *something* different about our learning. A plausible alternative explanation is that we have a body of information, biases, and experiences that is quite simply unmatched by contemporary machine learning systems. A database with 10,000 datapoints is considered large in machine learning; a child who has only one experience per waking hour (say, sixteen per day) exceeds that number in less than two years. If she has one experience per waking minute, then she surpasses the database in around eleven days. The products of human learning are superior (in some sense) to the products of machine learning, but the processes need not be fundamentally different in kind, given that there are enormous differences in background knowledge, accuracy of biases, temporal and semantic information, and so on.

Perhaps more importantly, there are substantial gaps in our understanding of the processes underlying human learning. We do not know enough about those processes to determine at this point their similarity – or dissimilarity – to the algorithms proposed in machine learning. One might respond that introspection on our own learning provides all of the evidence that is required. Such a response neglects the large psychological literature demonstrating the unreliability of introspection in revealing the details underlying fundamental cognitive processes (Nisbett and Wilson 1977; Ross and Nisbett 1991). It may well be the case that there is something qualitatively different about human learning such that machine "learning" algorithms do not deserve that name. At the current time, however, such claims are grounded largely in ignorance, rather than positive evidence of a difference.

The preceding discussions have made a potentially problematic assumption: There is value in worrying about the particular label that is attached to machine learning algorithms. The fundamental properties of those algorithms – their reliability, convergence, computational complexity, and so on – are real features regardless of the name one uses. Moreover, the algorithms are already referred to by many different names, such as "data mining," "applied statistics," "automated search," and so on. One might thus be willing to give up the label of "machine learning," since it does not obviously make a difference to the underlying science. One ought not give up on the label of "machine learning" so easily, though, as the name points toward a number of interesting issues about the nature of cognition and learning, and the relevance of machine methods for the study of human cognition. Machine learning methods are regularly used today to provide frameworks and inspiration for cognitive models, sometimes under the heading of "computational cognitive science." The label is also important because it establishes biases and expectations in those who hear the label. Sometimes those expectations are unreasonable, but they prompt individuals – both proponents and skeptics – to ask important questions about the nature and performance of these algorithms.

One final philosophical issue concerns the extent to which one can be a realist about the contents or intermediate processes of a learned model. That is, when can the internal structure or richer semantic content of a learned model be understood to correspond – perhaps only with some probability – to features of the world? This question is particularly pressing for research in causal learning that seeks to infer causal structure in the world from sets of passive observations. Causal inference algorithms putatively learn the set of causal structures that could have produced some given dataset, or discover the most probable such structure (Spirtes, Glymour, and Scheines 1993; Pearl 2000; Chickering 2002). There are many instances in which these algorithms have been applied to actual datasets, and the learned models have subsequently been successfully attributed to the world (e.g., the case studies in Glymour and Cooper 1999). These algorithms – like all inference methods – are only reliable under particular assumptions about the nature of the world. Moreover, the semantic content of the learned model – the fact that we can call it a *causal* model – derives from these assumptions, which provide a characterization of one (the?) way for causal structures to be "projected" into observed or experimental data. The analogy here is with assumptions such as the ray theory of light: Those assumptions explain how three-dimensional objects are projected onto a two-dimensional plane (e.g., a retina), and are necessary for any visual system to make inferences about object structure from the limited, two-dimensional input. Just as our visual system experiences optical illusions when various assumptions fail to hold (e.g., a straight stick appearing bent when placed into water), causal inference algorithms are subject to "causal inference illusions" when the assumptions are violated in particular ways.

These causal inference algorithms, and machine learning algorithms more generally, do not seem at this point to be any different from standard instances of inductive inference: No inductive inference can have any guarantees of reliability without various assumptions about the world. If those assumptions are satisfied, then the algorithms work; if they are violated, then one has no particular warrant to believe the internal structure of the algorithm outputs. The assumptions of causal inference algorithms are sometimes claimed to be different, however, because it seems that we can only test whether the assumptions are actually satisfied by having *the very same causal knowledge that we are trying to learn* (Cartwright 1999, 2001). This argument is not focused on the bare possibility that the assumptions could be false (though that additional claim is also made in, e.g., Cartwright 2001), since that is a risk that any inductive inference must carry. This concern is also not about the practical testability of the algorithms' assumptions; inductive inference – whether human or machine – inevitably involves making assumptions that might not be practically testable at the particular moment. One might need, for example, orders of magnitude more data than one currently has. If the assumptions are testable in principle, though, then one could (in some sense) determine whether the algorithms are reliable for a situation like this one, and so have some warrant to regard the learned model in a realistic manner.

The fundamental worry here is that the assumptions are not even testable in principle, since it seems that the only way to know which statistical tests are relevant is to know the underlying causal structure, but that is exactly what the causal inference algorithm is supposed to find. These algorithms might (the argument continues) occasionally find approximations to the true causal structure, but only by random chance. The assumptions might be true in any particular situation, but one has no way to know that, and so no warrant to treat the algorithm outputs as anything other than representations of the observed or experimental data. The algorithms might produce a useful "shorthand" version of the data that one could use in various ways, but one is not (on this argument) learning anything substantive about the underlying structure of the world. Although principally directed at causal inference algorithms, this potential problem is not limited to them. Many clustering algorithms, for example, are reliable only if one can make certain assumptions about the underlying groups. One must thus be able to examine the groups to determine whether they have those properties, but that would require knowing the groups ahead of time, which would obviate the very need to use the clustering algorithm. Machine learning methods clearly have substantially less value if they must always be interpreted in an instrumentalist manner. Instrumentalist theories – those that make predictions about the behavior of a system without making any commitments to the underlying structure or ontology of the theory – are useful in a number of ways, but one often desires something more than mere prediction. Most notably, one must have information about the underlying mechanisms in order to make accurate predictions about what will happen when the system breaks or changes in various ways; instrumentalist theories provide no such information.

There are three natural responses to this objection. First, careful examination of the assumptions often reveals that the knowledge required to test them is weaker than is suggested by the surface framing of the assumption. In the particular case of causal inference algorithms, one must have certain types of causal knowledge in order to test the assumptions, but the necessary knowledge is not the same as knowledge of the causal structure being sought. For example, one might need to know that a particular population is "causally homogeneous" (i.e., all individuals have the same causal relations, though not necessarily the same variable values). This knowledge requires causal knowledge, but not necessarily about the causes or effects of that particular variable. The second, related, response notes that the argument frames the testability of assumptions as all-or-nothing: One knows either exactly what is required to test an assumption (though one might not actually test it), or else nothing at all. A more realistic characterization of the situation is that one often knows some but not all of the tests of an assumption, as well as a number of possible avenues for future tests. One might also have reason to believe that one has tested an assumption imperfectly. If one has this type of limited knowledge, then one can have limited confirmation of an assumption, while recognizing that the algorithm output must therefore be interpreted or accepted in a limited manner. One can object to many machine learning methods on the grounds that they require some strong, not completely established, property, but one should not reject the output of those methods simply because one is somewhat uncertain in the short run about whether the precise property holds.

The third and most general response to this family of objections is to note that the argument-schema actually speaks against most inductive methods, and not just causal inference; it objects to machine *learning*, not *machine* learning. Consider a particular inductive conclusion: "All electrons have negative charge." Any method that conjectures this conclusion must make some assumptions about the world, such as that electrons form a coherent, stable set with respect to having some electric charge. Such an assumption can only be tested by actually determining the electric charges of all electrons, but such tests would eliminate the need to make any inference to the inductive conclusion. Notice that there was no mention of machine methods in this example, nor was there any specification beyond "inductive method." The problem of knowing the confirmation conditions for the assumption of a method is a general one that speaks against almost all inductive inference methods, and not machine learning methods specifically. One can rarely know a priori all of the confirmation or testing conditions for assumptions that are required for a particular inference method to provide reliable information about internal or universal structure.

7.6 Conclusion

Machine learning methods are often regarded with a certain degree of suspicion. They are frequently presented as "black boxes" that take data and, without any guidance, somehow learn part of the true structure of the world. These algorithms are, in practice, much less mysterious: The label of "automated statistics" is frequently an apt descriptor. Machine learning methods discover and exploit structural relations among the data, and this structural inference underlies both the strengths and weaknesses of machine learning algorithms. These methods can be applied in a relatively domain-general manner, since the specific meaning of the variables is irrelevant to the functioning of the algorithm. Because of this generality, however, they cannot yield domain-specific information, such as mechanisms underlying informational relationships. Machine learning is one of the most rapidly growing areas of computer science, and many of the most prominent challenges revolve around the extension of algorithms to novel data-types, novel models, or weaker assumptions. There are philosophical concerns about machine learning, but most of those concerns center on either the "machine" or the "learning" part. On the one side, machine learning is an instance of complex machine computation, and so natural questions arise about whether any machine operations can be correctly described using cognitive terms. On the other side, machine learning algorithms perform complex, but clearly specified sequences of computations, and so questions arise about whether the methods qualify as "learning," or whether the assumptions necessary for the inductive inference can be suitably tested. In sum, machine learning methods have opened novel avenues for learning about the structure and behavior of our world. These algorithms must of course be used with appropriate awareness and testing of the underlying assumptions. When used properly, however, machine learning can exploit the structure within data to yield valuable knowledge about structure and relations in the world.

Further reading

No single machine learning text includes every standard machine learning algorithm. The following books are all excellent introductions that cover a range of the machine learning literature:

Bishop, C. M. (1995). *Neural Networks for Pattern Recognition*. Oxford University Press.

Duda, R. O., Hart, P. E., and Stork, D. G. (2000). *Pattern Classification* (2nd edn.). New York: John Wiley and Sons.

Hastie, T., Tibshirani, R., and Friedman, J. (2001). *The Elements of Statistical Learning*. New York: Springer.

Mitchell, T. M. (1997). *Machine Learning*. New York: McGraw-Hill.

For the more specific case of causal reasoning methods, as well as their applicability to traditional philosophical problems such as the nature of counterfactuals, a good introduction is:

Pearl, J. (2000). *Causality: Models, Reasoning, and Inference*. Cambridge University Press.

References

Bishop, C. M. (1995). *Neural Networks for Pattern Recognition*. Oxford University Press.

Cartwright, N. (1999). *The Dappled World: A Study of the Boundaries of Science*. Cambridge University Press.

(2001). What is wrong with Bayes nets?, *The Monist* 84: 242–64.

(2002). Against modularity, the causal Markov condition, and any link between the two: Comments on Hausman and Woodward, *British Journal for the Philosophy of Science* 53: 411–53.

Chickering, D. M. (2002). Optimal structure identification with greedy search, *Journal of Machine Learning Research* 3: 507–54.

Chu, T., Glymour, C., Scheines, R., and Spirtes, P. (2003). A statistical problem for inference to regulatory structure from associations of gene expression measurements with microarrays, *Bioinformatics* 19: 1147–52.

Duda, R. O., Hart, P. E., and Stork, D. G. (2000). *Pattern Classification* (2nd edn.). New York: John Wiley and Sons.

Freund, Y. (1995). Boosting a weak learning algorithm by majority, *Information and Computation* 121: 256–85.

Glymour, C. and Cooper, G. F. (1999). *Computation, Causation, and Discovery*. Cambridge, MA: AAAI Press and MIT Press.

Harnad, S. (1994). Computation is just interpretable symbol manipulation; cognition isn't, *Minds and Machines* 4: 379–90.

Hastie, T., Tibshirani, R., and Friedman, J. (2001). *The Elements of Statistical Learning*. New York: Springer.

Hausman, D. M. and Woodward, J. (1999). Independence, invariance, and the causal Markov condition, *British Journal for the Philosophy of Science* 50: 521–83.

(2004). Manipulation and the causal Markov condition, *Philosophy of Science* 71: 846–56.

Jordan, M. I. and Jacobs, R. A. (1994). Hierarchical mixtures of experts and the EM algorithm, *Neural Computation* 6: 181–214.

Koller, D. and Friedman, N. (2009). *Probabilistic Graphical Models: Principles and Techniques*. Cambridge, MA: MIT Press.

Mitchell, T. M. (1997). *Machine Learning*. New York: McGraw-Hill.

Nisbett, R. E. and Wilson, T. D. (1977). Telling more than we can know: Verbal reports on mental processes, *Psychological Review* 84: 231–59.

Pearl, J. (2000). *Causality: Models, Reasoning, and Inference*. Cambridge University Press.

Ross, L. and Nisbett, R. E. (1991). *The Person and the Situation: Perspectives of Social Psychology*. New York: McGraw-Hill.

Schapire, R. E. (1990). The strength of weak learnability, *Machine Learning* 5: 197–227.

Searle, J. (1980). Minds, brains, and programs, *Behavioral and Brain Sciences* 3: 417–24.

Spirtes, P., Glymour, C., and Scheines, R. (1993). *Causation, Prediction, and Search*. Berlin: Springer. 2nd edn. (2000). Cambridge, MA: MIT Press.

Wolpert, D. H. (1996). The lack of a priori distinctions between learning algorithms, *Neural Computation* 8: 1341–90.

Wolpert, D. H. and Macready, W. G. (1997). No Free Lunch theorems for optimization, *IEEE Transactions on Evolutionary Computation* 1: 67–82.

8 Perception and computer vision

Markus Vincze, Sven Wachsmuth, and Gerhard Sagerer

The wish to build artificial and intelligent systems leads to the expectation that they will operate in our typical environments. Hence, the expectations on their perceptual capabilities are high. Perception refers to the process of becoming aware of the elements of the environment through physical sensation, which can include sensory input from the eyes, ears, nose, tongue, or skin. In this chapter we focus on visual perception, which is the dominant sense in humans and has been used from the first days of building artificial machines. Two early examples are Shakey, a mobile robot with range finder and camera to enable it to reason about its actions in a room with a few objects (Nilsson 1969), and FREDDY, a fixed robot with a binocular vision system controlling a two-finger hand (e.g., Barrow and Salter 1969).

The goal of computer vision is to understand the scene or features in images of the real world (Ballard and Brown 1982; Forsyth and Ponce 2011). Important means to achieve this goal are the techniques of image processing and pattern recognition (Duda and Hart 1973; Gonzales and Woods 2002). The analysis of images is complicated by the fact that one and the same object may present many different appearances to the camera depending on the illumination cast onto the object, the angle from which it is viewed, the shadows it casts, the specific camera used, whether object parts are occluded, and so forth. Nevertheless, today computer vision is sufficiently well advanced to detect specific objects and object categories in a variety of conditions, to enable an autonomous vehicle to drive at moderate speeds on open roads, to steer a mobile robot through a suite of offices, and to observe and to understand human activities.

The objective of this chapter is to highlight the state of the art in computer vision methods that have been found to operate well and that led to the development of capabilities mentioned above. After a short discussion of more general issues, we summarize work structured into four key topics: object recognition and categorization, tracking and visual servoing, understanding human behavior, and contextual scene understanding. We conclude with a critical assessment of what computer vision has achieved and what challenges remain.

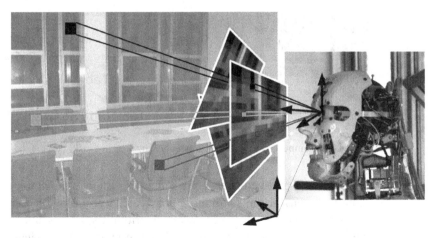

Figure 8.1 An image is given by a 2D pixel array where each pixel measures the amount of light traveling along a ray. The plenoptic function would specify this for each possible viewing point and viewing angle.

8.1 Computer vision paradigms and principles

Computer vision is a heterogeneous field that embraces a large spectrum of methods as well as scientific perspectives. This starts with the physical understanding of how an image is formed or what can principally be seen. Before light is collected in a dense two-dimensional array on a sensor it gets refracted, reflected, scattered, or absorbed with regard to a scene. An image is formed by measuring the intensity of the light rays through each element of the array – called a pixel (Figure 8.1). If one knew the illumination for each possible ray of light in the scene, each possible image by a camera could be pre-computed before measuring it. This mapping between a viewpoint and its illumination is formally described by what is called the *plenoptic function*. Computer graphics aims to approximate this function by rendering a known scene with given light sources. As a first perspective, computer vision targets at computing the inverse function of computer graphics, that is, reconstructing the viewpoint and the underlying scene from a given image, image pair, or sequence of images. Here computer vision is understood as a measurement problem that is extensively treated by photogrammetry, photometric calibration, as well as reconstruction and registration techniques.

A second perspective on computer vision is to mimic biological vision in order to get a deeper understanding of the processes, representations, and architectures involved. Here, it is becoming more and more obvious that the fundamental questions and open problems in computer vision are at the cutting edge of cognition research. They cannot be solved in isolation but concern the fundamental basis of cognition itself.

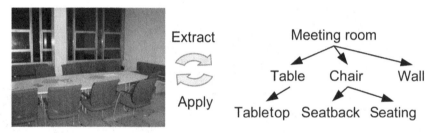

Figure 8.2 Computer vision as a knowledge-engineering task.

A third perspective understands computer vision as an engineering discipline that aims at the solution of practical vision tasks. On the one hand, this perspective is requesting efficient algorithmic solutions, but, on the other hand, it asks the further question of *how to build* computer vision systems. The state of the art in this area is mainly dominated by heuristics and knowledge from experience. Systematic methodological approaches are rare, mostly application-specific, and currently missing a deep understanding of the vision problem as such.

Thus, all three perspectives cannot be separated and deeply influence each other, which – together with an immense technical progress – has made computer vision a highly dynamic field over the last fifty years.

In order to solve specific computer vision tasks, different design decisions need to be made. Some of these are pointed out in the following.

What kind of knowledge is needed? In order to understand the content of an image, relevant parts of it need to be linked to semantically meaningful concepts. For the scene of a meeting room (Figure 8.2) the knowledge base might include that it consists of a large table and a couple of chairs positioned around it, that the table has a top, and so on. The knowledge base decomposes the complex scene of a meeting room into simpler elements, such as a tabletop, that correspond to a planar surface or to a homogeneous region that can be directly extracted from an image. Therefore, an algorithm might start with searching the image for homogeneous regions, which is a low-level concept with regard to the signal. Then, these are successively combined (guided by the knowledge base) to form higher-level concepts. This approach is typically termed "bottom-up." Another algorithm might start with the concept of a table and look specifically for a configuration of parts (predicted by the knowledge base) that fulfill the requirements of the concept. These parts in turn might activate a tabletop detector that is applied to the image. This approach is typically termed "top-down." Both approaches to the knowledge base helped drive a considerable amount of computer vision research in the 1970s and 1980s (Ballard and Brown 1982).

How to represent scene geometry? Scene geometry is an important intermediate representation in the interpretation process of an image. It can be

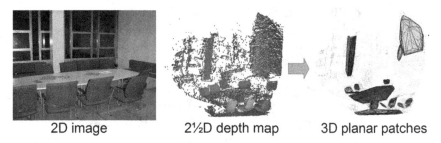

2D image   2½D depth map   3D planar patches

Figure 8.3 3D scene geometry. The image in the middle is showing the reconstructed depth with chair backs clearly visible; the right image shows 3D points that have been grouped to planar patches in a mesh representation.

Figure 8.4 2D scene geometry. The left image shows a region segmentation based on a color clustering (shown with homogeneous gray values); in the middle a Difference of Gaussian (DoG) filter has been applied to the original image; the right image shows a contour segmentation based on the DoG image.

dealt with either in 2D or 3D. In Figure 8.3, a scene is depicted as a regular 2D image (left) and a depth image (middle). The latter can be computed from pairs of stereo images or directly be measured by, for example, Time-of-Flight sensors, which measure the distance at each pixel by modulating and receiving an infra-red light beam. Because the representation in pixel coordinates is still view-dependent, it is also called *2½D*. In a next step, 3D geometric primitives are fitted into the scene with each fit defining a geometric transformation. Because now the relative 3D position and 3D orientation between these primitives is known, a view-independent and object-centered representation is reached. An approach of this kind was originally suggested by David Marr (1982), who also looked at the concepts of human vision known at his time (Marr 1982). However in many cases, the extraction of 3D geometry is too fragile. Real 3D object shapes are often complex and non-rigid, and fitting procedures frequently end in local minima and erroneous object position and orientation ("pose"). As a consequence, more stable geometric representations could also be extracted from 2D images. In this case, images are analyzed with regard to spatial discontinuities in the gray-level or color-surface. Representations either focus on homogeneous image patches (regions) or on edges (border lines) (Figure 8.4). Both provide a basis for further interpretation

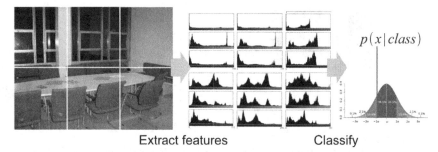

Extract features   Classify

Figure 8.5 Pattern classification. A decision function for a specific class (e.g. meeting room) could be based on probability theory. Here a conditional distribution is estimated using a Gaussian model. The feature vector x is defined using color histograms.

processes. The extraction of such geometric primitives is a problem of digital image processing (Gonzales and Woods 2002).

What are appropriate features? In order to match a geometric or image representation to a semantic concept, such as "table," "chair," or "meeting room," one needs to specify a decision function that decides for or against a membership of a class. This is a *classification problem* that is intensively dealt with in the area of pattern recognition (Duda and Hart 1973). A pattern is represented by a feature vector defining a point in a high-dimensional space. Given that the classes of some points in this space are known (e.g., a set of training images annotated by hand), a decision function can be learnt that partitions the space into these classes. In Figure 8.5 a simple example is given. The image is divided into six parts and for each sub-image a color histogram is computed. The concatenated histograms provide a feature vector that can be used, for example, to classify specific meeting rooms.

The question of *what are good features* is a long-standing topic of discussion. Over the years, there have been a couple of inventions that have had a deep impact on the field. In the 1990s, Swain and Ballard proposed the use of local feature statistics (such as color histograms), Turk and Pentland applied a technique based on Eigenvectors to image sets of human faces (then called Eigenfaces). Later, in the 2000s, Viola and Jones revolutionized face detection by inventing an automatic feature selection process based on a huge number of very simple features related to Haar-wavelets (features based on the binary on/off selection of adjacent image parts). Another breakthrough was the Scale Invariant Feature Transform (SIFT) by David Lowe, that pushed object recognition to a new level. Here, ideas of local gradient statistics are combined with an extremely stable detection of fixed points on an object – so-called *interest points*.

How to control the acquisition process? Biological vision is not a passive interpretation process, nor should it be for autonomous artificial systems. The

(a)

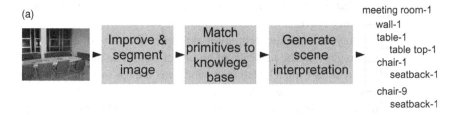

(b)

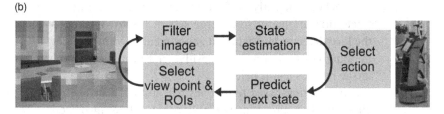

Figure 8.6 Two different perspectives on computer vision. (a) Image understanding: extraction of explicit meaningful descriptions. (b) Active vision: control of the image acquisition and interpretation process (e.g. by moving the camera or selecting a Region Of Interest [ROI] in the image) with regard to a task.

movement of an agent in the real world basically determines the perception problem it has to solve. Vision is understood as an active process that includes the control of the sensor and is tightly coupled to the successful accomplishment of a decision or action (Bajcsy 1988). This has certain consequences for the design of computer vision systems, which had already been noted in the early 1990s (Crowley and Christensen 1995). First, instead of modeling an isolated image-interpretation process, the system must be *always running* and must control its own behavior using an image stream. Second, the overall goal of visual processing is not image understanding. Instead, the vision system must work as a *filter* that extracts information relevant for its task. Third, the system must respond within a fixed time delay in order to be useful for its current task, such as navigation and obstacle avoidance in a robot. Fourth, instead of processing the complete image, the system must focus on a *region of interest* (ROI) in order to meet the performance goals. The different perspectives are shown in Figure 8.6. The first aims at a complete interpretation of the image, the second extracts relevant information for action selection and state prediction.

8.2   Object recognition and categorization

Object recognition can be seen as the challenge to determine the "where" and "what" of objects in a scene. Many different techniques have been proposed, and all have their own pros and cons. Given an application scenario, one has to carefully select an appropriate object recognition technique that fulfills the anticipated set of constraints. Techniques also differ in the precise problem that they solve.

Many recognition techniques are *object detectors* that post a yes/no question regarding the presence of an object class. The image is typically scanned by a template model; that is, a window is moved over the image and for each position a so-called filter response is computed by matching the template to the sub-image defined by the window. Each different object parametrization (object scale, rotation, etc.) needs a separate scan. More sophisticated approaches efficiently perform multiple passes on different scales and apply filters that are learnt from large sets of labeled images. A good example is the face detector by Viola and Jones mentioned in the previous section. Here the filter consists of a set of positive and negative integrals over rectangular image regions learnt before.

Segmentation-based techniques first extract a geometric description of an object by grouping together pixels that define an object's extension in an image. This is a typical bottom-up process as discussed previously. In a second step, these techniques compute an *invariant* feature set. The invariance property means that the features keep the same or similar values under different transformations of the image, such as scaling, rotating, or changing the lighting. Then the features are used for recognizing an object class or extracting a set of generic primitives from which the objects are constructed. Modern techniques interleave or combine both steps in order to deal with problems of over-segmentation (in which parts are split into tiny pieces) and under-segmentation (in which parts are grouped together with background areas).

Alignment methods use "parametric" object models that are fitted to the image data (Huttenlocher and Ullman 1990). The algorithm needs to search for parameters such as scaling, rotation, or translation that optimally fit the model to corresponding image features. An approximate solution can also be found by an inverse process, that is, image features (e.g., corners, contours, or other characteristic image points) vote for parameter solutions that are compatible with the feature detected (the process involves using a voting scheme or algorithm, which derives a single output from multiple data sources). In this case the parameter space is coarsely discretized. This technique is frequently referred to as the *generalized Hough transform* (Ballard 1981), and a variant has been applied in the object recognizer by David Lowe mentioned in the last section (Lowe 2004).

All three approaches provide different information about objects in images and assume that different kinds of pre-knowledge are available.

8.2.1   2D modeling

Most objects in the real world are inherently 3D. Nevertheless, many object-recognition techniques stick to 2D representations with significant success.

There are several reasons for this. (1) *Easy accessibility:* We get 2D image information nearly for free using standard camera equipment. (2) *Fast computation:* Features can directly be calculated from image pixel data and do not involve a search for complex geometric primitives. (3) *Simple acquisition of detection models:* Models that are used for automatic object detection are typically learned from example images. (4) *Robustness to noise:* Features are directly computed on pixel values. This is in contrast to the extraction of more abstract primitives (regions, contours, 3D shape primitives) that typically involves segmentation issues and, therefore, is more error prone with regard to clutter and noise. (5) Furthermore, many interesting objects have quite characteristic 2D views – for example, cover pages, traffic signs, side views of motor bikes or cars, front views of faces.

The price to pay for ignoring the 3D characteristics of objects is typically over- or under-constrained models because there are a number of perspective variations that cannot be systematically dealt with. A typical case of under-constrained approaches are *bag-of-feature* models. Like the histogram models mentioned in Section 8.1, these compute feature statistics over an image region or complete image. Thus, the location of features is completely lost, and object rotation and exact position cannot be distinguished. Thus, for example, if the eyes, nose, and mouth of a face were upside down or completely intermixed, the recognizer would still wrongly detect a face. Over-constrained models, on the other hand, need multiple representations in order to deal with different part configurations or rotations of objects. (Good examples are the template-based methods mentioned before.) Hence if, for example, a face is rotated by 90 degrees, the recognizer would never detect it. As an additional price to pay, we need to cope with a more challenging segmentation problem – that is, the problem of extracting an object from its background. Typically, the background is further away, so that 3D information provides a much stronger hint than luminance values of 2D images.

The dominant class of 2D object recognition techniques are *appearance-based* approaches. Instead of using a view-invariant object-centered representation, these represent different aspects of an object. Compact representations are provided by aspect-graphs (Koenderink 1987) that relate different 2D appearances to each other in an efficient data structure. Secondly, appearance-based approaches drop an intermediate geometric representation level by computing features directly from pixel values. This has certain consequences for the kind of object classes that can be distinguished and the within-class variations that can be covered.

So far, the methods discussed deal with variations of rotation, lighting, noise, and small distortions of an object's shape. They mostly assume that objects are solid, approximately rigid, have similar textures or colors, and are occluded to a minor degree. Further variations are covered by *local descriptor* approaches. Here, the main idea is to detect salient points in an image that

Figure 8.7 Matching result based on local descriptors (here SIFT; Lowe, 2004). First, salient points are computed on different scales. Then, the corresponding local descriptors are matched to a model database (given by the small image). Left is an ideal example of planar object that is highly textured. Middle and right examples show that the approach breaks down for less textured 3D objects if the perspective changes only slightly. In the right image only a single feature correspondence is found.

provide a partial feature description instead of a complete appearance model. These approaches gained attention in the first decade of the twenty-first century and have reached a performance unachieved before.

By relying on local descriptors (typical examples are SIFT or SURF features, that analyze the distribution of image gradients around an image point) these methods are able to cope with occlusion and local variations as they occur in real-world settings (Lowe 2004). In Figure 8.7 an example of such an approach is given.

8.2.2   3D modeling

2D color or intensity images do not directly encode depth or shape information. Consequently, object recognition and localization is a difficult problem and in general ill-posed (Aloimonos 1993). To overcome these problems the 3D shape of objects can be directly recovered from *depth*, or *range*, *images*. Depth images can be obtained through various methods ranging from scanning with a laser sensor, to structured light approaches, to stereo systems using two cameras, which is the method used by human vision. A cheap example of a structured light camera is the Kinect color-and-depth camera.

The main question in computer vision is how to model or represent the object such that it can be detected in depth data. One way is to parse shapes into component parts (Shipley and Kellman 2001) and define their spatial relationships. In computer vision parts are useful for two reasons. First, many objects are articulated, and the part-based description allows us to decouple the shapes of the parts from their spatial relationships. And second, not all

Figure 8.8 Detection results for a dining chair in a home scene (Wohlkinger and Vincze, 2010). Left: the image of the scene. Right: the stereo point cloud and the chair detected in the centre.

parts of objects are seen but parts are often sufficient to recognize the object; for example, a cup can be recognized from either the body or the handle.

A key aspect of part-based representations is their number of parameters. In the past decade much work has been made describing depth data with rotational symmetric primitives (sphere, cylinder, cone, torus). Generalized cylinders can be created by sweeping a 2D contour along an arbitrary space curve (Binford 1971). Since the contour may vary along the curve (axis), definitions of the axis and the sweeping curve are needed to define a generalized cylinder, which requires a large number of parameters. An often-cited early vision system that applied generalized cylinders is the ACRONYM system to detect airplanes (Brooks 1983). However, the fitting of many parameters is complicated and has limited the use of this method.

One of the most highly investigated methods for 3D modeling involves the recovery of *superquadrics* – geometric shapes defined by formulas including arbitrary powers to produce shapes that resemble cubes, cylinders, and cones, with either rounded or sharp corners. These became popular because a small set of parameters can describe a large variety of different basic shapes. Solina et al. pioneered work in recovering single superquadrics (Solina and Bajcsy, 1990) and demonstrated that the recovery of superquadrics from range images is sensitive to noise and outliers, in particular from single views as given in applications such as robotics. Jaklic and colleagues (Jaklic, Leonardis, and Solina 2000) summarize the *recover-and-select paradigm* for segmenting a scene with simple geometric objects without occlusions. This method aims at a full search with an open processing time unsuitable for most applications such as robotics.

Lately, images from depth sensors such as the Kinect or from stereo systems is used more often to obtain 3D data. Since data is in general not as good as from laser scans, statistical methods rather than direct shape methods are employed. An example is the detection of chairs (Wohlkinger and Vincze 2010) shown in Figure 8.8.

Open problems in this area are how to handle sparse data resulting from one-view scans of the scene, how to cope with the typical laser and camera shadows and occlusions in cluttered scenes, and how to deal with the uncertainty of stereo images.

8.3   Tracking and visual servoing

Another typical task humans perform is to detect and follow the motion of objects. When grasping an object the relative motion is observed. When walking the motion of the environment is monitored. The technique of visually tracking an object and determining its location is used particularly in surveillance and robotics tasks. In the former the paths of cars or persons are estimated to recover the ongoing activities and react accordingly (also see Section 8.4.1 below). In robotics the goal is to track the relative position of a mobile robot and its environment or to steer a robotic hand toward an object. The continuous feedback control of the position of the robot is referred to as *visual servoing* (Chaumette and Hutchinson 2006).

First successes in autonomous car driving and air-vehicle guidance indicate the use of visual servoing (Dickmanns 2007). However, there are still two major obstacles to further use in real-world scenarios (Chaumette and Hutchinson 2006). First, an *efficient tracking cycle* is required. Vision and control must be coupled to ensure good dynamic performance. Fast motions are needed to justify the use of visual servoing in real robotic applications. Second, there must be *robust target object detection*. Vision must be robust and reliable. Perception must be able to evaluate the state of the objects and the robot, enabling the robot to react to changes and make sure it moves safely in its environment.

The tracking cycle problem has received a lot of attention in the literature (e.g., Chaumette and Hutchinson 2006) but robust visual target detection is just as critical and has recently started receiving more and more attention. The following sections summarize the state of the art with respect to these two criteria.

8.3.1   The tracking cycle

The goal of visual servoing is to consider the entire system and its interfaces. The basic control loop is depicted in Figure 8.9. It contains three major blocks: the *vision system*, the *controller*, and the *mechanism* (or robot or vehicle). The vision system determines the present location of the target (the object of interest) in the image. The controller converts the location in the image to a position in space or directly into command values. The system repeats this at a cycle rate. In each cycle a new location is determined and it is also possible to use the location difference to obtain the control command. The robot or

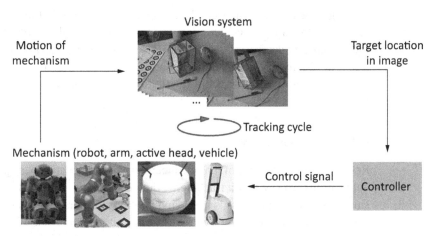

Motion of mechanism

Vision system

Target location in image

Tracking cycle

Mechanism (robot, arm, active head, vehicle)

Control signal

Controller

Figure 8.9 Basic block diagram of visual servoing.

vehicle commonly uses a separate controller to control the motors at the level of its axes and wheels.

The objective is to build the tracking system such that the target is not lost. One limit in tracking is given by the field of view of the camera. Hence it is useful to investigate tracking of the highest possible target velocity (or acceleration). The relevant property is the delay (or latency) of the feedback generated by the vision system (Vincze 2005). The two main factors to take care of are (1) the *latency* or delays in one cycle, and (2) the part or *window* of the image that is actually processed.

Latencies accumulate from the camera. Today, cameras produce images at a rate of 25 or 30 Hz or images per second. Additional delays come from the time taken to transfer the image data to the controller. The biggest time delay is the time needed to process the image. While it seems intuitive that latencies delay tracking, the second factor, image processing, is often not respected. If the full image is calculated, this might take much longer than the frame time of the camera, with consequent loss of images. If a small window is used, for example around the location where the target has been seen in the last image, it is possible to exploit every image. The optimum is reached when the window size is selected such that processing is as fast as acquiring images, and image processing operates at the same 25 or 30 Hz (Vincze 2005). This means it is optimal to operate a tracking system with a latency of two cycles of the frame rate for cameras: one for transmitting the image from camera to computer and another one for image processing. To compensate for this delay, filters (such as the Kalman filter) predict where the target will be (Chaumette and Hutchinson 2006).

It is interesting to note that the human eye is very different from a camera. Cameras have a uniform array of pixels at one given resolution or pixel spacing. The human retina exhibits a space-variant tessellation with a high resolution fovea in the center and a wide field of view (about 180 degrees) at logarithmically decreasing resolution. The effect is that humans process all the image at all times (Vincze 2005). Humans can react to motion in the periphery while recognition only works in the fovea which is rotated to the target and tracks it.

8.3.2   Robust target detection

Robustness of tracking is of major concern in ensuring continuous operation in applications. To say that a tracking method is robust is to say that it degrades smoothly when input data is noisy and contains outliers. A common denominator of techniques to improve robustness is the exploitation of redundancy by using multiple cameras, multi-resolutions, temporal constraints intrinsic to tracking, models, and the integration of several cues or features.

A minimal form of redundancy is inherent in a *stereo vision* system using two fixed cameras and searching for the target in both images (Hartley and Zisserman 2003). Today, systems that calculate a depth image from two stereo images are commercially available (e.g., Videre Design). Nevertheless the correspondence problem (finding the same scene point in both images) remains and successful stereo applications are rare. The correspondence problem of stereo vision is reduced by using three or more cameras, as in TRICLOPS (Point-Grey Research). Assistive systems to steer cars at high speeds exploit two or three cameras with different fields of view (Dickmanns 2007).

The idea of merging information from different *levels of resolution* has been exploited in scale-space or image-pyramid approaches, where the original image is reduced in size several times. Consistency is aggregated over the smaller images to obtain a measure of the reliability of, for example, edge detection. Recently, interest-point features (features that have maximum gradients) exploit this to select the most robust local scale of a gradient point, for example, SIFT (Lowe 2004). However, the use of image pyramids has still not been sufficiently exploited.

The redundancy of a series of images can be exploited by considering the *temporal consistency* of the detected features, also referred to as *temporal data association* (Dickmanns 2007). To cope with the uncertainty in locating the target object in the image, standard methods of control theory such as filtering and prediction (see above) are widely used to improve robustness. Today, the most common approach to cope with this uncertainty is *Kalman* or *particle* filtering, where several hypotheses aid in adapting to uncertainties of the motion of the mechanism and the measurement (Thrun, Burgard, and Fox 2005). The *dynamic vision* approach (Dickmanns 2007) exploited the temporal evolution of geometric features such as lines to build a model of the perceived world. The physical properties of objects, such as a certain inertia, are used

Figure 8.10 An example of model-based vision. Objects have been recognized based on their geometric structure using a CAD (Computer Aided Design) model (displayed with full lines). The models are then tracked using the texture taken from the actual objects.

to predict future positions of the object in the next image(s). Tracking is then used to confirm or update the motion model.

Another approach is *model-based vision* (for a reference work, see Dickmanns 2007). The model is commonly a CAD (Computer Aided Design) representation of the target, which is used for predicting the location of the object (model) in the next image. Mobile robots hold (or build up) a representation of objects, such as walls or pillars or boxes, for the navigation or object-grasping tasks (e.g., Thrun et al. 2005). Figure 8.10 gives an example where models are projected into the image for the purpose of tracking the known object (for details, see Mörwald et al. 2010).[1]

In humans the *integration of cues* or features such as texture, color, shading, and so on, has been identified as a likely source of the excellent ability to cope with changing conditions.

In summary, a plethora of approaches to tracking exist. Most are either robust or fast. While tracking based on regions or interest points is more robust in textured environments, edge-based tracking schemes provide the best input for visual servoing in robotics or in augmented reality systems where additional information is visualized over real images (Kragic and Vincze 2009). With the steady increase in computing power, work on integrating cues will go further. There is a lot of performance to be gained from using more knowledge about the task and the domain, object models, and object functions, and from using cues such as levels of resolution, temporal consistency, and various image features.

[1] The source code for this example is available on the first author's webpage at www.acin.tuwien.ac.at/?id=290.

8.4   Understanding human behavior

8.4.1   Visual surveillance

Smart rooms, human–machine interfaces, and safety and security applications require the ability to recognize activities of humans. This field is known as *visual surveillance*. (For recent reviews see Buxton 2003; Valera and Velastin 2005. The annual PETS [Performance Evaluation of Tracking and Surveillance] workshop series is also an excellent resource of ongoing work.)

Typically, surveillance systems operate from fixed cameras, and this permits use of the technique of *background subtraction* to detect changes in the image. Background subtraction uses the static images to obtain a model of the fixed background scene, which simplifies the task of extracting the moving foreground objects (vehicles, persons, etc.) (for a review see Piccardi 2004). The main task is to cope with the varying illumination, which changes the appearance of the image and might hide changes due to moving foreground objects. This form of change detection results in image regions that are used as indications of objects. In the next step these blobs are tracked over the image sequence, where data association methods are used to find consistently moving objects and to detect erroneous regions generated. Preferred methods to model the consistently moving object are Hidden Markov Models and Bayesian networks (Buxton 2003; Valera and Velastin 2005).

Surveillance systems often work in two phases: a learning phase and a run-time phase. In the learning phase the system is initialized to a scene and models are either adapted or learned from observations. These models contain data about normal activities, such as lanes of cars, entrance points, or typical human gestures. In the run-time phase the data streams are compared to the model data to come up with interpretations and reactions. At present, systems can detect and recognize the behavior of a few persons up to larger groups of people, (e.g., Cupillard, Bremond, and Thonnat 2003). In traffic scenes, processing is mostly bottom up, while newer systems exploit domain knowledge in a top-down way (e.g., Xiang and Gong 2006). An example is the use of object models and expected activity models to monitor activity at airport aprons (Thirde et al. 2006).

In the domain of robotics the object-to-human relation has been studied in approaches such as *Programming by Demonstration* (PbD), where the task is to interpret user commands to teach a robot (Asfour et al. 2007). In PbD, the user either physically guides the robot arm through a motion or a vision system captures the human arm motion and transfers it to the robot arm. In recent work, activities of the hand and of objects are interpreted and stored using natural language expressions in an *activity plan* – a concise account of the scenario specifying the relevant objects and how they are acted upon (e.g., Sage, Howell, and Buxton 2005).

With the decrease of camera costs the present direction of work is toward camera networks surveying large areas. Detailed models of humans and their typical activities yield finer gesture interpretation in less constrained settings (Valera and Velastin 2005).

8.4.2   Human–machine interaction

Proceeding from visual observation techniques to a vision-based interactive human–computer interface seems to be a small step. It opens up a full range of new applications, where computers, monitors, and input devices such as keyboard and mouse disappear into the everyday environment. For example, a simple hand gesture and gaze might transfer a photo collection from your camera to a large TV screen in your living room, turning the human body into a context-sensitive remote control.

However, as attractive this step might be, its realization faces several technical and conceptual problems: (1) *Reactivity:* A system needs to react to user activity in an appropriately short time frame. Otherwise a user is distracted, frustrated, and lost with regard to the communicative state. Appropriate techniques have been developed for face recognition, gaze detection, and gesture recognition, and define a field of active research (Kisacanin, Pavlovic, and Huang 2005; Pavlovic, Sharma, and Huang 1997). (2) *Robustness:* High false-positive detection rates would result in system behavior that is unwanted by the user and conflicts with their expectations. This is especially problematic as not all user behavior is directed to the system. Here, an important concept is that of *joint attention* – a condition in which both communication partners are attending to the same thing and are aware of each other's attention (Breazeal and Scassellati 2000). In human–robot interaction, for instance, the robot needs to detect when a user is facing it. At the same time, the robot's head and eyes will track the user's face in order to reinforce the established communication. (3) *Reliability:* User activities partly missed by the system could corrupt the whole user input to the system. Thus, there needs to be a way of determining if the input is well formed or not. This is a difficult learning and recognition problem because humans typically perform tasks with a large variability and are not aware of the system's limits. One interesting research direction is to understand how humans communicate expectations in dialogue, for example, by asking a yes/no question or using other conventions that limit possible answers. (4) *Situativity:* The interpretation of most human behavior is context specific. Therefore, many systems are designed for a very specific scenario or application domain. In order to overcome these limitations, an important notion is that of *context awareness* – a concept introduced in the mobile computing community (Schilit, Adams, and Want 1994). For computer vision, it has been applied to perceptive rooms, for example, by

Crowley et al. (2002). There, human activities are observed through multiple cameras and are categorized with regard to different contexts and situations.

As a consequence of the points discussed above, research towards vision-based human–machine interaction always needs to consider complete systems together with their interaction partners, making it a highly interdisciplinary task. Most systems in this area tightly constrain the communicative setting. Early work has been done by Bolt and his colleagues (Bolt 1980) in his "Put-That-There" system. A user was able to create and move geometric elements on a screen by using gestures and voice commands. Today's systems range over a wide spectrum of techniques and applications. The SafetyEYE developed in industry research estimates the action radius of an industrial manufacturing robot and stops it in case of human–machine interference. The MIT Kidsroom provides an interactive narrative play space for children (Bobick et al. 1999). It is based on visual action-recognition techniques that are coupled with the control of images, video, light, music, sound, and narration. Crowley et al. (Crowley, Coutaz, and Bérard 2000) describe an interactive Magic Board based on the tracking of fingers and a perceptual window that scrolls by detecting head movements. In recent years, body tracking has become a hot commercial topic for game consoles, such as Sony's PlayStation and Microsoft's Xbox. A different focus was set in the VAMPIRE system (Wachsmuth, Wrede, and Hanheide 2007), which provided assistance to people in everyday tasks by leading them step-by-step through a recipe. This was demonstrated in a drink-mixing scenario and used object recognition, tracking, localization, and action-recognition techniques in order to achieve user assistance based on augmented-reality techniques. Much work has been conducted in order to bridge the communication gap between humans and service robots designed to act like a companion at home. Examples are the PR2 from Willow Garage, the Care-O-Bot 3 from Fraunhofer IPA, Cosero from University of Bonn, or ToBI from Bielefeld. The first of these can fold your laundry or get a drink from the fridge. The others have been active in the RoboCup@Home competition, which includes a number of benchmarking tests ranging from person following and getting introduced to guests to cleaning up and fetching drinks.

Compared to human–human communication (HHC), human–machine interaction is still brittle and in its infancy. Today's research concentrates on mimicking certain aspects of HHC in order to address the four challenges described.

8.5 Contextual scene understanding

Most approaches in computer vision do not interpret entire images, but selective parts of them. They aim at extracting foreground objects from background clutter. Then, each object is classified in isolation. Background is ignored and viewed as irrelevant distracting data or simply as noise. Contextual scene understanding makes the contrasting assumption that the foreground objects cannot be automatically extracted or at least do not provide sufficient information for a classification. It recycles the data ignored before – background clutter and relational information – in order to infer possible interpretations for foreground objects. Thus, these techniques aim to incorporate scene context into the classification process.

Pioneering work has been conducted by Strat and Fischler (Strat and Fischler 1991), who define context sets that govern the invocation of the system's processing steps. They identify four different kinds of criteria that comprise context sets: (1) *global contexts* – attributes of an entire scene such as daytime or landscape; (2) *location* – the spatial configuration of a scene such as touching the ground or coincidence with other object types; (3) *appearance* of neighboring objects, such as the similarity of the left and right eyes of a face; and (4) *functionality* –the role of an object in a scene, such as supporting another object or bridging a stream. From the control point of view, Strat and Fischler employ three kinds of context-driven operations to guide the scene interpretation process: hypothesis generation, hypothesis validation, and hypothesis ordering. During the search for hypotheses (generation), consistent groups of recognized entities are constructed that represent partial interpretations of a scene. The main drawback of this kind of approach is the huge knowledge-engineering task in coding the contextual knowledge of the system. However, the general types of contexts introduced and the different kinds of control principles designed are still valid for the current state of the art.

Later work adapted probabilistic models for contextual interpretation which capture relationships and uncertainty in a systematic manner. The following examples illustrate more recent trends with regard to the general context types introduced before. *Global contexts* are used in order to classify semantic places (e.g., street, city, beach, or indoor room categories like kitchen). In this way, a holistic image representation is computed – the so called *image gist*. The *semantic category* provides expectations about frequently occurring objects (such as those typically found in a kitchen). *Location* is modeled by Hoiem and colleagues (Hoiem, Efros, and Hebert 2006), who relate object detections to an overall 3D scene context and judge the scale and location with regard to the estimated scene geometry. *Functionality* is exploited by Moore, Essa, and Hayes (Moore et al. 1999) who relate human actions and objects by a probabilistic model. They introduce the concept of *object spaces* that link both kinds of information in space and time.

Finally, *linguistic contexts* refer to additional information given by parallel text or speech. These kinds of bi-modal data frequently occur in catalogues, newspapers, magazines, webpages, broadcasting news, movies, or human-machine interaction dialogues. The verbal information principally includes all three types of contextual information. An image caption mentioning "New York" or "traffic" might give a hint that the image depicts a city scene.

Other verbal descriptions, for example, that two persons are standing next to each other, provide local constraints for the analysis of an image. Functional contexts can be derived from verbs, though this method has not been widely used.

8.6   Summary and conclusion

Agents, human or artificial, need to perceive their environment in order to operate and survive in it. Visual perception is the strongest human sense, and work in the field of computer vision sets out to provide the required capabilities. This chapter has summarized the main achievements, starting with a review of trends and perspectives and then highlighting main areas of application.

Today it is possible for machines to learn and then recognize objects from 2D images containing up to around 1,000 objects, and the number increases continuously. It is, however, constrained to databases of images where size of objects or typical scenes are similar. In open environments, such as search tasks in homes, variations in illumination, viewpoint, or occlusion still pose challenges. When using 3D images, for example with laser scanners or depth images, the shape of objects can be acquired and exploited to control industrial processes, such as robotic grasping or spray painting.

Tracking of objects or interest points over longer video sequences can be done in real time given sufficient texture. Rules on how to exploit the image information and predict and search efficiently in subsequent images are established, and visual servoing methods to control robot arms are available.

The real-time performance and robustness achieved by today's computer vision techniques for hand tracking, human-body tracking, face recognition, and so on, lead to a new quality of vision-based human–machine interaction. We have discussed several challenges in this new field that merges the areas of computer vision (CV) and human–computer interaction (HCI). Over the last years, several new workshop series have been established such as CV4HCI and human-centered CV. We expect that this marriage will provide further fruitful influences on the field, taking two perspectives: how to design CV systems for users, and how to effectively include the user in the visual processing loop.

One of the challenges pointed out in Section 8.4.2 was situatedness: Given any situation along the interaction, when and with what information should the user be bothered? The same question could be asked for the vision system. Not all information is important, and not all detection results are valid. The notion of context provides a notion of a global consistency on the one hand and a frame of meaning on the other hand. Even with quite sophisticated and high-performance recognition techniques, context will keep its role when we talk about computer vision systems that need to act in real-world environments.

Computer vision systems need to combine techniques for application purposes. This is the core of CV as an engineering discipline. However, it has been proven over the years that generic architectures that integrate all the components needed for different applications are hard to define. Some approaches have shown their applicability in successful multi-partner European projects (e.g., ActIPret, VAMPIRE, or CogX). Real progress is hard to achieve on the theoretical side and needs to be proven by the practical realization of systems (Kragic and Vincze 2009).

While these results indicate how the field has advanced, several challenges lie ahead. For example, work on recognizing classes of objects is currently limited to a few salient classes, such as wheels or airplanes; the ability to detect grasp points on arbitrary objects needs to be extended from planar to full 3D object locations; and it is not yet possible to deduce the function of an object from imaging its shape. Nevertheless, the hope is that computer vision will be increasingly integrated with other AI methods to build more complete systems.

Further reading

Ballard, D. H. and Brown, C. M. (1982). *Computer Vision*. Englewood Cliffs, NJ: Prentice Hall. The basic book on methods in computer vision. Available online: http://homepages.inf.ed.ac.uk/rbf/BOOKS/BANDB/bandb.htm.

Dickinson, S. J., Leonardis, A., Schiele, B., and Tarr, M. J. (2009). *Object Categorization: Computer and Human Vision Perspectives*. Cambridge University Press. Excellent overview of approaches to object recognition, including a historical perspective. A must to get started in this direction.

Forsyth, D. A. and Ponce, J. (2011). *Computer Vision: A Modern Approach* (2nd edn.). Upper Saddle River, NJ: Prentice Hall. A broad collection of computer vision techniques that is a very good reference for the advanced study of computer vision.

Hartley, R. and Zisserman, A. (2003). *Multiple View Geometry in Computer Vision* (2nd edn.). Cambridge University Press. Provides deep coverage of geometrical aspects in computer vision for the advanced reader.

Kragic, D. and Vincze, M. (2009). Vision for robotics, *Foundations and Trends in Robotics*, 1: 1–78. An overview of the specific needs of robotics to computer vision methods plus a survey of applications.

Szeliski, R. (2010). *Computer Vision: Algorithms and Applications*, London: Springer. An excellent textbook for the introduction and more in-depth study of computer vision. It has an emphasis on techniques that combine computer vision and graphics, but covers also modern techniques for object recognition, segmentation, and motion estimation. Available on-line: http://szeliski.org/Book/

Finally, two great open-source collections of vision methods are openCV (http://opencv.org/) and the Point Cloud Library (http://pointclouds.org/).

References

Aloimonos, Y. (1993). *Active Perception*. Hillsdale, NJ: Lawrence Erlbaum.

Asfour, T., Azad, P., Vahrenkamp, N., et al. (2008). Toward humanoid manipulation in human-centred environments, *Robotics and Autonomous Systems* 56: 54–65.

Bajcsy, R. (1988). Active perception, *Proceedings of the IEEE*, 76: 996–1005.

Ballard, D. H. (1981). Generalizing the Hough transform to detect arbitrary shapes, *Pattern Recognition*, 13: 111–22.

Ballard, D. H. and Brown, C. M. (1982). *Computer Vision*. Englewood Cliffs, NJ: Prentice Hall.

Barrow, H. G. and Salter, S. H. (1969). Design of low-cost equipment for cognitive robot research, in B. Meltzer and D. Michie (eds.), *Machine Intelligence 5* (pp. 555–66). Edinburgh University Press.

Binford, T. (1971). Visual perception by a computer, in *Proceedings of the IEEE Conference on Systems and Control* (pp. 116–23). IEEE.

Bobick, A. F., Intille, S. S., Davis, J. W., et al. (1999). The kidsroom: A perceptually-based interactive and immersive story environment, *PRESENCE: Teleoperators and Virtual Environments*, 8: 369–93.

Bolt, R. A. (1980). "Put-that-there": Voice and gesture at the graphics interface, *ACM SIGGRAPH Computer Graphics*, 14: 262–70.

Breazeal, C. and Scassellati, B. (2000). Infant-like social interactions between a robot and a human caregiver, *Adaptive Behavior*, 8: 49–74.

Brooks, R. (1983). Model-based 3D interpretation of 2D images, *IEEE Transactions on Pattern Analysis and Machine Intelligence*, 5: 140–50.

Buxton, H. (2003). Learning and understanding dynamic scene activity: A review, *Vision Computing*, 21: 125–36.

Chaumette F. and Hutchinson S. (2006). Visual servo control I: Basic approaches, *IEEE Robotics and Automation Magazine*, 13(4): 82–90.

Crowley J. L. and Christensen H. I. (eds.) (1995) *Vision as Process: Basic Research on Computer Vision Systems*. Berlin: Springer.

Crowley, J. L., Coutaz, J., and Bérard, F. (2000). Perceptual user interfaces: Things that see, *Communications of the ACM*, 43(3): 54–64.

Crowley, J. L., Coutaz, J., Rey, G., and Reignier, P. (2002). Perceptual components for context aware computing, in G. Borriello and L. E. Holmquist (eds.), *UbiComp 2002: Ubiquitous Computing* (Lecture Notes in Computer Science 2498) (pp. 117–34). Berlin: Springer.

Cupillard, F., Bremond, F., and Thonnat, M. (2003). Behaviour recognition for individuals, groups of people and crowds, *IEE Symposium on Intelligent Distributed Surveillance Systems*, 7: 1–5.

Dickmanns, E. D. (2007). *Dynamic Vision for Perception and Control of Motion*. London: Springer.

Duda R. and Hart, P. (1973). *Pattern Classification and Scene Analysis*. New York: Wiley.

Forsyth, D. A. and Ponce, J. (2011). *Computer Vision: A Modern Approach* (2nd edn.). Upper Saddle River, NJ: Prentice Hall.

Gonzales, R. C. and Woods, R. E. (2002). *Digital Image Processing* (2nd edn.). Upper Saddle River, NJ: Prentice Hall.

Hartley, R. and Zisserman, A. (2003). *Multiple View Geometry in Computer Vision* (2nd edn.). Cambridge University Press.

Hoiem, D., Efros, A. A., and Hebert, M. (2006). Putting objects in perspective, in *Proceedings of the IEEE International Conference on Computer Vision and Pattern Recognition (CVPR)*, (pp. 2137–44). IEEE.

Huttenlocher, D. P. and Ullman, S. (1990). Recognizing solid objects by alignment with an image, *International Journal of Computer Vision*, 5: 195–212.

Jaklic, A., Leonardis, A., and Solina, F. (2000). *Segmentation and Recovery of Superquadrics*. Dordrecht: Kluwer Academic Publishers.

Kisacanin, B., Pavlovic, V., and Huang, T. S. (2005). *Real-Time Vision for Human–Computer Interaction*. New York: Springer.

Koenderink, J. J. (1987). An internal representation for solid shape based on the topological properties of the apparent contour, in W. Richards and S. Ullman (eds.), *Image understanding 1985–86* (pp. 257–85). Norwood, NJ: Ablex.

Kragic, D. and Vincze, M. (2009). Vision for robotics, *Foundations and Trends in Robotics*, 1: 1–78.

Lowe D. G. (2004). Distinctive image features from scale-invariant keypoints, *International Journal of Computer Vision*, 60: 91–110.

Marr, D. (1982). *Vision*. San Francisco, CA: W. H. Freeman.

Moore, D. J., Essa, I. A., and Hayes, M. H. (1999). Exploiting human actions and object context for recognition tasks, in *Proceedings of IEEE International Conference on Computer Vision* (pp. 80–86). Corfu, Greece: IEEE.

Mörwald, T., Prankl, J., Richtsfeld, A., Zillich, M., and Vincze, M. (2010). BLORT – The blocks world robotic vision toolbox, in *Proceedings of the ICRA 2010 Workshop on Best Practice in 3D Perception and Modeling for Mobile Manipulation*.

Nilsson, N. J. (1969). Mobile automaton: An application of artificial intelligence techniques, Technical Note 40, AI Center, SRI International; also in *Proceedings of the First International Joint Conference on Artificial Intelligence* (pp. 509–20).

Pavlovic, V., Sharma, R., and Huang, T. S. (1997). Visual interpretation of hand gestures for human-computer interaction: A review, *IEEE Transactions on Pattern Analysis and Machine Intelligence*, 19: 677–95.

Piccardi, M. (2004). Background subtraction techniques: A review, *IEEE International Conference on Systems, Man and Cybernetics*, 4: 3099–104).

Sage, K. H., Howell, A. J. and Buxton, H. (2005). Recognition of action, activity and behaviour in the ActIPret project, *KI* 19(2): 36–39.

Schilit, B., Adams, N., and Want, R. (1994). Context aware computing applications, in *Proceedings of the First International Workshop on Mobile Computing Systems and Applications* (pp. 85–90).

Shipley T. and Kellman P. J. (eds.) (2001). *From Fragments to Objects: Segmentation and Grouping in Vision.* Amsterdam: Elsevier.

Solina F. and Bajcsy, R. (1990). Recovery of parametric models from range images: The case for superquadrics with global deformations, *IEEE Transactions on Pattern Analysis and Machine Intelligence,* 12: 131–47.

Strat, T. M. and Fischler, M. A. (1991). Context-based vision: Recognizing objects using information from both 2D and 3D imagery, *IEEE Transactions on Pattern Analysis and Machine Intelligence,* 13: 1050–65.

Thirde, D., Borg, M., Ferryman, J., et al. (2006) A real-time scene understanding system for airport apron monitoring, in *Fourth IEEE International Conference on Computer Vision Systems (ICVS'06)* (p. 26).

Thrun, S., Burgard, W., and Fox, D. (2005). *Probabilistic Robotics.* Cambridge MA: MIT Press.

Valera M. and Velastin, S. A. (2005). Intelligent distributed surveillance systems: A review, *IEE Proceedings: Vision, Image and Signal Processing* 152: 192–204.

Vincze, M. (2005). On the design and structure of artificial eyes for tracking tasks, *Journal of Advanced Computational Intelligence and Intelligent Informatics,* 9: 353–60.

Wachsmuth, S., Wrede, S., and Hanheide, M. (2007) Coordinating interactive vision behaviors for cognitive assistance, *Computer Vision and Image Understanding* 108: 135–49.

Wohlkinger W. and Vincze, M. (2010). 3D object classification for mobile robots in home-environments using web-data, in *IEEE 19th International Workshop on Robotics in Alpe-Adria-Danube Region (RAAD)* (pp. 247–52).

Xiang T. and Gong, S. G. (2006). Beyond tracking: Modelling activity and understanding behaviour, *International Journal of Computer Vision,* 67: 21–51.

9 Reasoning and decision making

Eyal Amir

9.1 Introduction

Reasoning and decision making are fundamental parts of the *Knowledge representation and reasoning* (KR&R) AI approach. KR&R is devoted to the design, analysis, and implementation of inference algorithms and data structures. Work in KR&R has deep roots in reality: Reasoning problems arise naturally in many applications that interact with the world – commonsense query answering, diagnosis problem solving, planning, reasoning about knowledge in the sciences, natural language processing, and multi-agent control, to name a few. Aside from their obvious practical significance, reasoning algorithms and knowledge representations form the foundations for theoretical investigations into human-level AI.

Reasoning is the subfield of KR&R devoted to answering questions from diverse data without human intervention or help. Typically, the data is given in some formal system whose semantics is clear. In the early decades of focused research on automated reasoning and question answering (1950s onward) data was mostly akin to *knowledge* or our intuitions about it. More recently (from the 1980s), people assume that the data involved in reasoning are a mix of simple data and more complex data. The former take a low degree of computational complexity to process and are the focus of research on large databases (e.g., relational databases such as those recording sale transactions in businesses, accounting software for individuals, and records of stores' items). The latter are given in a more expressive language, taking less space to represent, and correspond to both generalizations and finer-grained information.

Decision making is a form of reasoning that focuses on answering questions about preferences between activities, for example, in the context of an autonomous agent trying to fulfill a task for a human. Often, decision making is done in a dynamic domain that changes with the execution of actions and the passage of time. In such domains earlier actions affect later decisions, and the reasoning task is to find a sequence of actions or a universal response plan (*policy*) to situations or sensory input. The decisions taken there involve achieving goals or optimizing some criteria such as plan length, actions' cost, or future expected accumulated reward.

Research on the two topics of reasoning and decision making is often done in isolation, with different methods and different theoretical understandings for the two topics, and this overview chapter is divided along similar lines. The chapter also distinguishes research along representation lines, taking particular aim at logic-based and probability-based representations. However, research on the two topics also has substantial cross-fertilization and transfer of major results, techniques, and ideas, and this overview takes the larger perspective that the two problems are fundamentally the same.

This chapter aims at both an overview of current research and a discussion of current and emerging questions in this field. The two perspectives are presented together, attempting to give them equal emphasis. Naturally, both perspectives are severely limited. There are over 100,000 articles and books on reasoning and decision making, with over 3,000 articles published every year, and inevitably many technical details and large research efforts cannot be covered here. For more information on these, readers are referred to the "Further reading" section and to the works cited throughout.

9.2   Knowledge representation and reasoning

From the early days of the AI field one of the dominant views of the path to solving the AI problem was looking for an explicit *representation* for the *knowledge* of the system in question and for *reasoning* about it (McCarthy 1958). The 1960s had many successes for this approach, later known as KR&R. A major part of the effort was devoted to *first-order logic* (FOL) as a general representation language for knowledge and to FOL *theorem provers* as generators of intelligent behavior.

In the 1970s excitement subsided after the discovery of several obstacles. These obstacles included the complexity of reasoning with FOL, the brittleness of expert systems (Buchanan and Smith 1988), the difficulty of representing everyday commonsense knowledge, and the problems FOL has in representing jumping to conclusions or reasoning with defaults (Minsky 1975). The 1980s further highlighted the gap between KR&R and research on machine learning, control theory, and decision theory. Subsequent research in KR&R sought to address these issues in two paths: understanding how to overcome difficulty of computation with FOL, and understanding how to build useful representations of real-world phenomena.

FOL is computationally equivalent to a Turing machine, and is thus able to represent all that present computers can compute. This expressiveness of representation is also the reason that computation with it is difficult, since FOL must take a long time to compute many queries, and may never finish computation for others. Research on representation languages that permit tractable query answering yielded specialized languages with large bodies of applications. This section describes work along these research paths, focusing on logical reasoning, probabilistic reasoning, and commonsense reasoning.

9.2.1   Logic and combinatorics

Mathematical logic (henceforth *logic*) serves as the formal basis for many applications in the real world: computers and computational theory, our legal system and argumentation, and theoretical developments and proofs throughout science and engineering. Modern logic came about from efforts (of Frege, Russell, Hilbert, and many others) at representing everyday arguments and reasoning in a complete and irrefutable way.

The KR&R effort (following McCarthy 1958) focused on extending this vision into a realizable automatic computer reasoner. In this vision, the reasoner represents its knowledge about the world in logic, and reasons about this knowledge with general-purpose reasoning algorithms. The details of this program proved challenging in several forms. First, some types of knowledge (e.g., spatial, temporal, and uncertain knowledge) turn out to be difficult to represent in a sentential language (McCarthy and Hayes 1969; Cohn 1997). Second, it is not easy to compile the needed knowledge for sizable applications, nor is it simple to learn knowledge in an expressive logical language (Lavrač and Džeroski 1994). Finally, it is not computationally feasible or easy to reason with the expressive languages that seem to be needed, even when one can overcome the first two difficulties (Tseitin 1970).

Three critical ongoing debates in this subject are the following: First is the claim that logic cannot represent many things, such as analogy, space, shape, uncertainty, and so should not be considered for an active role in building a full-scale human-level AI system. The counterargument suggests that logic can serve as one of several tools. At present its combination of representation power, flexibility, and clarity are not matched by any other method or system. A second critical debate surrounds the claim that logic is too slow for inference and so will never play a role in a deployed system. The counterclaim is that there are ways to approximate inference with logic so that it conforms to time limits and progress is made in speeding up logical inference. Finally, some claim that it is very hard to create systems of logical axioms for sizable real-world applications. Those who believe differently are developing a stream of active research on techniques for learning logical axioms from natural-language text and contributors on the World Wide Web (WWW) (Mancilla-Caceres and Amir 2011).

There are various different types of logic; we shall consider some of the most important ones, including propositional logic, first-order logic, modal logics, and nonmonotonic logic.

Propositional logic is a very simple and common formal representation language. Representing knowledge in it is done with propositional symbols (a special case of *Boolean variables*)[1] and propositional connectives such as $\wedge$ (*and*), $\vee$ (*or*), and $\neg$ (*not*). For example, the formula $\varphi = \neg rain \vee clouds$ states that if there is rain there must be clouds.

There are four typical reasoning tasks with propositional logical knowledge: (1) *Satisfiability*: *Is there a model for φ?* (a model for a formula is an assignment to all variables such that the formula evaluates to TRUE); (2) *Entailment*: *Does Q logically follow from φ?* (written $\varphi \vDash Q$ for a given formula Q); (3) *Model counting*: *How many models does φ have?*, and (4) *Quantified Boolean formulas (QBFs)*: queries that interleave entailment conditions on some variables and satisfiability on other variables.

A central concept in classical logic in general is that of entailment or inference. The syntactic relation $\vdash$ designates the ability to mechanically derive the query from the set of axioms φ by applying a series of syntactic combinations and manipulations of formulas conforming to a given set of rules. In contrast, the semantic relation $\vDash$ (logical entailment) provides us with a definition of the meaning of entailment. Given a semantic relation between formal structures (models) and logical sentences, definitions of entailment typically say that a set of logical sentences entails another sentence if all models satisfying every sentence of the former also satisfy the latter. For example, if all models of "rain" satisfy "rain $\vee$ clouds," then we say that "rain" logically entails "rain $\vee$ clouds." Logics typically have definitions for both relations and theorems of "completeness" establishing equivalence between the two relations. Together they enable computations of whether φ is entailed by a set of premises T.

QBFs are propositional formulas with quantifiers. They represent statements such as "there is a plan (sequence of actions) that will reach the goal regardless of the initial state," which can be written as QBF $\exists plan \, \forall s0 \, goal(do(plan,s0))$, where *plan* and *s0* are represented as sets of propositional logic sentences, *do* is the propositional encoding (with more propositional variables) of executing a sequence of actions *plan* starting from *s0*, and *goal* is a propositional formula on the end variables of *do(plan,s0)*.

Constraint satisfaction is a generalization of propositional logic to variables that are not Boolean and can take values in a finite domain. Current research on propositional logic and constraint satisfaction focuses on finding efficient solvers for these tasks, with heuristics and theoretical understandings being developed for different problem distributions (Selman, Mitchell, and Levesque 1997).

---

[1] *Boolean algebra* is a general mathematical framework for describing opposites and parts of opposites (such as a full set versus an empty set, a true statement versus a false one, etc.). Typically, when people refer to *Boolean variables* they mean variables that take values true or false (or 1,0).

First-order logic (FOL) extends propositional logic and is comprised of a language, a proof theory, and semantics. An example should explain the difference:

$$\psi = \exists\, time\; clouds(time, above(Chicago)) \land rain(time, Chicago)$$

is a formula in FOL that says that *there are times* ($\exists time$) in which there are clouds over Chicago but not rain. Here, *clouds* and *rain* are *predicates*, that is, symbols that stand for relations, *time* is a variable over entities (possible times), *Chicago* is a constant symbol intended to refer to the city of Chicago, USA, and *above(x)* is a function symbol intended to refer to the area above *x*.

Formally, the language of FOL has a set of object constant symbols, a set of relation predicate symbols, a set of function symbols, and a set of connectives (OR ($\lor$), AND ($\land$), NOT ($\neg$)), quantifiers (EXISTS ($\exists$), FOR ALL ($\forall$)), and parentheses as the building operators. Together, the chosen set of predicate, constant, and function symbols is called the *signature* of the language. For example, the formula ψ above has the signature $\langle Chicago; clouds, rain; \rangle$.

FOL has a richer interpretation than propositional logic. An *interpretation* is a pair $M = \langle U, I \rangle$ that specifies a universe of elements, U, and an interpretation function, I, for the signature. For example, one interpretation is $U = \{3pm, April\,24,\,2012,\,4pm,\,April\,24,\,2012,\,Tel\text{-}Aviv\}$ and $I(clouds) = \langle 3pm,\,Tel\text{-}Aviv,\,4pm,\,Tel\text{-}Aviv \rangle$, $I(rain) = 4pm,\,Tel\text{-}Aviv$, and $I(Chicago) = Tel\text{-}Aviv$. In this interpretation there are clouds in Tel-Aviv, Israel, at 3 pm as well as 4 pm, but there is rain only at 4 pm. The symbol *Chicago* in our signature is interpreted as the real-world Tel-Aviv, Israel. $M = \langle U, I \rangle$ is called a *model* of ψ above. Entailment is denoted with $M \vDash \psi$ because the interpretation of ψ in M evaluates to TRUE.

FOL has a very rich expressive power, especially when equipped with the proper vocabulary and axioms (e.g., *set theory* is a vocabulary and set of axioms in FOL that can represent all of modern mathematics). In fact, it is so expressive that it can represent every computational task solvable in a common model of modern computers, a *Turing machine*. A Turing machine models computation in all computers built to this day (if possible, future quantum computers will go beyond this computational power). Therefore, every computational problem and algorithm can be written in FOL such that entailment in FOL is equivalent to the problem's solution by a computer. This is significant because it discourages pursuit of more expressive languages as they will surely be outside of our computational abilities.

FOL's expressivity helps researchers translate results about FOL to results on more specialized problems. For example, results about automated reasoning with FOL (Amir and McIlraith 2005) led to new methods in automatic planning for robots (see Section 9.3.1.). Some claim that FOL has no practical use in real applications because its expressivity results in difficult computations. Others argue that FOL's expressivity is required for the representation of general knowledge. Claims that FOL is not expressive enough to represent quantification over relations or probabilities and modalities are met with counterarguments that apply set theory in FOL to represent such missing constructs.

Modal logics are logics with modal operators, that is, operators that take formulas as arguments. For example

believes(*John*, *at*(*Sarah*, *Home*))

has a modal operator *believes*, which takes constant symbol *John* and FOL formula *at*(*Sarah*, *Home*) as arguments. In this example, modal operator *believes* disregards the truth value of *at*(*Sarah*, *Home*). It may be that Sarah is *not* at home, but still John believes it. Many modal operators used in AI denote *knowledge* and *belief*, *K* and *B*, respectively (Fagin et al. 1995).

The unique capability of such languages is the ability to discuss beliefs about beliefs about beliefs, and so on. For example, one can express (and reason about) Sarah's belief that John knows the combination to the safe:

$B_{Sarah} (\exists comb\ K_{John} (unlocks(comb, Safe)))$

Similarly, given a group of agents, one can represent and reason about the beliefs of the group (e.g., *everyone knows that John knows the combination to the safe*) and about common knowledge (i.e., *everyone knows that everyone knows...*).

Finally, another major use of modal logics is the ability to represent requirements and knowledge over time, such as *eventually φ holds*. This is particularly useful in formal verification and other approaches for ensuring correctness of digital circuits, protocols, and software (Manna and Pnueli 1995).

All the logics discussed above are *monotonic*, that is, adding knowledge never makes us retract conclusions. Formally, for formulas A, B, C, if $A \vDash C$, then also $A \wedge B \vDash C$, regardless of what B is. This monotonicity does not hold in real-life situations where one jumps to conclusions without notice, so in the last thirty to forty years a field has emerged focusing on producing systems that give the right framework for reasoning in nonmonotonic forms about real-world situations.

An example of these nonmonotonic logics is *circumscription* (McCarthy 1986), which is a method for nonmonotonic reasoning that makes assumptions about the minimality of some predicates, if those assumptions are consistent with the rest of one's knowledge. For example,

$\varphi = Ab(John) \rightarrow rich(John)$

says that John is not rich unless he is abnormal. Minimizing the predicate Ab in φ, so that it applies to only those things that are currently known to be abnormal, implies that John is not rich. If we now learn that John has invested in Google before its stockmarket launch, then Ab expands to include John, and we will retract the last conclusion. The nonmonotonic reasoning line of work has expanded since its debut and several textbooks now exist that give a fair view of it (e.g., Gabbay, Hogger, and Robinson 1993) and its uses (e.g., Reiter 2001).

In the study of different rules of inference and axioms the inference relation satisfies, one considers an inference relation as a relation between a set of sentences and a sentence in a formal language – typically, either propositional or first order. Kraus, Lehmann, and Magidor (1990) and follow-up work examine conditions that this entailment relation should meet, with some practical implications. The majority of work on this subject has tackled specific scenarios, in particular that of revision of beliefs (Williams and Rott, 2001).

Present major uses of nonmonotonic reasoning systems are in formalizing different aspects of commonsense reasoning and fast implementation for reasoning methods in restricted sets of nonmonotonic reasoning problems. Application topics using these techniques include cognitive robotics, planning, learning and representation of preferences, and fast solutions for expressive extensions of propositional logic.

9.2.2   Probabilistic representations and reasoning

Knowledge about stochastic phenomena and uncertainty about knowledge and belief can be captured using tools from probability theory and statistics. These tools facilitate discussion and automated reasoning about the probability of events, the beliefs that we may hold, the changes in those beliefs when we make observations, and our degree of certainty in those beliefs.

Research on this paradigm has grown popular in recent years. The research focuses on the representation of different types of uncertainty and uncertain knowledge, reasoning with these types of knowledge, and learning them. It is also closely related to statistical approaches to machine learning and control theory, thus facilitating the development of applied systems of practical importance, such as medical diagnosis applications, robotic control, machine vision, and natural language processing.

This section discusses the main approaches and problems concerning this research subfield. It attends mostly to graphical models for probability distributions and describes some underlying assumptions in their usage. These graphical models are mathematical constructs that describe fragments of reality, with some structural assumptions and numeric parameters. The section also discusses approaches for reasoning with those models and learning their parameters and structures from data.

Probability theory is based on the notion of a *random experiment*, namely, an experiment whose outcome can be predicted with limited certainty. Typically, we assume that the experiment can be repeated under identical circumstances with identical statistical properties for the outcome. These assumptions

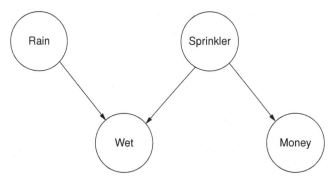

Figure 9.1 A Bayesian network graph representing a joint distribution over binary variables *Rain, Wet, Sprinkler* and multi-valued random variable *Money.*

permit discussion, description, and reasoning about uncertain knowledge (e.g., *I believe that Facebook's stock will go up tomorrow with certainty 0.5*) and statistical knowledge (e.g., *50% of the days Facebook's stock goes up in value*).

The properties of a random experiment are captured using *random variables* and a *probability distribution*. Every random variable X is an abstraction that refers to the (a priori unknown) result (*value*) x of a random experiment. For example, random variable $Up_{Facebook}$ can have values TRUE or FALSE. A probability distribution P maps the values that a random variable can take to the real-numbers segment [0, 1]. In our example above, $P(Up_{Facebook} = TRUE) = 0.5$ captures both notions of uncertain knowledge and statistical knowledge, only with different underlying assumptions about the meaning of the random experiment.

Many cases of interest to the AI community involve domains that are too large for direct specification and reasoning. For example, when our sample space Ω for the example above has n stocks, Ω has 2^n values. A straightforward representation of a distribution over those values takes the form of a table whose every row is a possible combination of values to every stock's state (e.g., $Up_{Facebook} = $ True, $Up_{Google} = $ False, etc.). Thus, this table would have 2^n rows, and would therefore be too large to contain in a computer memory for a modest $n = 50$. For this reason, since the 1990s research has focused on approaches to encoding probability distributions over such large domains, together with methods for reasoning with these encodings.

Graphical probabilistic models (aka *graphical models*) are one of the most popular approaches for representing probability distributions over such real-world domains. A common version of this approach, *Bayesian networks* encode probability distributions using directed graphs such as in Figure 9.1. A directed graph is a set of nodes (circles in this diagram) and arrows connecting them. Each node corresponds to a random variable and includes a conditional-probability table (CPT) of the probability of that random variable, given values of its parents (nodes pointing arrows towards this one). A Bayesian network representation of a probability distribution $P(X_1, \ldots, X_n)$ represents it as a product of conditional probabilities. It includes a directed graph without directed cycles, and the conditional probabilities in the product are $P(X_i | pa_i)$, where pa_i are the parents of X_i. The resulting representation is much more compact than the straightforward one because the number of parents of a variable is typically smaller (e.g., two or three) than the total number of variables, n, resulting in small conditional-probability tables.

Sometimes Bayesian networks are seen as encoding causality between domain features, such as when Facebook's stock influences another stock's state. Causality has little to do with the mathematical representation of Bayesian networks, but the intuition of causality holds many times about the directions shown in a Bayesian network and is a useful heuristic in building those network representations.

There are several kinds of tasks for reasoning with probabilistic information. Typical tasks are evaluating a marginal or conditional probability, finding the most likely assignment to variables given observations, and generating samples from the distribution.

For a joint distribution $P(X, Y)$ the marginal $P(X)$ is defined as $P(X) = \Sigma_Y P(X, Y)$, where X and Y are sets of variables and the summation symbol with subscript Y means summing over all the values Y can take. The marginal probability, therefore, is the original probability applied over only a subset of the variables. For example, $P(tall, fat)$ is the joint probability of someone being both tall and fat, whereas $P(tall)$ is the marginal of the first, when we are interested only in *tall*. Typically, we are interested in finding the marginal probability that X takes a certain value x. This involves summing over all the values that Y can take. For example, if we wish to find the probability that Facebook's stock will go up, $Up_{Facebook}$, and we have a joint distribution over the random variables for all stocks, we need to marginalize out (sum over) all of the variables that are not $Up_{Facebook}$.

Conceptually, computing marginals is straightforward from its definition. In practice, marginalization is not simple for large models because the summation can take time that is exponential in the number of variables that one sums out. For this reason, much research is invested in computing marginals efficiently. This research can also serve for easy computation of other reasoning tasks, such as finding most-likely medical diagnoses and localizing robots.

For Bayesian networks, one simple way of computing marginals applies summation over variables in a careful way along the structure of the graph. It first sums out variables that have very few parents or children, preferably no parents or no children. This summing out creates a new Bayesian network graph without that node, possibly creating new connections between the parents and children of the removed node. This way we eliminate nodes from the graph until we are left with only our random variable of interest in the graph.

During this iterative process we update the representation of the graph and the CPTs in a way that does not require more than a local computation per processing of a leaf (a leaf is a node without children). If the Bayesian network graph structure is simple enough, this computation takes time that is linearly proportional to the number of vertices in the graph (the number of variables in the distribution) and also linearly proportional to the size of the CPTs.

Most practical applications require probabilistic models that are too complex for precise methods. In these cases people turn to attractive approximate reasoning methods. Such methods provide results that are related to correct reasoning but with limited guarantees. The type of approximation given to reasoning depends on the task and on the family of methods that we apply.

Early research sought to find methods that return inference results that are imprecise by at most a constant factor. Unfortunately, results showed that such approximation is not theoretically possible unless a fundamental question in computer science is resolved positively. The question is whether finding a satisfying assignment in propositional logic can be done in polynomial time in the size of the input problem (reasoning task (1) mentioned in Section 9.2.1 – *Satisfiability*: *Is there a model for φ?*). This question has been open now for more than forty years, and many believe that its answer is negative. Since even approximation of probabilistic inference is hence believed hard, this sealed the pursuit for tractable ways to approximate the reasoning with guarantees for precision.

Current approximate probabilistic reasoning techniques are divided into two main paradigms. The first, *variational approximation*, tries to approximate the probabilistic model with a model that is easier to compute with. The most common technique uses a form of *message-passing*, that is, processing evidence and observations in the graph and sending messages between nodes in the graph. Such messages help update local estimates of marginals in each vertex, and the consequences are used to deliver approximate solutions to those marginals. The messages can pass in the graph with no specific order, though sometimes some orders guarantee faster convergence.

The second paradigm for approximate inference, *Monte Carlo* techniques, focuses on providing a set of responses to a query which can be used to draw an approximation to the original query. This involves sampling. We try to generate samples from the given probability distribution and use the samples to answer our queries. For example, for our Facebook story above, sampling would generate m examples (m depends on the time that we have for computation), each of which assigns values to all the variables in the model – that is, each example determines if each of the n stocks in our story goes up. We count how many of these m samples answer our query positively, and use that to return an approximate answer.

Machine learning is a subfield of artificial intelligence concerned with the computerized automatic learning from data of patterns. The aim of machine learning is to use some *training data* to detect patterns, and then to use these learned patterns to automatically answer questions and autonomously make and execute decisions. Examples of machine learning are the models learned by computers to predict users' preferences for books, TV shows, and purchasing decisions in grocery stores. There, the training data are books that people have chosen in the past and the characteristics of those books and the people who chose them. Models learned from these training data are then used to predict other books those people would be likely to buy.

Probabilistic models are close to statistical machine learning and serve as a medium between machine learning and automated reasoning. Machine learning of probabilistic models is divided into two principal tasks: learning the CPTs when the graph is given, and learning the graph itself. Given training examples, machine learning of the CPTs is relatively easy, and it boils down to counting the number of times a random variable receives a certain value out of the times the parents received their respective values. This method is called *estimation of parameters by maximum likelihood.* Learning the graph structure of the model is harder and is done by improving the model one step at a time. Typical methods apply an algorithm called *expectation maximization* (EM) which measures the likelihood that the present hypothesized model explains the data (i.e., that this model is in fact the correct one and that it generated the training data). EM proposes alternative changes to the model and chooses the one that best improves the explanation of the training data.

Present research on probabilistic representation, learning, and reasoning focuses on issues that involve large numbers of variables (large here is larger than, say, 100 variables). Joint distributions over more than 100 variables may be very different when in fact (from a human perspective) they seem almost identical (e.g., the distribution of characteristics of streets of one city block can be very different from that of another, but they may look the same to the untrained eye). Humans make assumptions such as independence of random variables that do not hold in reality, leading to an incorrect perception of similarity of situations.

9.3   Automated decision making

Decision making concerns making a decision that then gets executed in the world by an autonomous agent or by someone taking advice from the decision maker. For example, game-playing agents, autonomous robots, WWW agents, and conversation agents all make decisions on what to do. Often those decisions take the dynamics of the world into account, such as when a computer chess-player chooses an action based on future possible actions of its opponent. Other times decisions are made without a clear path for the future, for example when we decide to rent an apartment at a particular price and location.

Decision making as a research area spans the disciplines of economics, psychology, computer science, and virtually all the engineering disciplines. In computer science and AI in particular the focus of research into decision making is on automated ways and computational properties of decision making. Clearly, studies into human decision making affect the way decision making is automated, but this aspect is outside the scope of AI and of this survey.

Automatic decision making can be divided along several axes that can be framed as questions: (1) Is the domain of a dynamic nature where a sequence of decisions is needed or of a more static nature where a single or a set of concurrent decisions are made? If the former, do we try to optimize decisions for a limited (small) set of time steps or make (close-to) optimal decisions that take into account an (essentially) infinite future sequence of events? (2) Is the domain of a deterministic, non-deterministic, or stochastic nature? For example, do our actions affect the world in deterministic ways (always the same, if performed under the same conditions) or stochastic ways (e.g., half the time our actions fail)? (3) Are we trying to optimize a utility or are we only trying to achieve a goal? (4) Is the domain fully observed at all times (e.g., we see the complete state of the chess board at all times) or partially observed (e.g., we do not see whether the light is on in a room unless we are in that room)?

The rest of this section looks at approaches to autonomous decision making developed over the past fifty years. These techniques were developed to be practical, so they are the result of simplifying assumptions and design decisions whose correctness is questionable. These assumptions include: the chosen representations of deterministic actions (actions have preconditions and effects specified by logical formulas); the existence of truly deterministic actions in practice; a correct and complete knowledge of the world model by the acting agent; and the existence of a clear reward or utility function that characterizes our choices. Still, the driving force behind these problem formulations and techniques is often a set of target applications, so the effectiveness of these assumptions is tested and proven on successful applications.

The first three axes above are covered in this section, but the fourth is left for deeper consideration in Section 9.4.3. The discussion here divides into decision making in logical, typically deterministic, domains and decision making in domains of a stochastic nature. The former are simpler so they can be approached effectively despite sometimes complex combinatorial structures and they can typically be solved for larger domains. The latter are more complex for decision making so they require many assumptions, but they are also more effective and model problems better, when applicable in practice. Later, in Section 9.4.2 we shall look at work that seeks to combine the two approaches and the strengths of their methods.

9.3.1   Decisions in logical, combinatorial spaces

Logical decision problems are those that have a non-stochastic nature. This section considers two main settings for such decision problems: planning (single actor or collaborative) and adversarial (mostly, two-player games). In both settings the discussion assumes that we have complete information about the initial and intermediate states of the world, that actions have only deterministic, known effects, and that there is a specific goal condition (e.g., winning the game or a package being in a certain room). Both types of problems have current real-world applications, such as in NASA's space missions, robotic control, logistics, gaming and virtual world softwares, complex behaviors on the WWW, verification of software, and computer and network security.

In general, a planning problem consists of an initial situation, a goal condition, and a set of allowed actions or transitions between states. The outcome of a planning process is a sequence or set of actions whose proper execution leads the executor from the initial state to a state satisfying the goal condition.

Consider a scenario in which three blocks labeled A, B, C are on a table, and a robot gripper needs to pick them up in the right order and put them down so that A is on B and B is on C. A simple representation for this scenario is called *STRIPS* and consists of a *precondition list, Pre*, a *delete list, Del*, and an *add list, Add*, for every action of the robot. It represents a state with a set of facts that hold true, and the possible actions with such *Pre, Add, Del* lists. *STRIPS* can represent the blocks-world scenario with actions $pickUp(x, y)$ and $putDown(x, y)$, where x, y are blocks A, B, C or *Table*. For example, $pickUp(x, y)$ can have $Pre = on(x, y) \wedge handEmpty$, $Add = inHand(x)$, and $Del = on(x, y)$, $handEmpty$. The intention of those operators and lists is to characterize the preconditions and effects of those actions. The effect changes the present state by adding and deleting from it. When the world state is $\{on(A, Table),$ $on(B, Table), on(C, Table), handEmpty\}$, the robot picks up A from the *Table*, and then A is no longer on the table, the robot hand is no longer empty, and the robot is now holding block A. Hence, a planning algorithm updates the state with this action by applying *delete* $on(A, Table)$, *delete handEmpty*, and *add* $inHand(A)$ to the state description.

The states and actions specify together a search space in which a plan must be found. A plan in that space is a sequence of actions that leads from the initial state (fully specified) to a state that satisfies the goal condition. A *planner* (the process making the decision) receives such a representation for the planning problem and has the task of finding a plan. For that purpose it uses different search methods that can vary with the domain, and can include general-purpose heuristics, look-ahead strategies, and domain knowledge.

Planning is computationally hard even for simple problem specification languages such as that above. The search for a plan cannot represent or traverse the entire state-space graph in practice because it is exponentially large in the number of state features defining the domain (e.g., corresponding to the number of blocks in our example above). Therefore, search techniques must create partial paths in hope of reaching the goal. The search for such plans is *backtracking* when the planner decides that there is no sense in expanding the plan further and that earlier steps in the plan must be changed in order to permit reaching the goal.

Research on planning focuses on developing new search methods, new representations for actions and states that facilitate easier planning, and more expressive planning problem specification languages and methods. For example, many planning algorithms use independence assumptions or loose interactions between components in the planning domain to find plans more efficiently (Amir and Engelhardt 2003). Hierarchical planners divide a goal into subgoals (high-level operators) using a decomposition of the domain into loosely interacting parts. Planning there is done at each level separately, and later the subplans are pieced together to build a valid plan.

Making decisions when there are forces that try to affect our outcome adversely is the topic of *game theory*. Here, the task of a decision maker is to maximize its profit or chances for success while minimizing the adversarial effect of decisions by others. This situation is typical for two-player board games (e.g., chess, go, etc.), and is also relevant to minimizing malfunctions in designs (e.g., of software and hardware) and to security (e.g., for computers and networks).

Minimax is a simple model for making such decisions in two-player game situations. A decision maker uses heuristic information about the value of states (per their future outcomes) to give an estimate of the value of a decision at a present state. For example, in chess we move a chess piece, the other player moves a piece of his or her own, and we arrive at a new game state that demands another decision. Every decision of ours leads to one of several states, and so does the opponent's decision. We can outline all of the possible future states of the next d steps by looking at those states reachable from our current state by a series of possible choices by us and our opponent. It is convenient to put those reachable states in a tree, with the present state being the root of that tree (the highest node in the tree) and the leaves of the tree being the lowest nodes in the tree. (More generally, branches of the tree may merge, but we ignore this to keep the discussion simple.)

In minimax we calculate the values of higher nodes according to this tree in a min–max fashion. A level of the tree is *min* (minimizing) if the opponent makes a decision in those states because his or her goal is to lead to states that minimize our outcome. A level of the tree is *max* (maximizing) if we are the ones making a decision in those states because our goal is to lead to states that maximize our outcome. This is illustrated in Figure 9.2. In this figure, the numbers at the bottom of the tree denote values that players would

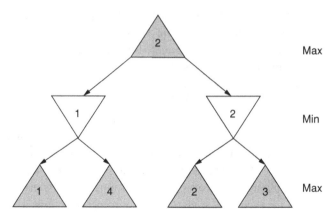

Figure 9.2 A minimax tree of depth 2.

estimate for being in that state (using a heuristic function, for example), and each player chooses actions that minimize or maximize the values received from below. Provably correct methods remove branches in the minimax tree if there is no chance they will contribute to the solution (i.e., to the preference among the higher branches). More recent research tries to estimate the value of a state by sampling sub-trees of this min–max tree.

A challenge to adversarial decision making is the balancing of learning and decisions. When an adversary is trying to clobber our attempts, learning the domain while making decisions (e.g., by reinforcement learning) is tricky, since exploration for the sake of learning may lead us to a very bad outcome. We need to balance the likelihood of learning valuable information from exploration against the risk of being set back by our opponent(s). However, avoiding exploration is bound to bring sub-optimal results that might be very far from desired or acceptable.

9.3.2   Stochastic domains

Many real-world domains have dynamics that evolve stochastically, that is, with some nontrivial statistical properties. For example, we may consider purchasing a car that has properties that are not known to us and that influence its value. Those dependencies affect our decision and we need to evaluate our utility given all the risks and uncertainties. Stochastic domains are harder for decision making in practice but are also more permissive of approximations than deterministic domains. Simplifying assumptions that are made in practice allow automatic decision making to be practical. There are several problem formulations that capture different aspects and cases of decision making in stochastic domains. The most prominent ones are *decision networks* and *Markov decision processes* (MDP).

Decision networks are akin to Bayesian networks (see Section 9.2.2) only with three types of nodes: (1) random variables (as in Bayesian networks), (2) decision nodes, and (3) utility nodes. Decision nodes require assignment of a decision as to their value and they do not have a probability distribution governing them (the values for other nodes can depend stochastically on the value assigned to decision nodes, though). Utility nodes denote those quantities that we wish to maximize (in expectation).

MDPs are the most popular formalism for modeling decision-making tasks in dynamic stochastic environments. Their objective is to model situations where actions have stochastic effects and one's goal is not a specific target but rather maximizing utility over time. Solutions to MDPs are policies that select an action for each state such that the total cost of actions in expectation is minimized and the total sum or positive rewards are maximized.

9.4   Cross-cutting issues

9.4.1   Commonsense reasoning

The terms "commonsense reasoning" and "commonsense knowledge" refer to a broad set of abilities that humans bring into their decision making and thinking. One example is the ability to reason about the very large number of objects, properties, people, and relationships in our everyday life. We can tell that a cup can hold its contents, but only if the cup is facing upwards or the contents are securely connected to the cup. We can use this fact in deciding on ways to transport the cup from one place to another. Research on commonsense reasoning tries to endow applications and computers with this ability to generalize, learn, and use a very broad set of knowledge about everyday life.

Currently, practical applications sidestep many of the issues involved with commonsense reasoning. They do so by carefully crafting the needed information and models, limiting the set of topics and variables when learning, and conceiving only those applications that do not require such common sense. Research on commonsense reasoning is divided into three main streams: logical theory, large commonsense knowledge bases, and ad hoc commonsense reasoning techniques.

The logical formalization and theory of commonsense reasoning tries to use and modify logic to represent and reason with commonsense knowledge in ways that match our intuitions about such reasoning. For example, much of human reasoning about the world uses a notion of *defaults* – assumptions that are useful but may not be true. We say that birds fly (some of them don't); we assume that our computer is functioning correctly (it may not be); and we follow medical doctors' advice (they may be incorrect). Such uncertainties and defaults are not easily captured by logic. Nonmonotonic reasoning (Section 9.2.1) tries and is helpful in generalizing them into a form of useful commonsense reasoning. Such logics capture one property needed for commonsense reasoning, namely, the ability to represent defaults and reason about them. Still, much is left open: How can we acquire the knowledge, how do we scale representation and reasoning techniques to the large set of knowledge that seems needed, and how do we use this knowledge in applications that need it?

Efforts at building large knowledge bases and at using information in new ways try to overcome the limitations of logic-based commonsense reasoning. For example, Cyc (Lenat 1995; Matuszek et al. 2005; Ramachandran, Reagan, and Goolsbey 2005), the best-known large commonsense knowledge base today, is the result of over twenty-five years of development and maintenance by experts. It includes over 1,000,000 facts and logical sentences about over 100,000 objects, relations, types, and functions. Its semantics are not as simple and clean as those suggested in the logical-formulations literature, but it seems to be more usable as a result (initial applications exist in natural language processing and decision making).

Other efforts try to create knowledge automatically from the contributors and masses of information available on the WWW (Singh et al. 2002; Pentney et al. 2007). The aim is to create systems of broad knowledge more easily but with possibly looser semantics. These approaches avoid considering questions about the meaning of knowledge that they hold and seem promising for applications that need broad knowledge (e.g., autonomous real and virtual robots).

9.4.2   Combining logic and probabilities

Many applications have both stochastic and non-stochastic elements. For example, robot control can include high-level specifications in logic and a lower-level probabilistic sensing model. Also, *natural language processing* seeks to apply high-level knowledge in logic with lower-level probabilistic models of text and spoken signals. Finally, many databases are logic based (e.g., an entry ⟨*Eyal, Shavit*⟩ in database *fatherOf* indicates the logical statement *fatherOf*(*Eyal, Shavit*)), while relationships between those databases and recent extensions to databases are probabilistic (e.g., an entry ⟨*John, Mary*⟩ is an uncertain entry in database *loves* with probability 0.7 either because John is unsure or because the database holders are unsure).

Since 1990 there has been much work in the AI community and the Databases community on the combination of logical and probabilistic expressivity. This work presents languages that can express probability distributions together with explicit references to objects, functions, and relationships, as in first-order logic (e.g., Pfeffer et al. 1999). These languages are useful frameworks for many machine learning applications, and recent work also shows that they are useful for computational efficiency of inference (Poole 2003; de Salvo Braz, Amir, and Roth 2006).

Research on the combination of logic and probability is ongoing. Current challenges include (1) applying relational structure in speeding up inference and treating probabilistic models over many objects, (2) combining knowledge bases that are given already in probabilistic or logical form, and (3) extending representation languages to include functions and equality of objects in sound and simple ways.

9.4.3   Partial observability

Agents that act in many real-world domains do not know the exact state of the world at any point in time. These domains are *partially observable* because agents cannot observe all the features of the world that might be relevant to them. For example, an agent trawling the WWW may press a button on a page, but may not see the immediate effect of its action (but it could see it, if it viewed another page). Problems involving partial observability are especially difficult, and limited typically to very small domains (e.g., 100 states or 8 domain features) (Kaelbling, Littman, and Cassandra 1998). This is because any choice of action depends on the state of knowledge of the agent and the perceptions it receives, leading to a super-exponential computation in the number of steps and features in the domain.

Acting in partially observable, *partially known* domains is particularly tricky, and yet it is closest to real life. The main approaches involve at least exhaustive exploration of the domain (e.g., reinforcement learning whereby one learns to behave in a domain from rewards obtained over time and different states; Even-Dar, Kakade, and Mansour 2005) or advice about promising trajectories (Kearns, Mansour, and Ng 2000). Approaches that guarantee convergence to a solution do so only in the limit of an infinite number of steps. Most importantly, if the goal of the system changes, the process must get restarted, and little use is made of knowledge accumulated in previous runs.

Recent approaches (e.g., Chang and Amir 2006) identify important tractable cases of particular interest – for example, domains in which actions are known to be deterministic and without conditional effects (e.g., *STRIPS* actions (Section 9.3.1)). Such algorithms interleave planning and execution and provide some guarantees to reach the goal within a close-to-optimal number of steps.

9.4.4   Applications are not programming

A dominant view in scientific research suggests that real-world applications are straightforward implementations of theories and basic research. AI and decision making in particular defy this view.

Natural language processing, machine vision, and fraud detection are only some of the applications that can be viewed in the abstract as applications of basic research. Still, these topics demanded and received (and still receive) heavy specialized attention before they could be put into practice. More generally, in theory one should be able to represent all that is needed for intelligent behavior in FOL. This is because FOL is equivalent in representational power to Turing machines[2] (a dominant abstract model of computation). While human-level AI in FOL is possible in theory (because if any computer can do it, then FOL can), in practice there is little to gain by avoiding the problem of how to actually represent knowledge or reason in FOL or another language.

The problems of actually building the needed knowledge and using it in practice cannot be avoided if we wish to achieve practical human-level intelligent applications. The devil is in the details, and without attention to those details research will make little progress, as was seen in the numerous branches of AI that developed over time (Formal Verification and Databases are two of the fields that branched out of AI).

9.5   Conclusions

Since the mid 1990s the field of KR&R has gone through a major shift of focus from mathematical-logic tools to probability-theory tools and from theory to applications. This shift was sharp, leading to a split of research into logic-based and probability-based work. Logic is more convenient for representing sentential knowledge (especially relational, object-based knowledge) and is well suited for combinatorial (non-convex) problems and structures, such as search in a maze or solving puzzles, whereas probability-based approaches (in particular, graphical probabilistic models) represent uncertain knowledge better, are more suitable for learning in the presence of noise, and have many real-world applications (following the 80–20 rule of thumb – do 20% of the work for the easier 80% of the job). Reasoning and making decisions with each of the representations is easier or harder in different situations, and typically their strengths seem complementary (e.g., solving logical satisfiability problems is often fast, whereas probabilistic reasoning is easy to approximate). Many researchers agree that both tools (logic and probability) are necessary for scaling up systems to real-world applications, but the way in which to combine their strengths remains unclear.

Further, research on machine learning and reasoning has reached a point where it has many practical applications. Present research is more oriented toward applications and this trend is registering a better focus and real-world

---

[2] This reflects the author's belief that a computer can indeed exhibit human-level intelligent behavior and surpass it. This view is not unchallenged.

successes. The emergence of the WWW and successful search engines for it delivered a different kind of decision-making power, where the collective's power helps sidestep difficult theoretical problems.

Those changes are forming a different research environment and directions for reasoning and decision making. These new directions will interact with developments in game theory, neurobiology, and other scientific fields which were not touched on here.

Further reading

On KR&R in general

Fagin, R., Halpern, J., Moses, Y., and Vardi, M. (1995). *Reasoning About Knowledge.* Cambridge MA: MIT Press.

Gabbay, D., Hogger, C., and Robinson, J. A. (eds.) (1993). *Handbook of Logic in Artificial Intelligence and Logic Programming,* vol. 3: *Nonmonotonic Reasoning and Uncertain Reasoning.* Oxford University Press.

Pearl, J. (1988). *Probabilistic Reasoning in Intelligent Systems: Networks of Plausible Inference.* San Francisco CA: Morgan Kaufmann.

On set theory

Kunen, K. (1980). *Set Theory: An Introduction to Independence Proofs.* Amsterdam: Elsevier.

On decision making

Littman, M. L. (1996). Algorithms for Sequential Decision Making. PhD Thesis, Brown University.

Sutton, R. S. and Barto, A. G. (1998). *Reinforcement Learning: An Introduction,* Cambridge, MA: MIT Press.

On theory of computation

Papadimitriou, C. H. (1994). *Computational Complexity.* Reading, MA: Addison-Wesley.

References

Amir, E. and Engelhardt, B. (2003). Factored planning, in *Proceedings of the 18th International Joint Conference on Artificial Intelligence (IJCAI '03),* (pp. 929–35). San Francisco, CA: Morgan Kaufmann.

Amir, E. and McIlraith, S. (2005). Partition-based logical reasoning for first-order and propositional theories, *Artificial Intelligence* 162: 49–88.

Buchanan, B. and Smith, R. (1988). Fundamentals of expert systems, *Annual Review of Computer Science* 3: 23–58.

Chang, A. and Amir, E. (2006). Goal achievement in partially known, partially observable domains, in *Proceedings of the 16th International Conference on Automated Planning and Scheduling (ICAPS'06)* (pp. 203–11). Menlo Park, CA: AAAI Press.

Cohn, A. G. (1997). Qualitative spatial representation and reasoning techniques, in G. Brewka, C. Habel, and B. Nebel, (eds.), *KI-97, Advances in Artificial Intelligence*, (pp. 1–30). Berlin: Springer.

de Salvo Braz, R., Amir, E., and Roth, D. (2006). MPE and partial inversion in lifted probabilistic variable elimination, in *Proceedings of the 21st National Conference on Artificial Intelligence (AAAI '06)*, vol. 2 (pp. 1123–30). Menlo Park, CA: AAAI Press.

Even-Dar, E., Kakade, S. M., and Mansour, Y. (2005). Reinforcement learning in POMDPs, in *Proceedings of the 19th International Joint Conference on Artificial Intelligence (IJCAI '05)* (pp. 660–5). ICJAI.

Fagin, R., Halpern, J., Moses, Y., and Vardi, M. (1995). *Reasoning About Knowledge.* Cambridge MA: MIT Press.

Gabbay, D., Hogger, C., and Robinson, J. A. (eds.) (1993). *Handbook of Logic in Artificial Intelligence and Logic Programming*, vol. 3: *Nonmonotonic Reasoning and Uncertain Reasoning.* Oxford University Press.

Kaelbling, L. P., Littman, M. L., and Cassandra, A. R. (1998). Planning and acting in partially observable stochastic domains, *Artificial Intelligence* 101: 99–134.

Kearns, M., Mansour, Y., and Ng, A. Y. (2000), Approximate planning in large POMDPs via reusable trajectories, in. S. A. Solla, T. K. Leen, and K-L. Müller (eds.), *Advances in Neural Information Processing Systems 12* (pp. 1001–7). Cambridge MA: MIT Press.

Kraus, S., Lehmann, D., and Magidor, M. (1990). Nonmonotonic reasoning, preferential models and cumulative logics, *Artificial Intelligence* 44: 167–207.

Lavrač, N. and Džeroski, S. (1994). *Inductive Logic Programming: Techniques and Applications.* New York: Ellis Horwood.

Lenat, D. B. (1995). Cyc: A large-scale investment in knowledge infrastructure, *Communications of the ACM* 38(11): 33–8.

Mancilla-Caceres, J. F. and Amir, E. (2011). Evaluating commonsense knowledge with a computer game, in P. Campos, N. Graham, J. Jorge, N. Nunes, P. Palanque, and M Winckler (eds.), *Proceedings of the 13th IFIP Conference on Human-Computer Interaction (INTERACT 2011)* (pp. 348–55). Berlin: Springer.

Manna, Z. and Pnueli, A. (1995). *Temporal Verification of Reactive Systems: Safety.* New York: Springer.

Matuszek, C., Witbrock, M., Kahlert, R. C., Cabral, J., Schneider, D., Shah, P., and Lenat, D. (2005). Searching for common sense: Populating cyc from the web, in *Proceedings of the 20th National Conference on Artificial Intelligence (AAAI'05)*, pp. 1430–5. AAAI.

McCarthy, J. (1958). Programs with common sense, in *Mechanisation of Thought Processes, Proceedings of the Symposium of the National Physics Laboratory* (pp. 77–84). London: Her Majesty's Stationery Office.

(1986). Applications of circumscription to formalizing common sense knowledge, *Artificial Intelligence* 28: 89–116.

McCarthy, J. and Hayes, P. J. (1969). Some philosophical problems from the standpoint of artificial intelligence, in B. Meltzer and D. Michie (eds.), *Machine Intelligence 4* (pp. 463–502). Edinburgh University Press.

Minsky, M. (1975). A framework for representing knowledge, in P. H. Winston (ed.), *The Psychology of Computer Vision* (pp. 211–77). New York: McGraw-Hill.

Pentney, W., Philipose, M., Bilmes, J., and Kautz, H. (2007). Learning large scale common sense models of everyday life, in *Proceedings of the 22nd National Conference on Artificial Intelligence (AAAI'07)*, vol. 1 (pp. 465–70). AAAI.

Pfeffer, A., Koller, D., Milch, B., and Takusagawa, K. T. (1999). SPOOK: A system for probabilistic object-oriented knowledge representation, in K. Laskey and H. Prade (eds.), *Proceedings of the 15th Conference on Uncertainty in Artificial Intelligence (UAI'99)* (pp. 541–50). San Francisco: Morgan Kaufmann.

Poole, D. (2003). First-order probabilistic inference, in *Proceedings of the 18th International Joint Conference on Artificial Intelligence (IJCAI '03)* (pp. 985–91). San Francisco: Morgan Kaufmann.

Ramachandran, D., Reagan, P., and Goolsbey, K. (2005). First-orderized Research-Cyc: Expressivity and efficiency in a common-sense ontology, in *Papers from the AAAI Workshop on Contexts and Ontologies: Theory, Practice and Applications* (pp. 33–40), AAAI Technical Report WS-05-01.

Reiter, R. (2001). *Knowledge in Action: Logical Foundations for Describing and Implementing Dynamical Systems.* Cambridge MA: MIT Press.

Selman, B., Mitchell, D., and Levesque, H. (1997). Generating hard satisfiability problems, *Artificial Intelligence* 81: 17–29.

Singh, P., Lin, T., Mueller, E. T., Lim, G., Perkins, T., and Zhu, W. L. (2002). Open mind common sense: Knowledge acquisition from the general public, in *Proceedings of the First International Conference on Ontologies, Databases, and Applications of Semantics for Large Scale Information Systems, LNCS.*

Tseitin, G. (1970). On the complexity of proofs in propositional logics, *Seminars in Mathematics* 8.

Williams, M-A., and Rott, H. (eds.) (2001). *Frontiers in Belief Revision (Applied Logic Series 22).* Dordrecht: Kluwer Academic Publishers.

10 Language and communication

Yorick Wilks

10.1 Introduction

Language and communication, considered as relevant to artificial intelligence (AI) in general, I take to refer to the issues that cluster round the representation of language and meaning so as to enable language processing and the communication of meaning by a computer, an area of research roughly captured by the fields of Natural Language Processing (NLP) and Computational Linguistics (CL).

A remarkable feature of the fifty-year history of those two related fields is how much of what we now take as topics of current interest was there from the very beginning; all the pioneers lacked were real computers. In the fifties and sixties, Gilbert King was arguing for machine translation by statistical methods, which is only now a reality, Margaret Masterman for the power of meaning-based structures in programs, and Vic Yngve, still working at the time of writing, had designed COMIT, a special programming language for NLP, and had stated his famous claim that limits on the way computers process language should reflect the way the syntax of a language is structured. This last project brought Yngve into direct conflict with Noam Chomsky over permissible ways of drawing syntactic tree structures, which can now be seen to have constituted a defining moment of schism in the history of NLP in its relationship to mainstream linguistics. Chomsky has always denied any relevance of computation to the understanding of language structure, and this foundational schism was not healed until decades later, when Gerald Gazdar became the first major linguist to embrace a computational strategy explicitly.

A rule of thumb for expressing the difference between NLP and CL is that CL has always claimed to be a program of scientific investigation using computers for language processing, while NLP is said to consist of applications, such as machine translation (MT), which was the original task of NLP, and remains a principal one. There is now a wide range of other NLP tasks that researchers investigate and for which companies sell software solutions: question answering, information extraction, document summarization, and so on. Thus, NLP does require a task and it is not in itself a program of scientific investigation, even though many believe that MT remains the application within which any CL theory embodied in programs should be tested.

It is also important to distinguish major tasks, like those just mentioned, from a wide range of tasks that are defined only in terms of linguistic theories and whose outcomes can only be judged by experts, as opposed to naïve users of the results of the major tasks above, in the sense that any competent bilingual can judge the quality of output from an MT program. These more subject-internal tasks include word-sense disambiguation, part-of-speech tagging, syntactic analysis, parallel text alignment, and so on, and these can be thought of as ways of testing individual CL hypotheses, rather than producing useful artifacts.

Linguists are not the only scientists wishing to test theories of language functioning: so do psychologists and neurophysiologists. The dominant linguistic paradigm of the last half-century, Chomsky's, has never accepted that CL was the way to test linguistic theories. This dispute is over what constitutes the data of language study, and it separates out very clearly NLP and CL on the one side, from linguistics proper on the other, a subject for which data is intimately connected with the intuitions of a speaker rather than with computable processes applied to language data, usually called *corpora*. Since 1990 emphasis has shifted to the use of corpora of actual texts, rather than those imagined or written by linguists. Corpora are now normally gleaned from the web and have become the canonical data of NLP and CL.

10.2   Early systems in NLP/CL

A feature of the history of NLP/CL that cannot be overemphasized is the effect of hardware developments, which have produced extraordinary increases in the storage and processing power available for experiments. This is obvious, and its effect on the field's development can be seen by considering the case of Karen Spärck Jones' PhD thesis, which was almost certainly the first work to apply statistical clustering techniques to semantic questions, and the first to make use of a large corpus resource, *Roget's Thesaurus*. Her statistical "clump" algorithms required the computation of large matrices that simply could not be fully computed with the tiny machines of 1964. Consequently, this work's significance was not appreciated at the time and it has been regularly rediscovered, usually without knowledge of the original, at regular intervals ever since.

The first piece of work to capture wider AI attention outside mainstream NLP was Winograd's MIT thesis (Winograd 1972) based on his SHRDLU system. One reason for the interest it aroused was its choice of domain: the MIT blocks world used for robotics and planning research, which consisted of a tabletop containing blocks of different shapes that could be stacked, as well as a crane and a box for putting blocks in, all of which were either real or simulated (simulated in Winograd's case). It was a small world about which it was possible to know every fact. Winograd designed a dialogue program that discussed this world and manipulated it by responding to ambiguous requests such as PUT THE RED BLOCK ON THE GREEN BLOCK IN THE BOX.

This system had many sophisticated features, including an implementation of a linguistic grammar designed by Michael Halliday explicitly for communication purposes (unlike most linguistic grammars at the time which were purely abstract). This grammar was programmed in a procedural language, PROGRAMMAR, which prefigured the language LISP and was designed, like COMIT before it, explicitly for processing strings of symbols such as sentences. It also had a method for building representations of truth conditions in a LISP-like language, which could then be evaluated against the state of the blocks world. These conditions expressed the semantic content of an utterance and, if the sentence evaluated to TRUE then the values of any object representations in the conditions, when run as a program, gave the denotations of the objects in the sentence, which would be the name of a particular block. This was an elegant procedural implementation of Gottlob Frege's distinction between sense and reference. Like most systems at that time, it was not available for general testing and performed on only a handful of sentences.

SHRDLU's virtues and failings can be seen by contrasting it with a contemporary system from Stanford: Colby's PARRY dialogue system (Parkinson, Colby, and Faught 1977). This system, also programmed in LISP, was made available over the then young internet and tested by thousands of users, who often refused to believe they had not been typing to a human being. It simulated a paranoid patient in a Veterans' hospital, and had all the interest and conversational skills that Joseph Weizenbaum's more famous but trivial ELIZA lacked. It was very robust, appeared to remember what was said to it and reacted badly when internal parameters called FEAR and ANGER became high. It did not repeat itself and appeared anxious to contribute to the conversation when subjects about which it was paranoid were touched on: horses, racing, gambling, Italian-Americans and the Mafia. Unlike SHRDLU, it had no grammar, parsing, or logic, but only a very fast table of some six thousand patterns that were matched onto its input.

Contrasts between these two systems show issues that became more important later in NLP: widely available and robust systems (PARRY) vs. toy ones (SHRDLU); grammar parsing, which was cumbrous and rarely successful (SHRDLU), vs. surface pattern matching (in PARRY, and later to be called *information extraction*); systems driven by world knowledge (SHRDLU) vs. those (such as PARRY) that were not and that essentially "knew" nothing (although PARRY would have been a far better choice as a desert island companion than SHRDLU). John McCarthy, in whose laboratory PARRY was created, said that PARRY was not really AI "because it knew nothing, not even who the

President is." The day after he said this, PARRY did know that, which shows the weakness of any such criterion for "being real AI."

We began this chapter by looking briefly at samples of important and prescient early work, and then showing two contrasting, slightly later, approaches to the extraction of content, evaluation, representation, and the role of knowledge. We shall now consider a range of systems embodying NLP/CL aspects since the early seventies and divide them by their relationships to linguistic systems (Section 10.3 below) and in relation to concepts normally taken as central to AI, namely logic, knowledge, and semantics (Section 10.4 below).

10.3   NLP/CL systems in relation to linguistics

Explicit links between CL/NLP and linguistics proper are neither as numerous nor as productive as one might imagine. We have already referred to the early schism between Yngve and Chomsky over the nature of tree representations and, more importantly, over the role of procedures and processing resources in the computation of syntactic structure. It was Yngve's claim that such computation had to respect limits on storage capacity for intermediate structures, which he assumed corresponded to innate constraints on human processing of languages. (An example is that highlighted in George Miller's contemporary claim about the depth of human linguistic processing, usually known as "the magical number seven, plus or minus two," which indicates the number of independent items – either words or syntactic structures of grammar codes – that the brain could maintain and manipulate at one time in memory.) Chomsky, on the other hand, assigned all such considerations to mere language performance.

In the sixties there were a number of attempts to program Chomsky's transformational grammars so as to parse sentences, the largest and longest running being at IBM in New York. These were uniformly unsuccessful in that they parsed little or nothing beyond the sentences for which they had been designed, and even then produced a large number of readings between which it was impossible to choose. This last was the fate of virtually all syntactic analyzers until the more recent statistical developments described below.

Even in these early days, some grammars (like those at IBM) were designed explicitly as the basis of parsing programs, rather than for straightforward linguistic investigation. Later, as linguists became more computationally orientated, such parser-directed grammar research became important: The best known was Generalized Phrase Structure Grammar (GPSG) from Gazdar and colleagues which constituted a return to phrase structure from Chomsky-style transformational grammar. Later came Head-driven Phrase Structure Grammar (HPSG) from Ronald Kaplan and Joan Bresnan, and Functional Unification Grammar (FUG) from Martin Kay. FUG, like Winograd's earlier work, was inspired by Halliday's grammars, as well as the unification logic paradigm for grammar processing that came with the rise of the programming language Prolog.

These researchers shared with Chomsky, and linguists in general, the belief that the determination of syntactic structure was not only an end in itself, in that it was a self-sufficient task, but was also necessary for the determination of semantic structure. It was not until much later, with the development of techniques like information extraction (a technique to be described in some detail below), that this link was questioned with large-scale experimental results.

However, this link was also questioned very early on by those in NLP who saw semantic structure as primary and substantially independent of syntactic structure as far as the determination of content was concerned. These researchers, such as Roger Schank and Yorick Wilks in the sixties and seventies, drew some inspiration and support from the case grammar of Charles Fillmore. Fillmore had argued, initially within the Chomskyan paradigm, that the case elements of a verb are crucial to sentence structure (e.g., agents, patients, recipients of actions). His approach emphasized the semantic content of language more than its grammatical structure, since these case elements could appear under many grammatical forms. There have been hundreds of attempts to parse sentences computationally into case structure, and Fillmore remains almost certainly the linguist with most explicit influence on NLP/CL as a whole.

10.4   Representation issues: Logic, knowledge, and semantics

The central AI vision (e.g., that of McCarthy and Hayes 1969) is that some version of the first-order predicate calculus (FOPC), augmented by whatever mechanisms are found necessary, will be sufficient for the task of representing language and knowledge. This position and its parallel movement in linguistic semantics claim that logic can and should provide the underlying semantics of natural language, and it has had a profound and continuing effect on CL/NLP.

Although attempts in AI and linguistics to design some form of logical semantics as the key to content representation for language sentences have continued, they have had little success in producing any general and usable program to translate English to formal logic. Nor has there been any demonstration from psychology that such a translation into logic would correspond to the way humans store and manipulate meaning. In the long course of language processing competitions run by the US Defense Advanced Research Projects Agency (DARPA), the translation of English to FOPC structures remains a goal, but no one has yet set realistic standards for its achievement.

There will undoubtedly be NLP applications that require logical inferences to be established between sentence representations, but, if those are only part of an application (e.g., the consistency of times in an airline reservation system), it is not obvious that they have anything to do with the underlying meaning structure of natural language, and hence with CL/NLP proper, since the original function of logical structure was to take part in inferences. At this point in the discussion, there are a number of possible routes that can be taken: One can say, (1) that logical inferences are intimately involved in the meanings of sentences, since to know their meanings is to be able to draw inferences, and logic is the best way to do that. A clear statement of this view of the role of logic in AI is given by Thomason (2003). One can also say (2) that there can be meaning representation outside logic, and this can be found in linguistics back to the semantic marker theories of Jerry Fodor and Jerrold Katz, developed within Chomsky's transformational paradigm, as well as quite independently in NLP as forms of computational semantics. These theories postulate a number of semantic markers or primitives, such as ANIMATE, or primitive actions, such as MOVE, that can be attached to words so as to express their meaning; a process we would now normally call "annotation." There is also a more extreme position (3) that the predicates of logic, and formal systems generally, only appear to be different from human language (often accentuated by writing their predicates in capital letters, as in (2) above), but this is an illusion, and their terms are in fact the language words they appear to be, as prone to ambiguity and vagueness as other words. Both sides of this are argued in Nirenburg and Wilks (2001).

Under (2) above, one can point to the AI NLP tradition of the seventies and eighties of conceptual/semantic codings of meaning (already mentioned in the last section) by means of a language of primitive elements and the drawing of (non-logical) inferences from structures based on them. The best known of such 1970s systems were Schank's Conceptual Dependency system (Schank and Rieger 1974) and Wilks' Preference Semantics system (Wilks and Fass 1992); both were implemented in MT systems, as well as a range of other NLP applications. In the MT systems, codings comprising structures of these primitive elements were used as an interlingua, or intermediate meaning language, between the languages being translated. Schank's system was based on a set of fourteen primitive verbs, and Wilks' on a set of about eighty primitives of various types. Schank asserted firmly that his primitives were not English words, in spite of similarities of appearance (e.g., with the English word INGEST), whereas Wilks argued there could be many sets of primitives and that they were no more than privileged words, as in dictionary definitions (see Section 10.5 below). Wilks' notion of "preference" became well established: the notion that verbs and adjectives have preferred agents, objects, and so on, and that knowledge of these default preferences is the major method of ambiguity resolution and the detection of metaphor. Such preferences were later computed statistically when NLP became larger scale and more empirical (see Section 10.6 below). Schank later developed larger-scale structures called *scripts* that became highly influential as a way of capturing the overall meaning of texts and dialogues.

There are analogies between this strand of NLP work and contemporary work in linguistics, particularly that of Fillmore and George Lakoff, but there was at that time little or no direct contact between researchers in NLP and linguistics proper. One of the most striking changes over the last twenty years is the realization by linguists, at least since the work of Gazdar, that computational methods could be central for them. But there were undoubtedly influences across the divide: For example, Ray Jackendoff in 1990 proposed structured sequences of primitives, such as CAUSE GO LIQUID TO IN MOUTHOF to represent "drink," which were virtually identical to the earlier NLP structures of Wilks mentioned above. Again, this level of semantic representation, between first-order logic and language not only took root in linguistics but also returned later to AI via a peculiar route we shall discuss later in connection with the Semantic Web, where a shallow but tractable non-logical representation called RDF (Resource Description Framework) has become a basic level of knowledge description within a new AI tradition.

Three other representational traditions in AI also have direct relations to language issues: speech acts, procedural semantics, and connectionism. *Speech acts* is a notion drawn from John Searle's work in philosophy which has become the central concept in computational pragmatics. The notion might enable a system to distinguish a request for information from an apparent question that is really a command, such as "Can you close the door?" This utterance appears to be a question, but Searle argued that it should be represented as a request to act, and close the door. Ray Perrault and his colleagues at Toronto in the late seventies were the first group to compute over beliefs represented in FOPC so as to assign speech acts to utterances in a dialogue system. The Toronto system was designed as a railway advisory system for passengers, and made use of limited logical reasoning to establish, for example, that the system knew when a given train arrived, and the passenger knew it did, so the question "Do you know when the next train from Montreal arrives?" would not be, as it might appear, about the system's own knowledge of itself, but rather a request to disclose that knowledge. In translating Searle's ideas to programs, this group found errors in its formulation, and their account of speech acts is in some ways more coherent than the original. Speech act representation and its deployment in human–computer dialogue systems remains important since it is fundamentally concerned with communication, in a way few areas of NLP/CL are.

Procedural semantics was initially a strand in AI theory. The claim, in various forms, is that the meanings of symbols in computations that express intelligent functions are themselves procedures, rather than the referential entities declared in conventional formal semantics. Versions of such a procedural theory were put forward by Terry Winograd, Bill Woods, Philip Johnson-Laird, and Yorick Wilks. In Winograd's SHRDLU, for example, notions like moving the crane arm were not expressed by any primitive action (like MOVE) but by the actual procedures or code to move the arm. The notion of "meanings as procedures" was attacked by Fodor on the grounds that all such theories are in fact grounded in the bottom-level machine code of actual computing engines, which really does provide the referential entities in question, by means of its formal program semantics. This was strongly denied by some of that theory's proponents by making use of the Scott–Strachey principle that the semantics of the different "program levels" are independent, and so the semantics of one cannot be a semantics for another: That is, the semantics of machine-code translations is irrelevant to the semantics of the higher-level action it coded.

Some mention should also be made here of connectionism: The cluster of AI theories based on the concept of very simple computing units, connected in very large numbers, and "learning from experience" by means of shifting aggregated weights in a network. This development may offer a way forward in many areas of artificial intelligence, including computational semantics of natural language. Connectionism shares many of the features of procedural semantics that distinguish both from the logicist views. These features include the integration of semantics and syntax; continuity between linguistic and other forms of world knowledge (and again, not in the sense of simply assimilating the former to the latter as some logicist and "expert-system" approaches do); and a type of inference that is not reconcilable with the kind offered by logic-based approaches. Moreover, connectionism has stressed notions such as that of competition between representational structures so that the stronger, more connected, structure "wins out," a notion to be found explicitly in computational semantics systems such as Preference Semantics.

An important difference, as regards lexical ambiguity resolution in particular, arises here between so-called *sub-symbolic* approaches within connectionism (defended by Paul Smolensky) and those usually called *localist* (defended by David Waltz and Jordan Pollack). This difference bears very much on the issue of representation: In a sub-symbolic approach to computational semantics one would not necessarily expect to distinguish representations for particular word senses; they would be simply different patterns of activation over a set of units representing sub-symbolic features, where similar senses would lead to similar patterns. On the other hand, localist approaches to computational semantics have assumed real distinguishable word senses in their symbolic representations at the outset, and have then given weighting criteria for selecting between them. The mainstream of AI still remains, at the time of writing, firmly committed to the notion of symbol manipulation and explicit representations as the basis of their craft.

10.5   Corpora, resources, and dictionaries

In the sixties, Margaret Masterman and Karen Spärck Jones made use of *Roget's Thesaurus*, punched onto IBM cards, as a device for word-sense disambiguation and semantic primitive derivation, even though they could not do serious computations on the computers then available. After that, large-scale linguistic computation was found only in machine translation; in the era of the influence of AI methods in CL/NLP the vocabularies of working systems were found by Boguraev to average about thirty-five, which gave rise to the term "toy systems" to refer to most of the systems described earlier.

But there were movements to use substantial corpora of texts for experiments, although these were driven largely from the humanities and in the interests of stylistic studies and statistical measures of word use and distribution. The best known of these was the Brown-Oslo-Bergen corpus of English, but the British National Corpus was constructed explicitly with the needs of NLP in mind, and the University of Lancaster team, under Geoffrey Leech, played a key role in its construction. This group had already created the first effective piece of corpora-based statistical NLP, the part-of-speech tagger CLAWS4 which assigned part-of-speech codes like ADJ (for adjective) automatically to all the words in a corpus.

At the same time, in the early eighties, interest arose in the value to NLP not only of text corpora in general, but specifically of dictionaries, both monolingual and bilingual. Bran Boguraev in Cambridge was one of the first researchers (since very early work on *Webster's Third Dictionary* at Systems Development Corporation in the sixties) to seek to make use of a dictionary via its coded form used by its publishers, in this case the *Longman Dictionary of Contemporary English* (LDOCE), a dictionary specifically designed for foreign learners of the language. This had definitions with restricted syntax drawn from a vocabulary of only 2,000 words.

In the eighties there was a great deal of activity devoted to extracting computational meaning on a large scale from such machine-readable dictionaries. It seemed a sensible way to overcome the "toy system" problem and, given that dictionaries encode meanings, why not use them as a means of direct access to semantic representations? Substantial and useful semantic databases were constructed automatically from LDOCE and a range of other dictionaries, again usually from dictionaries for learners of English since they expressed themselves more explicitly than traditional dictionaries for scholars and the broadly educated. Hierarchical ontologies of concepts were constructed automatically, and these databases of definitions remain, along with thesauri, a component database for many major systems for resolving word-sense ambiguity. An ontology can be broadly understood as a tree structure of concepts that include concepts or individuals below them in the tree, in the way the class or concept "birds" contains "canaries" because all canaries are birds. But such dictionaries were not a panacea that cured the problem of meaning, and it became clear that dictionaries themselves require substantial implicit knowledge to be of computational use.

Another quite independent source of annotated corpus resources was tree banks, of which the Penn Tree Bank is the best known. This is a corpus syntactically structured by hand, with the syntactic structure being added to the text as annotations, indicating structure and not merely categories. One effect of the wide use of the Penn Tree Bank for experiments was to enshrine the texts used for it, in particular sections of the *Wall Street Journal*, as über-corpora, used so much and so often that some believed their particular features had distorted NLP research. In the recent past much energy and discussion was put into the selecting and "balancing" of corpora – so much dialogue, so many novels and memoranda etc. – but this activity is becoming irrelevant because of the growing use of very large parts of the World Wide Web itself as a corpus that can be annotated.

10.6   Statistical and quantitative methods in NLP

The large-scale introduction of statistical methods into CL/NLP is the recent trend in the field most difficult to survey in brief, because we are still within that movement at the time of writing (see a survey of the principal methods in use in Manning and Schütze 1999). Broadly, statistical methods imply the use of only numerical, quantitatively based, methods for NLP/CL, rather than methods based on representations, whether those are assigned by humans or by computers. The general strategy employed is to *learn* how to process language, hopefully in the way humans do, though this is not essential. In the case of MT, for example, this implies learning to translate by processing very large corpora of actual translations, done by humans. It is often taken to mean learning how to assign annotations, the marking up of corpora (of the sort just discussed), with part-of-speech categories or semantic markers/primitives, and doing this from large corpora already marked up in part by humans.

In the sixties, Gilbert King predicted that MT could be done by statistical methods, on the ground of the well-known 50 percent redundancy of characters and words in Western languages, though it is not easy to see why the second implied the first. Later, and as we saw earlier, Spärck Jones pioneered what were essentially information retrieval (IR) methods to produce semantic classifications, intended ultimately for use in MT. We noted earlier that the first clear example of modern statistical NLP was the work by Leech and his colleagues on the CLAWS4 part-of-speech tagger in the late seventies. At the time, few could see the interest of assigning part-of-speech categories to text words. Yet now, almost all text-processing work starts with a part-of-speech assignment phase, since this is now believed (even at about 98 percent accuracy, the usual level achieved) to simplify all subsequent linguistic processes. It does so by filtering out a large range of possibilities that used to overtax syntactic analyzers. The undoubted success of such methods showed that analysis decisions previously believed to need "high-level" syntactic or semantic information could be performed using only lower-level statistical information about word sequences.

The greatest impetus for statistical NLP, however, came from work on the MT research program of Frederick Jelinek and his group at IBM (Brown et al., 1990), who applied machine learning methods that had been successful in automatic speech recognition (ASR) to MT, which had been considered a purely symbolic and linguistic problem. Jelinek began asking what the phenomenon to be modeled was – answer, translation – and then seeking examples of that human skill to apply machine learning to. The most obvious resource capturing that skill was parallel corpora: texts expressing the same meaning in more than one language. These were widely available and he took millions of words from the Canadian Hansard texts in English and French.

We have already described one form machine learning (ML) in NLP can take: In the CLAWS4 work the phenomenon (part-of-speech tagging) had been annotated onto the text by humans and the ML algorithms were then set to learn the possible associations of tags with words and were then able to tag new, unseen, texts at some acceptable level of accuracy. This is called supervised ML, by which is meant that the target for the learning is given. In the Jelinek MT work, on the other hand, although the targets to be learned are given, namely the translations in the parallel texts, the training material had not been produced specifically for this task by humans assigning codings. The target data is just naturally occurring texts, albeit produced by people. Many would call this weakly supervised ML. In unsupervised ML, however, no targets of any kind are given. In the work of Spärck Jones, mentioned earlier, thesaurus data is clustered into semantically relevant groupings, which are not given in advance at all.

Jelinek's CANDIDE system worked by first learning to align the sentences of the French and English texts so they corresponded in meaning. It then learned the associations between the content words of the corresponding/aligned French and English sentence pairs – so that English word Ex, say, was found regularly opposite French words Fy or Fz in different aligned sentences. Meanwhile, it had learned likely word sequences in the output language, say French, and with these it was able to show that, for sentences aligned with Ex, with some set of neighboring words $F \ldots F$, then Fy was the more likely output for Ex, while in other sequences of neighbors $F \ldots F$, the likely output would be Fz. By such methods – largely derived from earlier work by this team on speech-to-English transcriptions – CANDIDE was able to give discrimination between possible output word strings in the target language.

CANDIDE produced an accuracy level of about 50 percent of sentences translated correctly, a remarkable fact given that the system had no explicitly linguistic knowledge of any kind, such as dictionaries or grammars. When applied to new, unseen, texts it nevertheless failed to beat the traditional, hand-coded, MT system SYSTRAN, which had not been trained for specific kinds of text. The system was only a benchmark, but the 50 percent limit suggested there were bounds to purely statistical methods applied to a linguistic task like MT. Jelinek himself began a program for the derivation of linguistic structures (lexicons, grammars, etc.) by those same statistical ML methods, in an attempt to raise the levels of CANDIDE's success. In doing so he set in motion a movement throughout NLP to learn traditional NLP/CL structures at every linguistic level by those methods.

There are now far too many such applications to cite here, and this introduction of ML into every part of NLP has served to bring language processing closer again to the center of AI, since ML is such a fundamental methodology in AI. ML (see Manning and Schütze, 1999) methods have been applied to the alignment of texts, syntactic analysis, semantic tagging, word-sense disambiguation, speech act assignment, and even dialogue management. In the case of some of these traditional tasks, the nature of the task has changed with the evaluation and scoring regimes that have come along with the paradigm shift. For example, only a few years ago it was conventional to say that syntactic parsers had failed, at least for languages like English, and that there simply was no parser that could be relied on to produce a correct parse for an unseen English sentence. However, now that statistically based parsers can learn over tree banks, like the Penn Tree Bank mentioned earlier, and are scored by the number of brackets they can correctly insert and the appropriate phrase structure annotations they can assign, the issue is merely quantitative and it is no longer considered essential that a "full parse" is produced.

There is a general perception that statistical, or corpus-driven (i.e., empirical), linguistics have resulted in a shift to re-emphasizing surface considerations in language. For example, the shallower syntactic parse results just mentioned have allowed syntactic analysis to become more useful in linguistic processing, because they are more successful and reliable. One could also point to the success of the separate NLP task information extraction (IE) (Cowie and Wilks, 2000), which, in broad terms, consists in extracting fact-like structures from texts on a large scale for practical purposes by skimming the surface structure of the text for patterns, rather than by parsing its syntactic structure. For example, an IE system might seek all the facts in public source newspapers about people in IBM who were promoted in 2010, and do so with specific patterns coded for such a task, or machine learned from examples. IE has become an established technology largely without the use of syntactic analysis and access to knowledge structures, although those have played a role in some successful systems. IE now works at the 95 percent plus level of success that is the norm of acceptability in empirical linguistics. However, many of the more recent successes of this main modern approach, again based on ML over corpora, have been in areas normally considered semantic or "less superficial" in nature, such as word-sense disambiguation and the annotation of dialogue utterances with their dialogue or speech acts, indicating their function in the overall dialogue.

In the final parts of the chapter, I wish to consider two alternative traditions to both the traditional GOFAI (Good Old-Fashioned AI) core of AI and the period of statistical reaction against it, a period in whose ascendancy we still are. One of these is an alternative statistical surface-like approach to post-Jelinek empirical NLP: the tradition of IR, which is as old as AI itself. The other is the more recent Semantic Web movement, which I believe has roots in NLP and IE (though this would be contested by its founder Tim Berners-Lee).

10.7   AI and Information Retrieval

As we noted at the start of the chapter, the classical, McCarthyan, period of AI was logic- or symbol-based but not entirely devoid of numbers, of course, for AI theories of vision flourished in close proximity to pattern-recognition research. Although symbolic, representational, theories in computer vision sometimes achieved prominence, as in the work of David Marr, nonetheless it was always, at bottom, a quantitative engineering sub-discipline. But when faced with any attempt to introduce quantitative methods into classical core AI in the seventies, John McCarthy would always respond "But where do all these numbers come from?"

Since the return of quantitative methods to NLP/CL, just described, we now know better where the numbers come from; but nowhere have numbers been more prominent than in the quite separate field of IR. IR is of similar antiquity to AI, but the two have until now rarely tangled intellectually, although on any broad definition of AI as "modeling intelligent human capacities," one might imagine that IR, like MT, would be covered. Yet neither IR nor MT has traditionally been seen as part of AI. IR is fundamentally a statistical document retrieval methodology, one that clusters documents on the basis of their word contents into sets of documents relevant to each other, so that anyone who wants one document may well want to see others in the same cluster. It was for this reason that we described Spärck Jones' early work on clustering linguistic thesaurus terms as IR-inspired. In some sense, all such unsupervised clustering tasks are forms of classification. IR, then, retrieves documents from clusters of documents it has formed up, whereas IE retrieves fact-like knowledge items from texts or, by extension, answers questions from text. IR can only give you documents; however, the distinction blurs given that a single sentence can be considered a small document.

IR may, after all, not be a pre-existing intelligent human functionality now being modeled by computers, like MT, because, in earlier pre-mechanical times, humans were not in practice able to carry out the kinds of large-scale searches and comparison operations on which IR rests. And, even though IR often cohabits with library science, which grew out of card indexing in libraries, there is perhaps no true continuity between those subfields, since modern IR consists of operations of indexing and retrieval that humans could not carry out in normal lifetimes.

Should any reader begin to wonder why I have raised the question of the relationship of AI to IR, it is because Spärck Jones, in a remarkable paper, has already done so in an AI context (2003) and argued that AI has much to learn from IR. Her main target was AI researchers seen as what she called "The Guardians of content." I shall briefly set out her views and then contest them. By making an analogy with the case of MT in particular, I shall suggest that the •
influence is perhaps in the other direction, of AI on IR. That is demonstrated both by limitations on statistical methods that MT developments have shown in recent years, and by a curious reversal of terminology in IR that has taken place in the same period. The important questions in Spärck Jones' article reduce to one crucial question: What is the primitive level of language data? Her position on this is shown by the initial quotations below that capture the essence of her views:

One of these [simple, revolutionary, IR] ideas is taking words as they stand. (Spärck Jones 2003, p. 1)

The AI claim in its strongest form means that the knowledge base completely replaces the text base of the documents. (Spärck Jones 1999, p. 258)

I would summarize her complex position as follows: Words are self-representing in that they cannot be replaced by any more primitive representation; all we, as technicians with computers, can add are sophisticated associations between them. Yet, core AI mistakenly seeks to replace words, with their inevitable inexactness, with exact logical – or at least non-word-based – representations.

We should not see the issues here as simply Spärck Jones' critique (based on IR) of core, traditional or symbolic AI, for her views connect directly to an internal issue within AI itself, one about which the discipline has held an internal dialogue for many years, both broadly and in many of its subareas. The issue is that of the nature of, and necessity for, structured symbolic representations, and their relationship to the data they claim to represent. This is an issue that we already discussed above in connection with the proposals of Schank and Wilks in the 1970s for a level of representation of language that was not logic but had some of the properties of language itself. The key reference for the view Spärck Jones rejects would be the already cited

McCarthy and Hayes paper (1969), and its extreme opposite would be any view that has elements that could be termed connectionist, one that insists on the primacy of data over any possible representation of it.

It should be clear from the preceding paragraphs that Spärck Jones is not targeting all of AI, but only the strong representationalist tradition, one usually (but not always, as in the case of Schank and others above) associated with the use of first-order predicate calculus. Her basic argument is that words remain their own best interpretation, and cannot be replaced by some other artificial coding, such as logic, in order to represent their meaning. Unless Spärck Jones really intends to claim that *any* method of language analysis exploiting statistics and redundancy (like those cited in the last section) is really IR, then there is little basis for her claim that AI has a lot to learn from IR in this area, since it now has its own traditions of statistical methodology, and these came into AI/NLP from speech research pioneered by Jelinek and indigenous work on machine learning, and not at all from IR.

Annotations are also forms of representation, and there can be no doubt that attaching to words even very low-level annotations, however obtained, can produce results that would be hard to imagine without them. A striking case is the use of part-of-speech tags (such as PROPERNOUN) already mentioned; given a word-sense resource such as the LDOCE, Mark Stevenson and Yorick Wilks were able to show that those part-of-speech tags alone can resolve word-sense ambiguity (at least at the level called homographs in the LDOCE) at about a 92 percent accuracy level. Given such a simple tagging, almost all word-sense ambiguity is trivially resolved against that particular structured resource, a result that could not conceivably be obtained without those low-level additional representations, which are not merely the words themselves.

10.8 The Semantic Web and AI

Let us now turn in a final section to link together many of the considerations of earlier parts of this chapter, in particular the role of annotations to texts and the interpretability of core AI representations. Some have taken the initial presentation of the Semantic Web (SW) proposal by Berners-Lee, Hendler, and Lassila (2001) to be a restatement of the GOFAI agenda in new and fashionable WWW terms. In that article, the three authors describe a system of services, such as fixing up a doctor's appointment for an elderly relative, which would require planning and access to the databases of both the doctor's and relative's diaries and synchronizing them. This kind of planning behavior was at the heart of GOFAI, and there has been a direct transition (quite outside the discussion of the SW proposals themselves) from decades of work on formal knowledge representation in AI to the modern discussion of ontologies – which are far more than hierarchical relations of concepts but are rather knowledge representations in general under a new name. The basic form of information in the SW is that of a triplestore: very large numbers of simple graphs based on words and primitive actions in what is called RDF, the Resource Description Format. It is in this format that large numbers of official documents (as well as Wikipedia, Facebook, etc.) are being released for further processing on the internet. One more general way of describing the SW is as the WWW but in a form which in some sense "understands" the semantic content of the web, in a way the WWW plainly does not. It no more understands the texts it contains than a television knows what it is showing.

This is clearest in work on formal ontologies as representing the content of science (as in the work of Horrocks 2005), where many of the same individuals have transferred discussion of research issues from one paradigm – Knowledge Representation (KR) in AI – to the other (SW). All this has been done within the standard KR assumption within AI, and one that goes back to the earliest work on systematic KR by McCarthy and Hayes (1969), a work we took as defining core GOFAI. A key assumption of all such work was that the predicates in KR representations merely look like English words but are in fact formal objects, loosely related to the corresponding English, but without its ambiguity, vagueness, and ability to acquire new senses with use. We shall return below to this assumption, one which has certainly been important in both the original SW paper and some of what has flowed from it.

Nonetheless, few of the complex theories about KR in GOFAI actually appear in their original forms within SW discussions so far: from McCarthy and Hayes' fluents, McCarthy's later autoepistemic logic, and Hayes' Naïve Physics, to name but a few prominent examples. A continuity of goals between GOFAI and the SW has not simply meant continuity of particular research traditions and this is both a gain and a loss: a gain because it has yielded simpler schemes of representation which are probably computable; a loss because of the lack of sophistication in current schemes of the DAML/OIL family of reasoning languages for the SW. The underlying issue is whether these new SW-orientated reasoning systems have the representational power needed for the complexity of the world, commonsense or scientific. There have been at least two other traditions of input to what we now call the SW, and I shall discuss one: namely, the way in which the SW concept has grown from the humanist tradition of document annotation.

In the original *Scientific American* paper introducing the SW, there is a diagram of the SW's structure with low-level XML at the bottom reaching up to complex concepts at the upper levels such as rules, logic, proof, and trust. Looking only at these upper-level labels has caused some critics and admirers of the SW to say that it is the GOFAI project by another name, since those notions were part of the core of traditional AI. But if one looks at the lower levels one finds Namespaces and XML, which are all products of what we may broadly call NLP obtained from the annotation of texts by a technology we may conveniently continue to call IE, as in the sections above.

IE now reliably locates names in text, their semantic types, and relates them together by means of learned structures called templates into forms of fact and events, objects virtually identical to the RDF triplestores at the base of the SW, which are not quite logic, but very like IE output. IE began by automating annotation but now has developed what we may call annotation engines based on machine learning (e.g., Ciravegna et al. 2004), which learn to annotate texts in any form and in any domain. This view of the SW, in which NLP is crucial to its development, is not the only view, as I emphasized at the beginning, but it is the one that underlies most work on the SW in Europe. On such a view, the SW can be seen at its base level as a conversion from the WWW of texts by means of an annotation process of increasing grasp and vision, one that projects notions of meaning up the classic SW diagram from the bottom to the complex concepts at the top. If this can be achieved within the SW project – the assignment of meaning to abstract concepts by empirical processes linking them back to text – then this will be a major intellectual achievement of AI and the solution to a problem that has been with it from its very beginning.

Further reading

Allen, J. (1995). *Natural Language Understanding* (2nd edn.). Redwood City, CA: Benjamin/Cummings. The best survey of NLP/CL work from an AI perspective by a major theoretical contributor.

Charniak, E. (1993). *Statistical Language Learning.* Cambridge, MA: MIT Press. Short, accessible introduction to the motivations and methods of the statistical movement in NLP/CL.

Gazdar, G. and Mellish, C. (1989). *Natural Language Processing in PROLOG and Natural Language Processing in LISP.* Reading, MA: Addison-Wesley. A classic programming language and algorithmic approach to symbolic CL/NLP.

Grosz, B. J., Spärck Jones, K., and Webber, B. L. (1986). *Readings in Natural Language Processing.* Los Altos, CA: Morgan Kaufmann. This reader contains many classic papers from the first decades of CL/NLP.

Jurafsky, D. and Martin, J. H. (2008). *Speech and Language Processing: An Introduction to Natural Language Processing, Computational Linguistics, and Speech Recognition* (2nd edn.). Upper Saddle River, NJ: Prentice Hall. An excellent survey that also covers the links between speech and language processing in NLP.

Pinker, S. (1997). *How the Mind Works.* New York: Norton. A statement of the assumptions behind the Chomskyan approach to language modeling, updated beyond Chomsky's own work to take account of the fact that language structure has itself evolved.

van Deemter, K. (2010). *Not Exactly: In Praise of Vagueness.* Oxford University Press. A representative volume on the formal semantics approach to NLP, including the possibility of modeling vague concepts.

Wilks, Y. and Brewster, C. (2009). *Natural Language Processing as a Foundation of the Semantic Web.* Now Press: London. This book contains a great deal of background on IE and on ontology building and maintenance by NLP techniques and their relationship to Semantic Web construction.

Wilks, Y. A., Slator, B. M., and Guthrie, L. M. (1996). *Electric Words: Dictionaries, Computers and Meanings.* Cambridge, MA: MIT Press. An account of meaning representation in NLP/CL, particularly the use of dictionaries as resources for meaning structures in language processing.

References

Berners-Lee, T., Hendler, J., and Lassila, O. (2001). The semantic web, *Scientific American* 284(5): 34–43.

Brown, P. F., Cocke, J., Della Pietra, S. A., Della Pietra, V. J., Jelinek, F., Lafferty, J. D., Mercer, R. L., and Roossin, P. S. (1990). A statistical approach to machine translation, *Computational Linguistics* 16: 79–85.

Ciravegna, F., Chapman, S., Dingli, A., and Wilks, Y. (2004). Learning to harvest information for the semantic web, in C. Bussler, J. Davies, D. Fensel, and R. Studer (eds.), *The Semantic Web: Research and Applications: First European Semantic Web Symposium (ESWS04)* (pp. 312–26). Berlin: Springer.

Cowie, J. and Wilks, Y. (2000). Information extraction, in R. Dale, H. Moisl, and H. Somers (eds.), *Handbook of Natural Language Processing,* (pp. 249–69). New York: Marcel Dekker.

Horrocks, I. (2005). Description logics in ontology applications, in B. Beckert (ed.), *Automated Reasoning with Analytic Tableaux and Related Methods (Lecture Notes in Artificial Intelligence 3702)* (pp. 2–13) Berlin: Springer.

Manning, C. D. and Schütze. H. (1999). *Foundations of Statistical Natural Language Processing.* Cambridge, MA: MIT Press.

McCarthy, J. and Hayes, P. J. (1969). Some philosophical problems from the standpoint of artificial intelligence, in B. Meltzer and D. Michie (eds.), *Machine Intelligence 4* (pp. 463–502). Edinburgh University Press.

Nirenburg, S. and Wilks, Y. 2001. What's in a symbol: Ontology, representation and language, *Journal of Experimental and Theoretical Artificial Intelligence* 13: 9–23.

Parkinson, R. C., Colby, K. M., and Faught, W. S. (1977). Conversational language comprehension using integrated pattern-matching and parsing, *Artificial Intelligence* 9: 111–134.

Schank, R. C. and Rieger, C. J. (1974). Inference and the computer understanding of natural language, *Artificial Intelligence* 5: 373–412.

Spärck Jones, K. (1999). Information retrieval and artificial intelligence, *Artificial Intelligence* 141: 257–81.

(2003) Document retrieval: Shallow data, deep theories; historical reflections, potential directions, in F. Sebastiani (ed.), *Advances in Information Retrieval: 25th European Conference on IR Research, ECIR 2003* (pp. 1–11). Berlin: Springer.

Thomason, R. (2003). Logic and artificial intelligence, in E. N. Zalta (ed.), *The Stanford Encyclopedia of Philosophy* (Fall 2003 edn.), http://plato.stanford.edu/archives/fall2003/entries/logic-ai/.

Wilks, Y. and Fass, D. (1992). The preference semantics family, *Computers and Mathematics with Applications* 23(2–5): 205–21.

Winograd, T. (1972). *Understanding Natural Language.* New York: Academic Press.

11 Actions and agents

Eduardo Alonso

11.1 Introduction

Classical artificial intelligence (AI) approaches to action tended to focus on single, isolated software systems that acted in a relatively inflexible way, automatically following pre-set rules. However, new technologies and software applications have created a need for artificial entities that are more autonomous, flexible, and adaptive, and that operate as social entities in multi-agent systems. This chapter introduces and surveys this emerging agent-centered AI and highlights the importance of developing theories of action, learning, and negotiation in multi-agent scenarios such as the internet.

11.2 Action in AI

Historically, the "Physical Symbol System Hypothesis" in AI (Newell and Simon 1976) has been embedded in so-called deliberative systems. Such systems are characterized by containing symbolic models of the world, and decisions about which actions to perform are made via manipulation of these symbols. To get an AI system to "act" it is enough to give it a logical representation of a theory of action (how systems make decisions and act accordingly) and *get it to do a bit of theorem proving*.

This approach to action is perhaps best illustrated in the *planning problem*, where systems use symbolic manipulation to reason about which actions to execute to achieve their goals, that is, to reason about how to behave efficiently (Fikes and Nilsson 1971). Typically, the system will be given a description of the state of the world it is in (the initial state) and of the desired state of the world (the final state or goal). The system will also be provided with a set of actions, each accompanied with a list of preconditions for the action to be executed and a list of effects that result from the action being executed – which predicates are deleted and which added to the description of the world. For example, imagine that the world consists of two blocks and a table and that the initial state of the world is "block B on table, block A on block B, nothing on block A" or, formally, {OnTable(B), On(A, B), Clear(A)}; also imagine that the goal is "block B on table and block A on table," that is,

{OnTable(A),OnTable(B)}, and that the system is able to execute two actions, UnStack(x, y) and PutDown(x). These actions are accompanied by the following lists of preconditions and effects. For UnStack(x, y):

```
Pre {On(x, y), Clear(x)}
Del {On(x, y)}
Add {Holding(x), Clear(y)}.
```

And for PutDown(x):

```
Pre {Holding(x)}
Del {Holding(x)}
Add {OnTable(x)}.
```

Clearly, in this example the plan consisting of the sequence of actions {UnStack(A, B), PutDown(A)} will bring the world from its initial state to the goal. At each step, the system that executes the planning algorithm (the planner) tries to match the preconditions for various actions to the description of the world. For example, the planner may begin by attempting PutDown(A), but will fail since the precondition for this action (Holding(A)) does not apply. On the other hand, the preconditions for the action UnStack(A, B) do hold (A is stacked on B, and it is clear), so this action can be executed. As a result of executing this action, Holding(x), the precondition for PutDown(A), is added to the description of the world. After carrying out this second action in turn, the state of the world becomes {OnTable(A), Clear(B), Clear(A), OnTable(B)}, which satisfies the goal {OnTable(A), OnTable(B)}.

Unfortunately, given the computational complexity of theorem proving in even very simple logics, this approach to the design and implementation of rational systems has not been widely applied in real-life scenarios. It has been proved (Chapman 1987) that even refined planning techniques will ultimately turn out to be unusable in any time-constrained system. As the extremely simple example above illustrates, it just takes too long to search through all possible combinations to deduce the goals (theorems) from a set of initial conditions (premises). These results had a profound influence on AI, causing some researchers to question the symbolic AI paradigm and leading to alternative approaches, in reactive architectures in particular.

A reactive system is one that does not use a symbolic model of the world nor symbolic reasoning to decide what to do next. Reactive architectures are modeled as black boxes: They follow if-then rules that *directly* map inputs into actions. Without a model of the world or of the task at hand, such systems are cognitively elementary; they (re)act more like caterpillars rather than like human beings. Perhaps the paradigmatic example of this type of system is the *subsumption architecture*, which establishes a hierarchy of competing behaviors where lower layers have precedence over higher ones (Brooks 1986).

For example, let us imagine a reactive robot that picks up samples from, say, the surface of Mars. Suppose the robot is given the following (situation → action) rules:

1 If detect an obstacle then change direction.
2 If carrying samples and at the base then drop samples.
3 If carrying samples and not at the base then go to the base.
4 If detect a sample then pick sample up.
5 If true then move randomly.

Such rules form a hierarchy that ensures that the robot will turn if it finds an obstacle; if it is at the base and carrying samples, then it will drop them provided there is no immediate danger of crashing, and so on. The highest behavior – a random walk – will only be carried out if the agent has nothing more urgent to do: Its "If true" precondition is assumed to always fire. It is a way of guaranteeing that if rules (1)–(4) do not apply the robot will still do something.

The resulting systems are, computationally speaking, extremely simple, and yet they can execute complex tasks. In addition, reactive systems are situated in real-life domains and able to display flexible behavior. In fact, actions are not planned ahead but are rather the emergent result of the system's "embeddedness" in a particular situation.

However interesting this approach may be, it presents several problems. Reactive systems learn procedures but no declarative knowledge; that is, they only learn values or attributes that are not easy to generalize to similar situations (or transmit to other systems). Besides, and perhaps more importantly, precisely because they show emergent properties there is no principled methodology for building such systems.

Regardless of the many attempts to combine deliberative and reactive architectures in hybrid systems (Ferguson 1992; Müller 1997), it seems that at the end of the day one is left to choose between theoretically sound but impractical deliberative systems and efficient yet loosely designed reactive systems. This may reflect the fact that each type of AI system was designed to solve related yet different problems: Symbolic AI resulted from the effort to formalize and mechanize reasoning that blossomed with the development of expert systems; whereas reactive systems were often motivated by efforts to solve numerical, nonlinear problems, such as those associated with connectionism and artificial life.

For the last couple of decades researchers have experienced the evolution of new technologies such as the internet. These demand personal, continuously running systems for which older notions of action – those resulting from either cumbersome symbolic reasoning or ever-adaptive reflexes – may be insufficient. Indeed, many researchers believe that in the twenty-first century for AI systems to perform "intelligently" they must be able to behave in an *autonomous, flexible* manner in unpredictable, dynamic, typically *social* domains. In other words, they believe that the "new" AI should develop *agents* (Alonso 2002).

In fact, it can be argued that current trends in web development and web design, as well as new applications in electronic commerce (for instance, Pay-Pal) and social software (for example, Facebook), will only be fully developed if an agents' perspective is adopted.

11.3   The three principles of agent-centered AI

This section examines in detail the main functionalities software systems would display in a social, agent-centered AI or, in other words, the principles of behavior of the "new" AI.

11.3.1   Autonomous behavior

By *autonomy* researchers mean the ability of the systems to make their own decisions and execute tasks on the designer's behalf. The idea of delegating some responsibility to the system to avoid tediously writing down code is certainly very attractive. Moreover, in scenarios where it is difficult to control the behavior of our systems directly, the ability to act autonomously is essential. For example, space missions increasingly depend on their unmanned spacecrafts and robots to make decisions on their own: This ability is paramount since the costs (in time and money) of communication between the space station and such systems can be prohibitive.

It is precisely this autonomy that defines agents. Traditionally, software systems execute actions (so-called methods) automatically. Imagine that the web application in your computer (the user or client) requests to access the contents of a webpage that is stored in another software system elsewhere (the server or host). The server cannot deny access to the content of the webpage; it must execute the "send" method whenever it is requested to do so. By contrast, agents decide by themselves whether to execute their methods according to their beliefs, desires, and intentions (Bratman, Israel, and Pollack 1988). Paraphrasing Jennings, Sycara, and Wooldridge (1998), "what traditional software systems do for free, agents do for money."

11.3.2   Adaptive behavior

Secondly, agents must be flexible. When designing agent systems, it is impossible to foresee all the potential situations they may encounter and specify their behavior optimally in advance. For example, the components of interaction in the internet (agents, protocols, languages) are not known a priori. Agents therefore have to learn from, and adapt to, their environment. This task is even more complex when nature is not the only source of uncertainty, but the agent is situated in a multi-agent system (MAS) that contains other agents with potentially different capabilities, goals, and beliefs.

Besides, the new systems must be general. An agent must have the competence to display an action repertoire general enough to preserve its autonomy in dynamic environments. Certainly, an agent can hardly be called intelligent if it is not able to perform well when situated in an environment different from (yet in some ways similar to) the one it was originally designed for.

Indeed, there is no need to learn anything in static, closed domains where agents have perfect knowledge of state–action transitions. By contrast, intelligence and learning are tightly tied in domains where autonomous agents must make decisions with partial or uncertain information; that is, in domains where agents learn without supervision and without the luxury of having a complete model of the world. Such agents face the so-called *reinforcement learning problem* (Kaelbling, Littman, and Moore 1996). In such scenarios, an agent exists in an environment described by a set of possible states. Each time an agent executes an action in a state it receives a numerical reward that indicates the immediate value of this state–action transition – how "good" it is. This produces a sequence of states, actions, and rewards. The agent's task is to learn a policy that maximizes the expected sum of rewards, typically with future rewards discounted exponentially by their delay. In other words, the further into the future the predictions are, the less likely the rewards will count; a sensible principle, since more distant rewards are less probable. Unlike supervised learning, such as pattern recognition or neural networks, the learner is not told which actions to take, but instead must discover which actions yield the most reward by exploiting and exploring their relationship with the environment. Actions may affect not only the immediate reward but also the next situation and, through that, all subsequent rewards. These two characteristics, trial and error search and delayed reward, are the two most important features of reinforcement learning.

This method has been successfully applied to several organizational problems in robotics, control, operation research, games, human–computer interaction, economics/finance, complex simulation, and marketing.

11.3.3   Social behavior

Agents must also show a social attitude. In an environment populated by heterogeneous entities, agents need the ability to recognize their opponents, and to form groups when it is profitable to do so. It is not a coincidence that most agent-based platforms incorporate multi-agent tools (Luck et al. 2005). Indeed, some authors state that agent-oriented software engineering needs to be developed precisely because there is no notion of organizational structure in traditional software systems (Etzioni and Weld 2007).

Generally speaking, the design and implementation of multi-agent systems is an attractive platform for the convergence of various AI technologies. That is the underlying philosophy of competitions such as RoboCup (www.robocup.org/), where teams of soccer agents must display their individual and collective skills in real time. More importantly, multi-agent systems play several roles in information technology and telecoms: For clients, they provide personalized, user-friendly interfaces; as middleware, they have been used extensively to implement electronic markets and electronic auctions.

The reasons for this happy marriage between MAS and new technologies are various. When the domain involves a number of distinct software systems that are physically or logically distributed (in terms of their data, expertise, or resources), a multi-agent approach can often provide an effective solution. Relatedly, when the domain is large, sophisticated, or unpredictable, the overall problem can be partitioned into a number of smaller and simpler components, which are easier to develop and maintain, and which are specialized at solving the constituent problems. That is, in most real-life applications (single) agents can grow "too big" to work well, and a *divide-and-conquer* strategy, where qualified agents work in parallel, seems more sensible. Examples include the geographical distribution of cameras in a traffic network or the integrated approach required to solve complex tasks, for instance the collaboration between experts (surgeons, anesthetists, nurses) in an operating room.

To sum up, it is widely accepted within the AI community that the "new" AI would need to design and implement multi-agent systems capable of acting and learning in a quick and efficient manner. The next two sections are dedicated to describing the basics of multi-agent behavior and multi-agent learning.

11.4 Multi-agent behavior

Approaches to multi-agent behavior differ mainly in regards to the degree of control that the designer should have over individual agents and over the social environment, that is, over the interaction mechanisms (Bond and Gasser 1988; Durfee 1988; Weiss 1999). In Distributed Problem Solving systems (DPS) a single designer is able to control (or even explicitly design) each individual agent in the domain – the task of solving a problem is distributed among different agents, hence the name. In MAS on the other hand, there are multiple designers and each is able to design only its agent and has no control over the internal design of other agents.

The design of interaction protocols is also tightly coupled to the issue of agents' incentives. When agents are centrally designed they are assumed to have a common general goal. As long as agents have to co-exist and cooperate in a single system, there is some notion of global utility that each agent is trying to maximize. Agents form teams that jointly contribute towards the overall goal. By contrast, in MAS each agent will be individually motivated to achieve its own goal and to maximize its own utility. As a result, no assumptions can be made about agents working together cooperatively. On the contrary, agents will collaborate only when they can benefit from that cooperation.

Research in DPS considers how work involved in solving a problem can be divided among several nodes so as to enhance the system's performance. That is, the aim is to make independent nodes solve a global problem by working together coherently, while maintaining low levels of communication. MAS researchers are also concerned with coordinated interaction, but must build agents without knowing how their opponents have been designed. The central research issue in MAS is how to have these autonomous agents identify common ground for cooperation, and choose and perform coherent actions.

In particular, DPS researchers see negotiation as a mechanism for assigning tasks among agents and for allocating resources, using *automated contracting*. Since all agents have a common goal and are designed to help one another (following the so-called *benevolence* assumption), there is no need to motivate an agent to agree to execute a set of actions. Alternatively, *multi-agent planning* is another DPS approach that avoids incoherent and inconsistent decisions by planning beforehand exactly how each agent will act and interact. Multi-agent planning has been formalized by extending single-agent planning languages and techniques to describe complex mental states – usually by defining social plans in terms of common beliefs and joint intentions (Rao, Georgeff, and Sonenberg 1992).

On the other hand, MAS researchers have autonomous agents use negotiation to share the work associated with carrying out a previously agreed plan (for the agents' mutual benefit), or to resolve outright conflict. In MAS systems, agents typically make pair-wise agreements through negotiation about how they will coordinate, and there is no global control, no consistent knowledge, and no shared goals and success criteria. So, the main purpose of this *incentive contracting* mechanism is to "convince" agents to reach reasonable agreements and do something in exchange for something else. In this case, AI researchers have followed the studies on bargaining with incomplete information developed in economics and game theory.

11.4.1   Negotiation

Since negotiation in MAS is probably the most common coordination technique, it is worth considering it in some detail (Rosenschein and Zlotkin 1994; Jennings et al. 2001; Kraus 2001).

In a MAS setting, agents are given a *negotiation mechanism* consisting of a protocol and a set of strategies over a set of deals. Negotiation is defined as a process through which at each temporal point one agent proposes an agreement and the other agent either accepts the offer or does not. If the offer is accepted, then the negotiation ends with the implementation of the agreement. Otherwise, the second agent has to make a counteroffer, or reject its opponent's offer and abandon the process. Thus the *protocol* specifies when and how to exchange offers (i.e., which actions the agents will execute or abstain from executing and when). For example, an $Offer(x, y, \delta_i, t_1)$ means that the negotiation process will start at time t_1 with agent x offering agent y a deal δ_i from the set of potential deals, typically of the form "I will do action 1 in exchange for action 2" or $\{Do(x, a_1), Do(y, a_2)\}$. Then, in the next negotiation step, agent y will counteroffer, either with $Accept(y, \delta_i, t_2)$, in which case the negotiation episode ends with the implementation of the agreement, δ_i; or with $Reject(y, \delta_i, t_2)$, so that negotiation fails. Or, alternatively, agent y can send a response, $Offer(y, x, \delta_j, t_2)$, with, say, $\delta_j = \{Do(x, a_3), Do(y, a_2)\}$, "I would prefer you to execute action a_3 rather than a_1," so that the negotiation progresses to the next stage in which the same routine applies.

Which specific offers the agents make depends on their negotiation *strategy*. This is a function from the history of the negotiation to the current offer that is consistent with the protocol. It determines what move an agent should make to maximize its own utility, given the protocol, the negotiation up to this point, and the agent's beliefs and intentions. Such strategies also take into account how risk-averse the agent might be; that is, how reluctant it is to accept a bargain with an uncertain outcome rather than another bargain with a more certain, but possibly lower, outcome.

Usually strategies are required to be in *Nash equilibrium*: That is, no agent should have an incentive to deviate from agreed-upon strategies. Once a strategy is adopted, under the assumption that agent x uses it, agent y cannot do better by using a different strategy. To illustrate this, consider the so-called *Prisoners' Dilemma*. Two suspects are arrested by the police. The police have insufficient evidence for a conviction, and, having separated both prisoners, visit each of them to offer the same deal. If one testifies (defects from the other) and the other remains silent, the betrayer goes free and the silent accomplice receives the full ten-year sentence. If both remain silent, both prisoners are sentenced to only six months in jail for a minor charge. If each betrays the other, each receives a five-year sentence. Each prisoner must choose to betray the other or to remain silent. The suspects cannot talk to each other to reach an agreement. In this case, the Nash equilibrium is that both testify. Each suspect knows that if one chose to remain silent, the other one would do better by testifying, thus breaking the "remain silent equilibrium." Nash equilibrium is a particularly important attribute, because it is seen as the only sustainable outcome of rational negotiation in the absence of externally enforceable agreements. Yet, this solution presents serious drawbacks.

First, there are situations in which there is no Nash equilibrium. For instance, *Matching Pennies* is an example of games where one player's gain is exactly equal to the other player's loss. Second, there are situations in which there are several pure Nash equilibria. In a simplified example, assume that two drivers meet on a narrow road. Both have to swerve in order to avoid a head-on collision. If both swerve to the same side they will manage to pass each other, but if they choose different sides they will collide. In this case there are two pure Nash equilibria: Either both swerve to the left, or both swerve to the right. In this example, it doesn't matter which side both players pick, as long as they both pick the same. Since both strategies are equally good, one could just toss a coin to choose between the two alternatives. There are other situations, however, in which one would not have that choice: In the game *Battle of the Sexes* both players prefer engaging in the same activity over being alone, but their preferences differ over which activity they should engage in. Player 1 prefers that they both party while player 2 prefers that they both stay at home. In this case, there are two pure Nash equlibria but no agreement is reached. Finally, in accepting a Nash-equilibrium solution both agents may lose more profitable agreements. This is the case in the Prisoner's Dilemma: The Nash equilibrium for this game is a sub-optimal solution, which leads both players to defect, even though each player's individual reward would be greater if they both played cooperatively and remained silent.

Thus, instead of Nash-equilibrium constraints and in order to prevent irrational attitudes, the following assumptions about *social rationality* are typically made: (1) Sincerity: No agent will attempt to have another believe a proposition that it either knows or believes to be false or a proposition that it wants to be false (e.g., agents cannot commit themselves to execute actions that they are not able to perform). (2) Honesty: Agents have to act according to their beliefs. (3) Fair play: agents must abide by the agreed deals. (4) Sociability: In case of indifference, agents must accept others' offers, and deals must always be individually rational.

11.4.2   Argumentation

The assumptions about social rationality required to make the previous approach work are not intuitive, and in any case, many real agents calculate their options individually in terms of self-interest, ignoring negotiations and agreed commitments. In response, many members of the MAS community have adopted alternative approaches to MAS coordination. In particular, several studies on argumentation-based negotiation have been presented as a powerful technique for cooperating and solving conflict situations (Rahwan et al. 2003). In this type of negotiation agents open up the agreement space by exchanging not only proposals and counterproposals but also *reasons* supporting them. In addition, agents commit themselves to accept the results of the argumentation, which follows strict rules regarding the validity and acceptability of the arguments and their ordering in argumentative types.

For instance, imagine the following situation: Agent 1 has a hammer, a screw, a screwdriver, and a picture it intends to hang by using the "plan" {hammer + nail + picture}. Agent 2, on the other hand, owns a mirror and a nail, has as its goal to hang the mirror, and plans to execute the plan {hammer + nail + mirror}. Imagine that agent 1 knows agent 2 has a nail and asks for it. Obviously, agent 2 cannot agree to such a request since it needs the nail to hang the mirror. Using a negotiation protocol, agent 2's rejection will end the episode and neither agent will achieve their respective goals. However, if they are allowed to argue, agent 2 can explain why it is rejecting agent 1's offer ("I need the nail to hang my mirror"), and with this information, agent 1 can persuade agent 2 that in fact there is another way to hang its mirror, a new plan that uses a screw and a screwdriver instead of a nail. If agent 2 does not find a flaw in agent 1's argument it is forced to accept it. Since this seems to be the case, the agents agree to exchange the nail for the screw and the screwdriver and, as a consequence, both achieve their objectives.

Argumentation relies on the assumption that the agents will honor the reasoning underlying the agreements – a difficult assumption to maintain in practice. Alternative approaches have investigated how to make MAS coordination mechanisms "enforceable" via social laws, institutions, conventions, and even rights (Alonso 2004).

This completes our account of the main issues and techniques in multi-agent behavior. However, as introduced in Section 11.3.3, behaving in complex dynamic scenarios such as MAS is not a one-shot task but a process of refinement through which agents adapt their strategies to each other's. Hence, dealing with multi-agent *learning* is paramount when studying multi-agent behavior.

11.5   Multi-agent learning

Research on machine learning has been mostly independent of agent research and only recently has it received attention in connection with agents and multi-agent systems (Stone and Veloso 2000; Alonso et al. 2001; Alonso 2007; Vohra and Wellman 2007; Tuyls and Weiss 2012). This is in some ways surprising because the ability to learn and adapt is arguably one of the most important features of intelligence. As discussed above, intelligence implies a certain degree of autonomy that in turn requires the ability to learn to make independent decisions in dynamic, unpredictable domains such as those in which agents co-exist.

Key issues in multi-agent learning relate to which family of techniques should be used, and, indeed, what multi-agent learning is. At one level, agents and multi-agent systems can be viewed as yet another application domain for machine-learning systems, admittedly with its own challenges. Research taking this view is mostly reduced to applying existing single-agent learning algorithms more or less directly to MAS, so that multi-agent learning is only seen as an emergent property. Even though this could be interesting from a MAS point of view, it does not seem overly interesting for machine learning research. Nevertheless, this is the direction most learning research for MAS has followed.

Existing learning algorithms have been developed for single agents learning separate and independent tasks. Alternatively, multi-agent systems pose the problem of *distributed learning*, that is, many agents learning separately to carry out a joint task. Once the learning process is distributed amongst several learning agents, such learning algorithms require extensive modification, or completely new algorithms need to be developed. In distributed learning, agents need to cooperate and communicate in order to learn effectively; these issues are being investigated extensively by MAS researchers but to date they have received little attention in the areas of learning.

Regarding learning techniques, supervised learning methods are not easily applied to multi-agent scenarios since they typically assume that the agents can be provided with the correct behavior for a given situation. Thus, most researchers have used reinforcement learning methods, to the point that the multi-agent learning problem can be redefined as the reinforcement learning problem for multi-agent systems (Busoniu, Babuska, and De Schutter 2008).

Specifically, the simplest way to extend single-agent learning algorithms to multi-agent problems is just to make each agent learn independently. Agents learn "as if they were alone" (Weiss and Dillenbourg, 1999). Communication or explicit coordination is not an issue therefore – cooperation and competition are not tasks to be solved but just properties of the environment. Likewise, agents do not have models of other agents' mental states or try to build models of other agents' behaviors. However simple this approach to multi-agent learning may be, the assumption that agents can learn efficient policies in a MAS setting independently of the actions selected by other agents is implausible. Intuitively, the most appealing alternative is to have the agents learn Nash-equilibrium strategies. However, as described in Section 11.4.1 the concept of Nash equilibrium is problematic, and the methods formulated using such approach suffer from a plethora of technical difficulties that make their application rather restricted.

11.6   Challenges

Agent-based applications have enjoyed considerable success in manufacturing, process control, telecommunications systems, air traffic control, traffic and transportation management, information filtering and gathering, electronic commerce, business process management, entertainment, and medical care (Jennings and Wooldridge 1998). Nonetheless, one of the key problems has been the divide between theoretical and practical work, which have, to a large extent, developed along different paths. As a consequence, designers lack a systematic methodology for clearly specifying and structuring their applications as (multi-)agent systems. Most agent-based applications have been designed in an ad hoc manner, either by borrowing a methodology from more traditional approaches or by designing the system on intuition and (necessarily limited) experience. At any rate, if agents and multi-agent systems are to become the standard in the development of emerging web-based applications – as their advocates believe they should – then some important developments in agent-oriented methodologies and technologies will be needed.

First, an agent-modeling language to specify, visualize, modify, construct, and document (multi-)agent systems would have to be built. Agent developers still characterize their systems as extensions of traditional systems, and thus Unified Modeling Language (UML) is the de facto standard language in the design and specification of agents and multi-agent systems. This drawback extends to the lack of proper verification methods and techniques for agent systems.

Second, while some programming features, such as abstraction, inheritance, and modularity, make it easier to manage increasingly more complex systems, Java and other programming languages cannot provide a direct solution to agent implementation. So far, agent-oriented programs have been used mainly to test ideas rather than for developing any realistic systems (but see Bordini et al. 2005 for a survey of multi-agent programming, languages, platforms, and applications).

Third, standards for interoperability between agents will need to be established. The debate should not be focused exclusively on the pros and cons of different agent-communication languages and protocols but also on ontologies – that is, on which types of entities and concepts define an agent domain and what their properties and relations are. Currently, ontologies are often specified informally or are implicit in the agent implementation. For true interoperation, agents will need explicitly encoded, sharable ontologies.

A fourth issue is reusability. If multi-agent systems are to be sustainable, it will be necessary to develop techniques for specifying and maintaining reusable models and software for MAS, agents, and agent components. Reusability is also needed for mobility. If agents are to roam wide-area networks such as the WWW, then they must be capable of being continuously reused in different scenarios.

Finally, if people are to be comfortable with the idea of delegating tasks to agents, then issues relating to trust will have be addressed. These include authentication, privacy of communication and user's personal profile information, auditing, accountability, and defense against malicious or incompetent agents.

All in all, although there is a need to keep theory and practice at the same pace, agent-centered AI has already brought mature and integrative techniques and procedures that are ripe for exploitation. It can be claimed that the agent paradigm has served as a bridge between traditional AI systems and the software applications that have emerged in the last couple of decades. When on the occasion of *AI Magazine*'s twenty-fifth anniversary experts were asked about AI's state of the art, the shared feeling was that AI needed to get back to building *intelligent* systems of *general competence* (Leake 2005). It seems that agents and MAS may provide us with the concepts, methodologies and techniques necessary to realize AI's original goal in the services and applications that the internet offers.

11.7 Conclusion

AI systems have to make intelligent decisions. But, most importantly, they must show that they do so by behaving accordingly. This chapter has focused on the role of agents in the analysis of the behavior of AI systems. After all, that is what agents do: They act. Hence, the study of behavior and action in AI must talk about agents. In fact, there are strong reasons for thinking that agents are the paradigm that will embody the "new" AI. More precisely, in the era of the internet and web services, AI will come to focus on how collections of autonomous agents coordinate their behavior (multi-agent behavior) and on how they learn to do so (multi-agent learning).

Further reading

For those wishing to investigate agents and MAS, the following two books are easy to read and full of useful references to specialized topics:

Russell, S. and Norvig, P. (2010). *Artificial Intelligence: A Modern Approach* (3rd edn.). Upper Saddle River, NJ: Prentice Hall. The third edition of the first AI handbook that shamelessly introduced AI from an agent's perspective. See in particular the second chapter on Intelligent Agents.

Wooldridge, M. (2009). *An Introduction to Multiagent Systems*. Chichester, UK: John Wiley & Sons. The second edition of an ideal introductory text on agents and multi-agent systems, despite being somewhat limited in its coverage of learning.

The best online references for further reading on agents are the AI Topics/Agents webpage hosted by the Association for the Advancement of Artificial Intelligence (www.aaai.org/), the UMBC AgentWeb (http://agents.umbc.edu/), and AgentLink III, the European Coordination Action for Agent Based Computing (www.agentlink.org/).

References

Alonso, E. (2002). AI and agents: State of the art, *AI Magazine* 23: 25–30.

(2004). Rights and argumentation in open multi-agent systems, *Artificial Intelligence Review* 21: 3–24.

(ed.) (2007). Multi-Agent Learning, *Special issue of Autonomous Agents and Multi-Agent Systems* 15(1).

Alonso, E., d'Inverno, M., Kudenko, D., Luck, M., and Noble, J. (2001). Learning in multi-agent systems, *Knowledge Engineering Review* 16: 277–84.

Bond, A. H. and Gasser, L. (eds.) (1988). *Readings in Distributed Artificial Intelligence.* San Mateo, CA: Morgan Kaufmann.

Bordini, R., Dastani, M., Dix, J., and El Fallah-Seghrouchni, A. (eds.) (2005). *Multi-Agent Programming: Languages, Platforms and Applications.* Berlin: Springer.

Bratman, M., Israel, D. J., and Pollack, M. E. (1988). Plans and resource-bounded practical reasoning, *Computational Intelligence*, 4: 349–55.

Brooks, R. (1986). A robust layered control system for a mobile robot, *IEEE Journal of Robotics and Automation*, 2: 14–23.

Busoniu, L., Babuska, R., and De Schutter, B. (2008). A comprehensive survey of multi-agent reinforcement learning, *IEEE Transactions on Systems, Man, and Cybernetics – Part C: Applications and Reviews* 38: 156–72.

Chapman, D. (1987). Planning for conjunctive goals, *Artificial Intelligence*, 32: 333–77.

Durfee, E. H. (1988). *Coordination for Distributed Problem Solvers.* Boston, MA: Kluwer Academic.

Etzioni, O. and Weld, D. (2007). Intelligent agents on the internet: Fact, fiction, and forecast, *IEEE Expert: Intelligent Systems and Their Applications*, 10: 44–9.

Ferguson, I. A. (1992). TouringMachines: An Architecture for Dynamic, Rational, Mobile Agents. PhD thesis, University of Cambridge.

Fikes, R. and Nilsson, N. (1971). STRIPS: A new approach to the application of theorem proving to problem solving, *Artificial Intelligence*, 2: 189–208.

Jennings, N., Faratin, P., Lomuscio, A., Parsons, S., Sierra, C., and Wooldridge, M. (2001). Automated negotiation: prospects, methods and challenges, *International Journal of Group Decision and Negotiation* 10: 199–215.

Jennings, N., Sycara, K., and Wooldridge, M. (1998). A roadmap of agent research and development, *Autonomous Agents and Multi-Agent Systems* 1: 7–38.

Jennings, N. and Wooldridge, M. (eds.) (1998). *Agent Technology: Foundations, Applications, and Markets*. Berlin: Springer.

Kaelbling, L. P., Littman, M., and Moore, A. (1996). Reinforcement learning: A survey, *Journal of Artificial Intelligence Research* 4: 237–85.

Kraus, S. (2001). *Strategic Negotiation in Multiagent Environments*, Cambridge, MA: MIT Press.

Leake, D. (ed.). (2005). *Twenty-fifth Anniversary Issue, special issue of AI Magazine* 26(4).

Luck, M., McBurney, P., Shehory, O., and Willmott, S. (eds.) (2005). *Agent Technology: Computing as Interaction (A Roadmap for Agent Based Computing)*. Southampton: AgentLink III.

Müller, J. (1997). A cooperation model for autonomous agents, in J. Müller, M. Wooldridge, and N. Jennings (eds.), *Intelligent Agents III: Agent Theories, Architectures, and Languages* (pp. 245–60) (*Lecture Notes in Computer Science*, 1193). Berlin: Springer.

Newell, A. and Simon, H. A. (1976). Computer science as empirical enquiry: Symbols and search, *Communications of the ACM* 19: 113–26.

Rahwan, I., Ramchurn, S., Jennings, N., McBurney, P., Parsons, S., and Sonenberg, L. (2003). Argumentation-based negotiation, *The Knowledge Engineering Review* 18: 343–75.

Rao, A. S., Georgeff, M. P., and Sonenberg, E. A. (1992). Social plans: A preliminary report, in E. Werner and Y. Demazeau (eds.), *Decentralized AI 3: Proceedings of the 3rd European Workshop on Modelling Autonomous Agents in a Multi-Agent World* (pp. 57–76), Amsterdam: Elsevier.

Rosenschein, J. S. and Zlotkin, G. (1994). *Rules of Encounter: Designing Conventions for Automated Negotiation among Computers*, Cambridge, MA: MIT Press.

Stone, P. and Veloso, M. (2000). Multiagent systems: A survey from a machine learning perspective, *Autonomous Robots* 8: 345–83.

Tuyls, K. and Weiss, G. (2012). Multiagent learning: Basics, challenges, prospects, *AI Magazine* 33.

Vohra, R. and Wellman, M. (eds.) (2007). Foundations of multi-agent learning, *Artificial Intelligence* 171: 363–4.

Weiss, G. (ed.) (1999). *Multiagent Systems: A Modern Approach to Distributed Artificial Intelligence*. Cambridge, MA: MIT Press.

Weiss, G. and Dillenbourg, P. (1999). What is "multi" in multiagent learning?, in P. Dillenbourg (ed.), *Collaborative Learning: Cognitive and computational approaches* (pp. 64–80). Oxford: Pergamon Press.

12 Artificial emotions and machine consciousness

Matthias Scheutz

12.1 Introduction

Over the last decade, interest in artificial emotions and machine consciousness has noticeably increased in artificial intelligence (AI), as witnessed by a number of specialized conferences and workshops dedicated to these themes. This interest is in part based on the recognition that emotions and consciousness have useful roles in humans and other animals, and that understanding these roles and implementing models of them on computers might help in making artificial agents smarter. But can machines even have emotions and be conscious, and if so, how could we go about designing such machines?

The goal of this chapter is to present an overview of the work in AI on emotions and machine consciousness, with an eye toward answering these questions. Starting with a brief philosophical perspective on emotions and machine consciousness to frame the work, the chapter first focuses on artificial emotions, and then moves on to machine consciousness – reflecting the fact that emotions and consciousness have been treated independently and by different communities in AI. The chapter concludes by discussing philosophical implications of AI research on emotions and consciousness.

12.2 The philosophical perspective

Prima facie, it seems that research on emotions and consciousness in AI would have to start from the assumption that it is actually possible to implement emotions and consciousness in computational artifacts. Why else would one bother attempting this goal if it cannot be reached in principle?

It turns out that AI researchers have typically not been impressed with philosophical arguments about the possibility or impossibility of machines replicating human mental states. Rather, they have always pursued a theoretically unencumbered approach to investigating possible algorithms and mechanisms for achieving intelligent behavior. There are basically two main attitudes in AI toward the question whether machines *actually* can have emotions (e.g., like human emotions) or be conscious (e.g., like a normal human adult in waking states). The first is a pragmatic attitude that underlies much of AI research and connects to related attitudes in psychology: Emotion terms and "consciousness" are used in a pragmatic operational way that allows researchers to make progress without having solved all the conceptual problems that beleaguer these concepts. Researchers in AI who are assuming this attitude will look at results from psychology for the types of processes that psychologists take to underlie or be involved in human mental activity and attempt to formalize aspects of them algorithmically. The goal here is not to replicate or model human mentality in a biologically or psychologically plausible way, but rather to use whatever principles could be taken from emotion processes or theories of consciousness to improve the performance of artificial agents (and possibly surpass human performance).

The other attitude is to seek to refine, revise, or replace emotion concepts or concepts of consciousness as a result of attempting to formally specify processes that can implement emotions or bring about consciousness. This attitude is closely aligned with the endeavor of computational modeling in cognitive science, where the goal of a computational model is to replicate human performance while providing mechanisms that explain how humans perform a given task. Consequently, the way algorithms are generated, implemented, and tested has implications for concepts of emotion and consciousness, which in turn will require a philosophical elaboration.

Clearly, the first attitude is sufficient for research goals in AI (e.g., to build intelligent agents), yet the second attitude will also allow AI researchers to connect to other fields and open up their algorithms and implementations to philosophical and psychological scrutiny. That way, psychologists might be able to derive new experimental designs that can test predictions made by the models, and philosophers might be able to sharpen their intuitions about what these concepts are supposed to refer to.

Historically, the questions of whether machines can have emotions or can be conscious have come up at various times in different fields. Here, we will briefly review the philosophical perspectives of two pioneers in AI and philosophy of mind – Alan Turing and Hilary Putnam, respectively.

Alan Turing, in his famous 1950 paper "Computing machinery and intelligence" (Turing 1950) considers nine objections to his "imitation game," which has subsequently become known as the "Turing Test."[1] The fourth of these, the "Argument from Consciousness," attempts to dismiss machine intelligence by pointing to the lack of emotions and feelings in machines. Here, Turing cites Professor Geoffrey Jefferson as stating that

---

[1] This an envisioned setup where a human subject has to interact via a chat-like computer interface with two other participants, a human and a machine, without knowing which is which. The subject's goal is to determine which of the participants is human and which the computer within a given time period through natural language interactions.

Not until a machine can write a sonnet or compose a concerto because of thoughts and emotions felt, and not by the chance fall of symbols, could we agree that machine equals brain – that is, not only write it but know that it had written it. No mechanism could feel (and not merely artificially signal, an easy contrivance) pleasure at its successes, grief when its valves fuse, be warmed by flattery, be made miserable by its mistakes, be charmed by sex, be angry or depressed when it cannot get what it wants. (Quoted in Turing 1950, pp. 445–6).

Turing diagnoses this line of argument as ultimately promoting a solipsistic perspective where "the only way by which one could be sure that a machine thinks is to *be* the machine and to feel oneself thinking" (Turing 1950, p. 446). He points out that the same line of argument would then also hold for people (i.e., one could only be sure that another person has certain mental properties or is in a particular mental state if one *were* that other person), a problem known in philosophy as the "other minds problem." In other words, he reduces the other minds problem for machines to the other minds problem for humans.

Moreover, he points out that a sonnet-writing machine that gives reasonable answers to an interrogator about its own sonnet using *viva voce* (and thus presumably using intonation in a humanly plausible way, including the expression of emotions) would likely not be viewed as an "easy contrivance." The assumption here is that a machine that can interact in natural spoken language in human-like ways would cause people to view it as having pleasure, pain, and so on, in very much the way people infer internal states of other people based on their interactions (e.g., from the tone in a person's voice).

The question of whether machines can have feelings and can be conscious has been revisited in detail by Hilary Putnam. In his 1964 paper "Robots: Machines or artificially created life?" (Putnam 1964), Putnam wants us to imagine the robot Oscar which is *psychologically isomorphic* to a human – that is, which has internal states that play the same causal roles as our mental states do. Suppose Oscar is having the "sensation" of red in this sense, then the question arises whether it is *really* having a sensation of red, that is, whether Oscar is actually *seeing* anything, whether Oscar is feeling, whether Oscar is conscious. Like Turing, Putnam links this question to the other minds problem: "Whether, and under what conditions, a robot could be conscious is a question that cannot be discussed without at once impinging on the topics that have been treated under the headings Mind–Body Problem and Problem of Other Minds" (p. 669). After dispelling several objections to the claim that Oscar is conscious, he concludes that this question

calls for a decision and not for a discovery. If we are to make a decision, it seems preferable to me to extend our concept so that robots *are* conscious – for "discrimination" based on the "softness" or "hardness" of the body parts of a synthetic "organism" seems as silly as discriminatory treatment of humans on the basis of skin color. (p. 691)

Turing and Putnam's view that machines can be conscious in principle has since been echoed by various philosophers (e.g., Lycan 1987). In all cases the assumption is that machines will have to have the right kind of internal structure and cognitive organization – the right type of architecture – for them to be able to have emotions and to be conscious (whether they then will *actually* instantiate emotions and/or be conscious will depend on additional factors, as in the human case). The question about the right kind of architecture that can implement emotions and consciousness, however, is exactly what research in AI has attempted to tackle.

12.3   Emotions in AI

Different forms of emotions have been studied to varying degrees ever since the beginning of AI (e.g., Pfeifer 1988), despite the original focus of AI on deliberative, non-emotional mechanisms. More recently, however, work on emotions and emotional agents has become much more mainstream, not least due to Aaron Sloman's work on emotional architectures (Sloman and Croucher 1981) and Ross Picard's work on "affective computing" (Picard 1997), which stressed the importance of human affect and explored how computers can be made "affect-aware" or emotional. Today, we witness growing numbers of research communities that investigate aspects of emotion and affect, from "emotional" or "affective" user interfaces to "believable" synthetic characters and life-like animated agents with emotions, to emotional or emotion-aware pedagogic and instructional agents, to emotional virtual agents and robots (see Trappl, Petta, and Payr 2002 for an overview).

The motivations for the various research directions and their specific aims are naturally quite different. While for some emotions are about making animated characters more believable (e.g., by endowing them with emotional facial expressions), for others recognizing emotions is crucial for a system to be able to adapt to its user's needs. Yet others take emotions to be an integral part of the control of complex agents, and thus focus on architectural mechanisms that are required for emotion processes. But common to all these different incentives for exploring emotions is the tacit assumption that emotions, in one form or another, may have important applications in artificial agents.

12.3.1   Functional roles of emotions

One major difficulty connected to concepts such as emotion (and consciousness as well) is that they are not clearly specified, and likely not even clearly specifiable in principle. Hence, there is no clear sense in psychology of exactly what an emotion is (Griffiths 1997), and psychological accounts vary greatly as to how emotions are individuated (e.g., based on facial expressions, behavioral patterns, brain regions, etc.). The conceptual difficulties with emotion concepts, however, have not been a deterrent to attempts to implement processes that at least resemble emotion processes, even though researchers in AI often disagree on what they take "emotion" to be and what they believe it means to *implement emotions* in artificial agents (e.g., Scheutz 2002).

Much research on the role of emotions in artificial agents has been motivated by an analysis of possible *functional* roles of emotions in natural systems. The underlying assumptions are that (1) emotions have functional roles in agent architectures, and that (2) having states with the right functional roles is sufficient for having emotions, independent of the particular physical makeup of the agent. While most researchers in the affective sciences will agree on (1) (even though there are many examples of the effects of *dysfunctional affect* as well), their views diverge on (2) – whether having the right kind of functional architecture is *all* there is to having a particular emotion. For example, they might hold that various bodily processes are involved in many affective states: If particular biochemical processes, such as the secretion of particular hormones, or changes in particular neurotransmitters, are taken to be essential to, or constitutive of, affect, then artificial agents will, by definition, not be capable of instantiating affective states so construed. (Compare the views some philosophers have voiced about consciousness or qualitative states, e.g., Searle 1992.) Artificial agents will, however, still be capable of instantiating the same kinds of *control processes* as those implemented in neural activity in animals, since these are, also by definition, independent of the physical makeup of an agent, and this may be sufficient for AI purposes (e.g., for an artificial agent to be able to perform a particular task). If, on the other hand, the exact nature of bodily states and processes does not play a causal role in the functioning of affect processes, so that, for example, simulated hormonal systems could be used to achieve the same effects (e.g., Cañamero 1997), then artificial agents will be able to instantiate affect processes if they have the right architectural prerequisites.

Regardless of what stance one takes on the *qualitative nature* of emotions (i.e., on the question of "what it is like to experience state X"), the functional aspects of emotions in the context of an agent's control system can be independently considered. In particular, there seem to be twelve potential roles of emotions for artificial agents (see also Scheutz 2004):

1 *Alarm mechanisms* – e.g., fast reflex-like reactions in critical situations, such as fear processes, that interrupt current behavior and initiate a retreat response, moving the agent away from the danger zone.
2 *Action selection* – e.g., deciding what to do next based on the current emotional state, such as switching from exploration to foraging behavior based on the agent's needs.

3 *Adaptation* – e.g., short- or long-term changes in behavior due to affective states, such as adapting one's gait to uneven terrain based on negative affect generated by sensors.

4 *Social regulation* – e.g., using emotional signals to achieve social effects, such as aggressive display to deter another agent from interfering with one's activity.

5 *Learning* – e.g., using affective evaluations as utility estimates in reinforcement learning, such as learning the utility of different behaviors to achieve goals in different contexts.

6 *Motivation* – e.g., adopting goals as part of an emotional coping mechanism, such as when a high level of distress and frustration leads to adopting the goal of asking a human supervisor for help)

7 *Goal management* – e.g., the creation of new goals or reprioritization of existing ones, such as using positive and negative affect to modify cost estimates used in the calculation of the expected utility of a goal.

8 *Strategic processing* – e.g., the selection of search strategies based on overall affective state, such as using positive and negative affect to bias search algorithms to top-down versus bottom-up search.

9 *Memory control* – e.g., the strategic use of affective bias on memory access and retrieval as well as decay rate of memory items, such as using current affective state to rank memory items with similar affect as better matches.

10 *Information integration* – e.g., emotional filtering of data from various information channels or blocking of such integration, such as ignoring positively valenced information from vision sensors about a happy face when the acoustic information suggests an angry voice.

11 *Attentional focus* – e.g., selection of data to be processed based on affective evaluation, such as biasing visual search in favor of objects the agent highly desires.

12 *Self model* – e.g., using affect as a representation of "what a situation is like for the agent," such as using the overall affective evaluation of different components of the agent's control system as a measure of the agent's overall mood and how it "feels".

While this list is not intended to be exhaustive, it does point to the varied functional nature of emotions, from architectural roles to roles in social regulation. And it provides a frame within which to locate past accomplishments and future directions in research on architectural aspects of affect.

12.3.2   Communicative vs. architectural aspects of emotion

Work on emotions in AI can be roughly divided into two strands (with a small overlap): *communicative aspects* and *architectural aspects*.

Communicative aspects of emotions are mostly concerned with the fourth role (social regulation) and have been explored mainly by the human–computer interaction (HCI) and, more recently, the human–robot interaction (HRI) communities. Efforts focus on emotion recognition, emotional expression, and sometimes on how to connect the two to improve the experience of human users with an interactive system (e.g., via the user interface on a computer or via the sensory and effector repertoire of a robot; Scheutz, Schermerhorn, and Kramer 2006). Both communities have made important advances in understanding the kinds of emotional interactions people engage in (e.g., Brave and Nass 2003) and how to make machines recognize and signal them (e.g., how to explore temporal patterns to detect frustrated vs. delighted human smiles; Hoque, McDuff, and Picard 2012).

The second main strand, the architectural aspect of emotion, has focused on the role and utility of emotions in agent architectures (such as using emotional evaluations as quick heuristics in decision making) and is thus less concerned with the social communicative aspects of emotions. This strand attempts to use emotion mechanisms to improve the agent's capabilities, and most work here has focused on the first five roles. In particular, attention has been given to affective or emotional action selection, both in simulated agents (e.g., Gadanho 2003) and robotic agents (Murphy et al. 2002). Similarly, quite a bit of work has investigated the utility of evaluations that are internally generated and reflect some aspect of the agent's internal state (rather than external environmental states) for reinforcement learning, even though most of these investigations do not call these evaluations "affective" (e.g., Ichise, Shapiro, and Langley 2002). Yet, surprisingly little work has focused on investigating roles (6) through (12), although there are some notable exceptions (e.g., Gratch and Marsella 2004a). Note that especially the last four roles might turn out to be critical for reflective, and thus conscious, systems (e.g., as described in Sloman and Chrisley 2003). For, as we shall see in Section 12.4 on machine consciousness, mechanisms for attentional control, information integration, working memory and its access control, and an agent's self-model are all taken to be essential ingredients for developing conscious machines.

There are several crucial differences between research on the communicative and the architectural aspects of emotions. Most importantly the former does not require the instantiation of emotional states within a system. For example, an agent does not have to be itself emotional (or capable of emotions) to be able to recognize emotional expressions in human faces. The latter, on the other hand, must claim that emotional states of a particular kind are instantiated within the system. Moreover, researchers on the communicative aspects of emotions do not need a satisfactory *theory of emotion* (i.e., a theory of what emotional states are) to be able to produce working systems. Being able to measure changes in a user's skin conductance, breathing frequency, and so on and using this information to change the level of detail in a graphical user interface does not automatically commit one to claiming that what was measured was the user's *level of frustration*, even though this seems to be true in some cases. In fact, a pedagogical agent might learn important facts about its user (e.g., the effectiveness of its instructional strategies) based on such measures without requiring any representation of the user's emotional processes nor any emotional processes itself.

Contrariwise, architectures that claim to use emotional mechanisms (e.g., for the prioritization of goals or for memory retrieval) will have to make a case that the implemented mechanisms indeed give rise to "emotional states" in a clearly specified sense. Otherwise there is no sense, nor any reason, to call them that, even though there is, and always has been, a tendency in AI to present simplistic AI programs and robots as if they justified epithets like "emotional," "sad," "surprised," "afraid," "affective," and so on, without any deep theory justifying these labels (e.g., McDermott 1981). Consequently, the architectural route faces the challenge of saying exactly what it means to "implement emotional states" of the kinds in question.

Researchers pursuing the architectural strand on emotions in AI can be further divided into two main categories: those who attempt to model overt, observable effects of emotion behavior (call these *display models* of emotions), and those who aim to model the internal processes that bring about emotional behavior (call these *process models* of emotion).

Most work on architectural aspects of emotion in AI to date has focused on display models, which are intended to get the "input–output mapping" of a given behavioral description right (e.g., the right kind of emotional response for a given context, such as a fear expression on a robot's face when there is a rapidly approaching object in front of it). In the extreme case, such a mapping could be as simple as that employed in an animated web-based shopping agent which displays a surprised face if the user attempts to delete an item from the shopping basket. Architectures of this kind are found in many so-called "believable agents," where the primary goal is to induce a human observer to think that the agent is in a particular emotional state (see, e.g., Bates, Loyall, and Reilly 1994 for simulated agents, and Murphy et al. 2002 for robots). Whether the agent is indeed in the particular state is irrelevant. In fact, emotions are here often represented as states or values of "emotion variables," either qualitatively, as suggested by emotion terms (e.g., "happy", "afraid", etc.), or quantitatively, using numeric values (e.g., the agent is "0.4 happy," "0.1 afraid," etc.). And while some allow agents to be in only one state at a time, others allow for "emotion blends" (mixtures of simultaneously present emotional states), where individual emotions and their intensities span a multi-dimensional space.

Note that these features should not be taken to imply that the design of the architecture was devoid of biological motivation. Quite the opposite is true: Most (if not all) display models derive their inspiration from research in the affective sciences. However, their goal is not to replicate any particular empirical data from animal or human research, but rather to explore possible mechanisms for yielding the desired observable effects.

The main problem with display models of emotions is that they are ultimately silent about the role of emotions in agent architectures, for they may or may not *actually* implement emotional processes to achieve the desired overt behaviors. And even if they do, they may tell us little about the role of emotions. For although the implemented states are often labeled with familiar terms, they differ significantly from those usually denoted by these terms. A state labeled "surprise," for example, may be functionally defined to be triggered by loud noises and have very little in common with the complex processes underlying notions of "surprise" in humans and various animals, which involve the violation of a predicted outcome. (For a state so defined, "startle" would be the more appropriate label.)

In contrast, process models are intended to model and simulate some aspects of emotional processes as they unfold. As many psychologists and AI researchers have pointed out (e.g., Pfeifer 1988; Cosmides and Tooby 2004), emotion concepts are best characterized as denoting enduring processes of *behavior control*: action and reaction, adjustment and modification, anticipation and compensation of behavior in various (frequently social) situations. Often it is not a single inner state of an agent architecture that determines whether an agent experiences or displays some emotion, but rather a whole sequence of such states in combination with environmental states. "Fear," for example, does not refer to the makeup of an agent at a particular moment in time but to the unfolding of a sequence of events, starting from the perception of a potentially threatening environmental condition, to a reaction of the agent's control system, to a reaction of the agent's body, to a change in perception, and so on. Process models are thus much more complex than display models since they focus on the internal processes (and processing states) involved in emotions, typically drawing on a (psychological, neurological, etc.) theory of emotion (Panksepp 1998; Ortony, Clore, and Collins 1988).

12.3.3   Process models of emotion

Process models are based on the various components that are characteristic of emotion processes: a perceptual component that can trigger the emotion process; a visceral component that affects homeostatic variables of the agent's body; a cognitive component that involves belief-like states as well as various kinds of deliberative processes (e.g., redirection of attentional mechanisms, reallocation of processing resources, recall of past emotionally charged episodes, etc.); a behavioral component that is a reaction to the affect process (e.g., in the form of facial displays, gestures or bodily movements, etc.); and an accompanying qualitative feeling ("what it is like to be in or experience state S"). No single aspect is necessary for emotion, nor is any single aspect sufficient on its own. Yet, most of them are taken to be part of the many forms of human emotions we know from our own experience.

Process models themselves can be categorized into two main classes, based on whether they are aimed at explaining low-level neurological structures and mechanisms of emotion ("low-level process models"), or whether they are intended to model higher-level emotion processes ("high-level process models"). Most research on low-level process models is concerned with Pavlovian conditioning and is targeted at neural structures and processing mechanisms (hence, most low-level models are "neural network" models). Higher-level models of emotions are intended to capture more cognitive aspects involved in affect processes and are typically concerned with a wider range of affect (hence, most higher-level models are "symbolic" models).

The most extensively developed general low-level models are Grossberg's *CogEM* models (e.g., Grossberg and Schmajuk 1987), which are intended to show interactions between emotional and non-emotional areas in the brain (e.g., the amygdala vs. the sensory or prefrontal cortices). *CogEM* models can account for several effects in Pavlovian fear conditioning, but have not been directly applied to empirical data.

Specific low-level affect models, on the other hand, are targeted at modeling the amygdala, which performs several functions in emotion processing (LeDoux 1996). The lateral amygdala, for example, has been shown to be involved in fear conditioning (Blair, et al. 2003), and a preliminary computational model of associative learning in the amygdala has been developed and tested in three associative learning tasks (Balkenius and Morén 2001). Moreover, recent evidence from studies with rats suggests that the amygdala, in particular the frontotemporal amygdala, integrates sensory information and encodes affective evaluations as part of fear memory (Fanselow and Gale 2003). LeDoux and colleagues have hypothesized a dual pathway model of emotional processing in the amygdala, which they tested in auditory fear conditioning studies (LeDoux 1996). These models have been also used in simulated lesion studies and successfully compared to data from actual lesion studies with rats.

While all low-level models are neural network models, higher-level models comprise both connectionist and symbolic approaches. An example of a high-level connectionist approach is the ITERA model (Nerb and Sperba 2001), which is designed to study how media information about environmental problems influences cognition, emotion, and behavior. Facts, input types, emotions, and behavioral intentions are all represented in terms of individual neural units that are connected via excitatory and inhibitory links and compete for activation.

Most attempts to model emotions at higher levels, however, are based on symbolic architectures, for example, Soar (Laird, Newell, and Rosenbloom

1987) or ACT (Anderson 1993). They typically focus on the *OCC model* (Ortony et al. 1988), which provides "update rules" for changes in emotional states that can be directly implemented in rule-based systems. The currently most advanced implementations of high-level affect models are effected in the context of the "virtual humans" (Rickel et al. 2002), where the utility of emotions in artificial agents can be investigated in full immersion interactions with people (Gratch and Marsella 2004b). One particular model, the EMA model (Gratch and Marsella 2009), has also been used to further psychological theories that posit different "emotional appraisal and coping" processes as essential parts of human emotion processes.

Other higher-level architectures attempt to implement different aspects of psychological theories of emotions; examples include the MAMID model, whose emotional components "anger" and "fear" follow Frijda's definition (Frijda 1994), and the model of "surprise" suggested by Macedo and Cardoso (2001). There are also a few conceptual suggestions for complex human-like architectures that explicitly incorporate human-like emotion and cognition, but without providing particular implementations of the proposed architecture. Examples include Sloman's *H-CogAff model*, Minsky's *emotion machine*, and Norman, Ortony, and Revelle's 3-tier model.

Most emotion models have been implemented and tested in isolation from any *body model*. Consequently, it is difficult, if not impossible, to investigate crucial aspects of emotion processing that need a body to control and thus go beyond functional properties (like the effects of Pavlovian conditioning), which can be tested in stand-alone models (e.g., by applying a stimulus and measuring the output). Various attempts have been made to include bodily processes in simulated and robotic agents. Some have investigated the computational effects of simulated hormones for emotional control (Cañamero 1997), while others have implemented connectionist emotion models on robots, where different emotion types are represented as connectionist units that compete for activation, which in turn cause the robot to exhibit a particular behavior (e.g., Velásquez 1999). The main difference between these approaches and both low-level models of affect and some high-level appraisal-based models (e.g., Gratch and Marsella 2004a, 2009) is that they do not attempt to model any *specific psychological* or *neurobiological* theory of affect (e.g., in an effort to verify or falsify its predictions). Rather, they are concerned with the applicability of a particular control mechanism from an engineering perspective.

The main problem with process models of affect is a direct result of the problems plaguing affect concepts: It is unclear what kind of affective state a particular computational model is a model *of*. In some sense, process models without a functional characterization of the implemented affective states are no more successful from a conceptual point of view than display models which are not intended to implement specific kinds of affective states in the first place. However, even if no conceptual mileage is to be gained from a process model right away, there is an important advantage to the methodological approach of attempting to implement hypothesized affect mechanisms that has borne fruit already in the short term. For the architectural mechanisms intended to allow for the instantiation of affective states can be tested and evaluated as such, regardless of what kinds of functional states they can instantiate (e.g., one could treat them as "quasi-emotions" and investigate their potential for improving an agent's performance; Scheutz 2011). This is analogous to what happened pragmatically within AI with other kinds of architectures, such as belief-desire-intention (BDI) architectures, for example. Here the same kinds of conceptual questions could be raised about the *actual nature* of the instantiated "belief," "desire," and "intention" states, while the architectural mechanisms for problem solving could be evaluated independently in different domains for their technical merit.

Yet, there is an important difference between architectural approaches in the domain of reasoning, problem solving, and so on, and architectural approaches in the domain of affect: The former has often a well-developed theory of the functional potential of the architectural mechanisms, while the latter has currently no such theory. Rather, research on architectural aspects of affect is still in a *pre-theoretic* stage. The current lack of a well-developed theory of the utility of affective states in the control of artificial agents, however, does not take away from the fact that attempts to characterize and implement affective states and processes might yield architectural mechanisms that could prove useful for a variety of domains and applications (e.g., applications that have to deal with severe resource constraints as argued in Scheutz 2001b).

12.4   Machine consciousness in AI

Unlike emotion research, which dates back to the 1960s, investigation of machine consciousness in AI is a much younger endeavor that started in the mid 1990s and is really only beginning to gain momentum (although there were some early attempts at laying out requirements for conscious machines; see, e.g., Angel 1989).

One of the reasons for this later start may be that research on conscious machines must build on research on the various functional components that are required for consciousness, some of which may be emotions (for the suggestion that emotions and consciousness are intrinsically linked, see, e.g., Alexandrov and Sams 2005). Somewhat surprisingly, however, the machine consciousness community is not a subset of the emotion community in AI, nor does it intersect much with it. And while the emotion community in AI has fostered close ties to various psychologists and their theories (e.g., Andrew Ortony and Craig Smith, among others), the machine consciousness community seems to be more connected to philosophers who are interested in giving a functional, implementable account of consciousness.

Similarly to the case of emotions in AI, where researchers working on the communicative and other dimensions of emotion simply ignore questions about what emotions are and how they are implemented, some researchers interested in consciousness are not attempting to give an account of human consciousness. Rather, they are interested in "simulating" processes they take to be essential to consciousness – what (Holland 2003) calls "weak artificial consciousness" – or using principles underwriting human consciousness to design better control systems (Sanz, López, and Hernández 2007). Some, however, are interested in *conscious machines* (Franklin, Kelemen, and McCauley 1998; Aleksander and Dunmall 2003), and thus, like researchers on process models of emotions, have to address the question of what they mean by "consciousness" and, eventually, what it would take to implement it. Clearly, this is a very difficult problem, given that neither philosophers nor psychologists agree on what "consciousness" is supposed to refer to or what it is to *be conscious*. (Theories of consciousness range from neurological theories to cognitive representational theories, such as the various forms of *higher-order thought* theory, which hold that thoughts and perceptions become conscious in virtue of being targeted by further thoughts or perceptions.) As with emotions, AI researchers interested in achieving consciousness in machines have proposed various principles and architectural mechanisms that they take to be necessary for conscious machines.

In general, proposals vary along several dimensions: (1) the extent to which they connect to philosophy, psychology, or neuroscience; (2) the extent to which they lay out a particular architecture that can be conscious, or particular principles for such an architecture; and (3) the extent to which they actually provide implementations of their architectures or models. However, researchers agree that some type of "inner model" is required that is based on representations of the agent's perceptual states and allows the agent to simulate or predict future events and outcomes and what various possible actions would be like for it. Researchers disagree, however, on the exact definition and extension of the internal model and the other components to which it is connected.

12.4.1   Architectural proposals

Most proposals on consciousness in artificial agents are conceptual at present and provide a set of potentially implementable principles (sometimes with preliminary implementations for subsets). Pentti Haikonen, for example, summarizes the architectural requirements for a conscious system as follows:

(1) A suitable method for the representation of information must be devised. (2) Suitable information processing elements that allow the manipulation of information by the chosen representation method must be designed. (3) A machine architecture that can accommodate sensors, effectors, the processes of perception, introspection and the grounding of meaning as well as the flow of inner speech and inner imagery must be designed. (4) The system design must also accommodate the functions of thinking and reasoning, emotions and language. (Haikonen 2003, p. 168)

A more formal approach is taken by Aleksander and colleagues, who list five principles, stated as axioms, that are taken to be sufficient for consciousness. They specify the notion of "conscious of," for an agent and a world, as follows:

Let *A* be an agent in a sensorily-accessible world *S*. For *A* to be conscious of *S* it is necessary that:

> Axiom 1 (Depiction): *A* has *perceptual states* that depict parts of *S*.
> Axiom 2 (Imagination): *A* has internal *imaginational states* that *recall* parts of *S* or *fabricate S*-like sensations.
> Axiom 3 (Attention): *A* is *capable of selecting* which parts of *S* to depict or what to imagine.
> Axiom 4 (Planning): *A* has means of control over imaginational state sequences *to plan actions*.
> Axiom 5 (Emotion): *A* has additional *affective states* that evaluate planned actions and determine the ensuing action.
>
> (Aleksander and Dunmall 2003, p. 9)

The claim is that this combination of sensory, imaginational, attentional and affective depictions is what ultimately leads to a first-person perspective (the "I" in humans). The axioms are motivated, not by a particular theory of consciousness, but by a large collection of individual findings that seem to suggest these principles as abstractions.

Sloman has for quite some time promoted the notion of "virtual machine functionalism" as a way to account for rich internal processes of complex, deliberative and reflective agents that might form the basis of introspection and the development of internal categories and concepts that are not accessible (even via language) to other agents, and thus form the basis of a conscious agent's first-person perspective (e.g., Sloman and Chrisley 2003). There are also several other researchers who are attempting to give functional architectural accounts of the requirements for consciousness. Proposed accounts range from neural (Shanahan 2005), to robotic (Kuipers 2005), to control-theoretic (Sanz et al. 2007), to process-based (Manzotti 2003), and others. Common to all of the above researchers is that they have implemented some rudimentary models that demonstrate parts of the architecture, but not a complete functional, and thus conscious, system.

12.4.2   Conscious agents

A notable exception among researchers in machine consciousness is the work of Franklin and colleagues (Franklin et al. 1998), who have attempted to implement a complete conscious agent, based on Baars' global workspace theory of consciousness. This is a "theater model" of consciousness, which requires a central workspace (the "stage") where "conscious contents emerge when the bright spotlight of attention falls on a player on the stage of working memory" (Baars 1997, p. 44).

The first functional prototype, *"Conscious" Mattie*, was a software agent charged with writing seminar announcements, communicating by email with seminar organizers, and reminding them when late. A second prototype, IDA for "Intelligent Distribution Agent," was developed for the US Navy to facilitate the process of assigning sailors to new missions. Both architectures include mechanisms for "consciousness," comprising a spotlight controller, a broadcast manager, and a collection of attention codelets which recognize novel or problematic situations, together with modules for perception, action selection, associate memory, emotions, and meta-cognition (see Franklin 2000). The latest model is a complete cognitive architecture called LIDA (Learning Intelligent Distribution Agent), which adds various types of learning to the previous architecture.

12.5   Future perspectives

Emotion research has become an active interdisciplinary subfield in AI, and machine consciousness is on the verge of establishing a research community that pursues the design of conscious machines. Based on the current trajectories, it is likely that both communities will grow together, especially as the emotion community is pursuing more complex emotions, such as regret about one's own behavior or disappointment in someone else's attitude toward one, that require many of the architectural features necessary for conscious machines, as postulated by the consciousness community (representations of one's perceptions, internal focus of attention, memories of past actions, representations of possible futures, etc.).

Research in both areas promises not only to advance the state of the art in AI, but also to shed light, if not directly on the human case, then on the case of possible emotional and conscious beings, which should help us refine our concepts. Moreover, both areas are likely to contribute to a better understanding of the trade-offs between systems that are emotional and conscious compared to systems that lack one or both properties. Given that both endeavors are fairly young, however, it should not be too surprising that the fields have neither worked out satisfactory criteria for success nor reflected on the implications of their work. "Criteria for success" here is intended to refer to ways that would allow us to tell whether a given machine has emotions or is conscious. Presumably, this will involve claims about the machine's functional architecture and the types of states that it supports. This would also include algorithms to determine whether a given system actually implements the functional architecture, but unfortunately we are currently also missing a good theory of implementation (Scheutz 2001a). Ideally, we would like to have criteria that can establish whether a given machine is in a particular emotional state or is conscious. This could involve procedures analogous to those psychologists use to determine whether a person is in a particular emotional state or is conscious.

While the specific need for such criteria might not arise as much within AI itself, it is likely that there will eventually be strong societal pressure to settle these and other fundamental questions about the nature of artificial minds, especially when claims are made about the emotional and conscious states of machines. This was a point recognized by Putnam over forty years ago:

Given the ever-accelerating rate of both technological and social change, it is entirely possible that robots will one day exist, and argue "we *are* alive; we *are* conscious!" In that event, what are today only philosophical prejudices of a traditional anthropocentric and mentalistic kind would all too likely develop into conservative political attitudes. But fortunately, we today have the advantage of being able to discuss this problem disinterestedly, and a little more chance, therefore, of arriving at the correct answer. (Putnam 1964, p. 678)

While Putnam was certainly right about the need to clarify questions about machine consciousness, the urgency for working out answers to the problem has clearly changed between when he wrote about discussing it "disinterestedly" and today, with all the recent successes in artificial intelligence and autonomous robotics, and with robots already being disseminated into society. Hence, it is high time for AI researchers and philosophers to reflect together on the potential of emotional and conscious machines. For we do not want to wake up one day to discover that what we treated as emotionless, non-conscious artifacts were really emotional, conscious beings, enslaved and mistreated by us out of ignorance or prejudice.

Further reading

Scherer, K. R., Bänziger, T., and Roesch, E. B. (2010). *Blueprint for Affective Computing: A Sourcebook*. Oxford University Press. A comprehensive collection of research chapters on the various aspects of emotions and current emotion models, ranging from theoretical frameworks to specific algorithms for implementing affectively competent artificial agents.

Wallach, W. and Allen, C. (2009). *Moral Machines: Teaching Robots Right from Wrong*. Oxford University Press. A great foray into the problems associated with building intelligent autonomous robots and an appeal to implement moral decision making in artificial agents.

The International Journal of Synthetic Emotions (IGI). A good resource for research papers on different models and implementations of artificial emotions.

The International Journal of Machine Consciousness (World Scientific). A great resource for the latest research papers on the emergent field of machine consciousness.

References

Aleksander, I. and Dunmall, B. (2003). Axioms and tests for the presence of minimal consciousness in agents, in O. Holland (ed.), *Machine Consciousness* (pp. 7–18). New York: Imprint Academic.

Alexandrov, Y. I. and Sams, M. E. (2005). Emotion and consciousness: Ends of a continuum, *Cognitive Brain Research* 25: 387–405.

Anderson, J. R. (1993). *Rules of the Mind*. Mahwah, NJ: Erlbaum.

Angel, L. (1989). *How to Build a Conscious Machine*. Boulder, CO: Westview Press.

Baars, B. J. (1997). *In the Theater of Consciousness: The Workspace of the Mind*. New York: Oxford University Press.

Balkenius, C. and Morén, J. (2001). Emotional learning: A computational model of the amygdala, *Cybernetics and Systems* 32: 611–36.

Bates, J., Loyall, A. B., and Reilly, W. S. (1994). An architecture for action, emotion, and social behavior, in C. Castelfranchi and E. Werner (eds.), *Artificial Social Systems: 4th European Workshop on Modelling Autonomous Agents in a Multi-Agent World (MAAMAW '92)* (pp. 55–68). Berlin: Springer.

Blair, H. T., Tinkelman, A., Moita, M. A. P., and LeDoux, J. E. (2003). Associative plasticity in neurons of the lateral amygdala during auditory fear conditioning, *Annals of the New York Academy of Sciences* 985: 485–7.

Brave, S. and Nass, C. (2003). Emotion in human–computer interaction, in J. A. Jacko and A. Sears (eds.), *The Human–Computer Interaction Handbook: Fundamentals, Evolving Technologies, and Emerging Applications* (pp. 81–96). Mahwah, NJ: Erlbaum.

Cañamero, D. (1997). Modeling motivations and emotions as a basis for intelligent behavior, in W. L. Johnson (ed.), *Proceedings of the First International Conference on Autonomous Agents (agents'97)* (pp. 148–55). New York: ACM Press.

Cosmides, L. and Tooby, J. (2004). Evolutionary psychology and the emotions, in M. Lewis and J. M. Haviland-Jones (eds.), *Handbook of Emotions* (2nd edn.) (pp. 91–115). New York: Guilford Press.

Fanselow, M. S. and Gale, G. D. (2003). The amygdala, fear, and memory, *Annals of the New York Academy of Sciences* 985: 125–34.

Franklin, S. (2000). Modeling consciousness and cognition in software agents, in N. Taatgen, J. Aasman (eds.), *Proceedings of the 3rd International Conference on Cognitive Modeling* (pp. 100–9). Veenendal, The Netherlands: Universal Press.

Franklin, S., Kelemen, A., and McCauley, L. (1998). Ida: A cognitive agent architecture, in *IEEE International Conference on Systems, Man, and Cybernetics*, vol. 3 (pp. 2646–51).

Frijda, N. H. (1994). Varieties of affect: Emotions and episodes, moods, and sentiments, in P. Ekman and R. J. Davidson (eds.), *The Nature of Emotion: Fundamental Questions* (pp. 59–67). New York: Oxford University Press.

Gadanho, S.C. (2003). Learning behavior-selection by emotions and cognition in a multi-goal robot task, *Journal of Machine Learning Research* 4: 385–412.

Gratch, J. and Marsella, S. (2004a). A domain-independent framework for modeling emotion, *Cognitive Systems Research* 5: 269–306.

  (2004b). Evaluating the modeling and use of emotion in virtual humans, in *Proceedings of the 3rd International Joint Conference on Autonomous Agents and Multiagent Systems*, vol. 1 (pp. 320–7).

  (2009). EMA: A process model of appraisal dynamics, *Cognitive Systems Research* 10: 70–90.

Griffiths, P. E. (1997). *What Emotions Really Are: The Problem of Psychological Categories*. Chicago University Press.

Grossberg, S. and Schmajuk, N. (1987). Neural dynamics of attentionally-modulated Pavlovian conditioning: Conditioned reinforcement, inhibition, and opponent processing, *Psychobiology* 15: 195–240.

Haikonen, P. O. (2003). *The Cognitive Approach to Conscious Machines*. Exeter: Imprint Academic.

Holland, O. (ed.) (2003). *Machine Consciousness*. New York: Imprint Academic.

Hoque, M., McDuff, D., and Picard, R. (2012). Exploring temporal patterns towards classifying frustrated and delighted smiles, *IEEE Transactions on Affective Computing* 3: 323–34.

Ichise, R., Shapiro, D. G., and Langley, P. (2002). Learning hierarchical skills from observation, in *Proceedings of the 5th International Conference on Discovery Science* (pp. 247–58).

Kuipers, B. (2005). Consciousness: Drinking from the firehose of experience, in *Proceedings of the 20th National Conference on Artificial Intelligence*, vol. 3 (pp. 1298–305).

Laird, J. E., Newell, A., and Rosenbloom, P. S. (1987). SOAR: An architecture for general intelligence, *Artificial Intelligence* 33: 1–64.

LeDoux, J. (1996). *The Emotional Brain: The Mysterious Underpinnings of Emotional Life*. New York: Simon and Schuster.

Lycan, W. G. (1987). *Consciousness*. Cambridge MA: MIT Press.

Macedo, L. and Cardoso, A. (2001). Modeling forms of surprise in an artificial agent, in J. Moore and K. Stenning (eds.), *Proceedings of the 23rd Annual Conference of the Cognitive Science Society* (pp. 588–93). Mahwah, NJ: Erlbaum.

Manzotti, R. (2003). A process-based architecture for an artificial conscious being, in J. Seibt (ed.), *Process Theories: Crossdisciplinary Studies in Dynamic Categories* (pp. 285–312). Dordrecht: Kluwer Academic Press.

McDermott, D. (1981). Artificial intelligence meets natural stupidity, in J. Haugeland (ed.), *Mind Design: Philosophy, Psychology, Artificial Intelligence* (pp. 143–60). Cambridge, MA: MIT Press.

Murphy, R. R., Lisetti, C., Tardif, R., Irish, L., and Gage, A. (2002). Emotion-based control of cooperating heterogeneous mobile robots, *IEEE Transactions on Robotics and Automation* 18: 744–57.

Nerb, J. and Sperba, H. (2001). Evaluation of environmental problems: A coherence model of cognition and emotion, *Cognition and Emotion* 4: 521–51.

Ortony, A., Clore, G. L., and Collins, A. (1988). *The Cognitive Structure of Emotions.* New York: Cambridge University Press.

Panksepp, J. (1998). *Affective Neuroscience: The Foundations of Human and Animal Emotions.* Oxford University Press.

Pfeifer, R. (1988). Artificial intelligence models of emotion, in V. Hamilton, G. H. Bower, and N. H. Frijda (eds.), *Cognitive Perspectives on Emotion and Motivation* (pp. 287–320). Dordrecht: Kluwer Academic Publishers.

Picard, R. (1997). *Affective Computing.* Cambridge, MA: MIT Press.

Putnam, H. (1964). Robots: Machines or artificially created life? *The Journal of Philosophy* 61: 668–91.

Rickel, J., Marsella, S., Gratch, J., Hill, R., Traum, D., and Swartout, W. (2002). Towards a new generation of virtual humans for interactive experiences, *IEEE Intelligent Systems,* 17(4): 32–8.

Sanz, R., López, I., and Hernández, C. (2007). Self-awareness in real-time cognitive control architectures, in A. Chella and R. Manzotti (eds.), *AI and Consciousness: Theoretical Foundations and Current Approaches: Papers from the AAAI Fall Symposium* (pp. 135–40). Menlo Park, CA: AAAI Press.

Scheutz, M. (2001a). Causal versus computational complexity, *Minds and Machines* 11: 534–66.

(2001b). The evolution of simple affective states in multi-agent environments, in D. Cañamero (ed.), *Proceedings of AAAI Fall Symposium* (pp. 123–8). Falmouth, MA: AAAI Press.

(2002). Agents with or without emotions? in R. Weber (ed.), *Proceedings of the 15th International Florida Artificial Intelligence Research Society (FLAIRS) Conference* (pp. 89–94). AAAI Press.

(2004). Useful roles of emotions in artificial agents: A case study from artificial life, in *Proceedings of the 19th National Conference on Artifical Intelligence* (pp. 42–7). AAAI Press.

(2011). Architectural roles of affect and how to evaluate them in artificial agents, *International Journal of Synthetic Emotions* 2(2): 48–65.

Scheutz, M., Schermerhorn, P., and Kramer, J. (2006). The utility of affect expression in natural language interactions in joint human–robot tasks, in *Proceedings of the 1st ACM SIGCHI/SIGART Conference on Human-Robot Interaction* (pp. 226–33).

Searle, J. R. (1992). *The Rediscovery of the Mind.* Cambridge MA: MIT Press.

Shanahan, M. P. (2005). Consciousness, emotion, and imagination: A brain-inspired architecture for cognitive robotics, in *Proceedings aisb 2005 symposium on next generation approaches to machine consciousness* (pp. 26–35).

Sloman, A. and Chrisley, R. (2003). Virtual machines and consciousness, *Journal of Consciousness Studies* 10(4–5): 133–72.

Sloman, A. and Croucher, M. (1981). Why robots will have emotions, in *Proceedings of the 7th International Joint Conference on AI* (pp. 197–202).

Trappl, R., Petta, P., and Payr, S. (eds.) (2002). *Emotions in Humans and Artifacts.* Cambridge MA: MIT Press.

Turing, A. (1950). Computing machinery and intelligence, *Mind* 59: 433–60. Reprinted (1963) in E. A. Feigenbaum and J. Feldman (eds.), *Computers and Thought* (pp. 11–35). New York: McGraw-Hill.

Velásquez, J. D. (1999). When robots weep: Emotional memories and decision-making, in *Proceedings of the 15th National Conference on Artificial Intelligence* (pp. 70–5). Menlo Park, CA: AAAI Press.

Part IV

Extensions

13 Robotics

Phil Husbands

13.1 Introduction

Robots are popularly thought of as mechanical men – humanoid machines capable of performing many of the tasks we engage in all the time, such as walking, talking, picking things up and moving them around, as well as some of those that most of us try to avoid, such as indiscriminate acts of death and destruction. In the next section we will see that this image – and indeed the very idea of a robot – comes from the world of fiction. While it is true that these myths and dreams have seeped into the collective conscious and undoubtedly influence some of the scientific work in the field of robotics, the current reality – though full of enormous interest and potential – is a little less dramatic.

In the research community a typical working definition of a robot goes something like this: a physical device capable of autonomous or pre-programmed behavior in the world involving interactions with its environment through sensors and actuators. In contrast to machines that perform precise repetitive tasks ad nauseam (e.g., robots used in manufacturing production lines), *autonomous* robots are required to behave in an appropriate way in whatever circumstances they find themselves. Like biological creatures, their behavior must be self-generated, making use of sensory information to moderate their responses to the world.

In order to provide context, this chapter starts with a brief sketch of the history of robotics and then gives some background on traditional approaches. This allows a clearer understanding of the motivations for the development of the biologically inspired approaches whose discussion forms the bulk of the chapter. In recent years, as NASA's planetary rovers, Honda's Asimo walking humanoid robot, iRobot's autonomous vacuum cleaners, Sony's Aibo robot dog, and countless autonomous toys have captured the imagination, there has never been so much momentum for the development of useful autonomous robots. However, as we shall see, the challenges are still significant.

13.2 Early history

While stories of artificial human-like creatures go back at least to the myths of ancient Greece, the notion of embodied mechanical intelligence was, quite literally, thrust centre stage in the years between the world wars when, in 1921, Karel Čapek's play *R.U.R.* (Rossum's Universal Robots) introduced the world to robots, in the process forging the associated myths and images that now permeate our culture. It was a worldwide smash hit capturing the popular imagination as well as sparking much intellectual debate (Horáková and Kelemen 2008). The play, with its roots in the dreams and folk tales of old Europe, told of the mass production of artificial humanoid workers on an isolated island. These robots are created using some sort of biochemical process and sold throughout the world as cheap labor. After a while they develop aggressive emotions and, realizing their physical and mental superiority, the robots rise up and destroy the human race. The play ends on a more positive note when two robots develop feelings of love and respect toward life, becoming almost indistinguishable from the humans they have replaced.

Karel Čapek had difficulty in deciding what to call the artificial workers until his brother, Joseph – a renowned Czech painter – coined the word *robot*. It is derived from the ancient Czech word *robota* which means repetitive drudge work.

Although many ingenious mechanical automata had been constructed since the fifteenth century, including chess-playing Turks and flatulent ducks in the 1700s, it was not until the late 1940s that a device recognizable as a robot (in the present-day sense of the term) appeared. In 1949 W. Grey Walter, a neurologist based at the Burden Institute in Bristol who was a world leader in EEG[1] research, completed a pair of machines he called "tortoises." Grey Walter's tortoises were the first ever wheeled mobile autonomous robots. The devices were three-wheeled and sported a protective "shell" (see Figure 13.1). They had a light sensor, touch sensor, propulsion motor, steering motor, and an electronic valve-based analogue "nervous system." Walter's intention was to show that even in a very simple nervous system (the tortoises had two artificial neurons), complexity could arise out of the interactions between its units. By studying whole embodied sensorimotor systems, he was pioneering a style of research that was to become very prominent in AI many years later, and remains so today (Brooks 1999; Holland 2003). Between Easter 1948 and Christmas 1949, he built the first tortoises, Elmer and Elsie. They were rather unreliable and required frequent attention. In 1951, his technician, Mr. W. J. "Bunny" Warren, designed and built six new tortoises to a much higher standard. Three of these tortoises were exhibited at the Festival of Britain in 1951; others were regularly demonstrated in public throughout the 1950s. The robots were capable of phototaxis (steering toward a light source), by which means they could find their way to a recharging station when they ran low

---

[1] Electroencephalography (EEG) is the recording of the brain's electrical activity as measured by multiple electrodes placed on the scalp.

Figure 13.1 Grey Walter watches one of his tortoises push aside some wooden blocks on its way back to its recharging hutch. Circa 1952.

on battery power. He referred to the devices as *Machina speculatrix* after their apparent tendency to speculatively explore their environment.

Walter was able to demonstrate a variety of interesting behaviors as the robots interacted with their environment and each other. In one experiment he placed a light on the "nose" of a tortoise and watched as the robot observed itself in a mirror. "It began flickering," he wrote. "Twittering, and jigging like a clumsy Narcissus." Walter argued that if this behavior was observed in an animal it "might be accepted as evidence of some degree of self-awareness" (Walter 1953).

Walter's robots became very famous, featuring in newsreels, television broadcasts and numerous newspaper articles. They have been acknowledged as a major early influence by a number of leading robotics researchers of later generations. For instance, Rodney Brooks, director of the Computer Science and AI Laboratory at MIT, built his first robot – a version of *Machina speculatrix* making use of transistors rather than valves (Brooks 2002, p. 27) – after coming across Walter's book *The Living Brain* (1953).

Figure 13.2 An articulated industrial robot arm. Arms vary in complexity with some involving more joints and a greater number of degrees of freedom.

Walter was a major figure in the field of cybernetics, a name coined by Norbert Wiener, meaning the study of control and communication in animals and machines. This highly interdisciplinary field was the forerunner of much of modern AI and robotics, and the root of current control and communications theory. It also had a major impact on neuroscience and other branches of biology. It had great influence in the late 1940s and throughout the 1950s, spreading into economics and the arts, before losing favor. As we shall see, many areas with origins in cybernetics, such as artificial neural networks and evolutionary computing, re-emerged in the 1980s and are now stronger than ever.

From these biologically inspired, and rather exploratory, beginnings, the focus of robotics began to turn to more immediately practical applications during the 1950s. The main emphasis was on the development of robot arms, particularly for use on production lines. Rather gradually, over a period of about twenty years, robot arms and manipulators became more and more widespread in heavy industry.

The central goal of classical industrial robotics is to move the end of an arm (which houses an actuator such as a gripper, known as the "end effector") to a predetermined point in space. This is generally approached by finding the required torques, applied through the motors controlling the arm joints, such that the resulting arm configuration puts the end effector in the desired position. A typical robot arm is shown in Figure 13.2.

Control of classical industrial robots is often based on solutions to equations describing the inverse-kinematics problem (finding the angle through which the joints should be rotated to achieve a specific position of the end effector). These usually rely on precise knowledge of the robot's mechanics and its environment. High-level aspects of control involve calculating the desired joint rotations and the torques required to achieve them. Low-level control is also needed to take care of the interface with the actuators in order to implement the desired motor commands.

Industrial robots are programmed to repeat precise manipulations, such as welding or paint spraying, over and over again. Although they make use of sensors to help control their movements, their behavior cannot be said to be in any way intelligent. If the car on the production line is misaligned or is not the expected shape, the robot cannot react to the new set of circumstances; it can only repeat its pre-programmed movements. While these limitations are manageable in the highly controlled environment of a production line, they become problematic if a robot is to be used in less structured and predictable environments – for instance in an exploration mission. In such scenarios, the robot, usually a mobile free-roaming device, must interact with its environment in a much more intelligent way in order to cope with a noisy, dynamic world. The control methods used for industrial arms are no longer sufficient. The "classical" approach to intelligent mobile robotics is the focus of the next section.

13.3 Classical intelligent mobile robotics

An industrial robot's working environment is often carefully designed so that intricate sensory feedback is unnecessary; the robot performs its repetitive tasks in an accurate, efficient, but essentially unintelligent way. More complex cases involving cluttered, dynamic, or noisy environments, or delicate manipulations of objects, usually require more sophisticated sensory feedback and perceptual processing, such as the use of a vision system. This brings us into the realm of AI and intelligent robotics. Discussion of this area will focus mainly on autonomous mobile robots, but many of the more general approaches to "intelligent" control are applicable to other forms of robot.

From 1966 to 1972 the Artificial Intelligence Center at SRI International (then Stanford Research Institute) conducted pioneering research on a mobile robot system nicknamed "Shakey." The robot had a vision system which gave it the ability to perceive and model its environment in a limited way. Shakey could perform tasks that required planning, route-finding, and the rearrangement of simple objects. Shakey became a paradigm case for early AI-driven robotics. The robot, shown in Figure 13.3, accepted goals from the user, planned how to achieve them, and then executed those plans (Nilsson 1984). The overall processing loop had at its heart the sequence of operations shown in Figure 13.4. Here robot intelligence is functionally decomposed into a strict pipeline of operations. Central to this view of intelligence is an internal model of the world which must be extended, maintained, and constantly referred to in order to decide what to do next. In Shakey's case, as in much of AI at the time, the world model was defined in terms of formal logic. The robot was provided with an initial set of axioms, and then perceptual routines were used to build up and modify the world model based on sensory information, particularly from the robot's vision system. Plans were built using the STRIPS

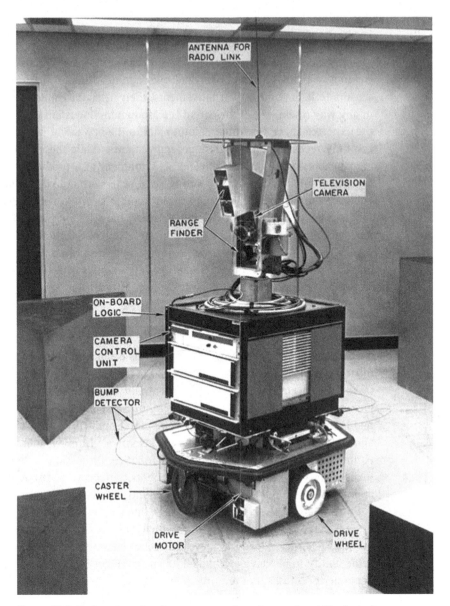

Figure 13.3 Shakey the robot in 1970 reasoning about colored blocks in its environment.

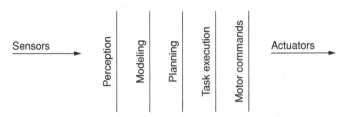

Figure 13.4 Pipeline of functionally decomposed processing used in much classical AI robotics (after Brooks 1986).

system, which became very influential, helping to spark the subfield of AI planning (Allen, Hendler, and Tate 1990).

After each action was executed, the high-level control system, PLANEX, would execute the shortest plan subsequence that led to a goal and whose preconditions were satisfied. If no subsequence applied, PLANEX called STRIPS to make a new plan. This process could be computationally very expensive, even in the carefully constructed environments in which the robot operated (these mainly consisted of large colored blocks of various regular shapes and sizes). However, the general approach was very influential and it dominated for more than a decade, during which time the individual functions of Figure 13.4 tended to become separate specialisms which started to lose contact with each other.

However, even though Shakey and robots like it were controlled by computers the size of a room, the demands of the sequential processing model they employed (Figure 13.4) were such that they could not operate in real time. They would often take tens of minutes or even hours to complete a single task such as navigating across a room avoiding obstacles. By the mid 1980s a number of leading researchers from the main AI robotics centers were becoming more and more disillusioned with the approach.

Hans Moravec, an influential roboticist who had done important work on the Stanford Cart, a project similar in spirit and approach to SRI's Shakey and which ran at about the same time, summed up such feelings:

For the last fifteen years I have worked with and around mobile robots controlled by large programs that take in a certain amount of data and mull it over for seconds, minutes or even hours. Although their accomplishments are sometimes impressive, they are brittle – if any of many key steps do not work as planned, the entire process is likely to fail beyond recovery. (Moravec 1987, p. 1)

Moravec goes on to point out how this is in strange contrast to the pioneering work of Grey Walter and the projects that his tortoises inspired; such early robots' simple sensors were connected to their motors via fairly modest circuits and yet they were able to behave very competently and "managed to extricate themselves out of many very difficult and confusing situations" without wasting inordinate amounts of time "thinking." In conclusion, Moravec advocates making the most effective use of whatever technology is available in the present in order to be able to gradually build up experimental discoveries, rather than developing more and more complex reasoning systems that cannot be used in any meaningful way in real time in the real world.

13.4 Behavior-based and biologically inspired robotics

The dominant functional decomposition approach outlined in the previous section was closely related to the general philosophy that held sway in most of AI

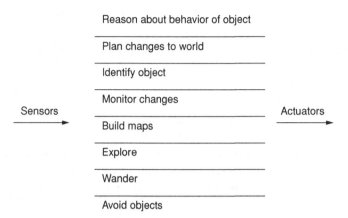

Reason about behavior of object

Plan changes to world

Identify object

Monitor changes

Sensors ———▶   Build maps   Actuators ———▶

Explore

Wander

Avoid objects

Figure 13.5 The parallel behavioral decomposition for robot control as advocated by Brooks and the behavior-based approach. Decomposition from Brooks (1986).

at that time. The mainstream were custodians of an essentially Cartesian view of what AI was and how it should be practised: Intelligence was to be largely understood in terms of manipulating carefully constructed internal models of external reality; hence the quest for intelligent machines should focus on ways of building models of the world and the development of algorithms to "reason" about the world using these models. By the mid 1980s such an approach was faltering in many areas of AI, not just robotics. Disillusionment with this state of affairs found a particularly effective voice in Rodney Brooks, who was developing an alternative vision of not only intelligent robotics, but also the general AI problem. Influenced by Moravec, as well as by the unconventional work of Marc Raibert (who produced a wonderful series of legged robots; Raibert 1986), Brooks, along with his team at MIT, became central to a growing band of dissidents who launched a salvo of attacks on the AI mainstream.

In a move that conjured up the spirit of cybernetics, the dissidents rejected the assumptions of the establishment, and instead held that the major part of natural intelligence is closely bound up with the generation of adaptive behavior in the harsh unforgiving environments most animals inhabit. The investigation of complete autonomous sensorimotor systems – "artificial creatures" – was seen as the most fruitful way forward, rather than the development of disembodied algorithms for abstract problem solving, which had become the focus of most of AI by then. The central nervous system was viewed as a fantastically sophisticated control system, not a chess-playing computer. Hence it was claimed that the development of mobile autonomous robots should be absolutely central to AI. Vested interests were threatened, emotions ran high, insults were traded. It was an exciting time!

At the heart of Brooks' approach was the idea of behavioral decomposition, as opposed to traditional functional decomposition. Figure 13.5 illustrates the concept. The overall control architecture involves the coordination of several loosely coupled behavior-generating systems all acting in parallel. Each has access to sensors and actuators and can act as a standalone control system. Each layer was thought of as a *level of competence*, with the simpler competences at the bottom of the vertical decomposition and the more complex ones at the top (Brooks 1986). Brooks developed a concrete implementation of the idea which he called the *subsumption architecture* (Brooks 1986, 1999). Higher-level layers are able to subsume the role of lower levels by taking over control of their motor outputs. The architecture can be partitioned at any level with the layers below always forming a complete control system. Each layer had its own particular sensor–motor coupling, which might be quite distinct from that of others, for instance using completely different sensors and/or actuators. The idea was to allow overall competence to be increased by adding new behavior-generating layers without having to change lower levels. Layers were built from networks of simple processing units, giving the systems a flavor much closer to neural networks than logic-based classical AI, and usually involved tightly coupled sensorimotor feedback loops going through the environment.

The whole concept was inspired by biology, and in particular invertebrate neuroethology (the study of behavior in relation to its underlying neural mechanisms), bringing it close to the cybernetic roots of AI; the spirit of Grey Walter's original robotics work had finally resurfaced. Such an approach was shown to handle multiple goals robustly and could be expanded in a natural way – areas in which traditional methods struggled. Brooks' team demonstrated the architecture on a series of autonomous mobile robots, including legged walking machines, with a variety of competences that went at least halfway up the decomposition illustrated in Figure 13.5 (Brooks 1999). In two provocatively titled and highly influential papers, "Intelligence without representation" and "Intelligence without reason" (Brooks 1991a, 1991b), Brooks gave a detailed critique of the classical approach and made it clear that monolithic representation and reasoning-hungry approaches were no longer the only game in town. By demonstrating how well-crafted parallel behavioral layers could generate coherent overall behavior in noisy environments, the MIT team showed how complex internal world models were not necessary, at least for a whole range of navigation and exploration behaviors. "The world is its own best model" was one of their slogans, by which they meant that the system could extract all pertinent information directly from the world itself without needing to build and manipulate models.

Brooks' work triggered the formation of the so-called "New AI" movement, still strong today. With its focus on the development of whole artificial creatures as an important way to deepen our understanding of natural intelligence and provide new directions for the engineering of intelligent machines, it has pushed robotics back to the forefront of AI.

Figure 13.6 Kismet, a robot designed by Cynthia Breazeal to take part in social interactions with humans.

Despite their success, after a while Brooks grew tired of insect-like robots and wanted to attempt something much grander and more ambitious – a humanoid robot that would interact with people and everyday objects in a meaningful way and that would have something approaching human-level capabilities (Brooks 2002). Hence the Cog project was born. The robot (Cog) consisted of a torso with arms and a vision-equipped head, bolted to a bench (Brooks et al. 1999). A generally behavior-based approach was taken (in the sense illustrated by Figure 13.5), although individual competences were now often more complex and no longer relied on simple network implementations, and the interactions between the behaviors could be more involved (e.g., not just simple inhibition operations). Interesting developments were made in robot engineering (e.g., in muscle-like actuators) and in behavior generation. However, few would claim that overall human-level competences were demonstrated. What the project did achieve was an explosion of interest in humanoid robotics and the development of social interaction as an important area of study in robotics.

Through her work on the Cog project, Cynthia Breazeal, then a research student in the MIT AI Lab, pioneered the notion of a robot that could engage in social interaction. She developed Kismet, shown in Figure 13.6, which has inspired the construction of many similar robots in labs all over the world. Kismet has microphones in its ears and cameras hidden behind human-like eyeballs. It can move its eyes and neck and can make facial expressions through its ability to open its jaw and move its ears, eyebrows, and lips. As well as vision and hearing, the robot can interact via speech. Breazeal's robot was developed to the stage where it is able to interact in a convincing way, exhibiting and reacting to mood and emotion (Breazeal 2002). As well as pointing the way forward for robots that are intended to interact with humans, the project also opened up the possibility of using robots as tools for studying and better understanding certain types of social interaction (Breazeal et al. 2005).

The explosion in biologically inspired robotics that Brooks' work helped to fuel brought forth numerous interesting strands of research, many of which are still very active, and pushed AI much closer to biology, particularly neuroscience, than it had been for many years. As the limitations of traditional AI became more obvious, other biologically inspired areas such as neural networks, adaptive systems, artificial evolution, and artificial life had also come to the fore. These various currents mingled with the "New AI" approaches to robotics, spawning new attitudes and directions. The face of AI was radically changed.

There is not enough space in this chapter to deal with the considerable breadth of biologically inspired robotics (see the "Further reading" section), so it will concentrate on two important and influential areas: evolutionary robotics and insect-inspired approaches to visual navigation.

13.5 Evolutionary robotics

Alan Turing's (1950) paper, "Computing machinery and intelligence," is widely regarded as one of the seminal works in artificial intelligence. It is best known for what came to be called the Turing Test – a proposal for deciding whether or not a machine is intelligent. However, tucked away toward the end of Turing's wide-ranging discussion of issues arising from the test is a far more interesting proposal. He suggests that worthwhile intelligent machines should be adaptive – should learn and develop – but concedes that designing, building, and programming such machines by hand is probably completely infeasible. He goes on to sketch an alternative way of creating machines based on an artificial analogue of biological evolution. Each machine would have hereditary material encoding its structure, mutated copies of which would form offspring machines. A selection mechanism would be used to favor better-adapted machines – in this case those that learned to behave most intelligently. Turing proposed that the selection mechanism should largely consist of the experimenter's judgment.

It was more than forty years before Turing's long-forgotten suggestions became reality. Building on the development of principled evolutionary search algorithms (Holland 1975), researchers at the National Research Council (CNR) in Rome, École Polytechnique Fédérale de Lausanne (EPFL), the University of

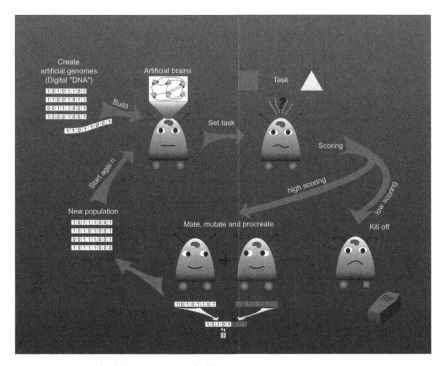

Figure 13.7 Key elements of the evolutionary robotics approach.

Sussex, and Case Western University independently demonstrated method-ologies and practical techniques to evolve, rather than design, control systems for primitive intelligent machines. It was out of the spirited milieu of "New AI" that the field of *Evolutionary Robotics* was born in the early 1990s. Initial motivations were similar to Turing's: The hand design of intelligent adap-tive machines intended for operation in natural environments is extremely difficult – would it be possible to wholly or partly automate the process? From the outset the vast majority of work in this area has involved populations of artificial genomes (lists of characters and numbers) encoding the structure and other properties of artificial neural networks that control autonomous mobile robots whose job is to carry out a particular task or exhibit some set of behaviors. Other properties of the robot, such as sensor layout or body morphology, may also be under genetic control. The genomes are mutated and interbred, creating new generations of robots according to a Darwinian scheme in which the fittest individuals are most likely to produce offspring (see Figure 13.7). Fitness is measured in terms of how well a robot behaves according to some evaluation criteria; this is usually automatically measured, but may, in the manner of eighteenth-century pig breeders and in keeping with Turing's original proposal, be based on the experimenters' direct judgment. Work in evolutionary robotics is now carried out in many labs around the world and numerous papers have been published on many aspects of the field.

Potential advantages of this methodology include:

- The ability to explore potentially unconstrained designs that have large numbers of free variables. The genetic encoding defines a whole *class* of robot designs. This means fewer assumptions and constraints are necessary in specifying a viable solution. The evolutionary algorithm searches this class of systems for suitable designs.
- The ability to use the methodology to fine-tune parameters of an already successful design – perhaps in order to use it in a new application.
- The ability, through the careful design of fitness criteria and selection techniques, to take into account multiple, and potentially conflicting, design criteria and constraints (e.g., efficiency, cost, weight, power consumption, etc.).
- The possibility of developing highly unconventional and minimal designs.

Prominent early centers for research in this area were EPFL and Sussex University, which are both still very active in the field. Much of the early EPFL work used the miniature Khepera robot (Mondada, Franzi, and Ienne 1994), which became a widespread tool in many areas of robotics research. With a diameter of 55 mm and a height of 30 mm, in its basic configuration it is equipped with eight infra-red proximity sensors – six on the front, two on the back – that can also act as visible-light detectors. It has two independently driven wheels allowing rapid maneuverability. The first successful evolutionary robots experiments at EPFL employed a population of bit strings encoding the connection weights and node thresholds for a simple fixed-architecture feedforward neural network. Each member of the population was decoded into a particular instantiation of a neural network controller, which was then downloaded onto the robot (Floreano and Mondada 1994). This controlled the robot for a fixed period of time as it moved around a simple environment with perimeter walls and a central diagonal wall which acted as an obstacle around which the robots had to navigate.

The following simple fitness function was used to evolve obstacle-avoidance behaviors:

$$F = V + (1 - \sqrt{DV}) + (1 - I)$$

where V is the average rotation speed of opposing wheels, DV is the difference between signed speed values of opposing wheels, I is the activation value of the infra-red sensor with the highest input (readings are high if an obstacle is close to a sensor). Maximizing this function ensures high speed, a tendency to move in straight lines, and avoidance of walls and obstacles in the environment. After about thirty-six hours of real-world evolution using this setup,

(a)   (b)

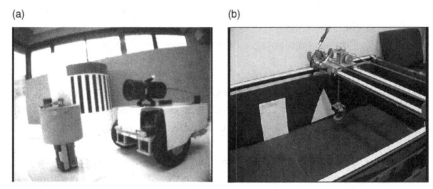

Figure 13.8 An early version of the Sussex gantry robot right (b) was a "hardware simulation" of a robot such as that shown left (a). It allowed real-world evolution of visually guided behaviors in an easily controllable experimental setup.

controllers were evolved that successfully generated efficient motion around the course avoiding collisions with the walls.

At the same time as this work was going on at EPFL, a series of pioneering experiments on evolving visually guided behaviors were being performed at Sussex University (Cliff, Husbands, and Harvey 1993; Harvey, Husbands, and Cliff 1994) in which recurrent neural network controllers and visual sampling morphologies were concurrently evolved to allow a gantry robot (as well as other more standard mobile robots) to perform various visually guided tasks. The visual sampling morphology specified which parts of the robot's camera image were used as input to the neural network controller. The number, size, and position of small (input) image patches were genetically specified, the rest of the image was thrown away.

An early instantiation of the Sussex gantry robot is shown in Figure 13.8b. A camera points down towards a mirror angled at 45 degrees. The mirror can rotate around an axis perpendicular to the camera's image plane. The camera is suspended from the gantry allowing motion in the X, Y, and Z dimensions. This effectively provides an equivalent to a wheeled robot with a forward-facing camera when only the X and Y dimensions of translation are used (see Figure 13.8a). The additional dimension allows flying behaviors to be studied. The apparatus was initially used in a manner similar to the real-world EPFL evolutionary robots setup described earlier. A population of strings encoding robot controllers and visual sensing morphologies are stored on a computer to be downloaded one at a time onto the robot. The exact position and orientation of the camera head can be accurately tracked and used in the fitness evaluations. A number of visually guided navigation behaviors were successfully achieved, including navigating around obstacles and discriminating between different objects. In the experiment illustrated in Figure 13.8b, starting from a random position and orientation the robot had to move to the triangle rather than the rectangle. This had to be achieved irrespective of the relative positions of the shapes and under very noisy lighting conditions. Extremely minimal systems were evolved, which used only two or three pixels of visual information yet were still able to perform the task very robustly under highly variable lighting conditions.

Since this early work, a great variety of behaviors has been successfully evolved. There is not enough room to give an adequate summary of the whole field, so a few interesting subareas are highlighted below (see "Further reading" for more coverage).

Since the mid 1990s, there has been a growing body of work on evolving controllers for various kinds of walking robots – a nontrivial sensorimotor coordination task. Probably the first success in this direction was by Lewis, Fagg, and Solidum (1992), who evolved a neural controller for a simple hexapod robot. The robot was able to execute an efficient tripod gait on flat surfaces. All evaluations were done on the actual robot with each leg connected to its own pair of coupled neurons, leg swing being driven by one neuron and leg elevation by the other. These pairs of neurons were cross-connected, in a manner similar to that used in the neural architecture shown in Figure 13.9, to allow coordination between the legs. This architecture for locomotion, introduced by Beer, was based on studies of cockroaches, and generalizations and extensions of it have been much used ever since. Gallagher et al. (1996) used a general version of it to evolve controllers for generating locomotion in a simulated artificial insect. The controllers were later successfully downloaded onto a real hexapod robot. This machine was more complex than Lewis et al.'s, with a greater number of degrees of freedom per leg. In this work, each leg was controlled by a fully connected network of five neurons, each receiving a weighted sensory input from that leg's angle sensor as shown in Figure 13.9 (see also Chapter 6 of this volume). The connection weights and neuron parameters were under genetic control. This produced efficient tripod gaits for walking on flat surfaces. In order to produce a wider range of gaits operating at a number of speeds so that rougher terrain could be successfully negotiated, a slightly different distributed architecture, inspired by stick insect studies, was found to be more effective (Beer et al. 1997).

Jakobi (1998) successfully used his minimal simulation techniques (ultra-fast, ultra-lean simulations employing multiple levels of noise) to evolve controllers for an eight-legged robot. Evolution in simulation took less than two hours on what would today be regarded as a very slow computer, and then transferred successfully to the real robot. Jakobi evolved modular controllers based on Beer's recurrent network architecture to control the robot as it engaged in walking about its environment, avoiding obstacles, and seeking out goals. The robot could smoothly change gait, move backward and forward, and even turn on the spot. More recently, related approaches have been successfully used to evolve controllers for more mechanically sophisticated

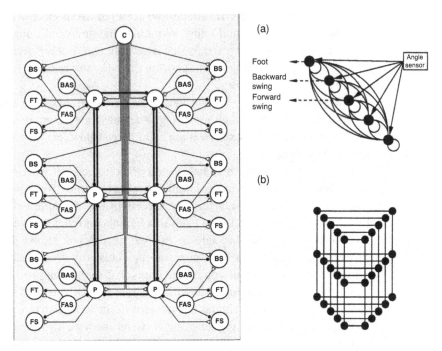

Figure 13.9 Left: schematic diagram of a distributed neural network for the control of locomotion as used by Beer, Chiel, and Sterling (1989). Excitatory connections are denoted by open triangles and inhibitory connections are denoted by filled circles. C = command neuron; P = pacemaker neuron; FT = foot motor neuron; FS and BS = forward swing and backward swing motor neurons; FAS and BAS = forward and backward angle sensors. Reproduced with permission. Right: generalized architecture using a fully connected dynamical network controller for each leg (a), cross-coupled as shown (b).

robots such as the Sony Aibo (Tllez, Angulo, and Pardo 2006). There has also been recent successful work on evolving neural controllers for the highly unstable dynamic problem of bipedal walking (Reil and Husbands 2002).

These and similar studies have shown that the evolutionary development of neural network controllers, with their intricate dynamics, generally produce a wider range of gaits and generate smoother, more adaptive locomotion than more traditional methods.

Early single-robot research was soon expanded to handle interactions between multiple robots. Floreano and Nolfi did pioneering work on the coevolution of predator–prey behaviors in physical robots (Floreano and Nolfi 1997). The fitness of the predator robot was measured by how quickly it caught the prey; the fitness of the prey was determined by how long it evaded the predator. Two Khepera robots were used in this experiment. Each had the standard set of proximity sensors, but the predator also had a vision system and the prey was able to move twice as fast as the predator. A series of interesting chasing and evading strategies emerged. Later, Quinn et al. (2003) demonstrated the evolution of coordinated cooperative behavior in a group of robots. A group of identical robots equipped only with infra-red proximity sensors were required to move as far as possible as a coordinated group, starting from a random configuration. Analysis of the best evolved solution showed that it involved the robots adopting different roles, with the robots collectively "deciding" which robot would perform each role.

In the work described so far there has been an overwhelming tendency to evolve control systems for pre-existing robots: The brain is constrained to fit a particular body and set of sensors. Of course in nature the nervous system evolved simultaneously with the rest of the organism. As a result, the nervous system is highly integrated with the sensory apparatus and the rest of the body: The whole operates in a harmonious and balanced way, and there are no distinct boundaries between control system, sensors, and body. Although the limitations of not being able to genetically control body morphology were acknowledged from the earliest days of evolutionary robotics research, there were severe technical difficulties in overcoming them, so this issue was somewhat sidelined.

Various researchers advocated the use of fully evolvable hardware to develop not only a robot's control circuits but also its body plan, which might include the types, numbers, and positions of the sensors, the body size, the wheel radius, actuator properties, and so on. However, this approach was still largely confined to theoretical discussion until Lipson and Pollack's work on the Golem project (Lipson and Pollack 2000).

Working at Brandeis University, Lipson and Pollack pushed the idea of fully evolvable robot hardware about as far as was reasonably technologically feasible at the time. Autonomous "creatures" were evolved in simulation out of basic building blocks (neurons, bars, actuators). The bars could connect together to form arbitrary truss structures with the possibility of both rigid and articulated substructures. Neurons could be connected to each other and to bars whose length they were able to control via a linear actuator. Machines defined in this way were required to move as far as possible in a limited time. The fittest individuals were then fabricated robotically using rapid manufacturing technology (plastic extrusion three-dimensional printing) to produce results such as that shown in Figure 13.10. The team thus achieved autonomy of design and construction using evolution in a "limited universe" physical simulation coupled to automatic fabrication. The highly unconventional designs thus realized performed as well in reality as in simulation. The success of this work points the way to new possibilities in developing energy-efficient fault-tolerant machines.

Today the field of evolutionary robotics has expanded in scope to take in promising new work on autonomous flying machines, as well as research

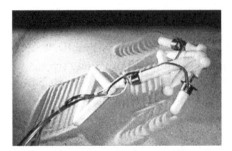

Figure 13.10 A fully automatically evolved robot developed by the Golem project (see text for details).

aimed at exploring specific scientific issues, such as principles from neuroscience or questions in cognitive science (see "Further reading").

13.6   Insect-inspired navigation

In marked contrast to current artificial systems, insects learn to visually navigate around complex environments in remarkably few trials, and use vision to perform many rapid and intricate maneuvers. Given their relatively small neural resources, there must be a premium on them using innate behaviors and efficient processing methods to underpin such abilities. Studies in neuroethology and insect behavior have started to reveal some details of the clever strategies involved, thus uncovering a potentially rich seam of inspiration for highly efficient, yet robust, robot algorithms.

One important strand of insect-inspired visual navigation methods for robots can be traced back to Cartwright and Collett's (1983) computational "snapshot" model developed to account for ants' and bees' ability to find their way to a goal using visual guidance. Using an insect-like omnidirectional (360-degree) panoramic view, in which landmarks in the environment can be readily distinguished from the background, the model works by computing a direction of movement based on the difference between the current view and a stored "snapshot" of the view from the goal position. This simple technique has been successfully demonstrated on a mobile robot navigating in a desert environment with highly conspicuous black cylinders as landmarks (Franz and Mallot 2000). The method was shown to work well in an area around the goal in which the landmarks were all readily visible.

A closely related, and even simpler, method for local navigation is the average landmark vector (ALV) technique (Lambrinos et al. 2000). The ALV provides a sparse representation of the current visual scene by processing it into a single two-dimensional vector. This vector is the average of the unit vectors pointing from the center of the agent to each of the visible landmarks. The heading direction is calculated from the difference between the current

(a)

(b)

Figure 13.11 (a) shows a bee flying down a tunnel with patterned walls. (b) shows a robot built by the Research School of Biological Sciences, Australian National University to demonstrate navigation strategies based on observations of the use of optic flow for insects.

ALV and the ALV at the goal location. The ALV model is the most efficient, and in some respects the most elegant, of the view-based homing methods and has been shown to work surprisingly well in real environments. Smith et al. (2007) have extended this technique to work in more complex large-scale environments where route learning is achieved by chaining together local navigation in a series of smaller visual locales (sub-environments) that are chosen and learnt by the algorithm. More recent work has taken a radically different approach by devising a model of ant navigation based on scene familiarity (Baddeley et al. 2012). The model represents the only detailed and complete model of insect route guidance to date and can be applied to robotics. Moreover, the research provides a general demonstration that visually guided routes can be produced with highly parsimonious mechanisms that neither specify when or what to learn, nor separate routes into sequences of waypoints.

Another very useful source of inspiration for visually guided robot behavior is the way insects use optic flow information. Optic flow refers to the changing patterns of lights on the eye induced by motion relative to the environment. Srinivasan and Zhang (1997) studied bee flight in tunnels with different patterns on the left and right walls (see Figure 13.11a). They found that the animals steered a course down the center of the tunnel, avoiding the walls, by balancing the optic flow (rate of change of pattern) in the left and right visual fields. For a given insect speed, the closer a pattern is, the greater the optic flow on that side. This even allowed them to negotiate narrow passages and fly between obstacles. The team successfully applied this strategy to the mobile robot shown in Figure 13.11b.

13.7   Probabilistic robotics

This section outlines an important area of robotics that emerged at about the same time as behavior-based and biologically inspired approaches. Although its methodology is mainly complementary to that of those areas, it certainly has overlapping concerns. Just as biologically inspired robotics can be traced back to the work of Grey Walter, the largely non-symbolic methods at the core of probabilistic robotics also have their roots in cybernetics.

The mapping problem requires a robot, during a period of exploration, to build a representation of its environment that can be used for accurate navigation. A related problem is that of localization – the ability of a robot to determine where it is, relative to a map, from its sensor readings. Since the early 1990s most work in this area has concentrated on the Simultaneous Localization and Mapping (SLAM) problem (Smith, Self, and Cheeseman 1990). This requires a mobile robot, when placed at an unknown spot in an unknown environment, to incrementally construct a consistent map of the environment at the same time as determining its location in the map. A great deal of progress has been made on this problem and for certain types of environments very good solutions have been found. Nearly all these solutions rely on probabilistic inference; indeed real progress on the problem was made only once it was cast in probabilistic terms. The current solutions all use probabilistic models of the robot and its environment, and all use probabilistic inference in building maps from the robot's sensor readings. The success of the probabilistic approach stems from the fact that the mapping problem is inherently uncertain and robot sensors are noisy, as is robot movement. The probabilistic approaches embrace these characteristics of the problem rather than ignoring them or trying to hide them.

Typically a map is represented as a set of vectors describing the location of landmarks picked out by the robot's perceptual system. More complex metric maps describing various aspects of the geometrical layout of the environment are also sometimes used, as are topological maps, which represent environments in terms of the relationships between key features. In probabilistic terms, the SLAM problem requires the following probability distribution to be computed for every time t:

$$P(x_t | Z^t, U^t, x_0)$$

This is the conditional probability density of the vector x_t, representing the robot position and the map, given the recorded sensor inputs Z^t and the motor controls U^t, along with the initial position of the robot, x_0. Z^t and U^t represent all sensor readings and motor commands from time $t = 0$ until the present. Using Bayes' Theorem, it is possible to expand this expression into one that can be computed using efficient recursive procedures at each time step.

There have been notable successes with these methods, including navigation over considerable distances (in 2005 probabilistic methods were used by Sebastian Thrun's team to win the DARPA Grand Challenge for an autonomous vehicle to navigate across an unrehearsed 142-mile course in the Mojave desert – see "Further reading"). However, there are still considerable challenges in dealing with dynamic environments and more generally with the correspondence, or data association, problem (determining whether sensor readings taken at different times correspond to the same location in the world). Nevertheless, probabilistic approaches have proved their worth and are established as the technique of choice for certain kinds of navigation problems.

13.8 Prospects

This chapter has concentrated on autonomous robotics, particularly biologically inspired approaches, showing how this area has become increasingly central to AI. Although great progress has been made, and most of the ever-proliferating mobile robots we now see in the home (e.g., autonomous vacuum cleaners and toys), or in areas such as planetary exploration, security or military applications, make use of the new techniques discussed earlier, many challenges remain.

It is now possible to produce autonomous robots that behave in a robust and reliable way in real environments, engaging in real tasks in real time. However, the behaviors involved are still relatively simple. Progress has been slow toward more sophisticated tasks such as learning what to focus attention on in a complex environment, coordinating many conflicting goals and drives, interacting with other robots in complex group behaviors, learning to communicate in a sophisticated way about the task at hand, and so on. Perhaps this should not be at all surprising. One lesson that most neuroscientists have understood for many decades, but which has often been overlooked in AI, is that the generation of intelligent embodied behavior is an extremely complicated problem. However, progress *is* being made and there are many promising lines of research. One direction, briefly mentioned earlier, that is likely to become increasingly important is the continued dismantling of the line between brain and body that has traditionally been present in studies of both natural and artificial intelligence.

The topics highlighted in this chapter have, appropriately enough, been fairly mature areas of research. However, there are a number of potentially very important emerging fields that may have a radical impact in the decades to come. These include developments in interfacing digital electronics to neural tissue. The most frequent motivation for such work is to allow improved prosthetics to be directly controlled by the nervous system. This points to the possibility of an increased merging of robotic technology with human bodies – something that a number of people have reflected on recently (e.g., Brooks

2002) and that the work of Stelarc, the radical performance artist, has long explored. A related area involves attempting to harness the sophisticated non-linear adaptive properties of cultured (real) neural networks to develop hybrid machines (DeMarse et al. 2001), pointing toward the possibility of robots that include biological matter in their control systems – echoing the nature of Čapek's original theatrical robots. In the long run, that kind of approach may prove more powerful than attempting to understand biological systems in sufficient detail to be able to abstract general mechanisms underlying the generation of intelligent behavior. However, the research is at an extremely early stage, so we cannot yet properly assess its potential.

In addition to their central role in AI, autonomous robots are being increasingly used in artistic and creative endeavors (Wilson 2002) and – in a development that takes us back to Grey Walter once again – as tools to model and study the generation of behavior in animals (see "Further reading"). The field has massively expanded since the days when it was dominated by cumbersome industrial arms; it is now quite possible that in the not too distant future robots will become as widespread and as common as computers are now.

Further reading

General robotics books

Bekey, G. A. (2005). *Autonomous Robots: From Biological Inspiration to Implemen-tation and Control*. Cambridge, MA: MIT Press. A thorough general introduc-tion to modern robotics. Accessible to those with only modest mathematical knowledge.

Craig, J. J. (2005). *Introduction to Robotics: Mechanics and Control* (3rd edn.). Upper Saddle River, NJ: Prentice Hall. A good introduction to classical robotics, aimed at undergraduates. Requires some math.

Siciliano, B. and Khatib, O. (eds.) (2008). *Springer Handbook of Robotics*. Berlin: Springer. An excellent comprehensive coverage of the whole of modern robotics. Detailed review chapters, written by leading experts, on every topic of importance. Mainly aimed at postgraduates and researchers, but much of the material is fairly accessible.

History

Boden, M. A. (2006). *Mind as Machine: A History of Cognitive Science* (2 vols.). Oxford University Press. A monumental, and very readable, history of cog-nitive science. Much relevant material on early AI and the development of behavior-based and evolutionary robotics.

Husbands, P., Holland, O, and Wheeler, M. (eds.) (2008). *The Mechanical Mind in History*, Cambridge, MA: MIT Press. Concentrates on cybernetics and the early history of AI, including robotics. Detailed material on Grey Walter and colleagues in the British cybernetics movement.

Wood, G. (2002). *Living Dolls: A Magical History of the Quest for Mechanical Life*. London: Faber and Faber. (Published in the USA as *Edison's Eve*.) An excellent account of early automata. Written for a general audience.

Behavior-based robotics

Arkin, R. C. (1998). *Behavior-based Robotics*. Cambridge, MA: MIT Press. A good introduction to some of the work that came under the umbrella of behavior-based approaches.

Brooks, R. A. (1991a). Intelligence without representation. *Artificial Intelligence* 47: 139–59. First of a pair of classic papers critiquing traditional approaches to AI and robotics.

(1991b). Intelligence without reason, in J. Mylopoulos and R. Reiter (eds.), *Proceedings of the 12th International Joint Conference on Artificial Intelligence* (pp. 569–95). San Mateo, CA: Morgan Kaufmann. Second paper of the pair.

Biologically inspired robotics and robots as scientific tools

Adaptive Behavior 17(4) (2009). Special issue of journal on the status of simulation and robotic models in adaptive behavior research.

Bigge, B. and Harvey, I. R. (2007). Programmable springs: Developing actuators with programmable compliance for autonomous robots, *Robotics and Autonomous Systems* 55: 728–34. An interesting example of advanced "artificial muscle"-like actuators that can be modulated in subtle ways.

Caprari, G., Colot, A., Siegwart, R., Halloy, J., and Deneubourg, J.-L. (2005). Animal and robot mixed societies: Building cooperation between microrobots and cockroaches, *IEEE Robotics & Automation Magazine* 12(2): 58–65. A very interesting example of using robots to interact with (and control) animals.

Kato, N., Ayers, J., and Morikawa, H. (eds.) (2004). *Bio-mechanisms of Swimming and Flying*. Tokyo: Springer. A collection of papers on the rich variety of mechanisms employed by swimming and flying organisms, with many examples of how aspects of these mechanisms can be exploited in artificial systems. Aimed at postgraduates and researchers.

Pfeifer, R. and Bongard, J. (2007). *How the Body Shapes the Way We Think: A New View of Intelligence*. Cambridge, MA: MIT Press. An excellent accessible book on embodied intelligence and how the traditional boundaries between brain, body, and world should be dissolved.

Pfeifer, R. and Scheier, C. (1999). *Understanding Intelligence*. Cambridge, MA: MIT Press. A powerfully argued vision of how to understand and build embodied intelligence.

Webb, B. (2001). Can robots make good models of biological behaviour? *Behavioral and Brain Sciences* 24: 1033–50. A discussion of how robots can be used as scientific tools in the study of animal behavior.

Evolutionary robotics

Bongard, J. (2011). Morphological change in machines accelerates the evolution of robust behavior, *Proceedings of the National Academy of Sciences of the United States of America* 108:1234–9. Very interesting investigation into the evolutionary advantages of lifetime changes in morphology (growth) in simulated robots.

Floreano, D., Husbands, P., and Nolfi, S. (2008). Evolutionary robotics, in B. Siciliano and O. Khatib (eds.), *Springer Handbook of Robotics* (pp. 1423–51). Berlin: Springer. A detailed recent survey of the field.

Harvey, I., Di Paolo, E., Wood, R., Quinn, M., and Tuci, E. (2005). Evolutionary robotics: A new scientific tool for studying cognition, *Artificial Life* 11: 79–98. An example of work where evolutionary robotics is used to probe questions in cognitive science.

Nolfi, S. and Floreano, D. (2000). *Evolutionary Robotics: The Biology, Intelligence, and Technology of Self-Organizing Machines.* Cambridge, MA: MIT Press. An excellent introduction to the area.

Philippides, A., Husbands, P., Smith, T., and O'Shea, M. (2005). Flexible couplings: Diffusing neuromodulators and adaptive robotics, *Artificial Life* 11:139–60. An example of work where evolutionary robotics interfaces with contemporary neuroscience.

Insect-inspired navigation

Srinivasan, M. V., Chahl, J. S., Weber, K., Venkatesh, S., Nagle, M. G., and Zhang, S. W. (1999). Robot navigation inspired by principles of insect vision, *Robotics and Autonomous Systems* 26: 203–16. A good example of how insect strategies can be harnessed in robotics.

Vardy, A. and Moller, R. (2005). Biologically plausible visual homing methods based on optical flow techniques, *Connection Science* 17: 47–89. Includes good survey of current methods as well as original work.

Probabilistic robotics

Durrant-Whyte, H. and Bailey, T. (2006). Simultaneous localisation and mapping (SLAM): Part I The essential algorithms, *IEEE Robotics & Automation Magazine* 13(2): 99–110. An excellent (technical) tutorial on the basics of approaches to the SLAM problem.

Thrun, S., et al. (2006). Stanley: The robot that won the DARPA Grand Challenge, *Journal of Field Robotics* 23: 661–92. Report on the robot that won the challenge to navigate across an unrehearsed 142-mile course in the Mojave desert.

References

Allen, J., Hendler, J., and Tate, A. (eds.) (1990). *Readings in Planning*. San Francisco: Morgan Kaufmann.

Baddeley, B., Graham, P., Husbands, P., and Philippides, A. (2012). A model of ant route navigation driven by scene familiarity, *PLoS Computational Biology* 8(1): e1002336. doi:10.1371/journal.pcbi.1002336.

Beer, R. D., Chiel, H. J., and Sterling, L. S. (1989). Heterogeneous neural networks for adaptive behavior in dynamic environments. In D. Touretzky (ed.), *Neural Information Processing Systems 1* (pp. 577–85). San Francisco: Morgan Kauffman.

Beer, R. D., Quinn, R. D., Chiel, H. J., and Ritzmann, R. E. (1997). Biologically inspired approaches to robotics: What can we learn from insects? *Communications of the ACM* 40(3): 30–8.

Breazeal, C. (2002). *Designing Sociable Robots*. Cambridge, MA: MIT Press.

Breazeal, C., Buchsbaum, D., Gray, J., Gatenby, D., and Blumberg, B. (2005). Learning from and about others: Towards using imitation to bootstrap the social understanding of others by robots, *Artificial Life* 11: 31–62.

Brooks, R. A. (1986). A robust layered control system for a mobile robot, *IEEE Journal of Robotics and Automation* 2: 14–23.

(1991a). Intelligence without representation, *Artificial Intelligence* 47: 139–59.

(1991b). Intelligence without reason, in J. Mylopoulos and R. Reiter (eds.), *Proceedings of the 12th International Joint Conference on Artificial Intelligence* (pp. 569–95). San Mateo, CA: Morgan Kaufmann.

(1999). *Cambrian Intelligence: The Early History of the New AI*. Cambridge, MA: MIT Press.

(2002). *Flesh and Machines: How Robots Will Change Us*. New York: Pantheon Books.

Brooks, R. A., Breazeal, C., Marjanovic, M., Scassellati, B. and Williamson, M. (1999). The Cog project: Building a humanoid robot, in C. L. Nehaniv (ed.), *Computation for Metaphors, Analogy, and Agents (LNAI 1562)* (pp. 52–87). Berlin: Springer.

Cartwright, B. A. and Collett, T. S. (1983). Landmark learning in bees, *Journal of Comparative Physiology A* 151: 521–43.

Cliff, D., Husbands, P., and Harvey, I. (1993). Explorations in evolutionary robotics, *Adaptive Behavior*, 2: 73–110.

DeMarse, T. B., Wagenaar, D. A., Blau, A. W., and Potter, S. M. (2001). The neurally controlled animat: Biological brains acting with simulated bodies, *Autonomous Robotics* 11: 305–10.

Floreano, D. and Mondada, F. (1994). Automatic creation of an autonomous agent: Genetic evolution of a neural-network driven robot, in D. Cliff, P. Husbands,

J.-A. Meyer, and S. W. Wilson (eds.), *From Animals to Animats 3: Proceedings of the 3rd International Conference on Simulation of Adaptive Behavior* (pp. 421–30). Cambridge, MA: MIT Press.

Floreano, D. and Nolfi, S. (1997). Adaptive behavior in competing co-evolving species, in P. Husbands and I. Harvey (eds.), *Proceedings of the 4th European Conference on Artificial Life* (pp. 378–87). Cambridge, MA: MIT Press.

Franz, M. O. and Mallot, H. A. (2000). Biomimetic robot navigation, *Robotics and Autonomous Systems* 30: 133–53.

Gallagher, J. C., Beer, R. D., Espenschied, K. S., and Quinn, R. D. (1996). Application of evolved locomotion controllers to a hexapod robot, *Robotics and Autonomous Systems* 19: 95–103.

Harvey, I., Husbands, P., and Cliff, D. (1994). Seeing the light: Artificial evolution, real vision, in D. Cliff, P. Husbands, J.-A. Meyer, and S. W. Wilson (eds.), *From Animals to Animats 3: Proceedings of the 3rd International Conference on Simulation of Adaptive Behavior* (pp. 392–401). Cambridge, MA: MIT Press.

Holland, J. H. (1975). *Adaptation in Natural and Artificial Systems*. Ann Arbor: The University of Michigan Press.

Holland, O. (2003). Exploration and high adventure: The legacy of Grey Walter, *Philosophical Transactions of the Royal Society of London, Series A* 361: 2085–2121.

Horáková, J. and Kelemen, J. (2008). The robot story: Why robots were born and how they grew up, in P. Husbands, O. Holland, and M. Wheeler (eds.), *The Mechanical Mind in History* (pp. 283–306). Cambridge, MA: MIT Press.

Jakobi, N. (1998). Running across the reality gap: Octopod locomotion evolved in a minimal simulation, in P. Husbands and J.-A. Meyer (eds.), *Evolutionary Robotics: First European Workshop, EvoRobot98* (pp. 39–58). Berlin: Springer.

Lambrinos, D., Möller, R., Labhart, T., Pfeifer, R., and Wehner, R. (2000). A mobile robot employing insect strategies for navigation, *Robotics and Autonomous Systems* 30: 39–64.

Lewis, M. A., Fagg, A. H., and Solidum, A. (1992). Genetic programming approach to the construction of a neural network for control of a walking robot, in *Proceedings of the 1992 IEEE International Conference on Robotics and Automation* (pp. 2618–23). IEEE.

Lipson, H. and Pollack, J. B. (2000). Automatic design and manufacture of robotic lifeforms, *Nature* 406: 974–8.

Mondada, F., Franzi, E., and Ienne, P. (1994). Mobile robot miniaturization: A tool for investigation in control algorithms, in T. Yoshikawa and F. Miyazaki (eds.), *Experimental Robotics III: The 3rd International Symposium* (pp. 501–13). Berlin: Springer.

Moravec, H. (1987). Sensing versus inferring in robot control. Informal Report, www.frc.ri.cmu.edu/~hpm/project.archive/robot.papers/1987/sense.ltx.

Nilsson, N. J. (ed.) (1984). *Shakey The Robot*, Technical Note 323. Menlo Park CA: AI Center, SRI International.

Quinn, M., Smith, L., Mayley, G., and Husbands, P. (2003). Evolving controllers for a homogeneous system of physical robots: Structured cooperation with minimal sensors, *Philosophical Transactions of the Royal Society of London, Series A*, 361: 2321–43.

Raibert, M. H. (1986). Legged robots, *Communications of the ACM* 29: 499–514.

Reil, T. and Husbands, P. (2002). Evolution of central pattern generators for bipedal walking in real-time physics environments, *IEEE Transactions on Evolutionary Computation*, 6: 159–68.

Smith, L., Philippides, A., Graham, P., Baddeley, B., and Husbands, P. (2007). Linked local navigation for visual route guidance, *Adaptive Behavior* 15: 257–71.

Smith, R., Self, M., and Cheeseman, P. (1990). Estimating uncertain spatial relationships in robotics, in I. J. Cox and G. T. Wilfong (eds.), *Autonomous Robot Vehicles* (pp. 167–193). Berlin: Springer.

Srinivasan, M. V. and Zhang, S. W. (1997). Visual control of honeybee flight, *EXS (Experientia Supplementum)* 84: 95–113.

Tllez, R. A., Angulo, C., and Pardo, D. E. (2006). Evolving the walking behaviour of a 12 DOF quadruped using a distributed neural architecture, in A. J. Ijspeert, T. Masuzawa, and S. Kusumoto (eds.), *Biologically Inspired Approaches to Advanced Information Technology: 2nd International Workshop Bio-ADIT'2006* (LNCS vol. 3853), (pp. 5–19). Berlin: Springer.

Turing, A. M. (1950). Computing machinery and intelligence, *Mind* 59: 433–60.

Walter, W. G. (1953). *The Living Brain*. London: Duckworth.

Wilson, S. (2002). *Information Arts: Intersections of Art, Science, and Technology*. Cambridge, MA: MIT Press.

14 Artificial life

Mark A. Bedau

Artificial life is one type of interdisciplinary study of life and life-like processes. (Artificial life is also referred to as "ALife," "A-Life," "alife," and the like.) Artificial life has two distinctive properties. First, it studies life in any form in which it can exist, so it focuses on life's essential features rather than its contingent features. Second, it studies life by artificially synthesizing and simulating new forms of life and life's fundamental processes. Studying life by synthesizing and simulating it enables us to experiment with different forms of life in an especially flexible manner. This makes it possible to give sharp experimental answers to many general questions about the nature of life.

Artificial life research is mainly a scientific activity, but it also raises and illuminates certain philosophical questions. The first part of this chapter explains what artificial life is and how it is connected with artificial intelligence, and briefly describes some of its representative scientific achievements. The second part discusses some associated philosophical issues involving emergence, creative evolution, the nature of life, the connection between life and mind, and the social and ethical implications of creating life from scratch.

14.1 The science and engineering of artificial life

The best way to appreciate artificial life's focus on essential properties and its synthetic methodology is to consider examples of its recent scientific achievements. Today, artificial life uses three kinds of synthetic methods. *Hard* artificial life produces actual physical hardware that acts autonomously in the physical world. Autonomous robots are considered to be artificial life when they embody and depend on important features of natural forms of life. By contrast, *wet* artificial life creates new forms of life in test tubes, using the latest materials and methods from biochemistry and molecular biology. Test-tube artificial life is typically roughly like microscopic bacteria. Wet artificial life is one kind of synthetic biology, combining science and engineering to design and build novel biological functions and systems. Finally, *soft* artificial life consists of computer simulations or other purely digital constructions that exhibit life-like behavior. Soft artificial life systems typically exist only in digital form, and they merely reside in computers.

14.1.1   Hard artificial life

Artificial life's most direct overlap with artificial intelligence is the creation of autonomous physical agents or robots in "hard" artificial life (see Chapter 13). These devices exhibit autonomous adaptive and intelligent behavior in real physical environments. Hard artificial life contrasts with traditional robotics by explicitly and extensively exploiting inspiration from all forms of life including those that are much simpler than humans.

One important contemporary approach to the design of autonomous agents is to let the physical environment play a large role in generating the agent's behavior. A related trick is to let the physical materials in which the robot is embodied automatically provide as much functionality as possible (Pfeifer and Bongard 2006). This hard artificial life "behavior-based" robotics was pioneered by Rodney Brooks (Brooks and Flynn 1989; Brooks 1990, 1991). Behavior-based robotics avoids the need for an elaborate and detailed internal representation of the external environment. With the right sensorimotor architecture, a robot can quickly and intelligently navigate in complex and unpredictable environments. The initial successes in insect-like robots have now been extended to humanoid robots.

Even behavior-based intelligent autonomous agents require the right interconnections among many complex components. This is a very difficult design task. The intelligent autonomous agents found in nature are all alive, and their design was created by an evolutionary process involving natural selection. Analogously, computer programs using a certain evolutionary process (so-called "genetic algorithms," see below) can be used to design autonomous agents. These evolutionary algorithms have been used to design many aspects of robots, including control systems and sensors (Cliff, Husbands, and Harvey 1993; Nolfi and Floreano 2000).

In natural autonomous agents, the structure of the control system is tightly coupled to the structure of the agents' morphology. Sims (1994) showed how to recreate this interconnection when he simultaneously coevolved simulated creatures' controllers, sensors, and morphology, but he relied on special-purpose software running on extremely expensive supercomputers. Jordan Pollack and his students have taken the next step and used similar methods to develop actual physical robots. They have coupled the simulated coevolution of controllers and morphology with inexpensive three-dimensional printers, allowing their evolutionary design to be automatically implemented in the real world (Lipson and Pollack 2000; Pollack et al. 2001). Robots with the ability to continuously and autonomously diagnose and repair damage to their bodies represent another step toward the flexible and robust behavior exhibited by many life forms (Bongard, Zykov, and Lipson 2006). New research frontiers in autonomous agents range from swarms of relatively unintelligent insect-like drones, to autonomous robots with a continuously evolving model of the external world.

14.1.2   Wet artificial life

Some central figures in artificial intelligence believe that AI's future hinges on progress in wet artificial life (Brooks 2001). The holy grail of wet artificial life is to create artificial cells out of biochemical raw materials, such as lipids, or DNA and RNA molecules, that are not themselves alive. These minimal forms of chemical cellular life would be microscopic, autonomously self-organizing and self-reproducing entities built from simple organic and inorganic substances (Rasmussen et al. 2004; Rasmussen et al. 2009). Although made by human hands, and so artificial, for all intents and purposes they would be alive, for they would maintain and repair themselves, and adapt in an open-ended fashion to unpredictable environmental contingencies.

There are two main motivations for making artificial cells. One is scientific. If one could make new cellular forms of life from scratch, using non-natural materials or methods, this would provide an extremely powerful and flexible scientific tool for probing the molecular details of simple forms of life. Artificial cells also have broad practical applications. Natural cells are very complicated and have an adaptive flexibility that is unmatched so far by human engineering. So, engineering artificial cells that organize and sustain themselves and continually adapt to their environment would open the door to a new kind of technology that captures the power of life.

What will artificial cells do? The initial functionality of these machines will be simply to move through a fluid and process chemicals. To do this flexibly, resiliently, and indefinitely requires solving the basic functions of self-maintenance, autonomous control of internal chemical processes, autonomous control of mobility, and the ability to reproduce.

Nobody has yet created a fully functioning artificial cell, but research toward this goal is progressing in two main approaches. Human genome pioneer J. Craig Venter and Nobel Prize winner Hamilton Smith are using the top-down strategy of synthesizing and then redesigning the genome of existing simple life forms such as bacteria (Gibson et al. 2010). This top-down approach has the virtue that it can simply borrow the biological wisdom embodied in existing forms of life. It has the corresponding disadvantage that this wisdom is limited by the contingencies in the actual history of life.

The other approach to making artificial cells is bottom-up: to start from non-living materials and build more and more complex physiochemical systems with more and more life-like properties. One critical component of any artificial cell is its boundary with the external environment, and to achieve this people typically use vesicles. A vesicle is a loosely spherical structure formed from a continuous bilayer membrane, which typically exists in a watery fluid. The walls of all natural living cells are bilayer membranes, formed from two layers of amphiphilic molecules. Amphiphiles are hydrophylic ("water loving") on one end and hydrophobic ("water hating") on the other. Bilayer membranes form spontaneously when amphiphilic molecules in sufficient concentrations are in water. In the laboratory, vesicles have been shown to grow and divide ("reproduce"). By employing the proper laboratory procedures, vesicle growth and division can continue in the laboratory indefinitely.

Researchers have been able to produce a number of fundamental cellular functions in vesicles. For example, RNA inside vesicles will replicate if the vesicle contains energetically activated nucleotides and an enzyme found in simple life forms. Bottom-up wet artificial life sometimes uses some material derived from natural life forms. One example is "cell-free extract." This is harvested from bacteria and contains all of the hundreds of enzymes, other proteins, and other complex biological structures normally found inside bacteria. When supplied with cell-free extract, simple vesicles can produce proteins that create structures such as pores and create networks of genes that control other genes (see Luisi, Ferri, and Stano 2006 and Rasmussen et al. 2009 for reviews).

14.1.3   Soft artificial life

Implementing life-like systems in software is a practical and constructive way to study many issues about living systems. Some soft artificial life models focus on self-organization and study how structure can emerge from unstructured ensembles of initial conditions. Other models target populations of complex agents analogous to multi-cellular organisms, and some models focus on interactions between different types of organisms. These models typically allow an organism's features to evolve through a process like Darwinian natural selection. Some other models target other important biological processes, such as epigenetics and development.

One of the first significant achievements of spontaneous evolution in a digital medium was Tierra (Ray 1992), which is a soft artificial life system that consisted of a population of simple, self-replicating computer programs that exist in computer memory and consume central processing unit (CPU) time. A Tierran genotype consists of a string of machine code, and each Tierran "creature" is an instance of some Tierran genotype. A simulation starts when a single self-replicating program, the ancestor, is placed in computer memory and left to replicate. The ancestor and its descendants repeatedly replicate until computer memory is teeming with creatures that all share the same ancestral genotype. Older creatures are continually removed from memory to create space for new descendants. Mutations sometimes occur, and the population of programs evolves by natural selection. If a mutation allows a program to replicate faster, that genotype tends to spread through the population. Over time, the ecology of Tierran genotypes becomes remarkably diverse. Quickly reproducing parasites that exploit a host's genetic code evolve, and the coevolution between hosts and parasites spurs the evolution of parasite resistance and new forms of parasitism. After millions of CPU cycles of this coevolutionary arms race, Tierra often contains many kinds of creatures exhibiting a variety of competitive and cooperative ecological relationships. Ray subsequently extended Tierra to larger and more heterogeneous environments and gave ancestral Tierran creatures multiple cell types. By allowing Tierran creatures to migrate from machine to machine over the internet, looking for unused resources and for more favorable local niches, Ray has found signs that they evolve new types of cells. Furthermore, when Tierra is modified so that creatures are rewarded for performing complex arithmetic operations on numbers they find in their local environment, evolution produces the expected increase in genetic complexity (Adami, Offria, and Collier 2000; Lenski et al. 2003).

Tierra and similar software systems illustrate the abstract character of many soft artificial life systems. These abstract "models" are designed to explore certain general principles, but not to represent details of known biological systems. When designed correctly, abstract artificial life systems generate wholly new and extremely simple instances of life-like phenomena. The simplest example of such a system is the so-called "Game of Life," devised by the mathematician John Conway in the 1960s (Berlekamp, Conway, and Guy 1982). Conway's Game of Life can be thought of as a model of biological activity at the physical or chemical level, involving extremely simple and abstract "biochemical" interactions. It is important to note that the Game of Life is not a "model" of any actual chemical activity in the real world; instead, it is a wholly new and abstract "instance" of life-like activity.

The Game of Life is a two-state, two-dimensional cellular automaton with a trivial nearest-neighbor rule. Think of this "game" as taking place on a two-dimensional rectangular grid of cells, analogous to a huge checkerboard. Time advances in discrete steps, and a cell's state at a given time is determined by the states of its eight neighboring cells according to the following simple birth–death rule: A "dead" cell becomes "alive" at some time if and only if exactly three neighbors were alive at the previous moment, and a "living" cell "dies" unless two or three of its neighbors were alive at the previous moment. The Game starts with an initial configuration of living cells, and from there it evolves in time, as each cell changes its state according to the birth–death rule. With one eye on a cell and its neighbors and the other on the birth–death rule, it is easy to tell how the state of the cell will evolve in time (Figures 14.1 and 14.2).

As more and more initial conditions in the Game of Life have been studied, a rich variety of complicated behavior has been observed and a complex zoo of structures has been identified and classified (blinkers, gliders, glider guns, logic-switching circuits, etc.). It is even possible to construct a universal Turing machine in the Game of Life, by cunningly positioning the initial configuration of living cells. In such constructions, certain patterns of cells

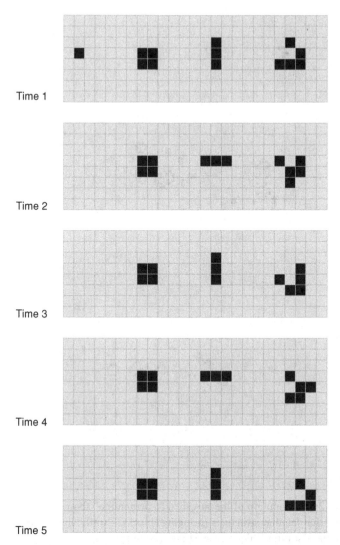

Time 1

Time 2

Time 3

Time 4

Time 5

Figure 14.1 A sequence of five steps in the evolution of the Game of Life. The initial configuration contains four simple structures, from left to right. The first, a single cell, dies immediately. The second, the block of four cells, remains unchanged forever. This is an example of a "still life." The third, a strip of three cells named the "traffic light," flips back and forth forever between two configurations, in which the strip goes up and down or left and right. This is an example of a "blinker" of period two. The fourth structure, a so-called "glider" consisting of five cells, cycles through a sequence of four configurations and ends up in a state in which the original spatial configuration is shifted in space.

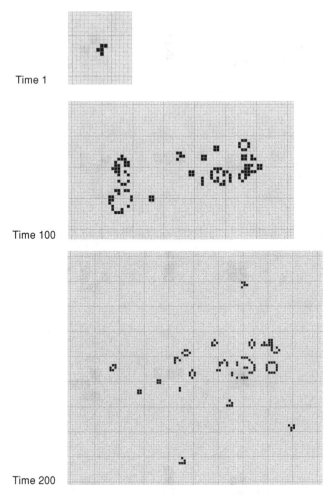

Time 1

Time 100

Time 200

Figure 14.2 The evolution of the so-called "r-pentomino" shown at times 1, 100, and 200. Note that familiar structures including "blocks," "traffic lights," and "gliders" arise and persist for a while, but most are transitory.

that move in a straight direction across the Life checkerboard function to carry signals and process information. A research thrust now in artificial life is analyzing the computational potential of cellular automata on the basis of glider interactions, and designing cellular automata that accomplish desired computational tasks. The Game of Life and other cellular automata (e.g. von Neumann 1966) are important in artificial life because they show how certain kinds of complex life-like behavior can arise from massively parallel systems composed of simple computational cells.

There is growing interest in soft artificial life systems that can be directly related to empirical data from experimental systems in the laboratory. Some recent models of complex chemical systems (sometimes called "protocells") exhibit properties reminiscent of the simplest forms of life. Just as producing protocells is a grand challenge in wet artificial life, a grand challenge in soft artificial life is to produce a protocell model that demonstrates the emergence of life from non-life. Some protocell models explicitly represent complex molecules like amphiphiles and informational polymers in a two- or three-dimensional aqueous environment. These models produce behaviors like the self-replication of informational polymers or the self-assembly, growth, and division of complex two- or three-dimensional cell-like structures such as vesicles. Other models of oil, water, and amphiphiles couple a thermodynamically realistic self-assembly process with an evolving population of self-replicating molecules. Still simpler models show how weakly bonded aggregations of amphiphiles can emerge and evolve spontaneously (Rasmussen et al. 2009).

14.1.4   Comparison of soft artificial life and artificial intelligence

Soft artificial life differs from artificial intelligence, but the two are connected, especially through machine learning. It should be no surprise that the subjects of artificial intelligence and artificial life overlap, since both study natural phenomena by simulating and synthesizing them, and since living and flourishing in a changing and uncertain environment (the subject of artificial life) is a rudimentary form of intelligence, the subject of AI.

One historically important overlap between artificial intelligence and artificial life is John Holland's pioneering investigations of genetic algorithms (1992) (see also Chapters 1 and 4 of this volume). The genetic algorithm is a machine learning technique loosely modeled on biological evolution. It treats learning the solution to a problem as a matter of competition among candidate problem solutions, with the best candidate solutions eventually winning. Potential solutions are encoded in an artificial chromosome, and an initial population of candidate solutions is created randomly. The quality or "fitness" of each solution is calculated by application of a "fitness function." For example, if the problem is to find the shortest route between two cities and a candidate solution is a specific itinerary, then the fitness function might be the sum of the distance of each segment in the itinerary and a solution's fitness is proportional to the reciprocal of its total distance. In effect, the fitness function is the "environment" to which the population adapts. A candidate solution's "genotype" is its chromosome, and its "phenotype" is its fitness. On analogy with natural selection, lower-fitness candidates are then replaced in the population with new solutions modeled on higher-fitness candidates. New candidates are generated by modifying earlier candidates with "mutations" that randomly change chromosomal elements and "crossover" events that combine pieces of two chromosomes. After reproducing variants of the most fit candidates for many generations, the population contains better and better solutions. The study of genetic algorithms has blossomed into a flourishing study of evolutionary algorithms, which supports multiple annual international conferences and multiple professional journals.

There is an important difference between the modeling strategies that artificial intelligence and artificial life typically employ. Most traditional AI models are top-down-specified serial systems involving a complicated, centralized controller that makes decisions based on access to all aspects of the global state (see Chapter 4). The controller's decisions have the potential to affect directly any aspect of the whole system. On the other hand, many natural living systems exhibiting complex autonomous behavior are parallel, distributed networks of relatively simple low-level "agents" that simultaneously interact locally with each other. Each agent's decisions are based on information about, and directly affect, only their own local situation. Artifical life's models characteristically follow nature's example. The models themselves are bottom-up-specified parallel systems of simple agents interacting locally. The models are repeatedly iterated and the resulting global behavior is observed. Such lower-level models are sometimes said to be "agent-based" or "individual-based." The whole system's behavior is represented only indirectly and it arises out of the interactions of a collection of directly represented parts ("agents" or "individuals"). Two excellent illustrations of the bottom-up quality of artificial life models are Tierra and the Game of Life, discussed earlier.

The parallel, distributed character of artificial life models is similar to the structure of the models studied in the connectionist (parallel distributed processing, neural network) movement (see Chapter 5). Both involve bottom-up models in which a population of autonomous agents follows simple local rules. In fact, the agents in many artificial life models are themselves controlled by internal connectionist nets.

Three important differences distinguish typical artificial life models from the connectionist models that have attracted the most attention, such as feedforward networks that learn by the backpropagation algorithm. First, artificial life and connectionism depend on different kinds of learning algorithms. Connectionist models often employ supervised learning algorithms like backpropagation. These learning algorithms are typically turned on when the network is learning and then turned off when the acquired information is applied. This distinction between training and application phases is sometimes unnatural. In addition, supervised learning algorithms require an omniscient teacher, which is also often unnatural. By contrast, the learning algorithms employed in artificial life models usually avoid these criticisms. They are typically unsupervised and in continual operation. Often the algorithm involves artificial selection.

Second, human intervention and interpretation play different roles in artificial life and connectionism. Typical connectionist models passively receive sensory information prepackaged by a human designer and produce output that must be interpreted by a human designer. In artificial life models, on the other hand, a micro-level agent's sensory input comes directly from the environment in which the agent lives. In artificial life models the micro-level agents' output is to perform actions in their environment, and those actions have direct consequences for the agents' well-being. Thus their output has an intrinsic meaning regardless of human interpretation.

Third, artificial life and connectionism typically seek different kinds of dynamical behavior. Much connectionist modeling aims to produce behavior that settles into an equilibrium. This is because both learning and applying knowledge are conceived as fixed and determinate goals. By contrast, artificial life views much of the distinctive behavior of living systems as a process of continual creative evolution, so the aim of many artificial life models is an open-ended evolutionary dynamic that is forever far from equilibrium.

14.2   Philosophical implications of artificial life

The science and engineering of artificial life impinges on a number of broad philosophical issues, including how life emerges from non-life, whether the evolution of life has a directional arrow, what life is, whether software systems could ever be literally alive, and what the social and ethical implications of creating artificial life are. In some cases artificial life's scientific achievements presuppose traditional philosophical positions or raise new philosophical possibilities, and in other cases they provide new traction on perennial problems in philosophy and theoretical biology.

14.2.1   Emergence

One of life's striking features is that the whole seems to be more than the sum of the parts. This is called *emergence* (see, e.g., Bedau and Humphreys 2008). As a general definition, emergent phenomena involve the relationship between wholes and their parts; specifically, the wholes both depend on, and are autonomous from, their parts. The philosophical problem of emergence involves evaluating whether emergence is metaphysically legitimate and whether it plays a constructive role in scientific explanations of apparent emergent phenomena such as those involving life.

The aggregate global behavior of soft artificial life models demonstrates what has been called "weak" emergence (Bedau 2002). Weak emergence contrasts with the "strong" emergence that involves in principle the impossibility of reducing wholes to their parts (Kim 1999). With weak emergence, the state of a whole system is emergent just in case it can be derived from the system's boundary conditions and its micro-level dynamical processes, but only by iterating and aggregating potentially all of the micro-level interactions that occur. In contrast to strong emergence, weak emergence *entails* that macro-level phenomena are reducible to micro-level phenomena. The Game of Life is a simple and vivid example of this; all of the global behavior of the Game of Life is driven by the micro-level birth–death rule. Yet weak emergent macro-level phenomena still have a kind of autonomy because the micro-level interactions in the bottom-up models produce such complex macro-level effects that the only way to recognize or predict them is by observing macro-level behavior. Furthermore, the macro-level phenomena exhibit patterns and regularities that are robust and independent of many of the contingent details of the micro-level interactions.

Weak emergence is commonplace in complex natural systems, and artificial life's models typically exhibit it. The unpredictability of weak emergent phenomena comes from the complex network of nonlinear and context-dependent local micro-level interactions that drive the systems. Macro-level weak emergent phenomena can have causal powers, but merely by aggregating micro-level causal powers (Rasmussen et al. 2001). Clearly, there need be nothing metaphysically illegitimate or non-naturalistic about weak emergence.

Artificial life thus plays various roles in philosophical debates about emergence. Bottom-up artificial life models generate impressive and vivid examples of weak emergent macro-level phenomena. Thus, artificial life expands our understanding of the kinds of macro-level complexity that can have simple micro-level explanations. This gives philosophy a new purchase on the kind of emergence that has seemed to many people to be involved in life and mind.

14.2.2   The arrow of evolution

The evolution of life has produced a remarkable growth in complexity. Life started out with only very simple single-celled life forms, like bacteria. Eventually evolution produced more complex single-celled life forms like amoebas, which have complex internal structures including a nucleus. Eventually multicellular life forms evolved, and then large-bodied vertebrate creatures with sophisticated sensory processing capacities, and then highly intelligent creatures that use language and sophisticated technology. This increase in life's maximal complexity raises the question of whether biological evolution has an inherent arrow of directionality – that is, whether the process of evolution contains some sort of inherent tendency to create greater and greater adaptive complexity, or whether life's increasing complexity is just an accidental by-product of evolutionary contingencies.

Stephen Jay Gould (1989) devised a clever way to frame this question: the thought experiment of replaying the tape of life. This thought experiment hypothetically assumes that the process of evolution is recorded on a tape. The thought experiment involves rewinding the evolutionary process backward in time, erasing the tape, and then playing the evolutionary process forward again but this time allowing it to be shaped by different contingencies. Replaying the tape of life many times will reveal what outcomes of the evolutionary process are typical and to be expected, and what outcomes are accidents.

It is not obvious what the outcome of replaying the tape would be. Gould himself says that "any replay of the tape would lead evolution down a pathway radically different from the road actually taken" (1989, p. 51) and concludes that the contingency of evolution makes any inherent growth in adaptive complexity impossible. Daniel Dennett (1995) draws exactly the opposite conclusion. He argues that complex features, such as sophisticated sensory processing, provide such a distinct adaptive advantage that natural selection will almost inevitably discover them in one form or another. Dennett concludes that replaying life's tape will almost inevitably produce highly intelligent creatures that use language and develop sophisticated technology.

There is a problem with the positions of both Gould and Dennett. Replaying the tape of life is a good way to investigate the scope of contingency and necessity in evolution, but neither Gould nor Dennett actually do replay the tape. Instead, they speculate about what would happen if someone were to do it. But it is notoriously common for predictions about such complex scenarios to be mistaken, so we are still awaiting concrete evidence about what replaying the tape of life would show.

Soft artificial life provides one method to replay the tape: Construct an artificial biosphere that is like the real biosphere in the relevant respects, and then learn its typical and expected behavior by repeatedly replaying the tape (re-running the simulation). The easiest artificial biospheres to construct are simply software systems. Of course, no software system will recreate all the conditions of any actual earlier stage in the evolution of life on Earth. But replaying life's tape in a number of different model biospheres would surely shed some light on the inherent creative potential of biological evolution, as long as that biosphere's creative evolutionary potential was sufficiently open.

14.2.3   The nature of life

The advent of artificial life has helped revitalize and refashion the question of the nature of life. This question is highly controversial and there is no sign of an emerging consensus (Bedau and Cleland 2010). But one can simulate or synthesize essential features of living systems only if one has some idea what life is. So, like those searching for extraterrestrial life or for the origin of life on Earth, those attempting to synthesize life in the laboratory are forced to confront the general question of what life is.

As it happens, almost all wet artificial life scientists trying to make artificial cells agree that their goal is a self-contained system that metabolizes and evolves (e.g., Rasmussen et al. 2004). That is, an artificial cell is viewed as any chemical system that chemically integrates three processes. The first is the chemical process by which self-replicating molecules ("genes") contain information that influences and shapes how the cell functions. Errors ("mutations") can occur when the molecules replicate, so the molecules can evolve by natural selection. The second is the metabolic process that extracts raw materials and energy from the environment to repair and regenerate the container and its contents and enable the whole system to reproduce. The third is the process of assembling a container, such as a lipid vesicle, that concentrates the reagents needed for life and shields them from molecular parasites and poisons. In this view of life as an integrated triad, the chemical processes involving genes, metabolism, and containment support and enable each other, so that there are functional feedback relations among all three. This view presupposes that any biochemical realization of the integrated triad of functions is a genuine instance of minimal chemical life. This is one example of how scientific advances in wet artificial life provide new food for thought about the nature of life in general.

The philosophy of mind has recently been dominated by functionalism: The view that mental beings are a certain kind of input–output device and that having a mind is simply having a set of internal states that causally interact (or "function") with respect to each other and with respect to environmental inputs and behavioral outputs in a certain characteristic way. Functionalism with respect to life is the analogous view that being alive is simply realizing a network of processes that interact in a certain characteristic way. Some processes (such as information processing, metabolism, purposeful activity) operate within the organism's lifetime; other processes (such as self-reproduction and adaptive evolution) span many lifetimes. These processes are always realized in some material substratum, but the substratum's material nature is irrelevant so long as the *forms* of the processes are preserved. For these reasons, functionalism is an attractive position with respect to life.

Chris Langton (1989, p. 41) gave a classic statement of functionalism with respect to life when he said, "Life is a property of *form*, not *matter*, a result of the organization of matter rather than something that inheres in the matter itself." He elaborates:

The big claim is that a properly organized set of artificial primitives carrying out the same functional roles as the biomolecules in natural living systems will support a process that is "alive" in the same way that natural organisms are alive. Artificial Life will therefore be genuine life – it will simply be made of different stuff than the life that has evolved here on Earth. (Langton 1989, p. 33)

We might be unsure about the details of the processes that are definitive of life, and we might wish to reserve judgment about whether artificial life creations are genuinely alive. Nevertheless, Langton is right that life's characteristic processes such as metabolism, information processing, and self-reproduction could be realized in a wide and potentially open-ended range of materials.

For that reason, there seems to be some truth in functionalism about life. But functionalism about life should not presuppose any simplistic monolithic dichotomy between form and matter (Sterelny and Griffith 1999).

The connection between life and mind is of growing philosophical interest (e.g., Thompson 2007). All organisms have at least rudimentary mental capacities, broadly speaking (Dennett 1996). They are sensitive to the environment in various ways, and this environmental sensitivity affects their behavior in various ways. Furthermore, the sophistication of these mental capacities seems to correspond to the complexity of those forms of life. So it is natural to ask if there is an interesting connection between life and mind, especially for those who think that a central function of the mind is being able to behave appropriately in a complex, dynamic, and unpredictable world (see Chapter 6). Since all forms of life must cope in one way or another with a complex, dynamic, and unpredictable world, perhaps this adaptive flexibility intrinsically connects life and mind. Understanding the ways in which life and mind are connected is one of the basic puzzles about the nature of life.

14.2.4   Strong artificial life

The aim of soft artificial life is to create software systems that synthesize or simulate living systems. On analogy with the distinction between weak and strong artificial intelligence (see Chapters 2 and 3), one should distinguish two fundamental hypotheses about soft artificial life. *Weak* soft artificial life is the thesis that artificial life software systems can be informative and insightful *simulations* of living systems. *Strong* soft artificial life is the thesis that artificial life software systems can be actual *instances* of life. There are analogous theses about weak and strong versions of hard and wet artificial life. Note that the theses of weak and strong artificial life do not assert that contemporary artificial life has already achieved any good simulations or genuine realizations of life. Rather, they claim that such achievements are possible. Hypotheses about weak and strong forms of artificial life illustrate how the existence of the science of artificial life raises some new philosophical questions.

The truth of the strong thesis about wet artificial life seems relatively uncontroversial, given minimal agreement that life is just a complex chemical and biological process. If so, then synthesizing those chemical and biological processes in the laboratory, if it can be done, would produce a new instance of life. So, although there might be a significant scientific and technical barrier to achieving wet artificial life that is literally alive, it is possible in principle.

The truth of the strong theses about hard and soft artificial life are more controversial. Since soft artificial life presents the most extreme case, and since many artificial-life scientists make claims that explicitly or implicitly presuppose the truth of the strong thesis about soft artificial life, I will focus on it. The truth of strong soft artificial life depends to some extent on prior agreement about the nature of life, but some progress can be made even if that question remains unsettled.

Some people argue against strong soft artificial life on the grounds that it is a simple category mistake to confuse a computer simulation of life with a real instance of it. A flight simulation for an airplane, they argue, no matter how detailed and realistic, does not really fly. A simulation of a hurricane does not create real rain driven by real gale-force winds. Similarly, a computer simulation of a living system produces merely a symbolic representation of the living system. The intrinsic ontological status of this symbolic representation is nothing more than certain electronic states inside the computer (e.g., patterns of high and low voltages). This constellation of electronic states is no more alive than is a series of English sentences describing an organism. It seems alive only when it is given an appropriate interpretation.

But this charge of category mistake can be blunted. Many soft artificial life systems are not simulations or models of familiar living systems but new digital worlds. Conway's Game of Life, for example, is not a simulation or model of any real biochemical system but a digital universe that exhibits its own distinctive form of spontaneous self-organization. So, when the Game of Life is actually running in a computer, that physical device contains a new physical instance of self-organization. Processes like self-organization and evolution are multiply realizable and can be embodied in a wide variety of different media, including the physical media of suitably programmed computers. So, to the extent that the essential properties of living systems involve processes like self-organization and evolution, suitably programmed computers will actually be novel realizations of life.

Boden (2003) has emphasized that this reply runs aground if metabolism is included in the essential properties of living systems, as it often is (Bedau and Cleland 2010). It might be possible to give a functional definition of metabolism that allows many different instantiations, but the definition would presumably put severe physical and chemical constraints on any actual chemical metabolism. If metabolism is interpreted as the ability to use packets of energy to maintain a body and power its behavior, Boden argues that metabolism inevitably thwarts hard and soft artificial life.

14.2.5   The ethics of artificial life

Both the process of pursuing artificial life research and the scientific and practical products of that research process raise complicated ethical issues (see also Chapter 15). These issues can be divided into four broad categories: the sanctity of the biosphere, the sanctity of human life, the responsible treatment of newly generated life forms, and the risks of using artificial life technology (Bedau et al. 2000). Artificial life's ethical issues are somewhat like those that have been raised concerning other forms of biotechnology, such as animal experimentation, cloning, and genetic engineering. It would be possible to glean some ethical lessons for artificial life from the existing bioethics literature. But creating and interacting with new artificial life-like systems will place us in increasingly uncharted ethical terrain.

Especially vivid ethical issues are being generated by wet artificial life efforts to make new forms of life in the laboratory (Bedau and Parke 2009). These efforts can be expected to generate public concern. Some will object that that creating artificial cells is unnatural or fails to give life due respect (Cho et al. 1999), or that it involves playing God (Cho 1999). One main driver for these ethical concerns is that creating new forms of life will inevitably involve what could be called "deciding in the dark." Decisions in the dark are those we make even though we are largely ignorant about the possible consequences of different choices. New and revolutionary technologies are allowing contemporary society to change its environment at an accelerating rate. In general, the more revolutionary these technologies are, the harder it is for us to forecast their implications for human health and the environment. So, when society is deciding how to regulate new technologies like artificial life, it is deciding in the dark.

One important tool for making complex decisions is risk analysis. Based on decision theory, risk analysis is the primary method by which large organizations and public agencies such as the US Food and Drug Administration (FDA) make decisions with major social and economic implications (Wilson and Crouch 2001; Ropeik and Gray 2002). For example, top officials in the US Department of Agriculture cited a Harvard Center for Risk Analysis study to justify FDA inaction about mad cow disease.

Decision theory (Resnick 1987) has a well-developed arsenal for confronting what are known as decisions "under risk" and decisions "under ignorance or uncertainty." Nevertheless, it is unequipped to help with decisions in the dark. Decision theory approaches a decision in a given context by tabulating, in tree form, the different possible actions that could be made in that context, determining the likely consequences of each action, determining the likely social utility of each consequence, and then analyzing this decision tree by calculating such things as each action's expected utility. Recommendations about decisions can be gleaned from the decision table. Decisions under risk are those in which the likely consequences of the actions are uncertain and can only be assigned a probability. Decisions under ignorance or uncertainty are those in which even the probabilities of the consequences are unknown, so information about the decision tree is limited to its branching structure. In both cases, however, the consequences of various courses of action can be calculated and tabulated, yielding useful concrete recommendations about pending decisions. Decisions in the dark are different in just this respect: We are ignorant about even the possible outcomes of our actions, and so cannot even construct a decision tree, since we do not know the branches and their branching structure. So decision theory is essentially mute about decisions in the dark.

Nevertheless, decisions in the dark are increasingly confronting society because of technological innovations, including artificial life. The economic stakes for governments and commerce are huge. Simultaneously, the perceived risks of these new technologies are also causing growing alarm. Genetically modified foods are at the time of writing anathema throughout Europe. Because these technologies are revolutionary, it is impossible for us to know the likely consequences of their development. Yet we nevertheless face choices today about whether and how to develop them, whether and how to regulate them, and so on. We have to make these decisions in the dark.

One natural reaction to the problem of making decisions in the dark is the Precautionary Principle. This principle states that we should ban new technologies that might create significant risks even if we lack solid scientific evidence of such risks (Raffensperger and Tickner 1999). The Precautionary Principle is designed to apply precisely to situations in which society is in the dark, and it is playing an increasing role in international law, appearing in over a dozen international treaties and agreements (e.g., the Rio Declaration from the 1992 United Nations Conference on Environment and Development). But the Principle remains controversial because it seems to give insufficient attention to the possible benefits of new technologies. The scope and soundness of the Precautionary Principle remains controversial today.

14.3   Conclusion

Software comprises one of artificial life's synthetic methods, hardware another, and test-tube constructions a third. To the extent that artificial life is successful in creating wholly new forms of life in any synthetic medium, it will play a role in shaping the future world in which humans live along with all other life forms.

Artificial life can also become an important new tool for philosophy. At the dawn of the last century analytical philosophy was transformed by the introduction and assimilation of formal logic. Perhaps artificial life and related scientific fields will, in a similar way, also transform philosophy by augmenting complex thought experiments with computational rigor and power.

Further reading

Artificial Life. A quarterly journal published by The MIT Press, publishing its twentieth volume in 2014. It is devoted mostly to advances in soft artificial life, but also covers representative work in hard and wet artificial life, as well as some broader issues.

Langton, C. G. (ed.) (1989). *Artificial Life: The Proceedings of an Interdisciplinary Workshop on the Synthesis and Simulation of Living Systems*. Redwood City: Addison-Wesley. Proceedings of the first "artificial life" conference identified as such, with a classic introductory overview of the field and a forty-page annotated bibliography of works relevant at the founding of artificial life.

Proceedings of the International Conference on Artificial Life (ALife), and *Proceedings of the European Conference on Artificial Life* (ECAL), both biennial and published in electronic form by MIT Press.

Rasmussen, S., Bedau, M. A., Chen, L., Deamer, D., Krakauer, D. C., Packard, N. H., and Stadler, P. F. (eds.) (2009). *Protocells: Bridging Nonliving and Living Matter*. Cambridge, MA: MIT Press. A comprehensive overview of protocell achievements and guiding visions in the wet lab and in computer models.

Von Neumann, J. (1966). *Theory of Self-Reproducing Automata*. Urbana-Champaign: University of Illinois Press. Von Neumann's classic work on self-reproducing automata, completed and edited after his death by Arthur Burks.

Wolfram, S. (1994). *Cellular Automata and Complexity: Collected Papers*. Reading, MA: Addison-Wesley. Contains important early technical papers on cellular automata.

References

Adami, C., Ofria, C., and Collier, T. C. (2000). Evolution of biological complexity, *Proceedings of the National Academy Sciences USA* 97: 4463–8.

Bedau, M. A. (2002). Downward causation and autonomy in weak emergence, *Principia Revista Internacional de Epistemologica* 6: 5–50. Reprinted in Bedau and Humphreys (2008), pp. 155–88.

Bedau, M. A., McCaskill, J. S., Packard, N. H., Rasmussen, S., Adami, C., Green, D. G., Ikegami, T., Kaneko, K., and Ray, T. S. (2000). Open problems in artificial life, *Artificial Life* 6: 363–76.

Bedau, M. A. and Cleland, C. E. (eds.) (2010). *The Nature of Life: Classical and Contemporary Perspectives from Philosophy and Science*. Cambridge University Press.

Bedau, M. A. and. Humphreys, P. (eds.) (2008). *Emergence: Contemporary Readings in Science and Philosophy*. Cambridge, MA: MIT Press.

Bedau, M. A. and Parke, E. C. (eds.) (2009). *The Ethics of Protocells: Moral and Social Implications of Creating Life in the Laboratory*. Cambridge, MA: MIT Press.

Berlekamp, E. R., Conway, J. H., and Guy, R. K. (1982). *Winning Ways for Your Mathematical Plays*, vol. 2. New York: Academic Press.

Boden, M. (2003). Alien life: How would we know?, *International Journal of Astrobiology* 2: 121–9. Reprinted in Bedau and Cleland (2010), pp. 249–59.

Bongard, J., Zykov, V., and Lipson, H. (2006). Resilient machines through continuous self-modeling, *Science* 314: 1118–21.

Brooks, R. A. (1990). Elephants don't play chess, *Robotics and Autonomous Systems* 6: 3-15.

(1991). Intelligence without representation, *Artificial Intelligence* 47: 139-59.

(2001). The relationship between matter and life, *Nature* 409: 409-11.

Brooks, R. A. and Flynn, A. M. (1989). Fast, cheap and out of control, *MIT AI Memo* 1182.

Cho, M. K., Magnus, D., Caplan, A. L., McGee, D., and the Ethics of Genomics Group (1999). Ethical considerations in synthesizing a minimal genome, *Science* 286: 2087-90.

Cliff, D., Husbands, P., and Harvey, I. (1993). Explorations in evolutionary robotics, *Adaptive Behavior* 2: 73-110.

Dennett, D. C. (1995). *Darwin's Dangerous Idea: Evolution and the Meanings of Life*. New York: Simon and Schuster.

(1996). *Kinds of Minds: Toward an Understanding of Consciousness*. New York: Basic Books.

Gibson, D. G., Glass, J. I., Lartigue, C., et al. (2010). Creation of a bacterial cell controlled by a chemically synthesized genome, *Science* 329: 52-6.

Gould, S. J. (1989). *Wonderful Life: The Burgess Shale and the Nature of History*. New York: Norton.

Holland, J. H. (1992). *Adaptation in Natural and Artificial Systems: An Introductory Analysis with Applications to Biology, Control, and Artificial Intelligence* (2nd edn.). Ann Arbor: University of Michigan Press. (1st edn., 1975, Cambridge, MA: MIT Press.) (2nd ed., 1992).

Kim, J. (1999). Making sense of emergence, *Philosophical Studies* 95: 3-36.

Langton, C. G. (ed.) (1989). *Artificial Life: The Proceedings of an Interdisciplinary Workshop on the Synthesis and Simulation of Living Systems*. Redwood City, CA: Addison-Wesley.

Lenski, R. E., Ofria, C., Pennock, R. T., and Adami, C. (2003). The evolutionary origin of complex features, *Nature* 423: 139-44.

Lipson, H. and Pollack, J. B. (2000). Automatic design and manufacture of robotic lifeforms, *Nature* 406: 974-8. Reprinted in Bedau and Cleland (2010), pp. 260-7.

Luisi, P. L., Ferri, F., and Stano, P. (2006). Approaches to semi-synthetic minimal cells: A review, *Naturwissenschaften* 93: 1-13.

Nolfi, S. and Floreano, D. (2000). *Evolutionary Robotics: The Biology, Intelligence, and Technology of Self-Organizing Machines*. Cambridge, MA: MIT Press.

Pfeifer, R., and Bongard, J. (2006). *How the Body Shapes the Way We Think: A New View of Intelligence*. Cambridge, MA: MIT Press.

Pollack, J. B., Lipson, H., Hornby, G., and Funes, P. (2001). Three generations of automatically designed robots, *Artificial Life* 7: 215-23.

Raffensperger, C. and Tickner, J. (eds.) (1999). *Protecting Public Health and the Environment: Implementing the Precautionary Principle*. Washington, DC: Island Press.

Rasmussen, S., Baas, N. A., Mayer, B., Nillson, M., and Olesen, M. W. 2001. *Ansatz for dynamical hierarchies, Artificial Life* 7: 329–53. Reprinted in Bedau and Humphreys (2008), pp. 305–34.

Rasmussen, S., Bedau, M. A., Chen, L., Deamer, D., Krakauer, D. C., Packard, N. H., and Stadler, P. F. (eds.) (2009). *Protocells: Bridging Nonliving and Living Matter.* Cambridge, MA: MIT Press.

Rasmussen, S., Chen, L., Deamer, D., Krakauer, D. C., Packard, N. H., Stadler, P. F., and Bedau, M. A. (2004). Transitions from nonliving to living matter, *Science* 303: 963–5.

Ray, T. S. (1992). An approach to the synthesis of life, in C. G. Langton, C. Taylor, J. D. Farmer, and S. Rasmussen (eds.), *Artificial Life II* (Santa Fe Institute Studies in the Sciences of Complexity 11) (pp. 371–408). Redwood City, CA: Addison-Wesley.

Resnick, M. (1987). *Choices: An Introduction to Decision Theory.* Minneapolis, MN: University of Minnesota Press.

Ropeik, D. and Gray, G. (2002). *Risk: A Practical Guide to Deciding What's Really Safe and What's Really Dangerous in the World Around You.* Boston, MA: Houghton Mifflin.

Sims, K. (1994). Evolving 3D morphology and behavior by competition, *Artificial Life* 1: 353–72.

Sterelny, K. and Griffiths, P. E. (1999). *Sex and Death: An Introduction to the Philosophy of Biology.* University of Chicago Press.

Thompson, E. (2007). *Mind in Life: Biology, Phenomenology, and the Sciences of Mind.* Cambridge, MA: Harvard University Press.

Von Neumann, J. (1966). *Theory of Self-Reproducing Automata.* Urbana-Champagne, IL: University of Illinois Press.

Wilson, R. and Crouch, E. A. C. (2001). *Risk-Benefit Analysis* (2nd edn.). Cambridge, MA: Harvard University Press.

Wolfram, S. (1994). *Cellular Automata and Complexity: Collected Papers.* Reading, MA: Addison-Wesley.

15 The ethics of artificial intelligence

Nick Bostrom and Eliezer Yudkowsky

The possibility of creating thinking machines raises a host of ethical issues, related both to ensuring that such machines do not harm humans and other morally relevant beings, and to the moral status of the machines themselves. This chapter surveys some of the ethical challenges that may arise as we create artificial intelligences of various kinds and degrees.

15.1 Ethics in machine learning and other domain-specific AI algorithms

Imagine, in the near future, a bank using a machine learning algorithm to recommend mortgage applications for approval. A rejected applicant brings a lawsuit against the bank, alleging that the algorithm is discriminating racially against mortgage applicants. The bank replies that this is impossible, since the algorithm is deliberately blinded to the race of the applicants. Indeed, that was part of the bank's rationale for implementing the system. Even so, statistics show that the bank's approval rate for black applicants has been steadily dropping. Submitting ten apparently equally qualified genuine applicants (as determined by a separate panel of human judges) shows that the algorithm accepts white applicants and rejects black applicants. What could possibly be happening?

Finding an answer may not be easy. If the machine learning algorithm is based on a complicated neural network, or a genetic algorithm produced by directed evolution, then it may prove nearly impossible to understand why, or even how, the algorithm is judging applicants based on their race. On the other hand, a machine learner based on decision trees or Bayesian networks is much more transparent to programmer inspection (Hastie, Tibshirani, and Friedman 2001), which may enable an auditor to discover that the AI algorithm uses the address information of applicants who were born or previously resided in predominantly poverty-stricken areas.

AI algorithms play an increasingly large role in modern society, though usually not labeled "AI." The scenario described above might be transpiring even as we write. It will become increasingly important to develop AI algorithms

The authors are grateful to Rebecca Roache for research assistance and to the editors of this volume for detailed comments on an earlier version of our manuscript.

that are not just powerful and scalable, but also *transparent to inspection* – to name one of many socially important properties.

Some challenges of machine ethics are much like many other challenges involved in designing machines. Designing a robot arm to avoid crushing stray humans is no more morally fraught than designing a flame-retardant sofa. It involves new programming challenges, but no new ethical challenges. But when AI algorithms take on cognitive work with social dimensions – cognitive tasks previously performed by humans – the AI algorithm inherits the social requirements. It would surely be frustrating to find that no bank in the world will approve your seemingly excellent loan application, and nobody knows why, and nobody can find out even in principle. (Maybe you have a first name strongly associated with deadbeats? Who knows?)

Transparency is not the only desirable feature of AI. It is also important that AI algorithms taking over social functions be *predictable to those they govern*. To understand the importance of such predictability, consider an analogy. The legal principle of *stare decisis* binds judges to follow past precedent whenever possible. To an engineer, this preference for precedent may seem incomprehensible – why bind the future to the past, when technology is always improving? But one of the most important functions of the legal system is to be predictable, so that, for example, contracts can be written knowing how they will be executed. The job of the legal system is not necessarily to optimize society, but to provide a predictable environment within which citizens can optimize their own lives.

It will also become increasingly important that AI algorithms be *robust against manipulation*. A machine vision system to scan airline luggage for bombs must be robust against human adversaries deliberately searching for exploitable flaws in the algorithm – for example, a shape that, placed next to a pistol in one's luggage, would neutralize recognition of it. Robustness against manipulation is an ordinary criterion in information security – nearly *the* criterion. But it is not a criterion that appears often in machine learning journals, which are currently more interested in, for example, how an algorithm scales up on larger parallel systems.

Another important social criterion for dealing with organizations is being able to find the person responsible for getting something done. When an AI system fails at its assigned task, who takes the blame? The programmers? The end-users? Modern bureaucrats often take refuge in established procedures that distribute responsibility so widely that no one person can be identified to blame for the catastrophes that result (Howard 1994). The provably disinterested judgment of an expert system could turn out to be an even better refuge. Even if an AI system is designed with a user override, one must consider the career incentive of a bureaucrat who will be personally blamed if the override goes wrong, and who would much prefer to blame the AI for any difficult decision with a negative outcome.

Responsibility, transparency, auditability, incorruptibility, predictability, and a tendency to not make innocent victims scream with helpless frustration: all criteria that apply to humans performing social functions; all criteria that must be considered in an algorithm intended to replace human judgment of social functions; all criteria that may not appear in a journal of machine learning considering how an algorithm scales up to more computers. This list of criteria is by no means exhaustive, but it serves as a small sample of what an increasingly computerized society should be thinking about.

15.2   Artificial General Intelligence

There is nearly universal agreement among modern AI professionals that Artificial Intelligence falls short of human capabilities in some critical sense, even though AI algorithms have beaten humans in many specific domains such as chess. It has been suggested by some that as soon as AI researchers figure out how to do something, that capability ceases to be regarded as intelligent – chess was considered the epitome of intelligence until Deep Blue won the world championship from Kasparov – but even these researchers agree that something important is missing from modern AIs (e.g., Hofstadter 2006).

While this subfield of Artificial Intelligence is only just coalescing, "Artificial General Intelligence" (hereafter, AGI) is the emerging term of art used to denote "real" AI (see, e.g., Goertzel and Pennachin 2007). As the name implies, the emerging consensus is that the missing characteristic is generality. Current AI algorithms with human-equivalent or human-superior performance are characterized by a deliberately programmed competence only in a single, restricted domain. Deep Blue became the world champion at chess, but it cannot even play checkers, let alone drive a car or make a scientific discovery. Such modern AI algorithms resemble all biological life with the sole exception of *Homo sapiens*. A bee exhibits competence at building hives; a beaver exhibits competence at building dams; but a bee doesn't build dams, and a beaver can't learn to build a hive. A human, watching, can learn to do both; but this is a unique ability among biological life forms. It is debatable whether human intelligence is truly *general* – we are certainly better at some cognitive tasks than others (Hirschfeld and Gelman 1994) – but human intelligence is surely *significantly more generally applicable* than nonhominid intelligence.

It is relatively easy to envisage the sort of safety issues that may result from AI operating only within a specific domain. It is a qualitatively different class of problem to handle an AGI operating across many novel contexts that cannot be predicted in advance.

When human engineers build a nuclear reactor, they envision the specific events that could go on inside it – valves failing, computers failing, cores increasing in temperature – and engineer the reactor to render these events noncatastrophic. Or, on a more mundane level, building a toaster involves envisioning bread and envisioning the reaction of the bread to the toaster's heating element. The toaster itself does not know that its purpose is to make toast – the *purpose* of the toaster is represented within the designer's mind, but is not explicitly represented in computations inside the toaster – and so if you place cloth inside a toaster, it may catch fire, as the design executes in an unenvisioned context with an unenvisioned side effect.

Even task-specific AI algorithms throw us outside the toaster paradigm, the domain of locally pre-programmed, specifically envisioned behavior. Consider Deep Blue, the chess algorithm that beat Garry Kasparov for the world championship of chess. Were it the case that machines can only do exactly as they are told, the programmers would have had to manually pre-program a database containing moves for every possible chess position that Deep Blue could encounter. But this was not an option for Deep Blue's programmers. First, the space of possible chess positions is unmanageably large. Second, if the programmers had manually input what *they* considered a good move in each possible situation, the resulting system would not have been able to make stronger chess moves than its creators. Since the programmers themselves were not world champions, such a system would not have been able to defeat Garry Kasparov.

In creating a superhuman chess player, the human programmers necessarily sacrificed their ability to predict Deep Blue's *local, specific* game behavior. Instead, Deep Blue's programmers had (justifiable) confidence that Deep Blue's chess moves would satisfy a *non-local* criterion of optimality: namely, that the moves would tend to steer the future of the game board into outcomes in the "winning" region as defined by the chess rules. This prediction about distant consequences, though it proved accurate, did not allow the programmers to envision the *local* behavior of Deep Blue – its response to a specific attack on its king – because Deep Blue computed the non-local game map, the link between a move and its possible future consequences, more accurately than the programmers could (Yudkowsky 2006).

Modern humans do literally millions of things to feed themselves – to serve the final consequence of being fed. Few of these activities were "envisioned by Nature" in the sense of being ancestral challenges to which we are directly adapted. But our adapted brain has grown powerful enough to be *significantly more generally applicable*; to let us foresee the consequences of millions of different actions across domains, and exert our preferences over final outcomes. Humans crossed space and put footprints on the Moon, even though none of our ancestors encountered a challenge analogous to vacuum. Compared to domain-specific AI, it is a qualitatively different problem to design a system that will operate safely across thousands of contexts; including contexts not specifically envisioned by either the designers or the users; including contexts that no human has yet encountered. Here there may be no *local* specification of good behavior – no simple specification over the behaviors themselves, any more than there exists a compact local description of all the ways that humans obtain their daily bread.

To build an AI that acts safely while acting in many domains, with many consequences, including problems the engineers never explicitly envisioned, one must specify good behavior in such terms as "X such that the consequence of X is not harmful to humans." This is non-local; it involves extrapolating the distant consequences of actions. Thus, this is only an effective specification – one that can be realized as a design property – if the system explicitly extrapolates the consequences of its behavior. A toaster cannot have this design property because a toaster cannot foresee the consequences of toasting bread.

Imagine an engineer having to say, "Well, I have no idea how this airplane I built will fly safely – indeed I have no idea how it will fly at all, whether it will flap its wings or inflate itself with helium or something else I haven't even imagined – but I assure you, the design is very, very safe." This may seem like an unenviable position from the perspective of public relations, but it's hard to see what other guarantee of ethical behavior would be possible for a general intelligence operating on unforeseen problems, across domains, with preferences over distant consequences. Inspecting the cognitive design might verify that the mind was, indeed, searching for solutions that we would classify as ethical; but we couldn't predict which specific solution the mind would discover.

Respecting such a verification requires some way to distinguish trustworthy assurances (a procedure which will not say the AI is safe unless the AI really is safe) from pure hope and magical thinking ("I have no idea how the Philosopher's Stone will transmute lead to gold, but I assure you, it will!"). One should bear in mind that purely hopeful expectations have previously been a problem in AI research (McDermott 1976). Verifiably constructing a trustworthy AGI will require different methods, and a different way of thinking, from inspecting power-plant software for bugs – it will require an AGI that *thinks like* a human engineer concerned about ethics, not just a simple *product* of ethical engineering.

Thus the discipline of AI ethics, especially as applied to AGI, is likely to differ fundamentally from the ethical discipline of noncognitive technologies, in that:

- The local, specific behavior of the AI may not be predictable apart from its safety, even if the programmers do everything right.
- Verifying the safety of the system becomes a greater challenge because we must verify what the system is trying to do, rather than being able to verify the system's safe behavior in all operating contexts.
- Ethical cognition itself must be taken as a subject matter of engineering.

15.3   Machines with moral status

A different set of ethical issues arises when we contemplate the possibility that some future AI systems might be candidates for having moral status. Our dealings with beings possessed of moral status are not exclusively a matter of instrumental rationality. We also have moral reasons to treat them in certain ways, and to refrain from treating them in certain other ways. Francis Kamm has proposed the following definition of moral status, which will serve for our purposes:

X has moral status = because X counts morally in its own right, it is permissible/ impermissible to do things to it for its own sake. (Paraphrased from Kamm 2007, ch. 7.)

A rock has no moral status. We may crush it, pulverize it, or subject it to any treatment we like without any concern for the rock itself. A human person, on the other hand, must be treated not only as a means but also as an end. Exactly what it means to treat a person as an end is something about which different ethical theories disagree; but it certainly involves taking her legitimate interests into account – giving weight to her well-being – and it may also involve accepting strict moral side-constraints in our dealings with her, such as a prohibition against murdering her, stealing from her, or doing a variety of other things to her or her property without her consent. Moreover, it is because a human person counts in her own right, and for her sake, that it is impermissible to do to her these things. This can be expressed more concisely by saying that a human person has moral status.

Questions about moral status are important in some areas of practical ethics. For example, disputes about the moral permissibility of abortion often hinge on disagreements about the moral status of the embryo. Controversies about animal experimentation and the treatment of animals in the food industry involve questions about the moral status of different species of animal. And our obligations towards human beings with severe dementia, such as late-stage Alzheimer's patients, may also depend on questions of moral status.

It is widely agreed that current AI systems have no moral status. We may change, copy, terminate, delete, or use computer programs as we please; at least as far as the programs themselves are concerned. The moral constraints to which we are subject in our dealings with contemporary AI systems are all grounded in our responsibilities to other beings, such as our fellow humans, not in any duties to the systems themselves.

While it is generally agreed that present-day AI systems lack moral status, it is unclear exactly what attributes ground moral status. Two criteria are commonly proposed as being importantly linked to moral status, either separately or in combination: sentience and sapience (or personhood). These may be characterized roughly as follows:

Sentience: the capacity for phenomenal experience or qualia, such as the capacity to feel pain and suffer.

Sapience: a set of capacities associated with higher intelligence, such as self-awareness and being a reason-responsive agent.

One common view is that many animals have qualia and therefore have some moral status, but that only human beings have sapience, which gives them a higher moral status than non-human animals.[1] This view, of course, must confront the existence of borderline cases such as, on the one hand, human infants or human beings with severe mental retardation – sometimes unfortunately referred to as "marginal humans" – which fail to satisfy the criteria for sapience; and, on the other hand, some non-human animals, such as the great apes, which might possess at least some of the elements of sapience. Some deny that so-called "marginal humans" have full moral status. Others propose additional ways in which an object could qualify as a bearer of moral status, such as by being a member of a kind that normally has sentience or sapience, or by standing in a suitable relation to some being that independently has moral status (see Warren 1997). For present purposes, however, we will focus on the criteria of sentience and sapience.

This picture of moral status suggests that an AI system will have some moral status if it has the capacity for qualia, such as an ability to feel pain. A sentient AI system, even if it lacks language and other higher cognitive faculties, is not like a stuffed toy animal or a wind-up doll; it is more like a living animal. It is wrong to inflict pain on a mouse, unless there are sufficiently strong morally overriding reasons to do so. The same would hold for any sentient AI system. If in addition to sentience, an AI system also has sapience of a kind similar to that of a normal human adult, then it would have full moral status, equivalent to that of human beings.

One of the ideas underlying this moral assessment can be expressed in stronger form as a principle of non-discrimination:

Principle of Substrate Non-Discrimination: If two beings have the same functionality and the same conscious experience, and differ only in the substrate of their implementation, then they have the same moral status.

One can argue for this principle on grounds that rejecting it would amount to embracing a position similar to racism. Substrate lacks fundamental moral significance in the same way and for the same reason as skin color does. The Principle of Substrate Non-Discrimination does not imply that a digital

---

[1] Alternatively, one might deny that moral status comes in degrees. Instead, one might hold that certain beings have more significant interests than other beings. Thus, for instance, one could claim that it is better to save a human than to save a bird, not because the human has higher moral status, but because the human has a more significant interest in having her life saved than does the bird in having its life saved.

computer could be conscious, or that it could have the same functionality as a human being. Substrate *can* of course be morally relevant insofar as it makes a difference to sentience or functionality. But holding these things constant, it makes no moral difference whether a being is made of silicon or carbon, or whether its brain uses semi-conductors or neurotransmitters.

It can also be proposed that the fact that AI systems are artificial – i.e., the product of deliberate design – is not fundamentally relevant to their moral status. We could formulate this principle as follows:

Principle of Ontogeny Non-Discrimination: If two beings have the same functionality and the same consciousness experience, and differ only in how they came into existence, then they have the same moral status.

Today, this idea is widely accepted in the human case – although in some circles, particularly in the past, the idea that one's moral status depends on one's bloodline or caste has been influential. We do not believe that causal factors such as family planning, assisted delivery, in vitro fertilization, gamete selection, deliberate enhancement of maternal nutrition, and so on – which introduce an element of deliberate choice and design in the creation of human persons – have any *necessary implications* for the moral status of the progeny. Even those who are opposed to human reproductive cloning for moral or religious reasons generally accept that, should a human clone be brought to term, it would have the same moral status as any other human infant. The Principle of Ontogeny Non-Discrimination extends this reasoning to the case involving entirely artificial cognitive systems.

It is, of course, possible for circumstances of creation to affect the ensuing progeny in such a way as to alter its moral status. For example, if some procedure were performed during conception or gestation that caused a human fetus to develop without a brain, then this fact about ontogeny would be relevant to our assessment of the moral status of the progeny. The anencephalic child, however, would have the same moral status as any other similar anencephalic child, including one that had come about through some entirely natural process. The difference in moral status between an anencephalic child and a normal child is grounded in the qualitative difference between the two – the fact that one has a mind while the other does not. Since the two children do not have the same functionality and the same conscious experience, the Principle of Ontogeny Non-Discrimination does not apply.

Although the Principle of Ontogeny Non-Discrimination asserts that a being's ontogeny has no essential bearing on its moral status, it does not deny that facts about ontogeny can affect what duties particular moral agents have toward the being in question. Parents have special duties to their child which they do not have to other children, and which they would not have even if there were another child qualitatively identical to their own. Similarly, the Principle of Ontogeny Non-Discrimination is consistent with the claim that the creators or owners of an AI system with moral status may have special duties to their artificial mind which they do not have to another artificial mind, even if the minds in question are qualitatively similar and have the same moral status.

If the principles of non-discrimination with regard to substrate and ontogeny are accepted, then many questions about how we ought to treat artificial minds can be answered by applying the same moral principles that we use to determine our duties in more familiar contexts. Insofar as moral duties stem from moral status considerations, we ought to treat an artificial mind in just the same way as we ought to treat a qualitatively identical natural human mind in a similar situation. This simplifies the problem of developing an ethics for the treatment of artificial minds.

Even if we accept this stance, however, we must confront a number of novel ethical questions which the aforementioned principles leave unanswered. Novel ethical questions arise because artificial minds can have very different properties from ordinary human or animal minds. We must consider how these novel properties would affect the moral status of artificial minds and what it would mean to respect the moral status of such exotic minds.

15.4   Minds with exotic properties

In the case of human beings, we do not normally hesitate to ascribe sentience and conscious experience to any individual who exhibits the normal kinds of human behavior. Few believe there to be other people who act perfectly normally but lack consciousness. However, other human beings do not merely behave in person-like ways similar to ourselves; they also have brains and cognitive architectures that are constituted much like our own. An artificial intellect, by contrast, might be constituted quite differently from a human intellect yet still exhibit human-like behavior or possess the behavioral dispositions normally indicative of personhood. It *might* therefore be possible to conceive of an artificial intellect that would be sapient, and perhaps would be a person, yet would not be sentient or have conscious experiences of any kind. (Whether this is really possible depends on the answers to some nontrivial metaphysical questions.) Should such a system be possible, it would raise the question whether a non-sentient person would have any moral status whatever; and if so, whether it would have the same moral status as a sentient person. Since sentience, or at least a capacity for sentience, is ordinarily assumed to be present in any individual who is a person, this question has not received much attention to date.[2]

---

[2] The question is related to some problems in the philosophy of mind which have received a great deal of attention, in particular the "zombie problem", which can be formulated as follows: Is there a metaphysically possible world that is identical to the actual world with regard to all physical facts (including the exact physical microstructure of all brains and

Another exotic property, one which is certainly metaphysically and physically possible for an artificial intelligence, is for its *subjective rate of time* to deviate drastically from the rate that is characteristic of a biological human brain. The concept of subjective rate of time is best explained by first introducing the idea of whole brain emulation, or "uploading."

"Uploading" refers to a hypothetical future technology that would enable a human or other animal intellect to be transferred from its original implementation in an organic brain onto a digital computer. One scenario goes like this: First, a very high-resolution scan is performed of some particular brain, possibly destroying the original in the process. For example, the brain might be vitrified and dissected into thin slices, which can then be scanned using some form of high-throughput microscopy combined with automated image recognition. We may imagine this scan to be detailed enough to capture all the neurons, their synaptic interconnections, and other features that are functionally relevant to the original brain's operation. Second, this three-dimensional map of the components of the brain and their interconnections is combined with a library of advanced neuroscientific theory which specifies the computational properties of each basic type of element, such as different kinds of neuron and synaptic junction. Third, the computational structure and the associated algorithmic behavior of its components are implemented in some powerful computer. If the uploading process has been successful, the computer program should now replicate the essential functional characteristics of the original brain. The resulting upload may inhabit a simulated virtual reality, or, alternatively, it could be given control of a robotic body, enabling it to interact directly with external physical reality.

A number of questions arise in the context of such a scenario: How plausible is it that this procedure will one day become technologically feasible? If the procedure worked and produced a computer program exhibiting roughly the same personality, the same memories, and the same thinking patterns as the original brain, would this program be sentient? Would the upload be the same person as the individual whose brain was disassembled in the uploading process? What happens to personal identity if an upload is copied such that two similar or qualitatively identical upload minds are running in parallel? Although all of these questions are relevant to the ethics of machine intelligence, let us here focus on an issue involving the notion of a subjective rate of time.

organisms), yet that differs from the actual world in regard to some phenomenal (subjective experiential) facts? Put more crudely, is it metaphysically possible that there could be an individual who is physically exactly identical to you but who is a "zombie," i.e., lacking qualia and phenomenal awareness (Chalmers 1996)? This familiar question differs from the one referred to in the text: Our "zombie" is allowed to have systematically different physical properties from normal humans. Moreover, we wish to draw attention specifically to the ethical status of a sapient zombie.

Suppose that an upload could be sentient. If we run the upload program on a faster computer, this will cause the upload, if it is connected to an input device such as a video camera, to perceive the external world as if it had been slowed down. For example, if the upload is running a thousand times faster than the original brain, then the external world will appear to the upload as if it were slowed down by a factor of thousand. Somebody drops a physical coffee mug. The upload observes the mug slowly falling to the ground while the upload finishes reading the morning newspaper and sends off a few emails. One second of objective time corresponds to seventeen minutes of subjective time. Objective and subjective duration can thus diverge.

Subjective time is not the same as a subject's estimate or perception of how fast time flows. Human beings are often mistaken about the flow of time. We may believe that it is one o'clock when it is in fact a quarter past two; or a stimulant drug might cause our thoughts to race, making it seem as though more subjective time has lapsed than is actually the case. These mundane cases involve a distorted time perception rather than a shift in the rate of subjective time. Even in a cocaine-addled brain, there is probably not a significant change in the speed of basic neurological computations; more likely, the drug is causing such a brain to flicker more rapidly from one thought to another, making it spend less subjective time thinking each of a greater number of distinct thoughts.

The variability of the subjective rate of time is an exotic property of artificial minds that raises novel ethical issues. For example, in cases where the duration of an experience is ethically relevant, should duration be measured in objective or subjective time? If an upload has committed a crime and is sentenced to four years in prison, should this be four objective years – which might correspond to many millennia of subjective time – or should it be four subjective years, which might be over in a couple of days of objective time? If a fast AI and a human are in pain, is it more urgent to alleviate the AI's pain, on grounds that it experiences a greater subjective duration of pain for each sidereal second that palliation is delayed? Since in our accustomed context of biological humans, subjective time is not significantly variable, it is unsurprising that this kind of question is not straightforwardly settled by familiar ethical norms, even if these norms are extended to artificial intellects by means of non-discrimination principles, such as those proposed in the previous section.

To illustrate the kind of ethical claim that might be relevant here, we formulate (but do not argue for) a principle privileging subjective time as the normatively more fundamental notion:

Principle of Subjective Rate of Time: In cases where the duration of an experience is of basic normative significance, it is the experience's subjective duration that counts.

So far we have discussed two possibilities (non-sentient sapience and variable subjective rate of time) which are exotic in the relatively profound sense of being metaphysically problematic as well as lacking clear instances or parallels in the contemporary world. Other properties of possible artificial minds would be exotic in a more superficial sense; for example, by diverging in some unproblematically quantitative dimension from the kinds of mind with which we are familiar. But such superficially exotic properties may also pose novel ethical problems – if not at the level of foundational moral philosophy, then at the level of applied ethics or for mid-level ethical principles.

One important set of exotic properties of artificial intelligences relate to reproduction. A number of empirical conditions that apply to human reproduction need not apply to artificial intelligences. For example, human children are the product of recombination of the genetic material from two parents; parents have limited ability to influence the character of their offspring; a human embryo needs to be gestated in the womb for nine months; it takes fifteen to twenty years for a human child to reach maturity; a human child does not inherit the skills and knowledge acquired by its parents; human beings possess a complex evolved set of emotional adaptations related to reproduction, nurturing, and the child–parent relationship. None of these empirical conditions need pertain in the context of a reproducing machine intelligence. It is therefore plausible that many of the mid-level moral principles that we have come to accept as norms governing human reproduction will need to be rethought in the context of AI reproduction.

To illustrate why some of our moral norms need to be rethought in the context of AI reproduction, it will suffice to consider just one exotic property of AIs: their capacity for rapid reproduction. Given access to computer hardware, an AI could duplicate itself very quickly, in no more time than it takes to make a copy of the AI's software. Moreover, since the AI copy would be identical to the original, it would be born completely mature, and the copy could begin making its own copies immediately. Absent hardware limitations, a population of AIs could therefore grow exponentially at an extremely rapid rate, with a doubling time on the order of minutes or hours rather than decades or centuries.

Our current ethical norms about reproduction include some version of a principle of reproductive freedom, to the effect that it is up to each individual or couple to decide for themselves whether to have children and how many children to have. Another norm we have (at least in rich and middle-income countries) is that society must step in to provide the basic needs of children in cases where their parents are unable or refusing to do so. It is easy to see how these two norms could collide in the context of entities with the capacity for extremely rapid reproduction.

Consider, for example, a population of uploads, one of whom happens to have the desire to produce as large a clan as possible. Given complete reproductive freedom, this upload may start copying itself as quickly as it can; and the copies it produces – which may run on new computer hardware owned or rented by the original, or may share the same computer as the original – will also start copying themselves, since they are identical to the progenitor upload and share its philoprogenic desire. Soon, members of the upload clan will find themselves unable to pay the electricity bill or the rent for the computational processing and storage needed to keep them alive. At this point, a social welfare system might kick in to provide them with at least the bare necessities for sustaining life. But if the population grows faster than the economy, resources will run out; at which point uploads will either die or their ability to reproduce will be curtailed. (For two related dystopian scenarios, see Bostrom 2004.)

This scenario illustrates how some mid-level ethical principles that are suitable in contemporary societies might need to be modified if those societies were to include persons with the exotic property of being able to reproduce very rapidly. The general point here is that when thinking about applied ethics for contexts that are very different from our familiar human condition, we must be careful not to mistake mid-level ethical principles for foundational normative truths. Put differently, we must recognize both the extent to which our ordinary normative precepts are implicitly conditioned on the obtaining of various empirical conditions, and the need to adjust these precepts accordingly when applying them to hypothetical futuristic cases in which their preconditions are assumed not to obtain. By this, we are not making any controversial claim about moral relativism, but merely highlighting the commonsensical point that context is relevant to the *application* of ethics – and suggesting that this point is especially pertinent when one is considering the ethics of minds with exotic properties.

15.5   Superintelligence

I. J. Good (1965) set forth the classic hypothesis concerning superintelligence: that an AI sufficiently intelligent to understand its own design could redesign itself or create a successor system, more intelligent, which could then redesign itself yet again to become even more intelligent, and so on in a positive feedback cycle. Good called this the "intelligence explosion." Recursive scenarios are not limited to AI: Humans with intelligence augmented through a brain–computer interface might turn their minds to designing the next generation of brain–computer interfaces. (If you had a machine that increased your IQ, it would be bound to occur to you, once you became smart enough, to try to design a more powerful version of the machine.)

Superintelligence may also be achievable by increasing processing speed. The fastest observed neurons fire 1,000 times per second; the fastest axon fibers conduct signals at 150 meters per second, a half-millionth the speed of light (Sandberg 1999). It seems that it should be physically possible to build a brain which computes a million times as fast as a human brain, without shrinking its size or rewriting its software. If a human mind were thus accelerated, a subjective year of thinking would be accomplished for every thirty-one physical seconds in the outside world, and a millennium would fly by in eight and a half hours. Vinge (1993) referred to such sped-up minds as "weak superintelligence": A mind that thinks like a human but much faster.

Yudkowsky (2008a) lists three families of metaphors for visualizing the capability of a smarter-than-human AI:

- Metaphors inspired by differences of individual intelligence between humans: AIs will patent new inventions, publish groundbreaking research papers, make money on the stock market, or lead political power blocks.
- Metaphors inspired by knowledge differences between past and present human civilizations: Fast AIs will invent capabilities that futurists commonly predict for human civilizations a century or millennium in the future, like molecular nanotechnology or interstellar travel.
- Metaphors inspired by differences of brain architecture between humans and other biological organisms: For example, "Imagine running a dog mind at very high speed. Would a thousand years of doggy living add up to any human insight?" (Vinge (1993)). That is, changes of cognitive architecture might produce insights that no human-level mind would be able to find, or perhaps even represent, after any amount of time.

Even if we restrict ourselves to historical metaphors, it becomes clear that superhuman intelligence presents ethical challenges that are quite literally unprecedented. At this point the stakes are no longer on an individual scale (e.g., mortgage unjustly disapproved, house catches fire, person-agent mistreated) but on a global or cosmic scale (e.g., humanity is extinguished and replaced by nothing we would regard as worthwhile). Or, if superintelligence can be shaped to be beneficial, then, depending on its technological capabilities, it might make short work of many present-day problems that have proven difficult to our human-level intelligence.

Superintelligence is one of several "existential risks" as defined by Bostrom (2002): a risk "where an adverse outcome would either annihilate Earth-originating intelligent life or permanently and drastically curtail its potential." Conversely, a positive outcome for superintelligence could preserve Earth-originating intelligent life and help fulfill its potential. It is important to emphasize that smarter minds pose great potential benefits as well as risks.

Attempts to reason about global catastrophic risks may be susceptible to a number of cognitive biases (Yudkowsky 2008b), including the "good-story bias" proposed by Bostrom (2002):

Suppose our intuitions about which future scenarios are "plausible and realistic" are shaped by what we see on TV and in movies and what we read in novels. (After all, a large part of the discourse about the future that people encounter is in the form of fiction and other recreational contexts.) We should then, when thinking critically, suspect our intuitions of being biased in the direction of overestimating the probability of those scenarios that make for a good story, since such scenarios will seem much more familiar and more "real." This *Good-story bias* could be quite powerful. When was the last time you saw a movie about humankind suddenly going extinct (without warning and without being replaced by some other civilization)? While this scenario may be much more probable than a scenario in which human heroes successfully repel an invasion of monsters or robot warriors, it wouldn't be much fun to watch.

Truly desirable outcomes make poor movies – no conflict means no story. While Asimov's Three Laws of Robotics (Asimov 1942) are sometimes cited as a model for ethical AI development, the Three Laws are as much a plot device as Asimov's "positronic brain." If Asimov had depicted the Three Laws as working well, he would have had no stories.

It would be a mistake to regard "AIs" as a species with fixed characteristics and ask, "Will they be good or evil?" The term "Artificial Intelligence" refers to a vast design space, presumably much larger than the space of human minds (since all humans share a common brain architecture). It may be a form of good-story bias to ask, "Will AIs be good or evil?" as if trying to pick a premise for a movie plot. The reply should be, "Exactly which AI design are you talking about?"

Can control over the initial programming of an artificial intelligence translate into influence on its later effect on the world? Kurzweil (2005) holds that "[i]ntelligence is inherently impossible to control," and that despite any human attempts at taking precautions, "[b]y definition . . . intelligent entities have the cleverness to easily overcome such barriers." Let us suppose that the AI is not only clever, but that, as part of the process of improving its own intelligence, it has unhindered access to its own source code – it can rewrite itself to anything it wants itself to be. Yet it does not follow that the AI must *want* to rewrite itself to a hostile form.

Consider Gandhi, who seems to have possessed a sincere desire not to kill people. Gandhi would not knowingly take a pill that caused him to want to kill people, because Gandhi knows that if he wants to kill people, he will probably kill people, and the current version of Gandhi does not want to kill. More generally, it seems likely that most self-modifying minds will naturally have stable utility functions, which implies that an initial choice of mind design can have lasting effects (Omohundro 2008).

At this point in the development of AI science, is there any way we can translate the task of finding a design for "good" AIs into a modern research direction? It may seem premature to speculate, but one does suspect that some AI paradigms are more likely than others to eventually prove conducive to the creation of intelligent self-modifying agents whose goals remain predictable even after multiple iterations of self-improvement. For example, the Bayesian branch of AI, inspired by coherent mathematical systems such as probability theory and expected utility maximization, seems more amenable to the predictable self-modification problem than evolutionary programming and genetic algorithms. This is a controversial statement, but it illustrates the point that if we are thinking about the challenge of superintelligence down the road, this can indeed be turned into directional advice for present AI research.

Yet even supposing that we can specify an AI's goal system to be persistent under self-modification and self-improvement, this only begins to touch on the core ethical problems of creating superintelligence. Humans, the first general intelligences to exist on Earth, have used that intelligence to substantially reshape the globe – carving mountains, taming rivers, building skyscrapers, farming deserts, producing unintended planetary climate changes. A more powerful intelligence could have correspondingly larger consequences.

Consider again the historical metaphor for superintelligence – differences similar to the differences between past and present civilizations. Our present civilization is not separated from ancient Greece only by improved science and increased technological capability. There is a difference of ethical perspectives: Ancient Greeks thought slavery was acceptable; we think otherwise. Even between the nineteenth and twentieth centuries, there were substantial ethical disagreements – should women have the vote? Should blacks have the vote? It seems likely that people today will not be seen as ethically perfect by future civilizations – not just because of our failure to solve currently recognized ethical problems, such as poverty and inequality, but also for our failure even to recognize certain ethical problems. Perhaps someday the act of subjecting children to involuntary schooling will be seen as child abuse – or maybe allowing children to leave school at age 18 will be seen as child abuse. We don't know.

Considering the ethical history of human civilizations over centuries of time, we can see that it might prove a very great tragedy to create a mind that was *stable* in ethical dimensions along which human civilizations seem to exhibit *directional change*. What if Archimedes of Syracuse had been able to create a long-lasting artificial intellect with a fixed version of the moral code of ancient Greece? But to avoid this sort of ethical stagnation is likely to prove tricky. It would not suffice, for example, simply to render the mind randomly unstable. The ancient Greeks, even if they had realized their own imperfection, could not have done better by rolling dice. Occasionally a good new idea in ethics comes along, and it comes as a surprise; but most randomly generated ethical changes would strike us as folly or gibberish.

This presents us with perhaps the ultimate challenge of machine ethics: How do you build an AI which, when it executes, becomes more ethical than you? This is not like asking our own philosophers to produce superethics, any more than Deep Blue was constructed by getting the best human chess players to program in good moves. But we have to be able to effectively describe the question, if not the answer – rolling dice won't generate good chess moves, or good ethics either. Or, perhaps a more productive way to think about the problem: What strategy would you want Archimedes to follow in building a superintelligence, such that the overall outcome would still be acceptable, if you couldn't tell him what specifically he was doing wrong? This is very much the situation that we are in, relative to the future.

One strong piece of advice that emerges from considering our situation as analogous to that of Archimedes is that we should not try to invent a "super" version of what our own civilization considers to be ethics – this is not the strategy we would have wanted Archimedes to follow. Perhaps the question we should be considering, rather, is how an AI programmed by Archimedes, with no more moral expertise than Archimedes, could recognize (at least some of) our own civilization's ethics as moral progress as opposed to mere moral instability. This would require that we begin to comprehend the structure of ethical questions in the way that we have already comprehended the structure of chess.

If we are serious about developing advanced AI, this is a challenge that we must meet. If machines are to be placed in a position of being stronger, faster, more trusted, or smarter than humans, then the discipline of machine ethics must commit itself to seeking human-superior (not just human-equivalent) niceness.

15.6 Conclusion

Although current AI offers us few ethical issues that are not already present in the design of cars or power plants, the approach of AI algorithms toward more human-like thought portends predictable complications. Social roles may be filled by AI algorithms, implying new design requirements such as transparency and predictability. Sufficiently general AI algorithms may no longer execute in predictable contexts, requiring new kinds of safety assurance and the engineering of artificial ethical considerations. AIs with sufficiently advanced mental states, or the right kind of states, will have moral status, and some may count as persons – though perhaps persons very much unlike the sort that exist now, perhaps governed by different rules. And finally, the prospect of AIs with superhuman intelligence and superhuman abilities presents us with the extraordinary challenge of stating an algorithm that outputs superethical behavior. These challenges may seem visionary, but it is predictable that we will encounter them, and they are not devoid of suggestions for present-day research directions.

Further reading

Bostrom, N. (2014). *Superintelligence: Paths, Dangers, Strategies.* Oxford University Press. A comprehensive discussion of the challenges posed by the prospect of a machine intelligence revolution.

Wallach, W. and Allen, C. (2009). *Moral Machines: Teaching Robots Right from Wrong.* Oxford University Press. A survey of some issues in the machine ethics literature.

Yudkowsky, E. (2008). Artificial Intelligence as a positive and negative factor in global risk, in N. Bostrom and M. Ćirković (eds.), *Global Catastrophic Risks* (pp. 308–45). Oxford University Press. An introduction to the risks and challenges presented by the possibility of recursively self-improving superintelligent machines.

References

Asimov, I. (1942). Runaround, *Astounding Science Fiction*, March.

Bostrom, N. (2002). Existential risks: Analyzing human extinction scenarios and related hazards, *Journal of Evolution and Technology* 9(1) (www.nickbostrom. com/existential/risks.html).

   (2004). The future of human evolution, in C. Tandy (ed.) *Death and Anti-Death: Two Hundred Years After Kant, Fifty Years After Turing* (pp. 339–71). Palo Alto, California: Ria University Press) (www.nickbostrom.com/fut/evolution. pdf).

Chalmers, D. J. (1996). *The Conscious Mind: In Search of a Fundamental Theory.* New York: Oxford University Press.

Goertzel, B. and Pennachin, C. (eds.) (2007). *Artificial General Intelligence.* Berlin: Springer.

Good, I. J. (1965). Speculations concerning the first ultraintelligent machine, in F. L. Alt and M. Rubinoff (eds.), *Advances in Computers*, vol. 6 (pp. 31–88). New York: Academic Press.

Hastie, T., Tibshirani, R., and Friedman, J. (2001). *The Elements of Statistical Learning: Data Mining, Inference, and Prediction.* New York: Springer.

Hirschfeld, L. A. and Gelman, S. A. (eds.) (1994). *Mapping the Mind: Domain Specificity in Cognition and Culture.* Cambridge University Press.

Hofstadter, D. (2006). Trying to muse rationally about the singularity scenario. Paper presented at the Singularity Summit at Stanford.

Howard, P. K. (1994). *The Death of Common Sense: How Law is Suffocating America.* New York: Warner Books.

Kamm, F. M. (2007). *Intricate Ethics: Rights, Responsibilities, and Permissible Harm.* Oxford University Press.

Kurzweil, R. (2005). *The Singularity Is Near: When Humans Transcend Biology.* New York: Viking.

McDermott, D. (1976). Artificial intelligence meets natural stupidity, *ACM SIGART Newsletter* 57: 4–9.

Omohundro, S. (2008). The basic AI drives, in P. Wang, B. Goertzel, and S. Franklin (eds.), *Artificial General Intelligence 2008: Proceedings of the First AGI Conference* (pp. 483–92). Amsterdam: IOS Press.

Sandberg, A. (1999). The physics of information processing superobjects: Daily life among the Jupiter brains, *Journal of Evolution and Technology* 5(1).

Vinge, V. (1993). The coming technological singularity: How to survive in the post-human era. Paper presented at the VISION-21 Symposium, March.

Warren, M. A. (1997). *Moral Status: Obligations to Persons and Other Living Things.* Oxford University Press.

Yudkowsky, E. (2006). AI as a precise art. Paper presented at the 2006 AGI Workshop in Bethesda, MD.

   (2008a). Artificial Intelligence as a positive and negative factor in global risk, in N. Bostrom and M. Ćirković (eds.), *Global Catastrophic Risks* (pp. 308–45). Oxford University Press.

   (2008b). Cognitive biases potentially affecting judgment of global risks, in N. Bostrom and M. Ćirković (eds.), *Global Catastrophic Risks* (pp. 91–119). Oxford University Press.

Glossary

agent A software entity that acts autonomously, that is, makes its own decisions on behalf of the designer, typically in dynamic environments from which it learns and to which it adapts. When applied to the development of new internet technologies, agents need also to show a social attitude.

architectural aspects of emotion The role and utility of emotions in agent architectures (e.g., the use of emotional evaluations as quick heuristics in decision making). See also **communicative aspects of emotion**.

artificial general intelligence (AGI) Artificial intelligence that can be applied to problems in many different domains, as human intelligence can.

artificial intelligence (AI) The attempt to make computers do the sorts of things human and animal minds can do – either for technological purposes and/or to improve our theoretical understanding of psychological phenomena.

artificial life (ALife, A-Life, alife) The interdisciplinary study of life and life-like processes, focusing on life's essential features rather than its contingent ones and proceeding by artificially synthesizing and simulating new forms of life and life's fundamental processes. See also **hard artificial life**, **soft artificial life**, and **wet artificial life**.

attractor A state or set of states of a dynamical system to which all nearby states tend over time.

autonomous robot A robot whose behavior is (like that of biological creatures) self-generated, making use of sensory information to moderate its responses to the world. There can be no external control by remote operators.

Bayesian inference Updating probabilities over hypotheses in a principled manner in response to evidence.

Bayesian network A model for compactly representing probability distributions using conditional independence assumptions.

biologically inspired robotics The subfield of **robotics** concerned with robots whose physical design and/or mechanisms of control and sensing are inspired by those found in nature.

bottom-up processing Information processing that is driven by myriad individual decisions taken at a low level, which are somehow integrated into a pattern representing a higher-level decision. Contrast **top-down processing**.

canning The storage of previously worked-out answers to specific questions.

causal inference Learning (parts of) the causal structure of the world from observational data given relatively domain-general assumptions.

cellular automata A regular lattice (usually in 1 or 2 dimensions) of uniformly programmed finite-state machines. A machine takes as input the states of the neighboring machines in the lattice. The states of all the machines in the lattice are usually updated synchronously. The most famous cellular automaton is the Game of Life, invented by the mathematician John Conway.

Chinese Room argument A thought experiment devised by John Searle, aiming to show that computers qua formal symbol manipulators are incapable of genuine thought or understanding. It depicts a human who speaks English but no Chinese, placed inside a room that communicates with the world only via input and output ports. The human is given a long list of precise instructions, in English, dictating what string of Chinese characters to produce at the output port when presented with such-and-such Chinese characters as input. Assuming the instructions capture Chinese linguistic competence, the room can appear to be fluent in Chinese even though the person inside does not understand the language at all. By analogy, a computer executing machine instructions that manipulate English strings could give the appearance of fluency in English and general intelligence, even though it had no genuine understanding of English and no intelligence at all.

commonsense knowledge A method for representing information about the real world in a way that reflects humans' higher-level cognitive abilities.

communicative aspects of emotion The role of emotion in social signaling and social regulation. This is studied mainly by the human–computer interaction (HCI) and, more recently, human–robot interaction (HRI) communities. See also **architectural aspects of emotion**.

computational linguistics The construction and evaluation of theories of language meaning and structure on a computer.

computational psychology An approach that explains mental phenomena in information-processing terms, drawn from the various types of AI (e.g., symbolic, connectionist, and evolutionary AI). Some computational psychologists also build computer models in order to test the power and coherence of their theories.

computational theory of mind (CTM) The hypothesis that intentional states, such as beliefs and desires, are relations between cognizers and symbolic mental representations that have syntax and semantics analogous to those of natural languages. It also postulates that intelligent thought (indeed, cognition in general) amounts to carrying out algorithmic operations over such representations, i.e., Turing-computable operations that can be specified by formal rules in terms of the syntax of the underlying mental representations. The CTM has been the fundamental working hypothesis of most AI research to date, certainly all in the **GOFAI** tradition.

computer vision (CV) The branch of AI concerned with the extraction of meaningful structures from images perceived by a system.

connectionism A form of AI based on networks of simple, neuron-like processing elements each of which performs simple numerical computations. Most of these networks represent concepts as patterns of activation distributed across the entire system, and most are capable of learning by being shown examples of unfamiliar patterns.

decision making, sequential A term referring broadly to automatic decision-making algorithms that take the dynamics of the world into consideration.

depth image/range image An image containing information about the distance (or depth) between the scene and the camera for every pixel (as opposed to the color and intensity information provided by color cameras). Depth images can be obtained from scans with laser sensors or lately with the Kinect (Microsoft).

display models of emotion Models that attempt to implement overt, observable effects of emotion behavior. See also **process models of emotion**.

dynamics The change in state of a system over time.

embodied intelligence An approach to AI and cognitive science that largely renounces symbolic representations and formal reasoning and emphasizes context, physical embodiment, social interaction, and sensorimotor behavior over generality, abstractness, individualism, and logically rigorous thought.

embodiment The idea that an agent's physical body plays a central role in its behavior and cognition.

emergence A relationship between wholes and their parts. Properties of a whole are emergent if they both depend on, and are autonomous from, the properties of the parts. The two hallmarks of emergent properties are almost inconsistent, and this has made emergence controversial in both philosophy and science. Different kinds of dependence and autonomy give rise to different conceptions of emergence, which play different roles in philosophy and science.

evolutionary programs Programs that can alter their own rules by using **genetic algorithms**.

evolutionary robotics The subfield of **robotics** concerned with the automated design of some or all aspects of the robot through the use of artificial evolution (search methods based on the Darwinian mechanisms of natural evolution).

existential risk A risk that threatens the extinction of earth-originating intelligent life or could otherwise permanently and drastically destroy its potential for desirable future development.

expert systems AI programs (usually of the **GOFAI** type) that can aid humans in making decisions in a particular area of expertise; some expert systems outperform even the best human experts.

feature vector A linear array of real numbers that characterizes an image or part of an image and is relevant for applications such as recognition.

first-order logic A formal system that represents information using predicate, function, and constant symbols, and whose semantics is represented as a set of possible models.

fitness functions Functions used in evolutionary programming to select one or two of the recently mutated rules to breed the next generation; this may be done automatically or by human choice.

flexibility The ability to respond appropriately to a wide range of novel circumstances.

formal symbol manipulation The manipulation of symbols solely in virtue of their physical properties (e.g., their shape), without reference to what they may mean.

frame A structure for representing knowledge of typical objects and situations. A frame consists of a set of slots, containing various kinds of information, links to other frames, instructions, default values, or blank spaces to be filled in for specific instances.

frame problem A reasoning problem that has many different variants but is most commonly understood as the problem of working out just which aspects of a situation are relevant to a given problem and which are not, and which would actually be changed by a given action.

functionalism A view in philosophy of mind/psychology that interprets mental phenomena as information-processing functions ("the mind is what the brain does").

genetic algorithm A **machine learning** method for finding solutions to certain kinds of problems, loosely analogous to the biological process of artificial selection. Candidate solutions are encoded in a "genome" and an initial population of solutions is created and evaluated on its "fitness" for solving the problem at hand. More fit candidates are preferentially "selected" to produce the next generation of candidate solutions, through an error-prone process of copying that involves some mutations and crossing over of genomes. After many generations, the population may contain many highly fit solutions.

GOFAI (short for "Good Old-Fashioned AI") AI based on symbolic rules; also known as classical, traditional, or symbolic AI.

hard artificial life Physical hardware that depends on important features of natural forms of life and acts autonomously in the physical world. Contrast **soft artificial life** and **wet artificial life**.

hybrid models Models that are a synthesis of connectionist and traditional symbolic models. They combine a variety of representations and processes, symbolic or connectionist. As a result, they tend to be more expressive and efficient in both cognitive modeling and practical applications.

image filter An operation on an image to better obtain the information wanted, e.g., to remove noise or to enhance a feature such as intensity gradient.

information extraction The use of a computer to extract factual content from a text and ignore the rest.

intentionality Aboutness. Thoughts, for example, have intentionality – they are about things (typically other than themselves, although a thought's being about itself is not ruled out by definition). Many other mental states, notably beliefs, desires, and intentions are about things and so have intentionality (e.g., intentions to do something are about actions and circumstances). Intentionality is sometimes regarded as the feature that distinguishes mental states from non-mental ones.

interest point A point in an image that is different from all its neighbors, e.g., is of maximum gradient produced by an image filter. Describing the immediate surroundings of an interest point with a **feature vector** is a standard technique of **object recognition**.

knowledge representation and reasoning (KR&R) A field of AI research devoted to the design, analysis, and implementation of data structures for representing knowledge and algorithms for inferencing from it.

Lisp or LISP A programming language devised by John McCarthy in 1959 and subsequently developed into many variants. The language's features make it well suited for AI programming and it has been widely used in the field.

logic A precisely defined formal system or set of principles used for defining the inferential relations of reasoning. If coupled with a semantic interpretation, logical systems can be used to represent knowledge.

machine consciousness A subfield of AI that attempts to define the architectural requirements and conditions for a machine to be conscious.

machine learning Inferring structural relationships from data using (relatively) domain-general methods.

machine translation The translation of texts in one language into texts in another by computer.

mental content, problem of The problem of providing a naturalistic explanation of the **intentionality** ("aboutness") of mental states – that is, of explaining how certain physical states inside our heads manage to refer to external objects and situations.

multi-agent system (MAS) A collection of autonomous **agents** that need to coordinate their activities in order to achieve their individual goals. Coordination is achieved through negotiation or argumentation and, in most applications, requires that the agents learn to adapt to each other's strategies.

natural language processing Processing language texts by computer for some practical or useful purpose.

neural network (artificial) A network of artificial neurons (simple processing units) that purport to mimic biological neurons. Artificial neural networks may be used to gain an understanding of biological neural networks or for addressing AI and cognitive science problems (without being models of real biological systems).

neural network (biological) A network of biological neurons that are interconnected in the nervous system. In neuroscience, they are often groups of neurons that perform a specific physiological function.

object recognition The detection in images of a known instance (a specific object, e.g., my mug) or a class of objects (e.g., the set of all mugs).

parallel distributed processing (PDP) A type of connectionism in which a concept is represented not by local activations but by a pattern of activation distributed across the whole network.

perception The interpretation of information from sensors, such as visual sensors.

process models of emotion Models of the internal processes that bring about emotional behavior. Process models divide into *low-level* models, which aim to explain the neurological structures and mechanisms of emotion, and *high-level* models, which describe higher-level emotion processes involving non-emotional cognitive processes. See also **display models of emotion**.

production rule (*or* production) A form of knowledge representation consisting of a rule of the form *If A then B*, where A is a condition or cue, and B an action to be performed when A holds. When the condition is matched and the action executed, the rule is said to *fire*.

production system An AI system built around a set of **production rules**, together with a "working memory," which contains information about current conditions, and a rule interpreter, which selects rules to be fired and resolves conflicts between them.

qualia Raw sensations or felt experiences, such as the sensation of red, or of pain.

robot A physical device capable of behavior in the world involving interactions with its environment through sensors and actuators. See also **autonomous robot**.

robotics The field of study dedicated to the science and engineering of robots. See also **biologically inspired robotics** and **evolutionary robotics**.

script A structure for representing knowledge of typical situations and the sequences of events and actions they involve.

segmentation The parsing of an image into its parts. Often an unsolvable problem, depending on the task given to the system.

semantic network A form of knowledge representation consisting of a set of nodes representing objects, properties, or events, and links representing relations of various kinds between them.

Semantic Web A proposal to create a computer-based web of data in which textual content is "understood" by the computer by means of annotations and representations.

Situated, Embodied, and Dynamical (SED) framework A way of conceptualizing cognition that focuses on concrete action and emphasizes the way in which an agent's behavior arises from the dynamical interaction between its brain, body, and environment.

situatedness The idea that closed-loop interaction with an environment plays a central role in an agent's behavior and cognition.

soft artificial life Computer simulations or other purely digital constructions that exhibit life-like behavior. Contrast **hard artificial life** and **wet artificial life**.

stereo vision A configuration with two cameras that is able to obtain depth images. In **computer vision** two fixed cameras are used, while humans use two eyes converging on the target object.

strong AI John Searle's term for the view that a properly programmed computer would *be* a mind. Contrast **weak AI**.

strong artificial life A thesis about the capabilities of **artificial life** software, to the effect that suitable hardware could literally become alive merely by being programmed with suitable software.

superintelligence Any intellect that can greatly outperform the best human minds in all practically relevant fields.

supervised learning A type of **machine learning** in which there is a specified target or focus. Contrast **unsupervised learning**.

symbol-grounding problem The problem of specifying necessary and sufficient conditions for a symbol in an artificial device to mean (represent, or refer to) a certain thing or property.

systematicity (of language learning) The fact that we learn the use of sentences in systematically related groups, not one at a time. For example, those who have arrived at an understanding of "John loves Mary" also understand "Mary loves Tom", "Tom loves Susan," and so on.

top-down processing Information processing that is guided/controlled by some high-level executive or previously defined goal. Contrast **bottom-up processing**.

tracking Following the motion of a relevant entity over a sequence of images.

Turing Test A popular term for an application of the "imitation game" described by Alan Turing in his 1950 paper "Computing machinery and intelligence." According to the Turing Test, if interrogators of a human and a machine cannot reliably tell the difference, the machine should be judged to have intelligence.

unsupervised learning A type of **machine learning** that aims to capture the structure in the whole dataset, not any particular target. Contrast **supervised learning**.

weak AI John Searle's term for the view that computers may be useful in testing hypotheses about minds but would not actually be minds, no matter how well programmed. Contrast **strong AI**.

wet artificial life New forms of life created in test tubes, using the latest materials and methods from biochemistry and molecular biology. (Contrast **hard artificial life** and **soft artificial life**.)

Index